## About the Author

Dr Robert Biel took a History degree at the University of Cambridge before studying International Relations at the University of Sussex and the London School of Economics. For many years he lectured at Birkbeck College, where he taught courses on Development, and at the School of Oriental and African Studies (SOAS). He is currently a member of the Development Planning Unit, University College, London. He is the author of *Eurocentrism and the Communist Movement* (1987).

# Zed Titles on the Political Economy of Capitalism

Intellectual fashion continues to prompt changes in vocabulary. Today, 'globalisation' and the 'market' have become the dominant buzzwords. In reality, however, what is happening is an ongoing, perhaps accelerating, spread (as well as transformation) of the market nexus between members of society on the one hand and relations of exploitation of labour on the other. Whatever the terms different writers may use, the world's economic systems are, with the collapse of the socialist project, almost exclusively capitalist, and the political economy of capitalism remains a centrally important focus of social understanding. Zed Books has a strong list of titles in this area.

Samir Amin, *Capitalism in the Age of Globalization: The Management of Contemporary Society*

Asoka Bandarage, *Women, Population and Global Crisis: A Political-Economic Analysis*

Robert Biel, *The New Imperialism: Crisis and Contradictions in North–South Relations*

Michel Chossudovsky, *The Globalisation of Poverty: Impacts of IMF and World Bank Reforms*

Peter Custers, *Capital Accumulation and Women's Labour in Asian Economies*

Diplab Dasgupta, *Structural Adjustment, Global Trade and the New Political Economy of Development*

Graham Dunkley, *The Free Trade Adventure: The WTO, GATT and Globalism: A Critique*

Terence Hopkins and Immanuel Wallerstein et al., *The Age of Transition: Trajectory of the World-System, 1945–2025*

Arthur MacEwan, *The Failure of Neo-liberalist Economics and the Alternative*

Saral Sarkar, *Eco-Socialism or Eco-Capitalism? A Critical Analysis of Humanity's Fundamental Choices*

Hans-Peter Martin and Harald Schumann, *The Global Trap: Globalization and the Assault on Prosperity and Democracy*

Harry Shutt, *The Trouble With Capitalism: An Enquiry into the Causes of Global Economic Failure*

Kavaljit Singh, *The Globalisation of Finance: A Citizen's Guide*

David Woodward, *Foreign Direct and Equity Investment in Developing Countries: The Next Crisis?*

For full details of this list and Zed's other subject and general catalogues, please write to: The Marketing Department, Zed Books, 7 Cynthia Street, London NI 9JF, UK or e-mail: sales@zedbooks.demon.co.uk

Visit our website at: http://www.zedbooks.demon.co.uk

# The New Imperialism

## Crisis and contradictions in North–South relations

ROBERT BIEL

Zed Books
LONDON • NEW YORK

*The New Imperialism: Crisis and contradictions in North–South relations* was first published by Zed Books Ltd, 7 Cynthia Street, London N1 9JF, UK and Room 400, 175 Fifth Avenue, New York, NY 10010, USA IN 2000.

Distributed in the USA exclusively by St Martin's Press, Inc., 175 Fifth Avenue, New York, NY 10010, USA.

Cover designed by Andrew Corbett
Set in Monotype Garamond by Ewan Smith
Printed and bound in Malaysia

A catalogue record for this book is available from the British Library.

Library of Congress Cataloging-in-Publication-Data

Biel, Robert, 1945–
    The New Imperialism: Crisis and contradictions in North/South relations / Robert Biel.
        p. cm.
    Includes bibliographical references and index.
    ISBN 1-85649-746-1 (cased) – ISBN 1-85649-757-X (limp)
    1. Capitalism. 2. Developing countries—Dependency on foreign countries. 3. Competition, International. I. Title.

HB501.B494 2000
307'.09172'4–dc21

                                              99-055043

ISBN 1 85649 746 1 cased
ISBN 1 85649 747 X limp

# Contents

# Introduction

I intend this book to be useful in understanding capitalism at a time of approaching crisis, when several different outcomes are possible. It comes from my main discipline, international political economy, with a particular focus on North–South relations. Its theoretical concern is to understand how international systems undergo major changes. In this sense, the book is about development. It partly addresses development as conventionally defined – the escape from poverty in Asia, Africa and Latin America – but situates this within a broader definition of development: that of capitalism as a whole, and, broader still, the history of human social development, of which capitalism is only a part. The study then considers the origins and course of the present phase of international capitalism, from around the end of the 1970s. This is treated partly as a case study for building a more general understanding of large-scale systemic change; but its more immediate purpose is to identify possible directions of change in the period now beginning.

Since the task is to analyse a form of capitalism, I have used Marx's historical materialism as the main analytical tool. Unjustly neglected in recent years, it is the most critical of theories because it is not committed to apologising for the existing system. It can be rehabilitated only by applying it successfully to concrete problems. I consider the following aspects of the Marxist approach particularly important:

- Working people have the right to an independent statement of their class interests, free of any assumption that these are in harmony with the demands of capital accumulation. This must be combined with a recognition of the need to safeguard their immediate livelihood within the existing system, and to identify what outcomes of a period of transformation would be favourable to them.
- The dialectical method. At an objective level, dialectics is the recognition that the identity of a phenomenon is determined by the contradictory forces within it; thus, the act of describing something (in this case, a given structure of capital accumulation) is at the same time a statement of the conditions under which it must eventually change, and of the different possible directions such change might take. This leads on to the

subjective level of dialectics: development occurs through willed human action on the basis of a recognition of the objective possibilities in a given situation.

- A concept of capital accumulation different from that employed by conventional economics. This concept refers to alienated human labour, which acquires a momentum of its own. The function of those in power is to promote the expansion of this capital. Agents such as the World Bank are often criticised on the grounds that their policies do not promote development, but it should be understood that their function is to promote capital accumulation, which continues to entail a transfer of wealth from the South. Their premise is that the accumulation system is immutable and must be conformed to.

- The centre–periphery or dependency perspective, a great theoretical creation of an earlier generation of radical scholars. In my understanding, it goes back to radical black writers such as W.E.B. Du Bois a hundred years ago, through to more recent figures such as Walter Rodney. I view dependency theory as an important *form* of the centre–periphery perspective, applied to the situation during the 1960s–70s, which generated extremely important insights. I owe a particular debt to the work of Samir Amin. I have sought to pinpoint areas where earlier theories were mistaken, or where they correctly described a reality which no longer exists today.

While this work is firmly situated within the existing radical tradition, it must be recognised that there are major areas where radical theory has not been adequate. We need a broader model of political economy, one that comprehends the differential exploitation of groups of people according to 'racial' and gender determinations, and that sees the human socio-economic system in the wider context of an ecosystem that might be tipped into an instability from which it could not be rescued. While the problems addressed under these headings belong to the contemporary world order – and are thus in an immediate sense problems of capitalism – they are also in a more fundamental sense problems of the whole history of human development. I believe that in the current situation we face two crises, not just one: an immediate crisis of capital accumulation, and a more profound problem of exhausting the human and ecological bases of social development. The historical roots of these issues predate the origins of capitalism.

In short, we need our model to encompass four factors: class, 'race', gender and the environment, and to take these as a basis for the analysis of international systems. I indicate the need for such an approach and attempt some preliminary steps towards it. Such a unified model must avoid being eclectic, merely grafting in bits of different theories without a unifying principle. What can the guiding principle be? I make the controversial assumption that dialectical and historical materialism supplies such a principle. Its potential in this respect was inadequately developed in the work of Marx himself and of others in the radical tradition.

There is scope here for a systematic historical critique of earlier theory. In a previous book, *Eurocentrism and the Communist Movement*, I attempted this with respect to the 'race' factor within the history of Marxism. In the present book I deliberately adopt a different approach. Here, the point of reference is whether the theory generated serves to cast some light on contemporary reality, and to suggest future practice.

It is the struggles of people within the capitalist machine itself which really bring home this reality, and I have been guided primarily by what I have learned about the reality experienced by them. The encouraging feature of the present period is the huge range of popular movements. They are somewhat scattered at present, which is positive insofar as it reflects the existence of a vast vocabulary for the creation of new principles of social development; but the crisis will increasingly demand that they coalesce around some responses, both immediate and strategic. This will mean a massive debate around theoretical issues, to which I intend this book to contribute.

# 1

# Capitalist Development in Historical Context

## Capitalism within Humanity's Social History

The problems of the present international system are problems of the development of capitalism, more specifically, of accumulation, the process whereby capital expands in value, a process which takes on a momentum of its own that even those who benefit from it can only partially control.

Capitalism's apologists present the system as natural, or as a necessary product of development in general. There are different variants to this. Either capitalism was implicitly always there, its practices providing fundamental metaphors for life itself (thus organisms are said to 'invest' in the future of their genes, and so on); or, according to a 'stages' view of development, capitalism is the summation of human advance from primitive society to the Euro-American business world. These views are not consistent, and fashions change.[1] But the underlying assumption of, say, the World Bank and the IMF is that conformity with the dictates of capital accumulation is in tune with the laws of either nature or historical progress.

The function of this book is to subject these assumptions to critical scrutiny, focusing on the recent period. Yet some view of capitalism within the context of human development must be arrived at. This cannot be attempted in a systematic way, especially given the danger of over-generalisation (particularly wrong in a pre-capitalist[2] context, where heterogeneity was the rule); however, in this chapter I will assemble some elements of a conceptual 'toolkit' which may help to understand these wider developmental issues. Even in this brief survey, I hope it will be possible to avoid eclecticism and see how the different elements could be brought together into a composite picture.

How are we to regard 'traditional' (pre-capitalist) society? Typical of capitalism's response to this question has been the perspective known as 'modernisation', according to which tradition is negative and holds up development. This is rightly being questioned today. Taking the critique of modernisation to its logical conclusion, we could say that capitalism is the problem – it has lost sight of the strengths of traditional society, which we need to rediscover. One of the symptoms of crisis and change at present is the eruption of issues which capitalism tried to ignore because it had no response to them.

Probably the most important of these is the relationship between human society and nature. While it is complicated to define pre-capitalist societies, we can see some common elements in indigenous movements today (Australian aboriginals, tribal people in India, and so on), which may identify principles of social organisation that humanity has lost sight of under the present system: there is a sense of the natural world as a system to which human society has to adapt, respecting nature's fundamental balancing mechanisms; science is closely integrated with culture as a whole, and the development, diffusion and transmission of knowledge are immensely important; heterogeneity is regarded as something positive, a mechanism by which societies keep their developmental options open, for example by maintaining the widest possible variety of plant-strains, a principle which is only now acquiring mainstream recognition in the term biodiversity.[3] This plurality also existed *between* different cultures, guaranteeing for humanity diverse cultural raw material for future development. Since culture has taken over from biology as the chief mechanism of human adaptation to the environment, a wide vocabulary of different responses is crucial.[4]

Capitalist culture has lost sight of this. Capitalism altered the nature of development because the exclusive focus on capital accumulation for the first time overturned the sustainability principle. But while capitalism fundamentally changed the course of development it also developed on the basis of what went before. This implies that today's developmental problems have to be seen in three different aspects. First, the contradictions between human society and nature; second, problems inherent in the whole history of human social development (of which capitalism is part); and third, contradictions specific to capitalism itself. Let us look particularly at the second of these. A useful focal point for this argument is the division of labour.

## Traditional Approaches to Organising Society

Division of labour increases the *scope* of social organisation ('scope' referring to both the geographical area within which society can be organised, and the range of activities). This enables people to 'tame' the environment further (for example, through large-scale water management) for larger populations to be supported. But it also introduces a certain contradiction between the development of individuals and of social groups. In particular, the division of labour categorised people. Fundamental in this is the division of labour by sex, and feminist thought has been crucial in showing how socially constructed characteristics can be made to appear as part of nature. The term 'gender' focuses this socially constructed element. The sexual division of labour was based on apparently physical criteria (superior male strength for heavy work, and giving women jobs that could be combined with looking after children), but the social determination of roles is probably over-whelmingly more important than the biological.[5]

Divisions can be made to appear natural by using the same vocabulary to describe human social divisions and forces of nature. Traditional thinking was heavily imbued with dialectics – this was its strength. It saw nature as being in a process of constant change, impelled by contradictory forces within it. Philosophies such as Chinese Daoism used gender division – Yin and Yang – as a fundamental metaphor for the conflicting forces of nature, and in so doing arrived at powerful insights. But there is a potentially oppressive aspect to this, not just because social divisions appear natural, but more specifically because of the hierarchy often established within the dyads that made up typical traditional perspectives on nature and society. One can see this for example even in the division between 'left' and 'right'; in the case of gender divisions, the male principle was the active one.

Other divisions of labour also gave rise to supposedly innate determina-tions – notably caste – in some pre-capitalist societies. Here again, the division was never in practice between equal occupations, but hierarchical. Even divisions by colour may have a basis in traditional society. While racism in its modern form is certainly associated with capitalism – and a case can be made out that it did not exist in the ancient world[6] – there is also evidence that 'black' and 'white' were quite deeply ingrained in an inferior–superior relationship in pre-capitalist European societies.[7] Ancient Chinese referred to themselves as 'white' to confer superiority over both inferior social classes and other nationalities.[8]

What this amounts to is that the division of labour, which enhances social development, tends to limit that of people as individuals, and some more than others. In this way, the demands of social development tend to take on a momentum of their own, imposing restrictions upon the people who form that society. As I will argue, this is an absolutely central under-standing for the analysis of contemporary capitalism, in the sense that the imperative of capital accumulation subordinates everything else, and draws individuals into roles within its schema. But this is not peculiar to capitalism; it was inherited from earlier societies and given new forms.

This takes us on to the terrain of the academic approach known as 'structuralism', according to which social practices and expressed ideas have a deeper meaning determined by the rules characteristic of that society. This analytical approach is now out of fashion, but I believe it holds a core of truth which should be retained. In practice, the structuralist analysis of pre-capitalist societies is problematical because the writers who used it permitted their own Eurocentric and sexist biases to leak into the supposedly inductive definition of what the structures were (more on this in a moment). However, the core of truth is that people can be alienated from the social structures they create, because those structures take on a logic or momentum of their own and tend to circumscribe the significance of individual human actions. 'Alienation' can be understood in many ways. Here I am using it in a specifically economic sense, to refer to situations in which people, or their labour, are sold and become the property of someone else (in early forms of alienation it is the people themselves; in capitalism, it is their labour). People or their labour thus become objectified, turned into an object.

This image of humanity alienated from its own social system is powerful and has a certain value. But we cannot consider humanity homogeneous in this respect. The dominant social groups benefit from the alienation, at least in a narrow and immediate sense. This is the case with class, and with the pervasive 'racial' and gender determinations of dominant groups under capitalism. There are many arenas of struggle and resistance. I will draw attention to just one theme which emerges from the analysis of pre-capitalist society and seems important in understanding certain issues of socio-economic organisation which are becoming crucial today. This is the question of a dualism between an 'official' level of socio-economic organisation, and a grassroots level that the official world partly ignores but always presupposes.

## Grassroots and Official Spheres

Traditional societies often found a creative and developmental way of dealing with a duality within social organisation. Feminist discussion of the household – a valuable example being Nancy Hartsock's analysis of Homeric Greece[9] – has shown how the official world is the 'polis', where public life takes place, while women's labour within the household is 'hidden from history'. The alienation this implied restricted individual development, but it also generated struggles which strongly influenced social development. Orthodox structuralism is strong on recognising alienation but weak on recognising struggle. Having helpfully conceptualised 'reification' (turning people into things) through alienation (in the sense of people being both cut off from their potential and physically traded), structuralists tended to assume that women could only be passive: for instance, they assumed that exogamy reduced women to the status of objects, but failed to recognise that through exogamy women acquired an important role in mediating relations between communities.[10] In the same way, evolutionary views of the family one-sidedly emphasise the decline in women's power and state in 'scientific' form the assumption that woman's nature is essentially reproductive.[11] The linearity of a progression to patriarchy must be called into question.[12] In effect, family systems were complex, with overlapping forms. 'It was not a "harmonious dualism" between men and women in matriarchal systems or a corporate co-existence between matriarchal and patriarchal systems. In whatever system, men incessantly sought to control women and their services, and succeeded more often than not.'[13] But precisely because it was a struggle, different outcomes were possible. The variety that characterises pre-capitalist forma-

tions was not determined by natural conditions specific to particular population groups, but by social struggles taking place against the *background* of
these conditions, particularly important being the way the gender struggle
was resolved. This may explain why academic studies come to a puzzling
conclusion about 'contradictory combinations of high and low positions of
women in different areas of social life'[14] in natural social formations. A
feature of this phenomenon is that different types of inheritance overlapped
in the same social structure.[15]

It is possible to extrapolate from this point about the household and
official spheres and identify further dualities in socio-economic organisation.
Ruling groups have by definition to co-exist with a semi-autonomous popular
sphere which has its own economic–technical role. There was probably a
certain creative tension between the spheres, which constituted a developmental principle in its own right, and in this respect we can say that different
pre-capitalist societies acquired their own equilibria, which differed from one
to another (hence their heterogeneity). The popular sphere of socio-economic
organisation played a key role in social development for the following reasons.

EXPERIMENTATION  Oral cultures have always been the living foundation
for written ones.[16] Popular knowledge systems may have been good at
handling something which flows from their developmental character, namely
the fact that there was always a leading edge, an outer limit of knowledge.
The element of magic in traditional knowledge systems has often been seen
as anti-scientific, but Winch was right to point out that any civilisation has
to come to terms with its limitations, the point at which its science and
technology cease to be able to influence the natural environment; less 'advanced' societies possibly have a more transparent way of doing this, via
magic, than industrial society has.[17] Magic constitutes 'a reality in which faith
and skepticism easily coexist'.[18]

THE ORGANISATIONAL ASPECT  The independent grassroots sphere constituted a fundamental cell of economy in general. Here we encounter the
household again. Apart from the role of women within households, there is
the question of the relationship between the household as a whole and the
wider economy. Take, for example, peasant systems: while there is debate
about the existence or otherwise of a specific peasant mode of production,[19]
the peasant family unit can be seen as a powerful tool of economic organisation. It was not confined to the level of mere subsistence.[20] It was, therefore,
susceptible to yielding an 'extra' value which the wider, official economy
could appropriate. In particular, Chayanov's analysis of peasant households
is significant. It is gender-blind, and its full potential is realised only if we
bring it together with the feminist perspective. The important concept is
'self-exploitation'.[21] This reflects the way the household manages its own
labour, but can (in doing so) yield a surplus which some other level of

economic organisation can appropriate *without having to go to the trouble of organising the exploitation itself, directly*. This opens up a whole range of insights on the role of the informal economy under capitalism. But this began in traditional society, where the official world could control and draw value from something which it denies or considers itself vastly superior to.

The grassroots side of this duality can be seen not only at the level of the household, but at the level of the village economy. This was a sphere operating according to its own economic principles – characterised by an important level of self-management, common resources, and so on. The situation in pre-colonial India was one where 'The sovereign authority ... ruled over the whole territory, that is, *over* the villages, while what went on *within* them was a matter for the village communities to look after'.[22] So in a sense, large-scale official society was superimposed on to a sphere which had its own rules, funding itself by value extracted from that sphere. In the African context, the ruling dynasties may be seen as 'living off a communitarian society'.[23] But, while this is a kind of accumulation, it is not accumulation in the capitalist sense because it is static, without giving rise to self-reinforcing circuits. It is thus useful to view it as a 'tribute', an important term in the analysis of pre-capitalist societies.

Resentment about this tribute probably existed – in other words the grassroots has always had a rebellious streak. But this resistance did not call into question the fundamentals of social organisation. It rather reinforced the overall structure by ensuring that the balance was respected, that the official world did not undercut the basis for its own existence by squeezing the grassroots too far. Social criticism from below may in fact have provided society with a defence against the degeneration and parasitism of ruling groups. While dominant groups imposed their interpretation of history,[24] they also recognised the need for an independent guardian of tradition (such as the West African griots), who could criticise rulers who were degenerating. One of Amin's important contributions was to emphasise the importance of humour and satire in this respect.[25] It is a system that can benefit both ruler and ruled: the element of struggle is that lower orders want to stop official society exploiting them, and may be strong enough to limit this, and the element of harmony is that they are protecting not only themselves, but indirectly assuring the survival of the social grouping as well, by keeping alive its dynamism.

The functionality of protest is particularly evident in role-reversals, which most pre-capitalist societies had in the form of periodic festivals where class, age and gender hierarchies were reversed, and social proprieties suspended. In parts of India 'the most impure and exploited of all castes' were elevated to positions of authority in such festivals.[26] The social categories which formed the basis of economic organisation were reversed both as a safety-valve, and, more importantly, as a way of harnessing protest itself in not only preventing the degeneration of social systems but also promoting development. These reversals were, however, only reversals relative to norms which were heavily enforced; and there is no mobility for individuals between the social categories. The notion of impurity in caste systems, for example, prevented the permeability of these divisions. Among the Wolofs in West Africa, the griots, who were the ones permitted to make satirical criticisms of those in power, were also an impure caste. This is expressed in a peculiar myth which has them descended from an already dead man; when one of them dies the body instantly breaks out in great open sores and decomposes.[27] In a sense, the corruption they are exposing is transferred on to them.

The above are a few social issues which will be useful in understanding what subsequently happened with capitalism. I will now consider an aspect particularly relevant to the present study: the international dimension.[28]

## International Issues in the Pre-capitalist World

There is a tendency to over-emphasise the element of conflict and war in pre-colonial societies. This was fuelled by structuralism, which heavily emphasised the role of slave-hunting expeditions in the transition between egalitarian societies and systems of domination.[29] But this is one-sided, because early inter-group relations were characterised not just by the exclusion of the outsider, but also by peaceful cohabitation between groups whose culture permitted them to explore different natural resources within the same territory – for example, pastoralists and agricultural formations.[30] This could be seen as a kind of informal division of labour which did not require a state to organise it. But the economic dualism which existed within individual stratified societies came to exist at an international level, in the sense that the official economy reinforced its status by its role in trade and warfare.

Looking at the trade aspect, one can in some cases identify a situation where 'two economic systems coexisted within the same society but were situated in spheres apparently impervious to each other. These were the village subsistence economy on the one hand, and the economy based on international and even transcontinental commerce on the other.'[31] But élites were also fighting each other, and reinforced their status by the value they were able to appropriate. In effect, the élites of different states competed over who was to enjoy the tribute generated by the grassroots. This was compatible in principle with the creative economic dualism that recognised the autonomy of the 'lower' economic sphere: after all, there was no point destroying the source of the tribute over which élites were competing. An ancient Indian principle held that the cultivator was regarded as 'neutral and inviolable' and was strictly left alone by fighting armies;[32] to some extent, the grassroots perhaps did not care which empire it was part of.

The problem, however, is that competition on an international scale has always tended to generate its own dynamic, which can become uncontrollably destructive. The state abolishes disorder at one level by imposing the rule of law over a certain territory (for example, permitting trade to flourish), but the disorder recurs at a higher level, *between* state entities. International relations theory suggests that this situation gives rise to an objective or subjective process whereby the balance between these competing interests would become a principle of order; and indeed the later European development of a system of predatory states, characterised by an amoral 'realism'[33] and cynical *raison d'état*, was already anticipated in the pre-capitalist context. This could be limited by the creation of a special science of handling these problems, where a balancing principle between power-seeking entities prevails – hence the growth of diplomacy.[34]

Within expansionism, therefore, competition was counterbalanced by something else: a vocation to create order or harmony over a larger territory. The victory-seeking state was propelled by some definition of order which it sought to impose.[35] The moral problem which runs right through the history of international society is this: in a world of ruthless military entities, how can any one of them survive while justifying this action with reference to some principle of social harmony? In commenting on the ancient Chinese theory of inter-state relations, Cleary draws a useful connection with the spirit of martial arts, where the problem is to purify oneself so as to build conflict itself into a principle of harmony.[36] It then becomes the case that the aim of the victory-seeking state is not just to enjoy the tribute but to organise the socio-economic life of the new territory it aspires to control.

Large states, formed through conquest, could deploy an expanded level of economic organisation, including central management of the social division of labour. In the Inca empire, the emperor travelled throughout the territory he ruled; he built up the knowledge to keep large herds of llamas, and to maintain stocks of grain in strategic places to guard against famine, while mining was performed through a rotational labour-service system. This clearly follows a logic of apportioning the total resources of society in the most efficient way. When China was unified, economic organisation also moved to a different level. Conventionally, this is reflected in water conservancy, but really one could speak of macro-economic regulation, even from early times; for example, a sophisticated discussion was had about pricing policy for grain so as to balance incentives to farmers with a reasonable price to consumers.[37]

Here too, struggle from below could be an important mechanism for maintaining the necessary balances. Whatever the merits of these larger agglomerations, there was the risk of homogenising, eliminating the variety characteristic of indigenous systems, wasting the raw material of future development. This could meet with resistance on the part of local populations within the pre-capitalist empires,[38] where peoples fought to maintain their own identity, their own contribution.

## The Impact of Capital Accumulation

With the advent of capitalism, accumulation took over from everything else as the principle of social organisation. With respect to relationships within human society itself, the complex criteria of earlier societies – reciprocal obligations, moral order, the oral transmission of knowledge, the reproduction of the physical environment, and so on – were essentially replaced by only one – making money. At the same time, the element of balance between grassroots and official spheres was also lost. With respect to the relations between society and nature, the commitment to sustainability was lost. The primacy of capital accumulation meant abolishing the 'natural' ways of managing the relationship between the human social system and the physical world, which earlier societies had evolved over millennia.

There is thus a sense in which something that earlier societies had struggled to prevent became a reality with the advent of capitalism. Capitalism aspires to abolish the problem of constraints on the use of resources, but the problem will not go away. It is preserved in the act of its apparent destruction. It is probably the loss of the balancing mechanisms *within* human society which has undermined the balance *between* it and the natural world. This is why the problem of development today raises the issue of what Hegel called 'the negation of the negation': the progressive agenda, which is principally forward-looking and creative, must also include an element of *restoring* something which has been lost. The issue of balance within society and between it and nature is 'sublated' (the dialectical term for an act of destruction which is simultaneously one of preservation) within capitalism until it eventually reasserts itself on the agenda of progress. The 'good' side of this might have been that with the advent of a universal money relationship, personal determinants of servitude would gradually decline. But in practice this has not been the case. In particular, 'race' and gender determinations have been developed under capitalism, and acquired a central role *within* accumulation. It is important to understand why.

In analysing complex processes of change, we have to build an argument step by step. To do this, we must temporarily leave certain elements out of the model and re-incorporate them later. It will be useful first to consider the principles of social organisation most directly typical of capitalism itself. To do so, we can make these temporary assumptions: that it occurred first within a particular society, and second as a pure system characterised by a unified market and wage labour.

Capitalism 'modernises'. This term elides a dual reality. In the more favourable light, there are the aspects which appear progressive, such as the attack on personal, hereditary relations of servitude in order to have the labour market operating freely. These would be replaced by a new form of alienation, with market relations now governing relationships of people to each other, or to things. But there is an element of deception even within this level of the argument. The claim to be progressive hinges on having dissolved the restrictive, decayed structure known as feudalism; the pre-capitalist system in Europe was indeed (in contrast to tributary societies elsewhere in the world[39]) rather stagnant and fragmented. But the more profound thrust was to expropriate the knowledge of the immediate producers and to remove all restrictions on the consumption of resources. 'Tradition' (the opposite of modernisation) after all includes not only ossifying hierarchies, but also the grassroots systems of communal management, complete with their oral traditions, popular science, fertility-oriented belief systems, and so on. Such societies had a 'steady-state' aspect which is not to be equated with stagnancy or lack of dynamism, but purely with the sustenance of a mechanism that enabled them to adapt to change without undermining the foundations of their continued viability. The French Revolution, however, expressed a belief that it would be possible to restart the calendar from zero. There was to be a clear break with the past, which left no room for dialogue with the ancestors, or building on the work of previous generations.

Capital realised a once-and-for-all act of 'primitive' accumulation, grabbing the large amount of resources necessary to launch a development of a completely different kind, which could not be fuelled by the traditional trickle-up of tribute from the grassroots village or household economy, which had respected the principle of its self-regeneration. The process of primitive accumulation either set out *directly* to break up these structures in order to grab resources – as in the enclosure of the commons – or was responsible indirectly for their destruction as a byproduct of the accumulation process. 'Taboos', which were in fact reasonable limitations placed upon the plunder of mineral resources, were broken, and this implied undermining the *social* relations, including gender relations, in which these limits were embedded. The long-hidden history of how this happened is just being uncovered. The feminist critique, in particular the path-breaking work of Carolyn Merchant, has explained this well. The unbridled plundering of nature was explicitly analogous to a new sort of subjection of women.[40] Science was separated from popular knowledge systems, which it now entirely refused to respect.

It was obviously dangerous to break up a system which had proved its worth over millennia, so efforts were made to replace it with a new, internally consistent, self-reproducing structure. Whether or not these endeavours succeeded is a question that remains of crucial importance today. And it is to this that we now turn.

Traditional views of the harmony between human society and nature were abandoned; what took their place was a narrow concern to achieve something very important to capitalist development, namely, to maintain agriculture within a society increasingly focused around industry. The group of eighteenth-century French economists known as Physiocrats advocated policies to give food producers enough economic incentive, which were at the same time premised on some notion of a natural order (sufficient indeed for a later radical like Caldwell to find something positive in the Physiocrat philosophy[41]). But the idea of natural order was also conservative socially, and this was a problem for Enlightenment thinkers who were closer to industrial–commercial interests. Eventually a compromise emerged between the agricultural and industrial ruling classes that reflected the narrow economic dimension of the problem of capitalist development: that in order for the economy to expand, enough food must be produced by a limited rural population to feed growing numbers of industrial workers. This implied a certain systemic equilibrium, not in the sense of any balance between human and natural systems, but only in the narrow socio-economic sense that the agricultural sector of the ruling class must have enough incentive to produce.

The only way of getting fewer workers to produce more goods was by increasing 'productivity', which in turn means applying technology to agriculture. In effect, the scientific approach to agriculture has, historically, signified taking knowledge from the direct producers and turning it into an instrument of tyranny over them.[42] This is one of the bases for the structural dominance of official society (and later takes on a global dimension, as we shall see).

The population freed from agricultural labour would be both available and obliged to work in industry. They would have to accept low wages. This would lead to a rapid accumulation of capital, whose reproduction could be guaranteed by the progress of manufacturing industry. This system could only be considered self-reproducing if it was capable of restructuring itself from time to time, whenever fundamental change became necessary. And there were ways in which this could be achieved. Once development could no longer proceed by building more and more heavy industry, other changes could be made. For example, workers could be paid more so that they could consume their own *industrial* products, and then things which were not real goods, such as so-called services, could be turned into commodities. In this way capitalism could create its own momentum; accumulation could constitute a mechanism of development to replace the one destroyed by the break-up of traditional society.

This model is useful up to a point, if only to highlight the importance of the areas omitted from it, two of which must be emphasised: first, even if we assume that capitalism developed endogenously, it is not a pure system with unified market and wage labour; second, in most countries it developed through conquest.

CAPITALISM IS NOT A PURE SYSTEM Taking the first of these points, the assumption that the old personal form of alienation was *replaced* by the new monetary one is incorrect. At times capitalism added on to its own structure earlier forms of subservient economic organisation once they had been emptied of the functional aspect they used to have. In this sense, the overlapping of different economic spheres was not abolished by capitalism, but re-established in a new form.

Value was still extracted from an unrecognised and unremunerated segment of the economy. As the official world now identified itself as a monetary economy where exchange (including the payment of labour) was conducted more or less at its value, modernisation itself became an instrument of enslavement. It acted as a parasite upon a sector which was not fully monetary, not fully remunerated, and where people's roles were still determined by ascribed personal characteristics (gender, colour), dominating this sector precisely through the gesture of non-recognition implied in the supposed vocation to abolish it.

The household continued to play a key role under capitalism, and in some ways women's exploitation deepened. As long as the domestic economy had retained its independence as an economic sphere, women had derived an important social role from their position within it.[43] This changed with capitalism: 'In the past, marriage for many women had been some sort of business partnership in agriculture, trade or domestic industry, but in the reorganisation which accompanied the industrial revolution, the majority of married women lost their economic independence.'[44] The reproduction of wage labour came to be based on unremunerated household labour. In this sense, even capitalism at the centre, that is to say, the form of capitalism which develops from its own roots and not by conquest from outside, is not 'pure'.

THE COLONIAL FACTOR IN CAPITALIST DEVELOPMENT  The second defect of our model – the assumption of a closed national economy – must now be removed. In reality, capitalist development occurred in most places not through the spontaneous maturing of contradictions within individual societies, but through the external imposition of the rule of the white world. Two issues arise here: firstly, this international dimension was an essential condition for the development of capitalism at the centre; secondly, the colonies were fashioned in such a way that they would permanently service the accumulation needs of the fully capitalist economies.

Non-European societies were developing at the time of colonisation, and this development was cut short. In eighteenth-century India, shipbuilding and the textile industry were extremely advanced, and Indian steel was considered the best in the world.[45] There is a debate about whether India was actually on the way to developing its own capitalist relations;[46] but there certainly was, at the time of colonisation, a massive movement for social change, an *aspect* of which could have been the triumph of mercantile forces over traditional restraints, but which included also a wide range of lower-order movements, standing up for cultural pluralism and opposing the restrictions that traditional society had placed on personal development. This was also accompanied by innovation in economic organisation – the state was, for example, giving loans to peasants to grow particular kinds of crops.[47] Society was therefore developing a new contradiction and a new balance, a creative dynamic which produced quite deep reflection, both spiritual and secular, about issues of change. Colonialism, therefore, involved an externally imposed capitalism displacing an endogenous development which might have become either capitalism or something different.

The international policy of early capitalism is often associated with the term mercantilism. The initial form of European expansion, centred around trade, can be seen as an exploration, not just of geographical space but of possible exploitative relationships at an international level; these replaced the old regional patterns of trade with one that was purely extractive. But through trade, the organisational tools of an eventual post-mercantilist capitalism appeared; joint-stock companies could, for example, eventually become international corporations, which could, in turn, organise not just trade but production globally.

Under mercantilism the theory developed that colonies should be prevented from developing industry. Apparently, the reasoning for this was purely economic, in that the metropolitan country wished to export as much as possible. It was for this reason that the industrialisation of settler colonies like the USA was prevented. But the reality of international capitalism is much more racial than it is economistic. Ultimately, settler colonies were part of the white world; the American War of Independence marked a transition to a situation where the settler world became a leading force in international capitalist development. It became the white world as a whole which jealously guarded its manufactures. In effect, this became the core principle, which has survived many changes in form, and in a sense still exists today.

Eventually, organising principles quite different from the old mercantilism would be required, particularly when it became more profitable to *organise* industry in the periphery rather than prevent it. But there was a more immediate reason why mercantilism in the strict sense had to go: it prevented the dominant powers becoming economically interdependent. As long as the prohibition on development in the colonies depended on the policy of individual colonial powers, it reinforced the division of the white world into competing nationalisms. Logically, the next step would be towards an interdependent white world which inherited from mercantilism the commitment to stop the subject countries producing for their own consumption, but began to enshrine this in a *systemic* form, rather than in the policies of individual states. Looking further ahead, it could be policed by institutions (say, a world bank) apparently owing allegiance directly to the system rather than to individual national interests, and simply telling poor countries what to do to find themselves niches within the system.

This change could come about only as the result of a long historical process. Part of it was the self-reinforcing exploitative relationship created through the drain of value and of human resources from the South. Eric

Williams argued that slavery was a major condition for the growth of capitalism in Europe,[48] and he probably touched a raw nerve, since a whole school of writers emerged devoted to refuting his thesis. Secondly, the damage done to the exploited areas (in terms of restricted development, economic and personal) was even greater than the profit extracted; as Frank puts it, 'one may make a distinction between the costs – economic, social, cultural and psychic – to those who suffer, and the (no doubt) much smaller contribution to those who benefit'.[49] Eventually, capital accumulation established itself on a world scale, with the product of alienated human labour taking on a systemic dynamic of its own, appearing as an immutable logic to which one has no choice but to conform.

There is an ecological angle too: in this respect, the rise of capitalism reflects the victory of the principle of unbridled exploitation over the various checks which had existed in earlier social systems. There has always been a possibility for society to 'go wrong' in this way. There are probably many examples of earlier societies which failed for environmental reasons, but the failure concerned only them. If capitalism had been established in one small society in a small area it would consume itself in its unsustainability and cease to exist. But it is inherently *global*, and this is the problem. It has sucked the whole world and its resources into the role of covering up its own deficiencies, creating a vortex where the inevitable crisis of its own sustainability will tend to drag everything else down with it.

Capitalism always establishes its credentials by attacking tradition in the name of modernisation. At the same time, it retains non-monetary, non-modern elements, and exploits these in a special way, as inputs into the cost of subsistence and reproduction. It does this in both the centre and the periphery (as, for example, in African colonies, where taxes were deliberately introduced to force people to lay their hands on a certain quantity of money either through wage labour or cultivating cash crops). But – and this is crucial – the process does not happen in the same way. In the centre, local capitalism is reproducing itself, which means that it acts as a pole of attraction for the value generated by exploitation. But no such process is happening in the periphery, which as a result does not enjoy the benefits of capitalist expansion. Moreover, in building its power base in the periphery, the centre could take advantage of oppressive local social structures, which appeared to be 'traditional' but in which the functional aspects of the pre-colonial ruling class systems had been destroyed. So useful was this element of non-modernity that apparent tradition could in some cases even be *invented* by colonialism. In Malaya, for example, Indian labourers were maintained by British colonialism in a feudal form of submission patterned upon the relations prevailing in South India.[50]

Elements of duality thus *existed within* both central and colonial societies, but there was another duality which acted at the international level, between the North and the South. It is the overlapping of these two forms of duality which is crucial for interpreting the international political economy (IPE), which prevented the formation of a dynamic of accumulation between countries outside the capitalist centre. What occurred was thus not the uniform extension of the capitalist sphere at a global level, but the constitution of two fundamentally different *kinds* of capitalism. Capitalism expanded enough worldwide to break down self-dynamising socio-economic systems in the subject countries, but, since the impetus for this was external, it was not possible for new capitalist systems to 'take off' there in 'complete' form. Rodney coined 'underdevelop' as a transitive verb in order to highlight this issue,[51] and this explains key features of today's 'underdeveloped' nations:

- stagnant agriculture and its dislocation from the rest of the economy
- lack of industry (at least in the sense of an industry oriented towards a domestic market)
- unfavourable trade balance
- extraversion in terms of being forced to export primary products and import industrial products
- inability to accumulate effectively in the domestic economy because of general poverty and the dependent character of élites which *do* manage to accumulate.

The barrier between the two sorts of capitalism is essentially a 'racial' one. Human capacity is limited by a level of alienation quite different from that existing in earlier forms of exploitative society.

The optimistic view of capitalism would accept that early capitalism was mixed-up and messy, with hangovers from earlier systems, but would argue that we are, after all, talking about *development*, and that modernisation will gradually resolve these problems. But in this book I will present the opposite case: that duality was intrinsic to capitalism and was reproduced *by development itself*.

## The Inevitability of Mass Resistance

This duality can engender resistance as well as exploitation. Mass movements can seek to counter the subordination of their nations by reasserting the creative forms of dualism which existed in pre-colonial society and allowed the grassroots to develop according to its own logic, particularly locally. The official world – whether colonial or in the shape of subordinate local élites – had in most cases by then lost the element of benevolence or patronage characteristic of authentic traditional systems, and had become wholly oppressive. People at the grassroots could try to carve out their own sphere. This wouldn't change the overall economic order, but the grassroots sphere could separate itself to some degree. For instance, the official world was more or less entirely hostile to black populations in the Americas, and at the household and family level, according to Hogan's interesting argument, they

established a more or less distinct political economy.[52] It could be argued
that self-sufficient economic structures indirectly benefited the exploitation
system because labour was reproduced and furnished to the monetary economy without the latter having to meet its true cost. There is an element of
truth in this, but there are other factors that seem to me important in the
longer term: first, the empowerment that occurs when people get the white
economy off their backs and establish a semi-autonomous sphere cannot be
assessed purely in economic terms; and second, there are wider implications
in that these grassroots initiatives could point the way forward to a new
form of political economy at the more general level, in which an alternative
is offered to the key tendency of the present system, which is the subordination of everything to the market and to the expansion of the division
of labour.

Resistance can arise not just in households or families, but also at the
level of organised *movements*. Grassroots protest can appear negative, destructive, obstructive and bloody-minded. But what colonialist anthropologists
branded as primitivism was a stubborn refusal to comprehend a profit-
oriented rationale which indigenous peoples correctly perceived as absurd.
Against an invading economy that gave value only to commodities, societies
struggled to preserve their way of life oriented to use-value.[53] Sometimes
colonial ventures were met simply by withdrawal: a French scheme for
founding settler colonies in Indochina collapsed because the peasants retreated
to the hills and refused to work the land.[54] Struggles were often consciously
directed against economic symbols of colonialism. Thus, in the Maji-Maji
uprising against the German colonial regime in Tanzania, peasants defied
their leaders' advice to continue cultivating cotton and asked, 'How can we
start a war? How can we make the Germans angry? Let us go and uproot
their cotton so that war may arise.'[55] Enemy communications were also
targeted, as they were seen as a symbol of the extraction of raw materials.
In India, peasant rebels encouraged the smashing of railways which, even
though they provided employment opportunities, were viewed as a symbol
of colonial enslavement. The nineteenth-century Senegalese resistance leader
Lat Dior Joob concentrated his forces on preventing railway-building.[56]

These strategies are not merely negative, but imply the defence of an
autonomous system of production and consumption; this emerged clearly
when there was a possibility of controlling territory. Maroon communities in
Jamaica were able to assert their independence not just militarily but at the
level of a functioning political economy. In the Cauca region of Colombia
from colonial times until the end of the nineteenth century, this kind of
movement was endemic.[57] Using crops such as plantain, the land could be
productive according to a non-capitalist logic of sustainability, with high
yields in proportion to energy inputs.[58] Escaped slaves in many parts of the
Americas established self-governing communities with a functioning political
economy in all its aspects. What has been underestimated until recently was

the extent to which they collaborated and fused with Native Americans to create a new political economy incorporating techniques from both cultures.[59]

Although the above examples apply to sparsely populated regions, a similar point could be made with respect to the large area of China controlled by the Taiping Rebellion (1851–64). Britain's massive plunder of resources extracted such a surplus that the safeguards restricting exploitation within the old Chinese social system collapsed. The ruling élites, who reached a political agreement with the enemy, made the situation worse by also squeezing the masses. Peasants responded by seizing power over quite wide areas, and when they did so, they attempted to restore the old economy geared to what local people needed to consume; but since it was impossible to turn the clock back, they worked out new methods, such as redistributing land and organising different crafts in central workshops.[60] The system worked, and it was overthrown only by foreign intervention in collaboration with domestic propertied classes.

Although seeking to restore the self-managed communities of the past, these movements were also forward-looking because the situation had changed. In so far as traditional rulers reached agreement with the aggressors, they forfeited the right to represent the nation; democratic elements took over, and in effect *became* the nation. The restorationist aspect of popular struggles means the reassertion not of a particular set of social practices, but rather of the basic *logic* of traditional societies, with their sustainability and production geared to need. Many writers of international economic theory have attacked the notion that people should produce what they need to consume and consume what they produce, and have argued instead that specialisation and a heightened international division of labour are more efficient. I will examine this more fully later, but it should just be noted here that popular movements often find it easier than economists to cut through the verbiage to the heart of the issue: in the real world, international specialisation and division of labour are usually exploitative.

Grassroots protest movements always seem to be 'there', ready to flare up when conditions are right. In their ideologies, the slave-outlaws of Latin America or the Taiping movement articulated millenarian communistic ideas through a mixture of Christian and traditional symbolism, for the spectre of communism was by no means haunting only Europe in the mid-nineteenth century. But these ideologies should not be viewed (as conservative élites sometimes aver) as a foreign import; on the contrary, as Mariátegui pointed out (in the case of Peru), they have an indigenous basis in their concern to preserve communitarian solidarity structures within traditional societies. It might seem that the strength of these movements lies precisely in their links with the communitarianism of the past, and would wane once urbanisation and globalisation undermine these links. But there is a significant counter-argument, which I will take up later, that trends to self-sufficiency can be reproduced *within* capitalism, as a spin-off of the dualism that is an essential aspect of accumulation. In this sense, the grassroots element can also be 'reborn' in an urban context whenever the official economy fails, even in the North, where the element of continuity with pre-capitalist practices is very weak. Official society can repress these struggles, but cannot obliterate them.

## Capitalist Development Produces Communism

Capitalism gave rise to its most specific opposition in the form of Communism, which, while building on earlier grassroots struggles, created a lower-orders movement appropriate to capitalism itself. The Communist perspective was the sharpest in understanding capitalism because it was not oriented to inventing excuses for it and could be critical of its entirety, not just of individual parts. But while Communism envisages the possibility of replacing capitalism completely, it also acquired, through Marx, an approach to pursuing this goal through a *step-by-step* development based on a realistic assessment of the concrete situation at each juncture. This was facilitated by the dialectical method, according to which any phenomenon is defined by the contradictions within it, and the act of defining something is simultaneously to state how it can change; thus, the tendencies and possibilities within any particular period of capitalism can be understood by considering the specific contradictions within it. Dialectics brings the processes of human thought into line with the processes upon which it is reflecting – that is, change within the natural world. Indigenous peoples had always viewed themselves as part of the natural world, so that it seemed appropriate that human thought should work in the same manner as the world which it was seeking to apprehend, probing a reality which (as new developments in natural science continue to confirm) does not accept a rigid definition of categories. Dialectics was inherited from traditional society, but by an indirect route: Hegel developed it from pre-Socratic Greek philosophers who in turn absorbed it from African and Asian thinking. Marx applied dialectics to capitalism.

Historical materialism is an application of dialectics to the development of human society through its relationship with the natural world. It postulates that the structures through which the relationship between humanity and nature is organised have a developmental potential which leads to major qualitative changes. The 'mode of production' is a deeply established systemic relationship between a particular form of organising human society and the natural world. Sometimes official communism regarded the progression of modes as unlinear and inflexible,[61] or tended to push all societies into a Eurocentric mould;[62] some later writers, rebelling against the mechanistic distortion of modes of production, threw the whole concept out with the bath water.[63] But the concept, used in a flexible and not rigid way, remains important as a basis for understanding how social systems acquire definite patterns which prevail over a certain period, before undergoing a non-deterministic process of change, which can be influenced by human initiative.

It became a basic principle of communism to propel change in a direction favourable to working people, something which can be achieved only if different struggles, at both strategic and tactical levels, are closely co-ordinated. This involves the search for allies, brought together in a common endeavour to circumvent capitalism's ability to use its state and military power to massacre grassroots forces.

The emergence of modern communism was a sign that capitalism had reached maturity, because a set of relationships (exploitation through the wage relationship) existed in fully-fledged form. But, despite this, capitalism today still has developmental potential. At different points in history the contradictions within capitalism can push in two fundamentally different directions. They can be used in a revolutionary sense by the grassroots forces – but this is never inevitable, it depends on the subjective ability to grasp the opportunities available; or they can lead to a major restructuring *within* capitalism, with the aim of establishing a fresh basis for exploiting labour.

Why does capitalism have developmental potential when its relationships already exist in fully-fledged form? One of the most important reasons is that full capitalist relations exist alongside a range of other social relationships, including 'racial' and gender divisions, as well as relations with the natural world. This gives capitalism room to manoeuvre, both to find new forms of exploitation and to prevent radical forces linking up.

Since the official world is dominated by those who want to maintain the existing system, and because the forces of opposition are weak and scattered, there is an incentive for Communism to seek a unified strategic perspective, even a unified organisational core. For this reason, different sets of orthodox Communist ideas and organisational principles have become dominant at different times. While this is understandable, in practice it has given rise to certain trends which weaken Marxism's inherent ability to see through exploitative relationships. A key example is Eurocentrism: here it was assumed that capitalism had created large industrial armies focused in Europe where the workforce was collectivised and disciplined, and that these could be turned against their creator, capital, to create the core of a new society. The implications are clearly not just analytical but also organisational. And it is here that the weakness of this line of argument becomes apparent, for by establishing a definition of Communism centred on the specific social forces and struggles which arise on the basis of pure monetary economy, it neglected the whole range of social forces arising from the *informal* exploitative relationships which gave capitalism leeway to outflank factory organisation (in ways which we will describe later). But the setback was only temporary, for there has always been a critical tradition within Marxism that can help it to adapt to new problems, to analyse these more complex relationships, and eventually to formulate a new strategy and new tactics for the struggles to which they give rise.

Today the core ideas of Marxism remain dangerous to established interests.

The concept of accumulation is as relevant as ever in providing a model for understanding the operation (globally and within individual countries) of objectified and alienated human labour. Under capitalism, surplus – the ability of labour to produce more than is needed for subsistence – takes on a life of its own. Its expansion becomes self-propelling, acting independently of the will of individuals. There may have been a powerful sense of individual mission with the Victorian entrepreneur, but the process has become partly depersonalised with the operation of fund managers and the like in more modern forms of accumulation.

In considering accumulation, one of the main issues Marxism addressed was developmentalism. It benefits any exploitative system to keep people quiet and tell them to work hard, but under capitalism this is plausible because the system constantly creates great wealth, feats of engineering and ways of controlling nature; so it might well be assumed that at some point the wealth will be shared. Marx's answer was categorical: since capitalism is fundamentally fuelled by accumulation, the impoverishment of the working masses is a necessary component of the production of this wealth.

To understand accumulation we must dissect it, and this implies a simplification of reality. Whenever we do this, there is a risk of distortion of which we have to be aware. There are elements of both abstract logic and concrete historical analysis in the Marxist method;[64] an important example is the use of a single-country closed-economy model, which forms a necessary part of the development of the argument. Problems arise when the simplification is mistaken for the reality.[65] It becomes easy for Eurocentrism and sexism to creep in. Even more risky is the simplification which focuses on the monetary economy, leaving aside all the racial and household layers of exploitation.

But the tools for analysing the wider dimensions of exploitation are there. Particularly important is the centre–periphery theory, which allows accumulation to be understood in a wider sense. Raw materials can be grabbed from colonies, neglecting the preservation of nature or the reproduction of the local labour which goes into producing them. Cash-crops forcibly grown in colonies can be used to feed and clothe metropolitan workers, making their living costs cheaper so that capitalists do not have to pay them so much. The full cost of labour seems to be paid, but in reality it is subsidised by inputs which are not fully remunerated. So the pure monetary economy is partly an illusion, sustained by the unacknowledged informal, racial economy. Even the development of class relations in the centre was influenced by the international circuits of accumulation.[66] In all these ways, the impoverishment of the working masses in the periphery is intensified. The problem of poverty, which has become the central problem in development today, cannot be understood outside the context of capital accumulation, and fundamentally can never be resolved while capital accumulation is the ruling principle of the international system. Communism, in fact, acquired its wider historical sense of mission in linking up with the mass-based movements which flourished at the sharpest points of exploitation, precisely where capitalism was not pure.

# Notes

1. While some schools of thought (for example, sociobiology) have latched on to the fact that Darwinian views on the struggle for survival could be used to justify both competitive capitalism and developmentalism, there is a conflict with the Biblical aspects of Reaganism.

2. This term is problematical, because it implies a certain teleology – as if capitalism was waiting to happen; allowing for this danger, it is used in the absence of an obvious alternative.

3. Cf., for example, Shiva 1988.

4. Goonatilake 1982.

5. Cf. Bleier 1984.

6. Cf. Snowden 1991.

7. These are certainly deeply ingrained in vocabulary, as Shakespeare's sonnets attest.

8. The term 'ren' (people) was applied only to the majority Chinese nationality. This fused with the colour issue when African slaves began to be used widely; cf. Dikötter 1992.

9. Cf. Hartsock 1983.

10. Cf. the critique of Lévi-Strauss by Gerda Lerner 1987, p. 48.

11. Coward 1983.

12. Diop 1989.

13. Amadiume 1987, p. 84.

14. Whyte 1978, p. 120.

15. In Malaya, for example, there were elements of inheritance along male and female lines, and although men dominated the public sphere, women in practice had considerable economic power; Cecilia Ng and Maznah Mohamed, 'Primary but Subordinated – Changing Class and Gender Relations in Rural Malaysia', in Agarwal 1988b.

16. Edwards and Sienkewicz 1990.

17. Winch 1970.

18. Taussig 1980, p. 231.

19. See de Janvry 1981, Chapter 3.

20. D. Thorner, 'Peasant Economy as a Category in Economic History', in Shanin 1971.

21. Chayanov 1966; see, for example, pp. 6, 73.

22. Mukherjee 1974, p. 150.

23. Jaffe 1985, p. 33.

24. See, for example, the discussion by I. Roxborough in Archetti 1987.

25. Amin 1983, p. 4.

26. Guha 1983, p. 33.

27. Diop 1981.

28. I am using the term in a loose way, to refer to relations between population groups at different levels.

29. Cf., for example, Meillassoux 1986, p. 49.

30. Rigby 1985, p. 64.

31. Nnoli 1981, p. 96.

32. Pareti 1965, p. 441.

33. I am using 'realism' in the sense in which it is used in international relations theory to mean the pursuit of state interests in an international system, where the effective actors are states and where they relate to one another solely through power.

34. Cf., for example, Nag 1923.

35. Kautilya (attrib.) 1962.

36. Cleary 1988.

37. Hu Jichuang 1981, p. 39.

38. C. Sigrist, 'Akephale politische Systeme und nationale Befreiung', in Grevemeyer, ed., 1981.

39. Cf. Amin 1980.

40. Cf. Merchant 1990.

41. Caldwell 1977.

42. Cf. Marie Christine Zelem, 'L'Évolution des Techniques éfromagères dans le Cantal, France du XVIII au XIX Siècle', in Dupré, ed. 1991.

43. Joan W. Scott and Louise A. Tilly, 'Women's Work and the Family in Nineteenth Century Europe', in Amsden, ed. 1980.

44. Pinchbeck 1981, p. 312.

45. Goonatilake 1984, p. 53.

46. See Frank 1978, Chapter 4.

47. Cf. Mukherjee 1974.

48. Williams 1994.

49. Frank 1978, pp. 162–3.

50. Hua Wu Yin 1983, p. 46.

51. Rodney 1972.

52. Cf. Hogan 1984.

53. Trobriand islanders in Melanesia as described by Malinowski, or Bakweri of west Cameroun exasperated European traders and plantation-owners because they simply refused to take on board the logic of commodities; cf. Taussig 1980, pp. 19–20.

54. Cf. Scott and Tria Kerkvliet, eds. 1986.

55. G. Gwassa and J. Iliffe, eds., *Records of the Maji-Maji Rising* Part 1, Nairobi, 1968, quoted in Guha 1983, p. 144.

56. A. Sheikh, personal communication.

57. Taussig 1980, pp. 57–8.

58. This non-capitalist usage of the term 'productivity' will be explained in the chapter on the environmental perspective.

59. Cf. Forbes 1988.

60. *The Taiping Revolution* 1976, p. 44.

61. Cf Wu Dakun, 'The Asiatic Mode of Production in History as Viewed by Political Economy in its Broad Sense', in Su Shaozhi *et al.* 1983.

62. For a critique of this, see Amin 1980.

63. An example is Hindess and Hirst 1977.

64. Cf., for example, Ilyenkov 1982; Nabudere 1990.

65. On the dangers of assuming the national economy to be the real unit of analysis, see Szentes 1988, p. 23.

66. It has been shown, for example, how closely the formation of the proletariat in the textile industry – the key to the early industrial revolution – was conditioned by the fluctuations of colonial trade; see G. Morgan, 'From West to East and Back Again: Capitalist Expansion and Class Formation in the Nineteenth Century', in H. Newby, ed. 1985.

# 2

# Imperialism and the Issue of Large-Scale Changes in Capitalism

## Imperialism's Place in the History of Capitalism

Just as is occurring today, as will be discussed later in the book, there was also a massive change within capitalism last time there was a change of century. 'Imperialism' was the term then widely used to describe the new structure. Superficially, the term describes an increase of nationalism among the great powers, a scramble for colonies and furious competition which led eventually to the outbreak of world war in 1914. But it was also understood that there were deeper structural changes within capitalism, such as the formation of large companies, the growth of 'finance' capital, and an attempt to defuse social problems by uniting different classes behind ultra-nationalist slogans.

There are two reasons to study this period: first, while we have considered capitalism as an overall category within human development, there is also a dynamic of social development within capitalism. Imperialism is central to this. Second, it may be that we are still in the era of imperialism. From this angle, imperialism would be defined as a capitalism which has completed its initial development and become mature. I will argue that we have to consider imperialism in two senses. In one sense, imperialism constituted a defined stage in capitalist development (I will loosely use the term 'classic imperialism' to signify this) which has since been superseded; but in another sense it also permanently changed the course of development, introducing features that are still present. While capitalism has stopped growing (in the sense of growing up), even within this mature phase it can undergo large-scale structural development. To grasp this, we need to understand the deepest contradictions underlying capitalist development, which expressed themselves in a special form in imperialism.

## The Conflict between Nationalism and Globalism in Capitalist Development

Capitalism initially came into existence through the act of 'primitive accumulation', for example by abolishing local, non-monetary economies; once

24

established as a system, it needs to continue its development: it continues to accumulate, and this implies major structural change. In a simplistic view (although we will examine this critically in a moment), the fuel for this development appears to be the expansion of the capitalist market. This process gives rise to a number of contradictions, one of the most important of which is that between the national and global dimensions of capital accumulation. This surfaced in an acute form with imperialism, and in different ways it is still playing itself out today.

Historic capital accumulation had two dimensions: the establishment of a unified market within national boundaries, and the global dimension. The latter was present from the beginning, a fact often neglected in the contemporary discourse on globalism, which assumes it to be the result of capitalist development rather than its cause. If we consider the early phase of capitalist development, the national and global aspects seem to fit together quite neatly, because accumulation from international exploitation (the slave trade, colonialism) was used to strengthen the nation at the centre. But since these national economies were wholly competitive, the world system might be torn apart by a series of 'zero-sum' relationships in which there was no room for compromise.[1] Catastrophic violence between capitalist powers was bound to have come at some point if a way had not been found to transcend mercantilism. It is against this background that the idea of free trade was put forward at the beginning of the nineteenth century in the work of English economist David Ricardo. It advocated, in effect, a unified international market as a counterweight to the destructive tendencies inherent in a system of competing national economies.

The argument is presented in the form of an economic rationale which is, at first sight, seductive. One of the main advantages of establishing a national market was to eliminate a lot of local systems all doing the same thing, and to make possible a division of labour. The same argument could apply internationally: rather than having several national economies all producing everything, in an open economy each country would specialise in what it was 'best at' and trade with others to obtain the rest. Ricardo's widely quoted theoretical model (based on two countries and two commodities) pinpoints the savings that would result from such specialisation: even if one country could produce both commodities more cheaply than the other, it would still have an interest in specialising in the commodity in which, comparatively, its 'advantage' is greater, measured in the ease with which a product could be made. This is because it would gain more by maximising the output of the commodity with the greater comparative advantage, even if this entails importing the other commodity, which it could itself produce more cheaply, from the other nation.

This is still the argument used today to force developing countries to open up their economies, as we will see later. But it is important that Ricardo's model was never intended as a blueprint for newcomers to join the capitalist club; it was, rather, a plea for that club to regulate relations among its members in such a way that they would not tear international capitalism apart. The economic savings were not the fundamental motivation for the progression to free trade; they were a reward or compensation for abandoning nationalism. Free trade could push things towards a co-operative dynamic – interdependence – which would yield a positive outcome for all parties. Where mercantilism saw international economics as a 'zero-sum' relationship, free trade theory argues that one party's gain can also be a gain for the other party. This can be understood in an economic sense, on the assumption that interdependence brings greater efficiency, but the more fundamental gain is really political. This is in effect what Ricardo envisages when he says that free trade 'binds together by one common tie of interest and intercourse, the universal society of nations throughout the civilised world'.[2]

Such arguments look towards some concept of international society, but there are two hidden problems in this vision. First, is it a society where the actors (by analogy with citizens of a national society) are states, or one where economic actors (entrepreneurs, firms) operate directly within a global-ised space? In practice, Ricardian liberalism did not challenge the national economy head-on, but this may be its ultimate implication. Second, the international society in question could be an unequal one. From the North–South angle, there are two crucial questions: first, who appropriates the savings arising from a supposedly more efficient division of labour? There is no proof they will be divided evenly. On the contrary, the country with the higher productivity (which therefore uses less labour) may well in practice exchange a smaller value (measured in terms of labour-time) for a larger one. Second, once the 'civilised' world is thus bound together, what happens to the 'state of nature' outside? Can other countries break into the circle? The established national economies could cement themselves into a group which jointly acted to maintain its members' monopoly of high productivity.

In some sense, these tendencies are continuing today. The powerful actors are increasingly interdependent, are safeguarding their technological monopoly, and are pushing the world economy into a new phase, where the conventional mechanisms of national economic management are outdated. But this his-torical development has not been arrived at by a direct route. Instead of an abrupt transition from mercantilism to liberalism, there was an extended transitional period in which economic nationalism was strengthened, which allowed nations, behind protective barriers, to promote the growth of new forces that would ultimately populate the economic space, once the balance tipped towards globalism. But, at the time, none of this was apparent. And the debate between the 'free-traders' and the 'nationalists' raged fiercely.

Friedrich List, a German writing in the first half of the nineteenth century, encapsulates the nationalist argument against free trade. There are actually two different levels at which it operates, a contradiction of which List himself (and the nationalist discourse in general) showed little awareness. The most profound level is that the Ricardian argument about the inefficiency of overlapping national economies is true only in a rather narrow economic framework, which overlooks many features in the real world: it forgets not only about the economic costs of specialisation (transport, retraining and so on) but also the non-economic ones – the social alienation implied when people are producing things they don't consume. From this perspective, the nation, however artificial, appears as the last bastion of the real economy, guardian of the link between local production and consumption, an economics which puts social developmental interests above the short-term calculations which (according to liberal economics) are supposed to yield the best possible allocation of resources. This idea, constantly repressed in mainstream economics, is reflected in List's theory of 'productive powers',[3] as well as in the title of one of his works, 'The Natural System of Political Economy'. This line of argument implies that free trade should be limited permanently, rather than simply temporarily.

At a different level, the nationalist argument accepts the Ricardian goal, but believes it cannot be arrived at directly. If free trade were prematurely applied, the capitalist market would never be established at the level of the individual country; and if it was not established at this level, there would be no basis for an eventual international economy. So the national dimension must come first, and the rest would follow. Although the Listian argument does not directly address North–South issues, it has a racial subtext just as much as Ricardo's, in the sense that the collective dominance of the North is conditional on individual Northern economies' being 'complete', with a range of different industrial and agricultural sectors all more or less hanging together. These must be built at a national level first.

In some ways, this scenario appears to explain the actual development of capitalism quite well. By the beginning of the twentieth century, significant progress had been made in building national economies, and the forces pushing towards Ricardian interdependence could at last come to the fore. This helps to explain why it was at that particular time that America developed its sense of mission, of 'manifest destiny', which we will consider in a moment. And more recently, since the 1980s capital accumulation has indeed progressed by gobbling up the nation state along with all the industries and services which the statist dimension used to protect.

But there are flaws in this model which help to explain why in practice economic nationalism has been hard to shift. First, there is a fallacy in the analogy between the destruction of local communities to create a national market (and division of labour) and the weakening of the state to create a world market: the national market is capitalism's own creation, it serves a purpose as a focus for identities in a way that the world market could not possibly do. The 1980s thus opened up immense problems for the next stage of capitalist development, as I will argue later. Second, the capitalist nation is not really 'natural'; it built itself by an ever-increasing plunder of external natural and human resources, which had to be policed militarily. For both of these reasons, weakening economic nationalism is highly dangerous for capitalism, and was resisted for a long time. But we have leapt ahead in our argument. It is important first to examine the origins of the modern phase of capitalist development – imperialism – which began around 1900 under the auspices of an accentuated nationalism.

## Imperialism as a Deliberate Policy

The reason capitalism entered an extreme nationalist phase is not explicable on economic grounds alone. The newly created capitalist market, which fuelled growth endogenously, made sense in economic terms insofar as rising productivity in agriculture threw peasants off the land and forced them to accept inhuman conditions in the new industries, enabling extremely rapid capital accumulation to take place. But this process also created social contradictions that threatened to tear nascent capitalism apart. So a new problem arose: now that the old identities of traditional society had been destroyed, what could be created to replace them?

The initial response, which began in 1815, was a move towards highly conservative political systems throughout the capitalist world. In Britain, the most fully developed capitalist country, it was remarked (in an article published in 1870, considered to be influential in the movement towards imperialism) that no more than thirty thousand people had any sort of stake in the country.[4] Elsewhere, the new capitalist class tried to prevent a social crisis by reaching agreement with traditional forces: France, for instance, retained a class of agricultural smallholders, but, however effective socially, this option created its own problem in that it limited the economic development of a capitalism to rival England.

These responses, however, at best repressed dissent, without addressing its basic causes, and social radicalism remained very strong. In fact, Communists attempted a fusion of the co-operative element in grassroots traditional society with the new agglomerations arising through industrial work-discipline. They argued that the old community life could be restored only by destroying capitalism. In response, capitalism sought to develop a new concept of community, based on the idea of the nation, which would unite all classes in their support for the colonial endeavour. The idea was to evolve some sort of developmentalist philosophy which could co-opt the social protest movement with the argument that if the nation remained successful in international conquest, there would be a fund available for distribution. But not even then would consumption necessarily rise, for the fund could be channelled into public works or education, thus strengthening the means of social control imposed by capitalism.

## Imperialism as an Objective Process

In its response to social conflict, imperialism appears manipulative and deliberate. But there is another way of looking at it: capitalist development was also an objective process which spontaneously generated new organisational forms. The most important of these forms were the big corporations and finance capital. Those who envisaged progression to an eventual world market were not wrong in the sense that these new forces would eventually push in that direction. But the problem is that, in the short term, they actually strengthened the destructiveness of competitive nationalism.

To understand both how this happened and how it was eventually resolved, it is important to understand the cyclical development of capitalism. This is the most objective aspect of capitalist development, in that it is not a conscious strategy of the capitalist actors themselves.

Under capitalism, development is essentially uneven. This can be understood from three angles: first, it exploits groups of people differently according to 'race' or gender; second, it is spatially uneven; third – and this is what concerns us particularly here – it is uneven in time. The simplest form of this temporal unevenness is the business cycle. Capitalist development is cyclical in a special sense: whereas traditional society respects the cycles of the natural world, capitalism's reference-point is the self-expansion of profit. This happens through the profit from one phase of production being invested in the succeeding one, which attempts to be larger than its predecessor. However strategic it seeks to be, capitalist development can never altogether shed the narrowness of this preoccupation with realising the next increment of profit.

Now, this very narrowness is the cause of economic downturns. Since the driving force of capital is self-expansion, it does not respond to some pre-existing demand, as liberalism asserts. Rather, competition drives enterprises to increase their production through economies of scale, whether or not the demand exists to absorb the new mass of products. At the same time, capital accumulates by exploiting labour, which implies keeping down wages and thus limiting the consumption which could absorb the products. The result is a periodic flare-up of overproduction, leading to bankruptcies. This in turn undermines people's identification with the system by causing insecurity of employment. To manage the economy in such a way as to iron out these fluctuations is not easy, so in practice capitalism often plays the card of 'growth' in the hope that this will swallow up the fluctuations of the business cycle. This solution was attempted first in the case under consideration – imperialism – when countries competed frantically with each other in a race to expand into the colonies.

But although the crises of over-production were part of the problem, they were also at another level, potentially at least, part of the solution. Their repetitive nature brought about a qualitative change, since with each downturn smaller companies were eliminated. So suddenly there was a new situation: oligopoly (colloquially referred to as monopoly), where each branch of production was dominated by a few companies which could anticipate each other's decisions or even deliberately collude. But there was also the deeper phenomenon of 'socialisation', whereby the entire resources of a whole society could be mobilised in pursuit of capital accumulation, and investment capital separate itself from specific industries. This might provide a solution by raising the possibility of strategic decisions. For example, large firms could develop management doctrines, and the state could become a major player. The background against which these decisions might be taken is provided by the 'highest' level of cyclical development, namely, 'long cycles'. Capitalist development probably falls into major periods which are international in scope, lasting perhaps three decades, during which the different parameters – social, technological, economic management, international relations and so on – acquire a definite structure and definite patterns of relations to one another. In other words, they relate in a systemic way, maintaining their essential characteristics until eventually the system is no longer tenable and has to change fundamentally, along with many of its individual components.

So important are long cycles that capitalist theory itself seeks to understand them, but the discussion by orthodox economists is often quite reductionist, narrowing the issue to, for example, the role of technology.[5] Changes of structure are really a response to a number of mutually reinforcing imperatives, some economic and some socio-political. In conceptualising such interlocking solutions, the term 'regime of accumulation' is useful.[6] A characteristic form of international politics is a crucial part of this picture.[7]

Imperialism initially emerged through a process whereby different tendencies of capitalist development had felt their way towards a mutually compatible structure. This does not mean that the outcome was the only possible one or the 'best' one. It would be an interesting exercise to speculate about another possible resolution, but this would be difficult because any outcome has to emerge, as imperialism did, not as an *a priori* blueprint but as a result of many mutually influencing trial-and-error probes.

We can define a given long cycle by its characteristic contradictions, so the process of definition is also a statement of the conditions under which it will eventually move into crisis, and the possible options for the resolution of that crisis. This is the element in the toolkit which we will seek to apply in the concluding section of this work to the situation at the end of the twentieth century. In the case of imperialism, its definition includes a statement of the following limitations:

1. Industrial capital was effective in building heavy industry and infrastructure. At a particular point this finds a natural resolution in the form of a switch to consumer goods. But, however logical, this evolution is hard to realise in practice because exploitation tends to restrict the market. Imperialism did not show how this dilemma could be resolved.

2. The new monopolies evolved under the auspices of nationalism. Although in principle impatient with the limitations of nationalism, the new actors (firms, financial interests), operated for the moment within it, thus intensifying the self-destructive, zero-sum dynamic already visible under mercantilism; this was reflected both in the tendency of heavy industry, which was structured in such a way as to run a surplus, to find an outlet in militarisation, and in an excessive demand for raw materials, which each nation sought to obtain from its own colonies.

3. In retrospect, it can be seen that some form of dependent industrialisation of the colonies would constitute one of the most important ways of unleashing a vast new range of possibilities for capital accumulation. The classic phase of imperialism inhibited this.

These contradictions led eventually to the transition to a new phase. Such a transformation would simultaneously preserve the essential aspects of imperialism as a mature form of capitalism (parasitism, speculative capital) and get rid of the features merely characteristic of the long cycle begun in the late nineteenth century, in particular the extreme competition among capitalist powers.

## Can Capitalism Organise Itself?

What could the elements of such a solution be? It is at this point that we should consider some issues developed by left-wing analysts of imperialism in the early years of the twentieth century. There are two crucial issues: strategic decision-making, and the relationship of the capitalist market to pre-capitalist systems.

A paradox of capitalism is that a lot of its claims have been and still are based on the free market, but the free market is itself a myth. In fact, a more realistic claim for capitalism as a system with developmental potential might be derived from the very thing which free-market economics most strenuously denies – monopoly. At the beginning of imperialism, capitalism's apologists were less inhibited about making such a claim, and the implications of monopoly were openly debated. Part of the left sought to take this line of argument to its logical conclusions: the future might lead to a sort of 'ultra-imperialism' in which strategic planning would take over from national-competitive chaos. Lenin countered this with an important observation: it would be all very well if strategic decision-making was the only issue, but in reality it is increasingly accompanied by something equally important – parasitic finance capital, which essentially seeks short-term profit. Today's capitalism, dominated as it is by currency speculation, the futures market, and so on, has become parasitic in ways that Lenin could scarcely have imagined, strongly confirming his argument that these are characteristics of mature capitalism, which it will never shake off. In this sense it is still correct to see imperialism as 'the highest stage of capitalism'. But despite this, it is important to recognise that imperialism can still undergo large-scale change as it acquires new regimes of accumulation that allow it to be parasitic in new ways.

What we need to understand are the contradictions that could fuel such a development. It is here that we have to look at the relationship between the capitalist market and the traditional community from a different angle. Superficially, imperialism made it appear that capitalism was becoming more internationalised, because it burst out of its home base and grabbed even more colonies. The theoretical approach to imperialism did not fundamentally challenge the assumption of a linear growth of increasing internationalisation; it simply sought to look beneath the surface and pinpoint the causes, which were assumed to be something to do with the dynamic of capital accumulation within the centre. Part of this debate involved the 'underconsumptionist' model, put forward by Rosa Luxemburg and widely criticised.[8] She observed that capital accumulation could not proceed in a self-contained way at the centre. The destruction of the traditional economy had been viewed as a one-off act to generate the funds for an initial injection of investment which would afterwards become self-sustaining, but Luxemburg explained it as a continuing process, whereby 'overseas, [capital] begins with the subjugation and destruction of traditional communities, the world historical act of the birth of capital, since then the constant epiphenomenon of accumulation'.[9] It was not just primitive, but continuing, so capitalist development would need a store of traditional systems to break up, or otherwise it would grind to a halt.

In some respects the theory is simplistic, and Lenin in particular criticised the notion of underconsumption. The arguments he employed are still valid, as we will see in our subsequent enquiries.[10] He stated that the key contradiction within 'pure' capitalism was not economic, but essentially a social issue, the balance of power among classes. Capitalism 'could' invest everything domestically, but if it did so, it would not be able to avoid raising the status of the working class;[11] and it is for this reason – the political need to prevent the working class from gaining more power – that it internationalises. This has the strength of avoiding a mechanistic and economistic reading. And there is a lot in this which rings true today, in that the South continues to pay the price for central capitalism defusing its own social contradictions. As long as the increased exploitation of the periphery enabled capital to maintain its status relative to labour, new élites, who were not afraid of raising the status of the working class, could adjust the internal relations of pure capitalism so that it could consume its own product. Keynesianism was the proof of this. It is curious that the official communist movement after Lenin's death, while it religiously affirmed Leninism and attacked underconsumption, completely failed to take on board the possibility of such a solution.

But there is a wider perspective within which the issues raised by Rosa

Luxemburg are fundamental, and are not defeated by the criticism of 'under-consumption'. The seeming self-containedness of any possible structural solution is only superficial, since accumulation has to fuel itself through non-renewable inputs. Our analysis of the post-war long cycle and its crisis will illustrate this concretely. Such inputs include colonial labour, which is so heavily exploited as to undermine the conditions of its future reproduction, and resources from the natural world. The strength of Luxemburg's analysis was to focus on the non-renewable inputs into capital accumulation; the weakness was that she focused on the one area where capitalism has been relatively successful, for it has learned how to manufacture 'tradition'. But, whereas Lenin was right to emphasise the social dimension, it is no longer valid to restrict this dimension to the centre, as he did. For today, international capitalism must develop in such a way that it carries with it a set of class relations that is viable – that is, which facilitates exploitation – not only in the centre but *in the periphery as well*. Ultimately, this means it has to propagate some vision of 'development'. To understand how this vision could be created, it is important now to examine what was happening in the periphery in the nineteenth century.

## Southern Élites' Quest to Copy the National Capitalist Model

Grassroots movements in the periphery always tend to turn their back on the global economy and restore links between local production and consumption. Élites, on the other hand, will often seek to use the international system to their advantage. That system wants to exclude them, but if they hammer at it hard enough it may be forced to let them in. It was possible for the élites in the colonies in the nineteenth century to put forward a national development strategy which viewed the system as hostile but sought to accentuate the favourable aspects of it. In doing so, they explored many of the parameters of development that were to be addressed in a much less clear-sighted way after the Second World War.

Liberal economists at the time argued for a direct transition from mercantilism to a kind of precocious neo-colonialism in which the South could be exploited through the world market. In effect, this would benefit the overlords because they then wouldn't need to bear the costs of directly ruling the rest of the world, and in Britain, there had been arguments from as early as the 1860s that an empire was more trouble than it was worth. But perhaps it was more important that Britain, as the leading great power, had the most to gain from an open world market. There was no consensus within international capitalism as a whole that it was practical to implement liberalism at that time.

The fact that liberalism existed as an idea nevertheless opened up interesting prospects to Southern élites in a way that anticipates the arguments of the 1980s. Liberalism was hostile to mercantilism, and the crucial issue from the colonial point of view was that mercantilism prohibited the industrial development of colonies, something that the Southern élites strongly favoured. This can be seen in the case of India. The East India Company (typically mercantilist) teamed up with local fundamentalists who also opposed social change. The liberal lobby in Britain was its enemy, so independence-minded Indians, such as Rammohun Roy in the early nineteenth century, logically saw it as an ally. Liberalism, the Southern élites thought, could be used to kill two birds with one stone: it would break the international power of mercantilism while simultaneously weakening traditional constraints on development and enabling local capitalist forces to emerge.

But there was a flaw in this thinking, in that while there was clearly an existing structural inequality, there was no proof that the free market would eliminate it; it could, on the contrary, make it worse. It had seemed to Southern élites that whereas mercantilism prevented development, liberalism would permit it; but in a deeper sense the difference might rather be that one, mercantilism, would prevent development via policy, and the other, liberalism, would prevent it systemically. This issue was pinpointed in the latter part of the nineteenth century by another Indian economist, Dadabhai Naoroji, who, in doing so, introduced the important concept of 'drain': the transfer of accumulated surplus, he argued, prevented India from 'making' its own capital, and in the absence of indigenous fixed capital, trade was bound to be dominated by the established industrial power.[12] Nineteenth-century Indian economists also perceived that the problem was not only systemic at an international level, but there was also a crucial intermediate step which occurred within the subordinated country. They pointed out that the extreme poverty of peasants in the rural sector meant that they consumed very little, and that this, in its turn, meant that resources were not fixed locally, and could easily be siphoned into the port economy, itself closely linked with the colonial power; this intensified the lack of fixed capital, leaving India at the mercy of the international free market.

This was an extremely far-sighted analysis, infinitely deeper than the naive free-trade-oriented development theories of today. The pitfalls of attempting to use free trade to stimulate development in the South are still substantially the same; but by now everyone has forgotten these lessons, so it is safe for international capitalism to reinvent the free-trade discourse. But during most of the nineteenth and twentieth centuries, people in the colonies were understandably suspicious of free trade, so for the most part they adopted a different strategy: nationalism.

## The Attempt to Replicate the National Capitalist Model in the South

According to the nationalist approach to development, the international system is hostile to new development projects but if, in spite of the opposition, the nation in the South manages to get its project off the ground, the international community will accept it, as the whole system is premised on the nation-state. Objectively, capitalism was spreading through the incremental addition of national economies. At least since the time of Peter the Great's Russia, aspiring developers had been working out a method. They faced the problem of having an already established power (England) controlling the international market; but this could be counterbalanced by the 'advantage of the latecomer': once certain productive experience and technology existed, the learning curve could be shortened.

It made sense for the South to attempt the same thing. But this brings us back to the difficulty that the dominant industrial powers do not follow a purely endogenous accumulation dynamic. International capitalism will always need a South to exploit. If countries from this area were to become successful latecomers, the accumulation system would suffer a double blow: the size of the exploiting area would increase while the territory available for exploitation would shrink! This is the fundamental reason why all the talk about general-ised growth is pure nonsense. It is still possible that a few new countries will be admitted. But the problem is that whereas the European world more or less accepted that its own countries (even though they might fight among themselves) were entitled to join the club of industrialised countries eventually, this did not apply to countries of the South. They were prepared to intervene, jointly if necessary (as was several times the case in China), to cut short some development which might withdraw major areas of the South from the field of exploitation.

Over the past half-century this motivation has been veiled by a lot of hypocritical verbiage, but in the nineteenth and early twentieth centuries it was relatively explicit. Aspiring developers knew they were fighting an enemy determined to smash them. This had an influence on the latecomer models, which has proved quite lasting even when the original reasons were forgotten: they are strongly marked by authoritarianism and militarism.

For both military and economic reasons the window of opportunity for nations in the South was quite small; they had to prevent themselves from being invaded and at the same time force the pace of development, or otherwise the benefits of the primitive accumulation resulting from the liquidation of traditional society would be creamed off by foreign exploiters. Clearly, there was a risk that militarism could become an instrument of oppression,[13] but the threats to which it responds were real.

Much of the latecomer, nationalistic strategy revolves around the idea that for the South capitalist development cannot proceed at the 'natural' pace, which it would develop in the absence of international factors. If they could industrialise within a time warp, domestic entrepreneurs would expro-priate traditional society at their own pace and develop a level of technology appropriate to that particular stage. But it is not possible for them to ignore the advanced level of technology existing elsewhere and this meant forcing the pace. According to the latecomer argument, there is an advantage, in that they can copy technology. But there is the disadvantage of more difficult social relations: social change cannot be speeded up in the same way as technological change; the logical conclusion is that the state should act as proxy for a capitalist class, keeping its place warm.

Moreover, domestic social relations are inserted within international ones. This is a problem because the relationship with the world economy is a dependent one, but it is not inconceivable to imagine solutions: for example, it seems possible that the wealth generated by landowners exporting products onto the world market could be invested in local industry to meet the new demand in a way that is conducive to development.

Concrete cases show how these issues played themselves out in practice. Japan was the favourable case. The initial expansion of colonisers into East Asia in the mid-nineteenth century – the Opium War in China, Russian colonisation, US expansion into the Pacific – stimulated Japanese leaders to industrialise rapidly. They found a way to move quickly to the advanced organisational forms of capitalism without wasting decades at the intermediate stages. For example, after an initial phase in which state activity was focused on creating industrial capital, it sold this off to a growing capitalist class from about the early 1880s, and shifted its attention to laying the basis of finance capital, setting up a number of internal and colonial banks.[14] The state does not have to disappear once the bourgeoisie is in place, for the latter can use it as its own instrument.

The Japanese experience inspired other countries from outside the European world, and the question arises as to why there were not more Japans. International factors are an important part of the answer. Japan succeeded partly because, at the time it was industrialising in the 1860s, nations that might have intervened were tied down elsewhere.[15] More importantly, Japan itself entered the colonial scramble, extracting vast amounts of value to launch its own accumulation – the Sino-Japanese war in the 1890s ended with the seizure of Taiwan and the payment of a huge indemnity by China. It is thus illegitimate to use Japan as an example of endogenous accumulation, but this tended to get forgotten by its admirers.

But a more important factor is the international context of existing class relations. Whatever the theoretical possibilities for turning dependence into development, in practice it is very difficult to make this work because the indigenous social stratum which trades with the international monetary economy may be the one which has least interest in independence. There are occasions where a nationalist state can seek to break the power of these elements, but they may hit back by capturing the authoritarian state from within. From this point of view, Japan's greatest strength may have been that its earlier relationship with global capital was comparatively weak. The case of Egypt is interesting as a contrast. Capitalism in the Arab world developed under the auspices of foreign dominance.[16] Politically part of the Ottoman

(Turkish) empire, Egypt had in practice been economically penetrated by Europe for some time. With French capitalism seeking to compete with English, Napoleon decided to invade Egypt. The early nineteenth-century local ruler, Mohamed Ali, tried to develop a militaristic, state-monopoly model as a basis for resistance. Millions of workers were employed in workshops using advanced production methods and locally produced means of production. Productivity in the textile industry outstripped most European countries.

This type of model regarded the masses purely as cannon-fodder, in a war conducted at both a military and industrial level. It failed partly because of international factors, when the European powers closed ranks to shut out a possible competitor. But perhaps the more important factor was social. The state commercial structure under Mohamed Ali has been described as 'a pre-capitalist formation which was a transitional stage in Egypt's integration into the world market as a peripheral capitalist formation'.[17] How are we to interpret this? In the notional model of endogenous capitalism, the feudal class was simply a thing of the past, and modernisation could be expected to sweep it away, along with all the good things it was also sweeping away, such as grassroots co-operative structures. But in the real world – of a capitalism which was global from the beginning – segments of the landowning class were by then embedded in and protected by the capitalist economy, because they were selling cash-crops to the world market. In the Egyptian context, these provided a major source of weakness for the development drive.

Capitalist development (the development of the accumulation system) tended to maintain rather than destroy this dependent ruling stratum. A similar argument could be made with respect to Latin America. Frank argues that the reason Latin America eventually became underdeveloped is, paradoxically, that natural conditions there are far richer than in North America. In the USA, the plantation-owners (the slavers) were relatively weaker in comparison to the industrialists, and were eventually defeated in the Civil War, enabling the industrial interests to push for protection of the national economy. But in South America, the landowning aristocracy acquired so much wealth selling goods on the world market that it could, during the nineteenth century, defeat the nascent industrial class.[18] It became, therefore, in Mariátegui's words, a dominant rural class 'camouflaged or disguised as a republican bourgeoisie'.[19]

This dependence was reinforced by new structural factors, one of the most important being to get the developing countries into 'debt'.[20] This was already visible in the 1860s and 1870s, when both the Ottoman Empire and Egypt borrowed from western Europe, and at the beginning of the 1880s the colonial powers took direct control of the internal finances of these countries in a way which strikingly anticipated the actions of the World Bank and IMF a century later. But when structural factors did not suffice, there was often the alternative of military intervention. When, in the middle of the nineteenth century, a modernising regime in Paraguay challenged the British monopoly of railway-building, Britain incited Argentina and Brazil to launch a total war in 1865–70, in which 90 per cent of the male population of Paraguay was killed.[21] In a sense, it is recognisable as the contemporary pattern: a mixture of carrot and stick.

But it may well be that the balance between the two was different then, for the carrot was not yet well developed. International capitalism will always use military repression against the masses, but it is a sign of weakness if it does so against the bourgeoisie, for it is then making possible a cross-class alliance against it. In this sense, I would argue that, in the nineteenth century, *international capitalism was not yet mature*. This is precisely why, despite efforts to manage areas like Latin America, China and Egypt under proto-neocolonial systems, colonialism could not yet be abandoned as a general system.

## The Scope for Grassroots Democracy within a National Development Strategy

In the period before the Second World War, there was not even a superficially plausible argument for believing that the system would allow the South to develop; indeed the whole ideology of imperialism was saying that this wouldn't happen. In these circumstances, certain élites in the South looked for inspiration to the grassroots with an attitude that had a hint of genuine nationalism. They needed culture as a reference-point for building national identity against imperialist intervention, and sought this in mass society – albeit an élite perception of mass society. While it might be a good thing for development if modernisation destroyed the oppressive aspects of tradition, something would be lost if the popular basis of culture was annihilated as well.

The solution was not necessarily – or exclusively – a top-down parliamentarism, because this still emphasised official society, and the problem in the South was that official society, whether openly authoritarian or not, remained an appendage of the international capitalist world order which held down competitors from the South. What was needed, instead, was a system that recognised, to some extent, grassroots democracy. After analysing the Mohamed Ali experience in the Middle East, thinkers like Rifa'ah al-Tahtawi attempted to explore new ideas which led eventually to the emergence of a specific third-world form of sociology that challenged Western-imposed definitions of tradition;[22] these, as Abdel-Malek points out in his critique of structuralism, emphasised the dead weight of practices which prevented societies from 'looking forward, i.e. discovering the potentialities of phenomena'.[23] Instead, they showed that the grassroots contribution could be innovatory and pro-independence at the same time.

This socio-cultural dimension also implied an economic one. The problem with any form of development in the South seeking to break the industrial monopoly of the North is that industrial society does not fully reproduce itself without external inputs: colonial exploitation, raw materials etc. (This argument constitutes a powerful critique of contemporary newly industrialising countries (NICs), and we will return to it in chapter 10.) One possible solution would be for the country in the South to activate some productive factors which are not available to central capitalism, such as the creativity of the grassroots. Such an approach is discernible in the ideas of Gandhi in India: the 'current economy' in his writing stands for indigenous techniques, which he saw as inexhaustible. The 'reservoir economy' can be used in such a way as to give rise to exploitation, and it must therefore be subordinated to the natural economy,[24] leading to a social system in which 'I do visualise electricity, shipbuilding, ironworks and the like, existing side by side with village crafts. But the order of dependence will be reversed.'[25] A certain similarity between Gandhism and the later phenomenon of Maoism in China has been noted.[26] The strength of such an economics is that it partly immunises locally focused economies against the 'drain', both in its urban-centred and international forms. It can also lead to an attempt to re-invent, in a new form, the creative dualism of pre-capitalist class societies with juxtaposition of the two spheres – the urban élite and the peasantry. Although central capitalism acted like a parasite on this relationship to create drain and stagnation, it may be possible to envisage a new relationship which recognises the existence of this dualism but turns it in a positive direction.

But the upper-class pro-peasant lobby were most frequently building an idealised picture of the peasantry which was very different from a movement which might have arisen from the peasantry itself. Nationalist élites had no intention of mobilising peasants directly; Indian populist leaders worked only with what were seen as acceptable segments,[27] and Gandhi himself became quite worried when a real peasant movement attempted to develop its own agenda.[28] This is a wider problem with élite pro-peasant movements, whether in the Middle East,[29] or Russia for example. Élites also have a big problem coming up with a genuinely pluralist conception of national development. The capitalist model is inherently homogenising, its pretence of dismantling backward social structures translated in practice into an attack on all forms of locally rooted culture, language, and so on. While this would 'work' in narrow capitalist terms if it established a self-focused market within this homogenised nation, in the peripheral context it is more likely to weaken the positive forces of traditional society without destroying the negative ones, and leave behind a mess with no clear focus. The seemingly strong nation, which gains credibility from its apparent ability to withstand foreign intervention, is built from the ruins of what should be a nation's greatest asset – its plurality. In this sense, the 'nationalist' state is just as effective in destroying the healthy aspect of tradition as unbridled Western-dominated modernisation would be. An alternative vision would not only make sure that value generated in local communities remains in the region, but also appreciate the unique contribution of particular groups of inhabitants, whose systems of knowledge have evolved symbiotically with the evolution of the land they occupy. It can be argued that this vision is not utopian, but emerges logically out of a critique of the shortcomings of the various bourgeois conceptions of national development.

## The USA Re-establishes White Supremacy

Despite the weaknesses discussed above, nationalism in the oppressed countries was a real threat to the centre during the period of classic imperialism, because at that time systemic forces which could co-opt the bourgeoisie in the South were also weak. This explains how nationalism and revolution were able to form a potentially dangerous synthesis, which eventually came to a head with the policy of revolutionary Russia under Lenin.

At the same time, imperialism made it inevitable that conflagration between the great powers would break out. The claim that competing interests would stabilise the system through a balance of power between them became increasingly unconvincing.

It is against this background that we should consider American manifest destiny. In the late nineteenth century Republicans, like imperialists in other countries, advocated foreign expansion, whereas Democrats were more turned inward towards the home base. Then a new idea emerged: a new kind of outward-looking policy which, in contrast to the narrow competitiveness of classic imperialism, would work towards changing the international system itself. America had reached a point where its 'national interest' (in reality, the interest of its capitalists) could be realised only through the pursuit of systemic goals (known in international relations theory as 'milieu' goals). The USA became the advocate of something new because its own interests happened to coincide with those of capitalist development in a more general sense. This is, in effect, what 'manifest destiny' signifies.

For the industrialised, Euro-American world it meant abandoning colonial exclusivity. The joint sharing of resources would eventually imply a decisive step beyond the old narrow state-centricity, towards increasing North–North political interdependence and then, at a further stage, the growth of a form of official society at an international level to work on their collective behalf. Although the Cold War was later to serve as a convenient pretext, the economic rationale was already in place before then. For the South, on the other hand, the open world economy simply meant that they had to open up their resources to an exploitation which by then had become multilateral.

In reality, it is not likely that a state would change overnight from conventional national interest to milieu goals; instead, while seeking a long-term change it will also strive to maximise the benefits it gets from the current system, that is, to have its cake and eat it too. The USA sought to do this, for example by internationalising the Monroe Doctrine; this had originally been put forward in the early nineteenth century, nominally to prevent Latin America (following independence from Spain) from becoming the exclusive sphere of outside powers, but really to make it part of the USA's sphere of influence. When, at the end of the First World War, the United States took charge of redesigning the world system, it ensured that the Monroe Doctrine was written into the Covenant of the League of Nations in 1919.

Partly, the effect was to safeguard US regional power, but there were also wider systemic implications. US President Woodrow Wilson explicitly remarked that it became world doctrine by entering into the Covenant,[30] and advocated that 'the nations should with one accord adopt the doctrine of President Monroe as the doctrine of the world'.[31] What did the Doctrine signify in this systemic sense?

Ostensibly, it upheld the right of countries to decide on their own polity and way of development. Now, to an important degree this is hot air: the League of Nations' view of colonies as unable to 'stand by themselves under the strenuous conditions of the modern world' reflected a consensus among US leaders that the Americans' own principle of free consent of the governed could not be made to apply to 'lesser' peoples. Wilson had already argued in 1901 that to give Anglo-Saxon political institutions to underdeveloped peoples would not be appropriate because they were in the 'childhood of their political growth'.[32] Cold War interventionism – as with Henry Kissinger's statement on Chile, 'I don't see why we have to let a country go Marxist just because its people are irresponsible'[33] – follows naturally.

But it would be a mistake to view the self-determination issue within the Monroe Doctrine as mere verbiage. The substantive question behind the globalised Monroe Doctrine is the strategy of building *the world system itself* (ultimately based on the mechanism of capital accumulation) till it becomes strong enough for countries to be permitted 'freely' to choose their 'polity and way of development', safe in the knowledge that they won't step outside the bounds of what is acceptable to capital accumulation. In this sense, the World Bank's insistence today on democratisation, against the background of structural adjustment programmes (SAP), can be looked upon as the logical product of the Monroe Doctrine as world doctrine.

The new order was a way of reconstituting the racist North–South divide on a basis where capital accumulation itself did the job more efficiently than old-style colonialism. It is thus no accident that it was in 1900, at the precise moment when America was developing away from classic imperialism towards the modern form of racial liberalism, that the black leader W.E.B. Du Bois made the historic statement that 'The problem of the twentieth century is the problem of the colour line'.[34] He understood much more clearly than other left-wing critics of imperialism that, in a sense, imperialism was only at the beginning of its development.

## The Explanation for and Function of Japanese Success

While some form of colour line was a basic fact of the international system, the case of Japan poses the question as to whether some flexibility could be permitted in order to consolidate this division more effectively. Exploitative systems which have no mobility tend to be weak. One example of a country which has 'made it' might console the rest, and the leading caucus of the world system would be better able to present itself as a club of imperialists rather than as a club of white men! There is also a second argument which would apply more specifically with respect to Asia. The 'decline of the West' has been mentioned in one way or another since the advent of imperialism, as a dangerous fate which one either accepts with resignation or seeks to control and channel into an acceptable form. J.A. Hobson's influential book, written in the early period of imperialism, includes a lengthy discussion about Asia and imperialism's possible responses.[35] Hobson's discussion is so prescient that it seems appropriate to analyse it in Chapter 10 in the discussion of contemporary issues around NICs; but the main point is that ever since the advent of imperialism it has been inescapable that international capitalism must in some sense develop Asia, so the problem becomes how to control this development. It would clearly be useful to have an Asian power within the system.

This does not in any way deny the racial element built into the imperialist system from the outset. Wilson fought the 1912 election on a ticket of, as he put it, 'the national policy of exclusion',[36] that is, the exclusion of Asians. And the true significance of liberalism was revealed after the First World War when, during the drafting of the League Covenant, Japan proposed a clause establishing the principle of racial equality. It was an important decision for the international community: did liberalism signify the eighteenth-century humanitarian perspective of abolishing the personal determinants of servitude, or did it merely mean opening up sources of raw materials for exploitation? The answer was unequivocally to reject the former interpretation. Wilson strongly opposed the clause. Supporting him, British Foreign Secretary Balfour argued that the statement 'all men are created equal' was an incorrect eighteenth-century notion; it may be 'true in a certain sense that all men of a particular nation were created equal, but not that a man in Central Africa was created equal to a European'.[37] The idea of 'racial' equality was therefore scrapped. The essence of the international form of official society which was being created is summed up by this decision.[38]

Some people were fooled at the time into believing that Japan's admittance to the ruling caucus marked the end of race as an issue in world politics;[39] and such deception was precisely the purpose of the decision, which helped to consolidate a system which has in fact since then become increasingly racial, as nations within the white world have become more united, losing their sense of individual national interest. Despite repeated predictions that the West is declining and Asia taking over, the truth may rather be that the system works to accumulate from Asian development without ever letting the latter gain the upper hand. Today's Asian crisis may be the most recent expression of this essential truth.

This does not mean that the control mechanisms are foolproof; for example, capitalism in Japan might actually be more dynamic and innovatory than in the white nations, and it might even galvanise Asia as a whole to an unacceptable degree. We will examine the later manifestations of this elsewhere, but even in the inter-war period there was a hint of this. Japan certainly experimented with dependent industrialisation in the territories it controlled.[40] The two areas it colonised longest, Taiwan and Korea, did subsequently 'take off'. Japan also experimented with some issues of 'human resources', notably investing in education, and in increasing food productivity.[41] The objective was of course exploitative, but then this is the whole point: human resource development can be a good way of exploiting dependent countries, and it has taken the mainstream capitalist nations decades to learn this lesson. At a theoretical level, particularly significant was the 'flying geese' model of economic development put forward by Japan in the 1930s, according to which a fast-developing economy would tow others along in its slipstream, maintaining its technological edge while the others successively picked up its discarded, lower-value-added industrial sectors. Ideas such as this have come into their own more recently.[42] Even the notion of a specific Confucian–Buddhist approach to social organisation, another contribution of Japanese thinking around the time of the Second World War,[43] was eventually taken up by the mainstream. Capitalism needed this dynamism, and then had to invent new control mechanisms to prevent too much of the benefit going to Asia itself.

## Seeking the Developmental Principles of Mature Capitalism

Since the advent of imperialism, capitalism has continued to develop. But the structural ingredients for the development of mature capitalism have been unfamiliar and have had to be worked out. Although the Euro-American world may use the Japan–Asia connection as a laboratory from which it can copy certain elements, it seeks to maintain the focus of innovation within itself. During the period after the First World War, international capitalism was learning to create the building-blocks which might fit into a new accumulation regime.

The following elements were involved: first, a new social balance within each of the countries in the North. Classic imperialism had sought to co-opt the labour movement at an ideological level only (with the argument that *eventually* there would be more for all classes to share if the nation competed successfully with others), but it later became clear that the co-optation would be more effective if there were immediate material benefits. Now, to permit increased mass consumption would also be a way of ending the stagnation of the old industries and of promoting new ones. Such a solution was undoubtedly foreshadowed in the critique made by British economist J.M. Keynes of the Versailles peace settlement of 1919[44], which showed quite a strong consciousness of the link between social alienation and frustrated consumption. In practical terms, the production-line system created the possibility of greatly increased economies of scale, while Henry Ford promoted the idea that capitalism could create its own market by paying better wages. It began to be seen that the state's role could shift from infrastructural development towards social engineering, and this too was foreshadowed in America's response to the Depression, Roosevelt's New Deal. At the same time, tripartite (labour–state–management) negotiations under the auspices of the International Labour Organisation anticipated later 'social contract' approaches. This whole complex of innovations had tremendous possibilities.[45]

Second, some new *modus vivendi* between the capitalist powers would be necessary. Ideally, the process of homogenising the world market would retain a certain boundary, but this boundary would be the North–South colour line rather than the boundary between individual national economies. This would create the need both to police this frontier and to manage the development of an interdependent Northern sphere which had already begun to move beyond the safe haven of state-centricity. Both these imperatives meant that the Northern states had to learn to co-operate in a new way.

The problem could be addressed by the emergence of some international 'regimes' – using the term in a special sense, to denote the gradual establishment of informal co-operative structures which become valued because they provide a necessary service. Later events, notably the Marshall Plan, suggest that this could be achieved through the conscious channelling of capital accumulation in such a way as to promote interdependence. Something similar was anticipated by the Dawes and Young plans of the 1920s, through which the USA established a cyclical movement whereby capital flowed from America to Germany, then to Britain and France in the form of reparations for Germany's supposed war crimes, and then returned to America as the repayment of war loans. So even during the period of 'isolationism', the USA played an innovatory economic role.

The third and final aspect of experimentation was the search for a new method of managing the South. Since this is the main focus of our enquiry, I will consider it in more detail in the remainder of this chapter. To understand what happened, we need to consider capitalism's *economic* contradictions in the old system. As mercantilism and colonialism stopped the colonies producing, they also failed to increase demand for the metropolitan countries' manufactures. In this way, they were beginning to undermine capitalism's own development potential. In the early imperialist period, some groups of capitalists sought an answer to this problem. These tentative attempts can be studied in the context of the Dutch colony of Indonesia in the period leading up to the First World War. Capitalists who were producing goods in the Netherlands and wanted markets promoted an 'ethical' policy, also known as 'the moral way', the aim of which was to allow Indonesians more development and wealth, so that they could consume Dutch exports. But this strategy would make labour costs in Indonesia rise, so it was vigorously opposed by those Dutch capitalists who were investing in Indonesia.[46] Socialists in the period of the Second International were often misled into lining up with the 'ethical' faction of the bourgeoisie and promoting colonialism with a human face.[47] In the inter-war period, too, there was some attempt to evolve a strategy of deepening integration between metropolitan countries and colonies in which the latter's consumption would increase. In 1934–35 France called a 'Conférence économique de la France métropolitaine et de l'Outre-Mer' which advocated improving conditions in the colonies so that they could consume French exports.[48] It has to be remembered that in the pre-Keynesian era metropolitan markets were still quite restricted.

But it was ultimately a completely different strategy that prevailed – the American approach, which involved facilitating transnational corporation (TNC) investment in industrial *production* in the South. This change was to prove of crucial importance, since with the South's gradual shift from consumption to production of industrial goods, Southern poverty was no longer a constraint on the development of international capitalism as a whole. Once Keynesian–Fordist policies were applied in the North, it could constitute the market for the new production from the South, so the different elements of the equation would fit. And, in the South, the poverty of the most exploited sectors could go on increasing without it acting as a brake on capitalist development, which is empirically what has happened.

The motor industry was very important in pioneering the new structural features of capitalist industry. The assembly-line system espoused by Ford was effective in exploiting metropolitan labour, but General Motors jumped ahead with a system based on the internationalisation of production, and by the late 1920s 'a trend to replace trade in the final product with trade in the intermediate products was already underway in certain markets'.[49] US automobile manufacturers contributed to the dependent industrialisation of India in the period soon after the First World War. In the immediate term, this increased the wealth of local élites, thus increasing the market and enabling the goods to be consumed locally, all of which fitted in neatly with the political demands of decolonisation. But in the longer term, as imperialism theory had predicted, this policy also led to the export of industrial products to the North. In these circumstances, poverty, far from being a constraint on development (as it had been under mercantilism), became a good thing (for capital) because it kept wages low.[50] The motive for such investment is its impact on the rate of profit.[51]

The new set-up did not *replace* the earlier pattern, because in the later phases of imperialism, particularly after the Second World War, there was still a massive, in fact greatly increased, import of raw materials and cash crops which entered into the total consumption of metropolitan workers. But now the effect of technological progress in undermining the rate of profit within the centre could be offset by a much higher rate of profit available outside.[52]

We can thus identify a new systemic structure to succeed classic imperialism, the components of which more or less 'hang together' and are capable of revitalising capital. However, these did not cohere into a real structure prior to the Second World War. When a structural solution is necessary and cannot be found, capitalism cannot simply mark time, as the Depression showed. The effective collapse of the international economy between the World Wars even created the conditions for a kind of involuntary delinking, for example on the part of countries such as Argentina, Egypt and Turkey, where domestic industries developed to supply commodities that could not be imported. It became apparent that only the establishment of a fairly strong global economic sphere would prevent the emergence of elements of independent self-related capitalism. But the temporary enslavement of the monopolies to extreme nationalism, the absence of conditions for 'regimes' to be established, all made the solution hard to find. The international system was caught in a situation half way between the old set-up of national powers and half-hearted experiments in a more collective style of domination. This created openings for Nazism to profit from a consistent application of the old individualist power politics. Unable to discover the mechanism for a structural transition to a mass-consumption regime which would defuse social protest, capitalism connived at the growth of Nazism, perhaps under the assumption that transnationalisation of economic interests had advanced to a point where it would prevent the resurgence of the old conflictual international relations. It turned out to be a false assumption, and the Second World War was the result. It marked the end of the phase of classic imperialism. At the same time the fundamental issues of mature capitalism, which had emerged during imperialism, were now free to develop in earnest. In the next chapter, I will consider the beginnings of this new phase of capitalist development, the system after the Second World War, which takes us to where we are today.

## Notes

1. 'Zero-sum' means that the gains of one party are exactly equivalent to the losses of the other. Their relationship is thus purely competitive. The 'conflict resolution' approach often seeks to show that another, less immediately perceptible, strategy would lead to a positive outcome for both parties, who would thereby gain by co-operation.

2. Ricardo 1951, p. 134.

3. List 1983, pp. 34 ff.

4. Thornton 1959, p. 22.

5. As an example, see Freeman 1982.

6. Lipietz (1987) made an important contribution in popularising this term.

7. The term 'international politics' is used for convenience here, without prejudice to the question of whether it is describing relations between nation-states or conversely relationships within some globalised sphere of action.

8. Examples would be Day 1981, p. 30, and Brewer 1980, p. 63.

9. Luxemburg 1972, pp. 59–60.

10. I will argue later that a temporary element of underconsumption does indeed emerge in conditions of structural crisis which occur in the transition between major systemic regimes of capitalism.

11. See Lenin 1970, p. 73.

12. Naoroji 1962, p. 34.

13. The military dynamic, once established, probably transcends its original rationale, constituting a symbol of the 'nation' itself, with an immense 'opportunity' cost in terms of other things which are not done, thus undermining the development it is supposed to protect.

14. Lockwood 1954, pp. 249–50.

15. Britain was tied down with the aftermath of the violent Indian 'mutiny' of 1853–57; various powers were fighting the Taiping peasant rebels in China; there were also the Crimean War and the Civil War in America.

16. See Amin 1978a.

17. Gran 1979, p. 110.

18. Frank 1972.

19. Mariátegui 1971, p. 32.

20. The term 'debt' is placed in inverted commas in this work, to reflect the fact that the South has been plundered, and if anything is owed it would be some form of reparations by the North.

21. See Rouquié 1982, p. 233; Gaignard 1968.

22. See Rodinson 1972, pp. 101, 110.

23. Abdel-Malek 1972, p. 277.

24. See Madan 1966.

25. Quoted in Ganguli 1977, p. 255.

26. See Bandyophadyaya 1982.

27. Chandra 1979, p. 370.

28. See Kumar 1979–80, p. 71.

29. For example, Abdel-Malek 1983, p. 55.

30. Queuille 1969, p. 175.

31. Speech to Senate, 22 January 1917, in Latané and Wainhouse 1941, p. 599.

32. Quoted in Weston 1972, p. 19.

33. Quoted in Molineu 1986, p. 165.

34. Du Bois 1970, p. 125.

35. Hobson 1938.

36. Weston 1972, p. 32.

37. See Lauren 1988, p. 84.

38. Even settler-colonialism should not be permitted to dilute the power centres of

official society too far; thus soon afterwards, in 1920, the League of Nations also rejected a resolution by Argentina to recognise the principle of the equality of all states.

39. For a statement of this position, see, for example, Dutt 1936, p. 192.

40. See Myers 1996.

41. See Kobayashi 1996.

42. Hill and Lee 1994.

43. See arguments expressed by a variety of original texts from the late 1930s to early 1940s, in Lebra 1975.

44. See Keynes 1919.

45. As our subsequent analysis will show, this system would eventually run up against its own limitations, in the sense that workers remained strong through concentration in factories, and were now enabled or even encouraged to recoup part of the benefits of their productivity, and if this continued to grow there would be no intrinsic limits to what the demands might be. But the potential needed first to be exhausted before such limitations appeared.

46. Bruhat 1976, p. 65.

47. Many of the splits in the labour movement at that time did indeed mirror divisions between different factions of capitalists; see Haupt and Reberioux 1967.

48. Gbagbo 1978, pp. 12–13.

49. Foreman-Peck 1986, p. 147.

50. This is correct from a consumption point of view, but capitalist economics may also have to broaden out in the direction of a 'human resources' perspective, since poverty restricts workers' ability to work (and hence be exploited) to their full capacity. This will be discussed in the final chapter.

51. A single-country model for the expanded reproduction of capital takes the following form:

$$M - C \Big\langle \begin{array}{c} L \\ MP \end{array} - P - M + m$$

C: commodity   L: labour   M: money
MP: means of production   P: production

The quantity of money which emerges at the end of the process is bigger than what went in (M+m). It is assumed that the increase is entirely due to labour within the country in question. Now, in the real history of capitalism this has never been true. In the classic colonial pattern we can assume that investment essentially takes place within the metropolis. Even here, however, the amount of profit is influenced by inputs from outside: raw materials are obtained very cheaply, and the living costs (hence the wages) of metropolitan labour are reduced by the availability of cheap consumer goods.

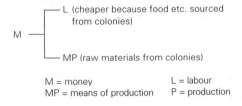

M ⌐ L (cheaper because food etc. sourced from colonies)
  └ MP (raw materials from colonies)

M = money          L = labour
MP = means of production   P = production

But the centre can benefit even more if it discovers a way to invest in a dependent form of 'development' of the periphery. In this case, it would embed the centre's higher productivity within a mutually interdependent accumulation structure:

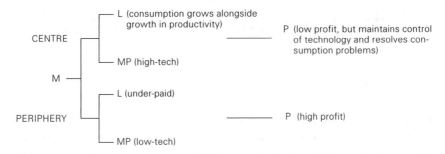

52. It is important to note that the relative importance of these spheres would depend in practice on motives which are political rather than purely economic: the point is always to defuse struggles at particular points by rewarding certain social strata with consumption.

# 3

# The Post-Second World War Era

In the post-war period, the elements of a solution to capitalism's stagnation, a solution which existed tentatively earlier but failed to cohere, now started to come together into a new system of accumulation. Capitalism was thus able to move into the modern phase of its development.

When one is looking at a major change like this (a similar point could be made about the beginning of imperialism), there are usually two key aspects: first, new conditions for capitalist development are opened up which then become available for all subsequent phases – North–North interdependence increased and capital in 1945 became more mobile, aspects of capitalist development which have continued ever since without any sign of abating; and second, a new long cycle begins, but here the conditions cease when the long cycle ends. I will deal first with how capital accumulation was organised within the centre, before examining the international conditions.

## Capitalism at the Centre Rescues Itself by Raising Consumption

A set of new economic policies, often loosely described as Keynesianism, provided the condition for the formation of a relatively stable central structure which could then control the South.

Implicitly, the colour line was defined in a new way, since rich countries developed a distinct system of economics premised on the abundance of capital, and involving rising mass consumption. It was one law for the rich and another for the poor, because developing countries were supposed to follow a different sort of economics, which I will outline in the next chapter.

The new developments occurred against a background of stagnation, which characterised capitalism before 1945, for capitalism had learned very well how to build heavy industry and infrastructure (railways and so on), but it had tended to 'over-accumulate' in these areas, locking up resources which were then not available for consumption; yet increased consumption was the only way of providing an outlet for new industries and thus getting out of the impasse. Capitalism was stuck in a situation where capital could safeguard its position only by squeezing workers, which resulted in a vicious circle: poverty meant there was low demand (since capitalism responds only to demand, and not to need), which, in its turn, meant capitalists had no incentive to invest, which, in its turn, meant low employment, which takes us back to the beginning – poverty.

Since capitalism was organised primarily at a national level, the accumulation problem also led to the duplication of capacity between national economies, which created a destructive, competitive dynamic. Here too a vicious circle developed, because countries competed with one another, which reinforced the downward trend. Capitalism got caught in a descending spiral of several interlocking vicious circles. Intuition suggested that a single key might unlock them all.

The fundamental problems in North–South relations during the post-colonial period did not necessarily form part of the same logic, but it seems obvious that if the centre could get its act together, it would be able to dominate the rest of the system more effectively.

These problems can be analysed from an economic viewpoint, but in many ways the key difficulty was social unrest: this can be seen clearly in the approach of the English economist J.M. Keynes, whose ideas were to play a role in the formulation of a new economic framework. The First World War had led to revolution in several countries, and this helps to explain why the key to resolving the impasse took the form it did – mass consumption. In *The Economic Consequences of the Peace* (1919), Keynes had observed that 'The war has disclosed the possibility of consumption to all and the vanity of abstinence to many.'[1] During the imperialist period, 'social-imperialist' policies had led to heavy spending on public works and education so that the masses would identify at an ideological and material level with the system, but this had done little to raise actual consumption.

The solution to these problems came from a major change in the capitalist way of thinking, in particular, a temporary move away from free market economics. The free market has always had an enormous significance in supplying the ideological basis of capitalism, as a seemingly objective, post-religious equivalent of divine order. Much of this is a lie, but that is precisely why it is useful. The premise is that the best allocation of resources occurs only on the basis of a multitude of micro-level decisions by individuals and firms. This conceals the big social issues (which had become too dangerous once the left had started putting forward its own analysis of these); it therefore seems impossible for society to make fundamental choices about the direction of social development.

But there are two problems with the free-market model: first, it leaves the field open for the left to put forward a broader, more socially aware economic theory; and second, just because the free market is a distortion, it deprives capitalism of a viable theory with which to analyse itself and to inform its own decisions. By and large, the ideological advantages probably outweigh these disadvantages, but in special circumstances this may not be the case: in the period in question, capitalism had immensely important strategic decisions to take, at a time when Soviet Communism was making a strong claim that central planning was a much better way of running the economy, rather than leaving it to the market (an exaggerated claim, as I will argue, but still influential at the time).

Of course, the free-market dogma could be criticised constructively in a number of ways, including the observation that, under conditions of imperialism, oligopoly means that for many decisions the 'free market' does not exist. It is also definitely the case that in market conditions 'bad' equilibria can arise which are very stable.[2] Keynes' analysis, though, was at the same time less damning of imperialism, but also in a way more sweeping in its criticism of *laissez-faire*: even without considering oligopolies, it points out that there is more than one possible self-reproducing equilibrium into which the market could settle if left to its own devices.

The issue Keynes directly addressed was the vicious circle mentioned above in the form of low demand → low investment → low employment → low demand. A certain increase in demand will stimulate more investment, hence employment will rise and, with more money to spend, demand will increase further. Of course Keynesianism was in its own way just as ideological as *laissez-faire*. The myth of the free market is replaced by that of the socially oriented, benevolent state. But Keynes' challenge to *laissez-faire* was nevertheless risky for capitalism in the long run because he showed that there could be debates about broad questions of economic orientation.

Keynes' ideas focused on the general theoretical problems of stimulating demand, rather than on the qualitative structural implications of a shift from heavy accumulation to consumer society. Nevertheless, in practice Keynesianism fits very neatly into the approach, often associated with the name of US motor manufacturer Henry Ford, of paying people enough to buy the products they themselves produce, which makes possible the emergence of a mass market for uniform consumer goods. Keynesianism–Fordism was the right combination at that point in history because it paved the way for a new accumulation structure where all the parts would fit together. It simultaneously solved both the general problem of stagnation through under-investment, and created the conditions for the qualitative changes required in the shift to a new long cycle (with new commodities, consumption strategies, and so on). What was particularly neat was that the economic and politico-ideological changes worked well together: social protest was defused not only through higher wages, but also because providing the masses with cheap consumer goods would encourage them to identify with the system.

## The Hidden Agenda of Keynesianism and its Limitations

Just because it was appropriate for a specific historical moment, Keynesianism had a limited shelf-life. In fact, its limitations were highlighted by the very developments it facilitated, for the following reasons:

FORESTALLING CRISIS  The prolonged economic crisis had created the problem, for it had fuelled the social unrest of the 1930s; it had also been a source of embarrassment for capitalism because the Soviets made a lot of the ability of their system to avoid crises. Keynesianism had offered a breathing space because it had mobilised hitherto dormant resources, but it had also created a fundamental problem in that crises could be expected to recur once resources had been fully mobilised. So the question became: what would happen when demand continued to rise and there was no more surplus labour to satisfy the investment that this required?

BUSINESS CYCLE  Keynesianism and *laissez-faire* share the assumption that the volume of production is determined by demand. But this makes it impossible to understand the real causes of a crisis. For in reality it is capital accumulation which determines the volume of production. This becomes clear from the following example.

At the simplest level entrepreneurs will seek the largest possible volume of production in order to expand their capital as much as possible and to benefit from economies of scale. This would lead to an infinite expansion of production, except that the products have to be sold and demand is finite. Capitalists compete over this finite market, but this only drives them to use more sophisticated technical methods of production in order to keep down the unit cost of their products, and thus maximise the market share that they can wrest from their rivals. The dynamic of this competition means that supply can easily outstrip demand. Since Keynesianism did not resolve this basic problem, it could be ditched (at the end of the 1970s) in favour of a new form of *laissez-faire*, which claimed to address the problem of the business cycle through monetarist policies.

NEW TECHNOLOGY  The goal of 'full employment' responded to the need to consolidate capitalism from a *political* angle after the war. Economically it justified itself by providing a market for a system of mass production whose development would be primarily quantitative rather than qualitative. But any technological breakthrough which was very radical would threaten this equilibrium by simultaneously creating unemployment and reducing *mass* demand. As technology was developing rapidly throughout the post-war boom period, this was another problem that could not be resolved by Keynesianism.

THE BALANCE OF CLASS FORCES  Further development under Keynesianism would create political problems. There are two major aspects: first, 'full employment' creates the threat that workers may win higher wages that can eat into the profits of capitalists and thus change the balance of power between the classes, and second, the factory system – as the Communist movement had always recognised – was a source of strength for organised workers. While the Fordist–Taylorist production line served to control and discipline labour at one level, it also provided opportunities for industrial action, since militant action somewhere along the line could bring the whole process to a halt. It also meant that organised labour could claim to be upholding society's own norms (that is, full employment) when it defended existing working practices.

The above are the Keynesian system's inner weaknesses, which in the long run would undermine it. These contradictions could, however, be kept under wraps during a period of prolonged expansion. This partly explains capitalism's concern to maintain continued quantitative growth in industrial economies, which in turn implied increasing exploitation of the South. The issues we have discussed so far go some way towards explaining the North's success in making itself internally strong and an effective controller of the world economy. But the usefulness of Keynesianism to capitalism would not have been anything like as great had there not been two other elements which were not explicitly recognised in the official theory.

SOCIAL ROLE OF THE STATE   According to the strictly economic rationale behind Keynesianism, the state merely fine-tuned the economy in pursuit of a favourable equilibrium. But in reality, its role was far more extensive, in that it played a managerial role of a new kind. One of the greatest hidden achievements of Keynesianism was to dissociate the managerial role of the state from economic nationalism. The state could at last be 'civilised' in an international sense; it could retain its repressive function, while no longer standing in the way of internationalisation.

This was accompanied by new elements of social control. Ideologically, the state appeared to represent society as a guarantor of social dialogue, and to be an actor which could influence social priorities and which radical forces might aspire somehow to capture or to influence. It was this view of the state that provided the basis for the idea in the industrial countries of the parliamentary road to socialism, 'convergence', the 'historic compromise', Eurocommunism, and so on. The welfare state was also beneficial to capitalism, not only because a large proportion of the value obtained by workers came in the form of the social wage (which they could not easily defend through workplace struggles of the conventional type), but also by making it look as though capitalism was developing in a more humane direction.

The other element is one which I will discuss in a more theoretical way in Chapter 7, but it is important to introduce the issues here:

NON-MONETARY FORMS OF EXPLOITATION   Economic analysis of the period recognised only relationships within the official, monetary world; indeed, with the rise of statism, official society seemed more triumphant, more all-consuming than ever. But this is actually illusory: official accumulation would not have lasted a single day without inputs from an economic sphere whose very existence was denied. There are two main aspects to this relationship, which was consolidated in a new form during this period.

First, the exploitation of women's unremunerated labour. Official society went to great lengths to restore the nuclear family and to create social control mechanisms which forced women to perform unremunerated labour in the home. The concept of full employment, central to Keynesianism, is actually the opposite of what was really happening, since women were forced out of the mainstream industrial jobs they had performed during the war. Keynesianism consolidated the elimination of women's labour from the officially recognised sphere of economics by popularising an apparently objective, statistical measure for the resources society is *seeking* to mobilise – the Gross National Product – which excludes all forms of housework.[3]

The policies of this period also expanded the relationship with the household into new territory. In particular, Keynesian economics claimed that consumption was simply a matter of providing people with the wherewithal to consume, but this was not true, for the system effectively forced people to consume through social pressures. It became an essential social requisite to have a car, a television, a washing machine, and the household was the key locus for performing this social conditioning.

The strategy of pushing women back into the household did not entirely eliminate them from the official economy. But the gender determination which clung to them from their supposedly natural identification with the household ensured that their labour in the official economy would also be under-remunerated. This happened in two main ways: women could be paid less on the grounds that they were only dipping a toe in the monetary economy because their main identity was still in the household; and women could be confined to distinct, lower-paid professions which reflected their supposed vocations, such as caring and catering. These areas of employment actually grew rapidly during the Keynesian era, with the rise of the service sector and the welfare state.

The exploitation of women was actually one of the main weaknesses of the Keynesian development model, because it hinged on a totally false family structure. Traditional patriarchal systems had built up family structures with clear economic roles and reciprocal obligations, which, however limiting on the development of the individual, worked at a social level. Capitalism has never really had a stable family system, and the normative certainties of the Keynesian era were in fact very hollow.

Second, the post-war political economy vastly expanded the scope of racial dualism within the centre. There are a number of ways in which this happened. Given that there was full employment among white males in the centre, it might have been possible for the class struggle to have reduced the rate of surplus value and of profit extracted by capitalism. But the availability of a reserve of labour from the oppressed nations closed off this opportunity.

Capitalists in a number of industrial sectors were even able to substitute cheap labour from the former colonies for machinery. The rate of profit was higher in these sectors because more labour was exploited and (since the rate of profit is averaged over the economy as a whole) this would benefit overall profitability. This applied not only in sectors like textiles but probably also in apparently more advanced sectors such as the motor industry, where technological improvements were kept in abeyance throughout the boom period. This was not a master-plan, for the employers' first response might have been to discriminate against black workers, but they were adaptive, and they learnt to make racism profitable by employing these workers in the worst jobs for less money.[4]

Finally, women and 'racial' minorities were both heavily employed in the new growth sectors characteristic of Keynesianism, such as the poorly paid sectors of the transport industry and the health service. Thus the sectors most *specific* to capitalist development in the Keynesian period were also the most dualistic. And the white and male biases of the organised labour movement ensured that anti-capitalist struggles did not converge.[5]

Growth was therefore conditional on a range of inputs which, in terms of mainstream economics, do not have a properly accounted cost. It should be noted that there is another crucial area in which this happened: the environment. Growth was such an article of faith that the environmental cost was not even considered.

In the above ways, capitalism had found a new way of managing its own accumulation which, within limits, hung together as a coherent system. But it would not have lasted without the *international* conditions.

## From Colonialism to Multilateralism

Although the North–South issue was probably the most fundamental international question, there was another issue of crucial immediate importance, both in its own right and as a condition for managing the North–South relationship: relations among the great powers. Although acute, violent conflict had been endemic since early mercantile days, it had intensified under imperialism. It was becoming clear to the capitalist nations that it would be far more convenient if, instead of fighting among themselves, they could co-operate in exploiting the rest of the world.

The United States of America took charge of the solution. To understand what went on, we should consider the relation between national interest and systemic goals in international relations theory. Some writers assume, somewhat simplistically, that the ruling interests in any state simply pursue their individual national interests, but I would argue that they usually also take into account the nature of the international system. Either nations like it and think they have a chance of maximising their interests within it, or they think it should be changed. Ever since the invention of 'manifest destiny' at the turn of the century, US leading interests had believed that capitalism needed a fundamental change of international system in order to develop. America was promoting change because it was the homeland of the rising forces of capitalism – transnational corporations and investment capital – which needed to rid themselves of the old restrictions. These new forces began to claim that they could carry out some of the organising functions required in this new phase of the world economy, to supplement or replace those formerly filled by the state.

The old imperial powers did not want change, precisely because they still held empires. But because the old order, particularly within the established powers, was seriously undermined by the Second World War, leaving America so dominant, conditions were right for the USA to *force* them to accept change. The American élite was right in perceiving that this would be in the long-term interest of capitalism as a whole, so all the exploiters would benefit. As far as the exploiters were concerned, capitalist development was not a 'zero-sum' game where the gains of one party were balanced against the losses of the other. All could gain from interdependence. But it was only the combination of the destructiveness of the war and the predominance established by the USA during the course of it that made it possible to impose a multilateral solution.

If the key aim was to establish an open world economy, then obviously Nazism was an enemy because it had no real vision of a supra-national economy, beyond that of establishing a command economy at a regional level.[6] But an equally important aspect of the war was that the US used it to start to break down the exclusive interests of the old colonial powers, even though these were America's allies. And change was opposed. For example, the French resistance forces, meeting in Algiers in 1943, took a decision to consolidate the empire first, before liberating France. The intention of this was to keep America out of their sphere of influence.[7] But US hegemony eventually foiled these plans.

To impose their view, the American élite had to claim to be supplying something of value to all central capitalist interests. An important element in this new vision was security. International politics tends to speak of security as if it were economically neutral, but in the real world security always creates conditions for the élites to enjoy their wealth. National systems of law and politics had long provided this at a national level, but now it was time to do it globally. Although part of the conditions for security was to get the rich actors behaving nicely to each other, the major aspect of any security system (national or international) has always been to protect them against troublesome have-nots. In practice this usually means that the have-nots are excluded from the security that the rich enjoy. The endemic violence that capitalism, as an inherently conflictual system, constantly generates tends to be borne by them.

The Second World War showed that the security system had gone seriously wrong. Nazism showed within the industrial world itself a kind of genocide and violence previously practised only against the colonies: 'a civilisation which justifies colonization ... calls for its Hitler, I mean its punishment'.[8] Nazism was the result of a historical process that has always excluded some people from its definition of humanity, in order either to displace the population to facilitate access to resources, or to super-exploit local labour. But by transferring this to the white world itself, Nazism was effectively subverting the North–South division. In a sense, therefore, the US-sponsored post-Nazi world order was actually more racist, because its definition of security restored the colour line – genocide would continue only on one side of it.

The open world economy would benefit industrial powers on the right side of the international divide. For the other nations, it would provide only conditions for accentuated exploitation. Concretely, it would mean first a structured system of world dominance by the North *as a whole* (replacing that of individual powers); second, a commitment to dismantling the protectionist tools which late developers had traditionally employed to promote their industry; and third, a demand that the nations of the South should make available their raw materials to the new internationalising economy and that they should allow corporations the freedom to invest in their economies and repatriate profits. All of this was to be granted without any compensating benefits.

The rhetoric of anti-colonialism made it seem as if the coalition of interests which won the war was not a selfish one. But in practice, all it led to was the dismantling of the barriers which had earlier inhibited their joint exploitation of the rest of the world. When US President Franklin Roosevelt argued that the allies could not 'fight a war against fascist slavery, and at the same time not work to free all peoples all over the world from a backward colonial policy', he immediately explained what he really meant: 'The structure of peace demands and will get equality of all people. Equality of peoples involves the utmost freedom of competitive trade'. This definition of equality meant that countries (that is, industrial ones) should have 'access, without discrimination and on equal terms, to the markets and to the raw materials of the world ... needed for their economic prosperity'.[9] What was being proposed was clearly a strategic solution in which, under the banner of attacking economic nationalism, interdependence in the North was consolidated and at the same time the South was enslaved. The US-sponsored League of Nations, inaugurated at the end of the First World War, had established the principle that colonial peoples could not 'stand by themselves under the strenuous conditions of the modern world'; and when the Charter of its replacement, the United Nations, was being drafted at San Francisco in 1945, American representatives argued for retaining this phrase, and only the opposition of some Arab delegates caused it to be dropped. Even then, the US managed to prevent the inclusion within the Charter of a commitment to independence.[10]

But, if the new order was in general simply a continuation of the old supremacy, the practical mechanics of exploitation had to be different because the vertically integrated colonial systems could not survive intact under conditions of multilateralism. The substantive new measures were multilateral ways to ensure access to resources. The war had, for example, created the system of 'reverse' lend-lease, whereby Britain compensated the US for its wartime finance by massive exports of raw materials, many of them from Africa.[11] And now, each of the bilateral treaties in the Marshall Plan contained a clause giving the USA the right to raw materials beyond what was needed for the country in question's own use and commercial export, while US citizens were also allowed access to the exploitation of raw materials on the same terms as nationals.[12]

But, in what is emerging as a persistent theme in our study, economics and politics do not necessarily coincide. In this case, the special privileges of individual colonial powers, however outdated economically, remained an indispensable tool in fighting liberation movements. In Africa, for example,

> To Roosevelt and his advisers, who were conscious that the *Pax Britannica* was being replaced with a sort of *Pax Americana*, it was perhaps tempting at first sight to try to take over Britain's imperial bases under the guise of inter-nationalisation; but in view of British opposition to internationalisation it seemed better in the long run to shore up the British ally and her empire and achieve security for as long as possible at second hand.[13]

And even in the longer term, it was more a question of superimposing a multilateral dimension in Europe (via the Marshall Plan and NATO) over a refurbished vertical colonial relationship. However competitive it seemed, the old colonial system had always involved a division of labour among the dominant powers in suppressing national movements. This was simply taken to a new level in the post-war system: Britain and France were free to undertake colonial repression while the growth of their domestic economies was provided for by Marshall Aid. This set-up also provided the United States with a safety mechanism: it was funding the other powers, so it could always pull the plug if one of them tried to restore exclusivity.

What was at stake, however, was not the simple refurbishment of colonial exploitation. A new strategy had to be formulated because the objective situation was different. This can be seen in two aspects:

INDEPENDENCE MOVEMENTS COULD NOT BE DENIED INDEFINITELY
There was no grand design for decolonisation. In the British empire in Africa, for example, the number of locals considered qualified to elect an eventual self-governing regime was tiny;[14] vague plans put forward in 1943 envisaged the independence of some African countries after 60–80 years.[15] It was only mass movements that eventually forced through change.[16] In a general way, oppressive systems tend to suppress protest until this is no

longer possible, and then to look for some way to co-opt the new movements. Ultimately, the new phase in capital accumulation implied a new kind of North–South relationship which was not just extractive, but permitted a limited degree of industrialisation in the South. But although some kind of neo-colonialism would have been in the long-term interest of the system, such a solution was not reached through strategic planning, which revealed the limitations of this approach. Instead, the North reacted to events and only eventually found an answer through improvisation.

GROWTH IMPLIED AN INCREASED CONSUMPTION OF RESOURCES
Capitalism in general has to expand or die, but this imperative took a special form under Keynesianism, where continued growth is necessary even under conditions of full employment. This implied intervention in the third world to make sure that raw materials kept coming and to undermine the pressures for an increase in the price of raw materials which normally would have occurred given the situation of high demand. This interventionist dynamic creates a new focus for militarism, to replace that formerly provided by competition *among* great powers.

In contrast to some of the systemic problems I have discussed in this chapter so far – which had been apparent at the turn of the century and the 1930s – these issues emerged gradually in the course of the early post-war period. It is against this background that we can appreciate the functional role played by the Cold War, something which evolved through trial and error as the post-war period unfolded.

## Dual Tactics towards the Communist States: Aggression and Co-optation

Communism as a mass movement is always anathema to capitalism, but at a state level the relationship was more ambiguous. If we look theoretically at the 'normal' situation (that is, outside the context of World War), it is clear that both capitalism and communism want security, the former so that it can increase exploitation and the latter so that it can build its social system. In these circumstances, it is possible that capitalism might draw some benefit from reaching some kind of agreement with communism.

In the Second World War, the situation was peculiar because Communism was an ally of the major capitalist powers. The post-war world order grew out of this, but in an indirect and pragmatic way, which was certainly not planned. It suited the capitalist powers to have the Soviet Union doing most of the fighting against the Nazis in Europe while they could concentrate on consolidating their positions in the third world. They always had their eye on the post-war order, for defeating fascism had never been an end in itself (for example, the US administration hushed up details of Nazi massacres because they did not want public opinion to lobby strongly in favour of a second front). The nuclear bombing of Japan was certainly envisaged as a way of consolidating American influence in the post-war world, as well as pre-empting, through the precipitation of an immediate Japanese surrender, the possibility of a negotiated surrender by Japanese forces to the radical national movements in countries such as Malaya and Indonesia.[17] Imperialism's long-term fascination with Asia was also reflected in the key role of China within America's wartime blueprints for a post-war order. The preservation of the 'open door' in China was a core interest for American policy-makers; key advisers argued that the bomb should be used against Japan in order to forestall a Soviet intervention in the war which could prejudice subsequent American economic interests in China.[18] Through the Yalta agreement, the US took advantage of the strong Soviet interest in state security by promising a kind of buffer zone in Eastern Europe in exchange for a commitment from Russia not to demand the large zone of influence which might have seemed justified on the basis of its predominant role in defeating Hitler.

The primary concern of the USA at this stage was not, therefore, to confront the Soviet Union – which had been kept out of the way behind its own security curtain – but rather to create a new world order which in the last analysis would guarantee the security necessary for capital accumulation. But although the thrust of this policy was not primarily aimed at the Soviet Union, the United States would inevitably come up against local communism, against radical grassroots struggles and even against nationalism in the third world. Recent studies based on newly declassified documents show that United States leaders formulated a very grand geopolitical theory of a disordered world which it was their responsibility to sort out and which, in its most extreme form, would have them virtually controlling the whole of the Atlantic and Pacific regions. These theories did not assume that the threat came from the Soviet Union, but they clashed with the Soviet Union's own views of security. When conflicts arose, US leaders were not ready to accept the legitimacy of Soviet demands and eventually, to justify their blueprint for world order, they deliberately ignored evidence of Soviet moderation.[19]

Eventually, the Cold War emerged. In a broad sense, we could say that it responded to America's key strategic objectives: it provided the best rationale for forcing the old capitalist powers into line in Europe, for suppressing labour and democratic movements, and above all for permitting increased intervention in the third world. This was made necessary by the two factors outlined above: the need for both huge quantities of resources at static prices, and a controlled transition to a post-colonial order so that radical forces would be unable to impose their own agenda.

But, once entrenched, the Cold War also altered the way the international system worked. One change was the impetus it gave to a new kind of militarism. Under conditions of Keynesian policies, military expenditure is 'safer' (economically!) than other forms of government spending because it provides a way of injecting money into the economy without increasing production in the civilian economy, where it might create enough production to cancel out the additional demand. For this reason, some economic analysts regard militarism as a central pillar of Northern economies.[20] But for the following reasons this does not seem to me a totally adequate explanation. First, militarism played a different role at different times. In the Cold War, the arms economy almost seemed to be absorbing or siphoning off technological innovations that would be too destabilising if they were allowed to burst into the rest of industry. It was necessary for capitalism to remain at the cutting edge of technical innovation, and, for this reason, the state was funding the investment. It would not, however, have been safe for the latest technology to penetrate too deeply into the civilian economy, at least while Keynesian options still prevailed. This is because it would have had a disastrous impact on employment levels. Second, we have to take account of the effect of militarism on the *international* system. The arms economy under classic imperialism certainly stimulated individual economies, but at the same time, when the major industrial powers were competing with each other, it tended to tear the system apart. In this sense, I believe the Cold War found a 'safe' (in terms of North–North relations) method of going ahead with militaristic development, in a way which would otherwise have been incompatible with the demands of international economics. The industrial economies could unite to face an external enemy in an endemic conflict, which meant the armaments industry could play its economic role without destroying the interdependence among the countries in the North that capitalism was trying to build. Third, the cost–benefit analysis of militarism cannot be confined to the North–North dimension of the international system, because it also played an indispensable role in other areas. It maintained the South in a subordinate position so that its resources could be exploited by international capitalism, as well as suppressing the radicals in that region. It also maintained an atmosphere of constant threat against the Soviet Union, forcing it to play a 'responsible' world role.

But militarism, however important, was only a symptom of something deeper. The Cold War was an important element within an international system which (as is probably a common characteristic of systems that maintain their hegemony over a long period) somehow turned its antagonisms and conflicts into a source of stability.

The new equilibrium was very different from the old. By abolishing the old power politics, capitalism had moved into completely uncharted territory. Under the old system, the antagonism between the great powers had been transformed into a source of stability, through the phenomenon (sometimes seen as a deliberate policy, sometimes as an objective process) of the 'balance of power', whereby the aggressive impulses of the ruling groups of different capitalist nations somehow neutralised each other. The American post-war agenda recognised that the 'balance of power' system had to be abolished, for it reinforced competitive nationalism and prevented the development of the interdependence now necessary for capitalist development. The new state of affairs was explicitly recognised by Roosevelt's Secretary of State, Cordell Hull, when he said that once the 'extreme nationalism' expressed in 'excessive trade restrictions' had been eliminated, there would 'no longer be need for spheres of influence, for alliances, for balance of power, or any other of the special arrangements through which, in the unhappy past, the nations strove to safeguard their security or promote their interests'.[21] This prescription left open the question of what precisely would replace the old system. It implied that a universal collaborative system bringing together all the industrial states would be set up, but this was an enormous change from past practice. And it failed to address the question of what would be the new source of 'constructive antagonism', which was required to create a new stabilising principle.

Initially, communism was defined as purely negative (evil) and it was not recognised as having rights and interests of its own. But already at this level it was functional in a systemic sense, because it reinforced the definition of the 'Free World' as its opposite, namely something entirely positive (good). In these circumstances, rollback (destruction of communism at a state level) would be counter-productive. At the same time, the mere threat of rollback forced the Soviet Union to consolidate its domination of the Eastern bloc. In order to hang on to its buffer zone, the Soviet Union was forced to reject the offer of Marshall Aid to Eastern Europe, which in economic terms would have virtually amounted to rollback, and to clamp down, enforcing total uniformity. This made it practically impossible for socialism to acquire a genuine popular base in the area, and it also reinforced capitalism's identity as the opposite of socialism.

There were both mythical and real aspects to the anti-communism of the Cold War. On the one hand, Soviet expansionism was, at least in the early period, a myth, and it was used as an excuse by the United States for attacking nationalist movements. On the other hand, it is perfectly true that popular liberation movements *were* part of Communism. This is because these movements were – and always will be – opposed to the US world order; this is a contradiction which is in principle entirely separate from whatever understanding the USA subsequently reached with the USSR at a state level. US policy reflected this dualism. On the one hand, it projected an image of communism as an all-encompassing force that would have to be fought everywhere. On the other hand, US interventionism was concentrated in practice in key areas, according to a 'strongpoint' idea, of (in George Kennan's words) 'adroit and vigilant application of counter-force at a series of constantly shifting geographical and political points'.[22] This, rather than the broader 'domino' theory, was the guiding principle behind US strategy.[23] But the broader concept remained because it could at times be useful; it was part of an over-arching vision of world order which allowed the USA to justify intervention anywhere, against countries, for example, which nationalised raw materials. In this way, the wartime conception of a world security order (in effect, security for capital accumulation) came to be implemented in the guise of the Cold War.

Attempts were made to harmonise these two elements into consistent policies for particular issues – for example, Indochina. But there was a problem in defining what was in essence to become the post-colonial order. For the new order was being established on behalf of the North as a whole, in areas that were not in the traditional US spheres of influence. Initially, the USA secretly supported the colonial ventures of the old established powers in areas where there was a genuine communist (though not Soviet-expansionist) threat. Its goal was to establish good conditions for exploiting the resources of such areas as today's Malaysia and Indonesia: 'The plantations of Malaya and the Netherlands Indies cannot be fully worked nor the rich resources of this area developed while guerrilla warfare rages.'[24] And US support for France in Vietnam aimed to lock Asian countries into a system which could 'stimulate the flow of the raw material resources of the area to the free world'.[25]

But a problem soon emerged in the distribution of the costs and benefits of the new order, in both the political and economic spheres. America claimed to be doing a good turn for its allies, since communist control over raw materials 'would endanger the stability and security of Europe',[26] but there was another way of looking at it, that, under the excuse of keeping raw materials out of communist hands, America was in a sense attempting to control Europe by controlling its sources of raw materials. Not surprisingly, resentment surfaced, coming to a head around the time of the Suez war, when some commentators in Britain viewed the US as 'the general enemy of British imperial interests'.[27] As well as this backward-looking imperial perspective, there was also a more modern way of calculating costs and benefits. Take, for instance, the Middle East. From the European point of view, US companies were taking advantage of the conflict to move in and squeeze out rivals. But from the American angle, they were bearing the burden of military intervention on behalf of all the others. European capitalists could reply that, with the dollar as the linchpin of the monetary system, America could finance its operations by printing money. The counter-argument on America's part was that, with the dollar overvalued, it was sacrificing its *industrial* development. These contradictions came to a head at the time of the collapse of the Bretton Woods monetary system in the early 1970s.

In many ways US policy appears classically imperialist, based on its individual nationalist interests. A good example is the coup promoted by the CIA in Iran in 1953, which overthrew the nationalist regime of Dr Mossadeq. Under the pro-Western regime which followed, American companies strengthened their hand at the expense of the British. And the link with the corporations is even clearer in the case of Guatemala in 1954, when the CIA launched a coup to overthrow the elected government of Jacobo Arbenz Gusmán, who was attempting to nationalise areas of unused land held by the United Fruit Company. Most of the US political establishment seems to have had a direct interest in that company.[28] With hindsight, it can be said that this kind of direct imperialism was characteristic of the transitional period. At that time, the 'Free World' was a melting-pot in which trans-nationals and other capitalist actors were forging a Northern dominance of a new type, predominantly multilateral. This was not always apparent at the time, and other industrial powers often reacted with old-style resentment over what the USA was doing. But these differences were eventually patched up, because ultimately it became clear that the US-inspired world order was, first of all, benefiting capital accumulation as a whole, and, second, promoting North–North interdependence. Little by little, the whole capitalist world became aware of these benefits.

But even if this solved the problem of the transition at a North–North level, the North–South dimension remained a problem. The *ad hoc* solution which had developed out of the Second World War, and was secretly sup-ported by America, was an uneasy compromise with old-style colonialism; it was scarcely adequate to the new order. A more stable solution was needed to enable the industrial world to continue exploiting the South without the direct costs of both administering it and repressing dissent. This required a transitional international system radically different from anything that had existed before.

## The Advent of Bipolarity

In practice, this was only achieved by trial and error. And I believe that the solution that eventually emerged explains the evolution of the Cold War in the direction of a mutually accepted bipolarity. Historically, this change is associated with the concept of *détente*. Conventionally, the period from the early post-war years to 1989 is brought together as the Cold War period, but I consider it more helpful to define the period from the mid-1950s to the end of the 1970s as one characterised by a mutually accepted bipolarity. As I will argue later, to end this period in the late 1970s makes it coincide much more closely with an important shift in *economic* structures than if we were to take 1989 as the finishing point. But what concerns us here is the beginning of the period, which was dominated by the need to move to some form of 'neo-colonialism'.

During this phase, international relations apparently became de-ideologised. It seemed as though, after a temporary interlude of ideological conflict, the international system was returning to the power politics which had tradi-tionally formed the best condition for stability and security. Rather than being the evil 'other', the Soviet Union became a normal power with its own interests. This would be different from the balance of power in the strict sense, which implies *several* more or less equal actors which can form temporary alliances with each other to cut down to size any power whose ambitions threaten the system's stability. But it was still possible to argue that this arrangement could provide stability, first because of the nuclear 'balance of terror', in which each would be inhibited from using the ultimate weapon, and second because, if there were only two superpowers with global interests, any dispute in the world would risk taking on a global dimension, so they would each have an interest in restricting conflicts to below a certain threshold. This balance serves stability in a systems-theory sense, according to which a stable system is one that retains its essential characteristics, does not lead to the elimination of any of the major actors and does not provoke the outbreak of a large-scale war.[29] It has even been argued that bipolarity was the stabilising factor, and the more bipolar the world became the better, because this reduces world politics to a single issue and prevents too much troublesome complexity.[30]

But this apparent shift from ideology to power is deceptive. The underlying purpose of the international system was not security *per se*, but security for capitalist exploitation. This takes us back to the fundamental elements in the definition of 'stability' and 'security' in the capitalist system. Poverty and malnutrition can develop apace under such a regime; indeed, they are certain to do so since they are the necessary product of the capital accumulation which the security protects. This, in turn, creates resistance, which is met with repression, which further increases the insecurity faced by working people. The problem that had to be faced in the new world order was to find a *modus vivendi* between an increasingly internationalised economy and the nationalist state; in other words, an arrangement had to be found in which nationalism could be enlisted to carry out a repressive function, but without this holding back the trend towards interdependence.

Under the auspices of the Cold War, the USA had the whole non-communist world as its arena. It could grab resources and promote its universalist way of life, which was supposed to attract people away from communism. As Richard Nixon put it in a 1950s speech,

> Nothing in our economic life so well symbolizes our constant desire for perfection and progress as does our annual showing of new models of powerful and comfortable automobiles. The struggle for the world will be finally determined by what happens to the millions of people now neutral who are trying to decide whether they will aline [*sic*] themselves with the Communist nations or with the free nations.[31]

Yet the assimilationist promise is no sooner made than it is contradicted. Nixon again:

> There are only seven per cent of the people in the world living in the United States, and we use thirty per cent of all the energy. That isn't bad; that is good. That means we are the richest, strongest people in the world, and that we have the highest standards [of] living in the world. That is why we need so much energy, and may it always be that way.[32]

Not only are there not enough resources to go round, but the South must be kept as a *purveyor* of these resources. This can be done only by restricting their development, which might lead to their consuming the resources themselves. The *consumer* appeal of assimilationism was thus basically flawed, and assimilation would inevitably have to rely more on the stick than on the carrot. Non-alignment became the enemy, because it would threaten to narrow the scope of capital accumulation. Hence the pronouncement of US Secretary of State John Foster Dulles that, 'Barring exceptional cases, neutrality today is an obsolete conception.'[33] Even British Prime Minister Harold Macmillan's 'Winds of Change' speech, delivered to the white South African parliament in 1960, and often taken as a far-sighted recognition of the historical process, is imbued with a fairly classic cold-war dualism, where 'the great issue in this second half of the twentieth century is whether the uncommitted peoples of Asia and Africa will swing to the East or the West'.[34]

But from the point of view of the South, this simplistic division of the world into two camps was not convincing; indeed, bipolarity appeared threatening because of the agenda it carried with it. And the non-aligned world developed rapidly on the basis of a sort of astrophysics view of the world: if the two blocs sucked in all the surrounding free matter this could launch a catastrophic clash between them; and this would be bad not only for the small actors, but also for everyone else in the system. Although this view was put forward by élites, there is a strong case for saying that they were articulating some deep aspiration of the mass movement for some avenues of development to be opened up that were free from the interference of outside powers. It is interesting to note that when representatives of Asian and African states met at Bandung in 1955, even though they issued a very sharp challenge to great-power domination, only perhaps half a dozen out of twenty-nine governments would be commonly considered radical (China, Egypt, Ghana, India, Indonesia and North Vietnam), and in at least twice that number the governments in place were strongly pro-Western in political terms. It was public opinion, it seems, that persuaded the Conference to adopt such a position.

It was the North's attack on neutralism that created a basis for cross-class unity in the South; but this effect was counteracted by other factors which, on the contrary, facilitated a political alliance between Northern capital and third-world élites. To understand these factors, we have to look at the role of the state at the time. The state monopolised violence both nationally and internationally. It could therefore be armed, nominally in pursuit of cold-war international security, but really to provide élites with a way of suppressing the mass movement. This could be given a semblance of development by rewarding ruling groups for their acceptance of US goals with 'aid' which they effectively appropriated. Co-operation between the USA and secret services of repressive regimes had been pioneered by the activities of the US Navy with the Guomindang in China during the Second World War.[35] At that time the US friends of the Guomindang had been considered a lunatic fringe by the US military establishment, but with the advent of the Cold War they *became* the establishment. Such a development also became prevalent in Latin America. For example, a resolution adopted by the Organisation of American States (a regional grouping dominated by the USA) in 1951 stated that 'The expansionist activities of international communism require the immediate adoption of measures to safeguard the peace and the security of the Continent.'[36] These measures, which involved strengthening the military and the secret services, deepened the insecurity of ordinary people's lives, as well as protecting not only international exploitation but also unequal property relations and distribution of wealth. Military power, apparently a symbol of sovereignty, became responsible for widespread repression of the people.[37] And in the 1960s it became clear that the US could afford to remain serene in the face of third-world rhetorical attacks, as long as it kept its hold over the military. Indonesia is a classic case: at the height of Sukarno's anti-imperialism in 1964–65, the United States was careful not to break off military aid, and in 1965 the right-wing military seized power, leading to the massacre of between half and one million people. And the Americans knew very well what they were doing. The following year a Senator put this question to Defence Secretary Robert McNamara: 'At a time when Indonesia was kicking us pretty badly – when we were getting a lot of criticism for continuing military aid – at that time we could not say what that military aid was for. Is it secret any more?' McNamara replied, 'I think in retrospect, that aid was well justified.'[38] In this way, militarism proved a good way of pandering to the nationalistic pretensions of élites and keeping them in power so that the flow of resources continued. Without militarism, nationalist élites with development plans that challenged the North's supremacy could have taken over.

The dual nature of state violence – national and international – gave rise to an interesting and complex state of affairs. At one level, the international facet (the supposed Communist threat associated with the Cold War) served as justification for a militarisation primarily geared to internal repression. But it was also possible for élites in the South to develop this dialectic one stage further by unfolding an international-level violence of a new kind. Having armed the third-world élites, the industrial world sometimes gets worried about the implications, and the élites, knowing about this concern, can brandish the threat of destabilisation to bargain for better terms. India is an example. In the 1950s and 1960s, the West quite openly approved of the Indian government massacring domestic revolutionaries and providing a military counterweight to China. When India obtained a lot of military aid from the Soviet Union as well, it was therefore impossible for the West to object. But the Indian élite had planned all along to use this situation to assert its regional dominance at the expense of one of America's staunchest third-world allies, Pakistan, and in the early 1960s the US administration secretly reassured Pakistan that, in the event of an Indian attack, 'there would be immediate US response'.[39] But when, in 1971, India eventually intervened militarily in the process which led to the dismemberment of Pakistan, the stakes had become so high that America was unable to do anything.

There are many complex contradictions in such processes. Certainly, in such situations the West was able to carry on exploiting economically all the countries concerned. But some stability was nevertheless needed at a politico-military level, as a precondition for continued economic exploitation. It became clear that the United States faced significant dangers in the dynamics of local conflict in the South and that it was only partially successful in its endeavour to use the Cold War to define them.

International capitalism obtained some successes during this period. It found a new structure to replace old-style colonialism, and the transition to this new system was secured under the auspices of a relatively stable international order, within which bipolarity played a crucial part. The relative success of this period nevertheless was achieved at the cost of several important contradictions, the results of which we are experiencing today. In some ways, neo-colonialism was itself only a transitional solution, which began to come unstuck around the time when the post-war long cycle came to an end at the beginning of the 1980s. The assimilationism of the South into the 'free world' was always on a weak footing insofar as the North failed to deliver tangible advances to the masses, and this problem could only get worse, as the plausibility of *national* economic development began to wane. Multifaceted violence, both national and international, had become an intrinsic feature of the post-colonial order, and this violence could take on a dynamic which no political forces could control. This problem was to be starkly exposed with the eventual repudiation of bipolarity, itself associated in a complex way with the shift in long cycles. In many senses, therefore, the world order is at the moment witnessing the unfolding of contradictions stored up during the post-colonial era.

## Notes

1. Keynes 1919, p. 19.

2. For example, game theory, which analyses both economic and international decisions, has clearly demonstrated at a logical level that situations where individual short-sightedness leads to the optimum result are the exception rather than the rule, and in many hypothetical situations the pursuit of purely selfish and non-cooperative strategies can lead to a stable equilibrium which is worse for all parties than a possible alternative combination of decisions.

3. See Waring 1988, pp. 46ff.

4. See Fevre 1985.

5. Certainly these divisions could be surmounted, but this could only be done by recognising and combating the reality of differences in people's day-to-day lives, access to education, health, life expectancy, job prospects, and so on, which were heavily embedded

in the post-war political economy. In this respect, the left-wing critique of 'post-Fordism' in the 1980s performed something of a disservice by taking at face value the predominance of the official economy during the earlier period.

6. See Harvey 1954. In theory, one could postulate an internationalised form of the Listian argument about the growth of the world economy, whereby the individual economy is transcended first at a regional level, before this occurs at a global one. However, this regionalism reflects the collapse of the globalising tendency in the world market, rather than something which would develop hand in hand with it.

7. Gbagbo 1978, p. 25.

8. Césaire 1972, p. 18.

9. Quoted in Keal 1983, p. 68.

10. El Ayouti 1971, pp. 22–3.

11. See Rodney 1972, p. 187.

12. In the case of the agreement with Britain, it was made clear that the United States could change its mind about the aid provisions if the more important colonies did not become part of it; see Text in *Keesings Archives* 9362, 1–3 July 1948.

13. Louis and Robinson 1982.

14. Cornevin 1980, p. 10.

15. Sekgoma 1982, p. 47.

16. See James 1982.

17. In Indonesia the Japanese had already offered negotiation, and the nationalist forces led by Sukarno had to enter into discussions with Communists about whether to accept. In Malaya, the popular movement had got out of control, all the more extraordinary since the leader of the Communist Party was a British intelligence agent! See Clutterbuck 1984; Caldwell and Utrecht 1979.

18. Westad 1993, p. 45.

19. See in particular Leffler 1994.

20. See, for example, Hunt and Sherman 1986, p. 161.

21. Quoted in Kolko 1969a, p. 317.

22. Quoted in Morris 1982, p. 486.

23. See MacDonald 1991.

24. Brookings Institution 1949, p. 17.

25. Sheehan 1971, p. 28.

26. Ibid.

27. Quoted in Epstein 1964, p. 56.

28. CIA head Allen Dulles was a former president of that company; his brother John Foster Dulles, the Secretary of State, was a former legal adviser; Walter Bedell Smith, Dulles' predecessor at the CIA, was made president after the invasion; and Henry Cabot Lodge was on the board of directors at the time when, as US ambassador to the UN, he was President of the Security Council when the latter rejected Guatemala's call for a UN debate on the invasion. See Julien 1972, chapter 4; Greene 1970, chapter 8.

29. See, for example, Crockatt 1993.

30. This is the neo-realist view, which we will examine more fully later.

31. United States Government 1957, p. 5.

32. Quoted in Kegley and Wittkopf 1979, p. 169 – no date is given for the quotation.

33. Quoted in Crabb 1965, p. 168.

34. Text in *Keesings Archives*, 20–27 February 1960, 17269.

35. See Schaller 1979, p. 250.

36. Ball 1969, p. 448.

37. In the period under discussion this occurred because arms were being imported. But local production does not fundamentally alter the problem, since resources still have to be diverted from other areas of the economy.

38. Quoted in Blum 1986.

39. Choudhury 1975, pp. 110, 112.

# 4

# Development: Theory versus Practice

## 'Development' as Part of the Growth of Global Capitalism

In this chapter, I will consider how post-war capitalist development as a whole was related to the development of the South.

Under capitalism, the aim of balancing human development with the needs of the natural world has been abandoned. Economic trends which see the goal of development as something real, such as improving agriculture or improving human resources – for example the Physiocrats, or List's theory of the natural economy – have been viewed with suspicion. Instead, development has become practically synonymous with capital accumulation, which effectively serves as both the means and the end. The prime focus of the development process has been the nation. Development has therefore come to mean 'modernising' society within national boundaries, in such a way that the traditional safeguards that used to stand in the way of unbridled accumulation have been removed. The new national economy becomes a unit which the international system both recognises and respects as one of its own.

All national economies in the North are engaged in international forms of accumulation which are in essence predatory. The transition from mercantilism to liberalism did not affect the substance of this predatory behaviour; all that changed was first the relationship of the established national economies to each other, and second their earlier practice of establishing exclusive spheres within which to conduct their predatory activities. The essential element that has remained constant is the way in which the international facet of the accumulation process has prevented the formation of new national economies. There are essentially two ways in which this has been achieved: by depleting resources and by exploiting cheap labour. In order to be able to do this, the economies in the North have stopped the economies in the South from erecting effective national boundaries. International exploitation is still a 'primitive' form of accumulation, because it does not pay full value for the things it consumes: resources are taken from the natural world without significant economic cost, and the human labour employed both in producing the resources and in processing them is reproduced on the basis of a partly non-monetary economy. This makes it impossible to 'modernise' the local economy in such a way as to create a fully-fledged capitalist national economy.

There is an interesting conclusion to be drawn from the above analysis. Since the capitalist national economy is a dubious blessing anyway – because it subordinates human and natural resources to accumulation – the South might actually be at an advantage in not being fully 'modernised', in other words, in not having all its relationships enslaved to the market. It might be possible to build a different sort of national economy which develops these non-market elements rather than smashing them, as happened in the central capitalist blueprint. This is an important possibility which I will consider in the final chapter. But it is one that has been largely ignored: most official development strategies have tried to copy what happened at the centre, i.e. constituting an accumulation system within national boundaries at the expense of the traditional/local economies. Precisely because this attempt to copy the old capitalist countries has been conducted under conditions of international accumulation, it has often resulted in an imitation national economy which, under the guise of autonomy, has served as a staging post in international accumulation. Nevertheless the process brings about a real change in the South's economy which needs to be understood.

It was crucial that the economy in the South had the appearance of becoming developed. Indeed, the new international economy imposed a form of development on the South which, although really reinforcing subordination, involved rapid and far-reaching changes which could easily appear as though they were leading to modernisation, and to the constitution of national economies. This was possible because there was still a lot of scope for change within the limits of subordination. The global accumulation system inherited by capitalism at the end of the Second World War was still marked by colonial/mercantilist relations with the South, and this had important implications for relations within the countries of the South. Society was predominantly rural. There were still many areas of the economy with no wage labour, little exchange, and so on. Mercantilism, which actively prevented colonies from developing their own industries so it could export to them, did not enter into terminal decline until after the Second World War. And the key changes in the post-war period, such as the growth of dependent industrialisation and the demand from the North for more cash crops produced by more efficient methods, all implied profound changes in the South: urbanisation, wage-labour in the rural sector and the growth of an exchange-oriented economy including services.

Development theory then stepped in to provide a relatively coherent body of ideas depicting these changes as though they were or could be part of a coherent, self-reproducing dynamic, thus reinforcing the illusion that these were symptoms of autonomous modernisation. I will analyse three key elements of this rationale: stages theory and the linked concept of trickle-down; urban–rural dualism; and import substitution.

## The Illusion of Development by Stages

Stages theory was widely accepted in the early post-war period. A useful, systematic statement can be found in the writings in the 1950s of Walt Rostow, an American economist who was also active in the politico-military establishment.[1] Essentially, the theory says that development proceeds through a linear succession of stages copied from the historical experience of existing industrial countries. The roots of linear developmentalism can be found in eighteenth-century ideas of progress.[2] There was a negative aspect to this idea of progress because it wrote off a country's sense of continuity with the past, but it was at least exciting in that it generated a feeling that the future was open-ended and injustices could be resolved. Post-war stages theory, on the other hand, was deterministic because the goal was predetermined – it was to be just like contemporary America. This is simultaneously teleological (pursuing a pre-existing goal) and assimilationist (following an external model). Society is heavily reified, and somehow acquires its own 'propensities', which embody this capitalist vocation. It assumes that latent entrepreneurial tendencies are already there, and that development is merely a matter of removing barriers to their self-expression. So the choice is effectively between one predetermined path to development and no development at all.

This theory assumes a closed-economy model which, though a legitimate tool of economics, lends itself to abuse. Here it leads to two basic errors: it eliminates entirely from the picture the whole issue of international exploitation, and even if we assume its model of past industrialisation experience to be accurate, it conceals the fact that huge changes occurred in the institutionalised and internationalised world economy in the post-war period, making it a totally different place.

Besides generally sanctifying the tyranny of the American way of life, the stages idea was socially conservative also in a more specific sense: it implied political repression within Southern societies because of the heavy degree of accumulation involved in take-off. This could only be achieved at the expense of consumption, so labour-movement campaigns for higher wages had to be suppressed.

Even so, the model's handling of the accumulation issue remains superficially persuasive even for those sceptical of its assimilationism and historical distortions. There are two aspects of the process of accumulation. First comes what could be seen as the negative facet of accumulation, that is the break-up of steady-state economics. Stages models are in this sense very much a continuation of the colonialist view, that it is necessary to liberate people from their old stagnant lives, where they would sit under a tree chatting once they had done enough work to feed themselves, rather than rushing to accumulate more. So for Rostow, it is a bad thing when people draw high levels of welfare from their land and natural resources,[3] and a qualitative, structural change is needed to break them away from this. This is the 'negative' aspect of accumulation, when it is necessary to break with the old situation but there are not yet sufficient conditions for something new. The second, positive aspect of accumulation is supplied by the idea of take-off into *self-sustained* growth, meaning that capital will establish its self-reproducing circuits within the national economy. Early models assumed that a ratio existed between the amount of savings (that is, what was not consumed) and a particular economic growth-rate.[4] The concept of take-off assumes that the change is a qualitative one. The metaphor of an aeroplane is used: it needs to acquire a critical speed if it is to leave the runway (traditional life) and leap into the air (the modern world). Large growth-rates, which are seen as qualitatively different from small ones, are required for take-off, and to achieve these, very big increases in savings are needed. To save, resources must be withdrawn from consumption, and the savings become accumulation only if they are concentrated in entrepreneurial hands. Rostow thought savings would need to be fifteen–twenty per cent to push the growth rate high enough to achieve take-off.

In its time, the stages idea was quite appealing and generated a broad consensus. The idea that poverty is a characteristic of an early stage of industrialisation (for example, Dickensian England) appeared plausible. The masses might therefore agree to limit their consumption so that future generations might enjoy the fruits. It also seemed to make a lot of sense that there might be two different sorts of economics. Keynesian economics dealt with a situation in which there was abundant capital, which could be mobilised through increasing demand. The South was not yet ripe for this, but it was a promise for the future. Rostow placed 'high mass consumption' at the pinnacle of his progression.[5] Although given an explicitly anti-Communist twist by Rostow, this was generally accepted by economists at the time.[6]

So developing countries were seemingly stuck with a special economics appropriate to their particular stage. And one of the key problems that emerged was how to link the destructive and constructive aspects of accumulation so that the value generated by the breakup of traditional society would feed into new self-reproducing circuits of accumulation.

## The Myth of the Benefits of Urban–Rural Dualism

Development economics, best expressed in the work of Arthur Lewis, claimed to provide an answer. It is interesting to note that Lewis, who was a contemporary of Rostow with whom he shared many presuppositions, came from the developing world (Jamaica); this in itself suggests the extent to which élites in the North and the South agreed at the time on a common agenda. Lewis' model focused on the fact that, while the North had abundant capital, the South apparently had surplus labour. It was perhaps the perception of rural life held by a town-dweller, who saw a lot of people hanging about with nothing to do, and ignored the seasonal character of rural labour. What is certainly true is that rural economies can sustain many people at a minimal level – which is not necessarily a bad thing, although modernisers perceived only the wasted resources.

The colonialists had already developed the concept of dualism, but they had seen the traditional sector as merely a dead weight holding back progress. Lewis thought that dualism, if handled correctly, could actually be a *favourable* factor for development. This was enormously bold and attractive, and it fitted in with an era in which independence had apparently permitted the South to take hold of its own destiny and disprove the negative ideas which the colonialists had used to hold them back. Lewis suggested that through its economic policies, the government should make it easy for entrepreneurs to tap into this pool of labour. The capital available at a particular time would be invested in a bout of productive activity, which would draw in from the rural areas a number of workers, paying them just enough to encourage them to migrate to the town. The profits from this cycle would then be reinvested, so the next cycle would draw in more workers. This would continue until all the surplus rural population has been absorbed, by which time a different sort of economy would have been established.

The theory implies that wealth would become concentrated.

> Many under-developed countries, awakening in the middle of the twentieth century to a strong desire for economic development, are embarrassed by what it seems to require in terms of inequality of income, whether it is between the 'middle' classes and the farmers, as between foreigners and natives, or as between profits and other incomes ... These, however, are part of the cost of development.[7]

But the theory also suggested that the wealth had to be in the hands of a dynamic stratum. 'It is the inequality which goes with profits that favours capital formation, and not the inequality which goes with rents.'[8]

In this discourse, the reactionary landlord system is equated with the rural economy overall. In effect, in the transfer of wealth from the rural to the urban areas, it is the whole of the former that is being robbed, not just the landlords (who are in a good position to safeguard their interests). In the new world, the capitalists become the dominant force, and the reciprocal relationship with the grassroots, found in traditional systems, is broken.

There are serious problems with this 'modernisation' model. It is true that the rural–urban relationship would be an essential basis for any successful capitalist development strategy. We can set this out in schematic form: if the circuits were really to be coherent and self-reproducing, the forced destruction of rural structures through enclosures would create a pool of labour which had no choice but to migrate, but this would occur as a spin-off from a process which rendered agriculture productive enough to feed the urban population. And even here it is coherent only within narrow limits: the destruction of sustainable social and knowledge systems (not the same thing as the destruction of landlordism) has become a problem at a world level; capitalist agriculture feeds the urban population with a level of artificial inputs that could not possibly be reproduced on a world scale. But within these narrow limits the model makes sense, if we assume the goal of capitalist development to be desirable.

However, with respect to the South, development theory neglected the fundamental importance of raising agricultural productivity as a precondition for the depopulation of the rural world; if this does not happen, the rise in urban population creates dependency on imported food. The neglect of agriculture was justified by a mechanical application of theories such as Engel's law,[9] according to which the lower a person's income, the greater the proportion spent on food. This law not only supplied additional reasons for transferring wealth to the rich (since the poor, according to this argument, do not save), it was also an argument for economic planners to neglect investment in agriculture since its proportional importance in the national economy would shrink as development occurs.

Apart from the two-sector model, the more general assumption of modernisation theory was that poverty could be turned into development because cheap labour would provide the basis for accumulation. But this assumption too was flawed.

Taking existing industrial countries as the model, it is assumed that poverty can be alleviated only by following the path of development in an inverted 'U', with poverty getting worse in the earlier stages and then declining. The conclusion is that people must tighten their belts for a generation or two, and then the situation will improve. The problem is, however, that, if poverty is structural, it can easily be *reproduced* by the process of development itself, and this in the end undermines the chances of real development in human terms. Keith Griffin has explained this well: first, existing inequalities form a basis for the allocation of resources which supposedly lead to new development, and second, national production is geared to the demand of those who already have the wealth to consume, and public investment generally supports these orientations. This undermines the assumptions of the Lewis model in concrete ways: for example, in a neutral economy without class interests it would be expected that investment would use the abundant productive resource, labour, because it is cheap. However, since the access to capital is in practice limited to those who are already rich and influential, interest rates are artificially low, and the incentive to invest in labour, rather than machinery, is eliminated.[10] In similar fashion, deficient rural income translates itself into a lack of incentive for food production, since in a capitalist set-up production is stimulated by demand, not need.

Even if hypothetically parts of the South appeared to be developing *as countries* in such a way as to narrow the gap with the North (at a state-to-state level) this would not necessarily mean that the gap was really being narrowed if internal polarisation within the countries in the South increased.

Consumption within the international capitalist economy as a whole would still mainly take place in the North, so the living standards of the masses in the South need never improve.

The conditions for the form of development which entrenches poverty are international. The dependency perspective (which is a radical critique of mainstream development theory) highlights these conditions by introducing a dangerous idea: it is not just that there is one group of countries in the world which happens to be developed and another which happens to be poor. The two are organically linked; that is to say, one part is poor *because* the other is rich. The relationship is partly historical – for colonialism and the slave trade helped to build up capitalism, and this provided the conditions for later forms of dependency – but the link between development and underdevelopment is also a process that continues today. As Amin pointed out, in what is perhaps the most important single idea of dependency theory,[11] the tendency to pauperisation – the acute poverty that is both the basis and product of capital accumulation, and thus of 'growth' – was transplanted to the periphery.[12]

But it is simplistic to see dependency simply as an international relationship, for it also requires a base in the social relations within Southern countries. Specifically, it is internalised in the form of incomplete capitalism. The contemporary critique of development theory by Paul Baran makes this clear. The problem is not the absence of development but its presence. The key proposition is that capitalism in the periphery arose in a special form; in Baran's words,

> all that happened was that the age-old exploitation of the population of under-developed countries by their domestic overlords was freed of the mitigating constraints inherited from the feudal tradition. This superimposition of business mores over ancient oppression by landed gentries resulted in compounded exploitation, more outrageous corruption, and more glaring injustice.[13]

In the traditional set-up, the tribute received by the ruling class was largely conditional upon the good functioning of the system they ruled. In the context of neo-colonial capitalism, by contrast, they receive what amounts to a kind of tribute arising from the malfunctioning of the system.

This is not to say that dependency theorists are 'against' the development of the third world along capitalist lines; indeed, if it were possible it might be supported, insofar as it weakened imperialism. But the problem is that it is very difficult to achieve because capitalism as it concretely arises in the periphery is of a special, truncated form, which inhibits the development of complete capitalism rather than promoting it: 'Far from serving as an engine of economic expansion, of technological progress, and of social change, the capitalist order in these countries has represented a framework for economic stagnation, for archaic technology, and for social backwardness.'[14]

Part of the weakness of mainstream development economics comes from imposing false closed-economy assumptions upon a reality which was really international. But it is also possible to formulate an approach which seeks to build upon the international dimension, and it is in this context that we should consider import substitution.

## Industrialising for the Domestic Market – Import Substitution

Although import substitution is often discussed as though it were mainly a policy adopted by Southern élites, it can be seen as a trend which arose within the world economy independent of their desires.

The classic colonial–mercantilist pattern was to stop any industrialisation in the periphery; local demand would be met by finished products from the metropolis. But this created a quandary for capitalism. If Southern demand depended entirely on the wealth generated by raw material exports, it would fall if the prices for these kept declining; as a result, capital accumulation would be harmed. But, at the same time, growth in the North required the prices of raw materials to be kept low.

A solution was required, and it arose from a parallel development in the North. In an important sense international capital had increasingly been moving in a direction where the developed countries consumed their own product. Keynesianism had set the seal on this. But, as Lenin had realised, the absence of underconsumption did not necessarily mean the absence of a drive to export capital; on the contrary, it is precisely because the product is increasingly consumed at the centre that the export of capital is increasingly necessary. This is because, first, the rising incomes needed to consume the product mean that profit will fall unless new sources of cheap labour can be found; and, second, a safety-valve in the form of capital export was necessary if capitalism's relative position in the balance of class forces was not to be weakened.

The answer to both problems was to exploit cheap labour in the South. Two conditions of the Ricardian model no longer applied: labour could be remunerated at different rates, and capital could become mobile. Multinational capital could obtain a higher rate of profit in the periphery and transfer this value to the centre.[15]

There was therefore a strong argument for a post-mercantilist inter-nationalisation of production. In its fundamental implications, this might take no account of the national dimension. As I argued earlier, capitalism had already, in the inter-war period, been feeling its way towards a solution where it could 'replace trade in the final product with trade in the intermediate products'.[16] This really took off in the more recent period, when it soon became a strategic concern for corporations to focus increasingly on 'the international production of goods and services, rather than traditional export/import trade'.[17] The critical period for this change came immediately after the Second World War. The term 'import substitution' is used as part of the internal planning vocabulary of TNCs, meaning that it is cheaper to manufacture something on the spot than to import it in finished form. In itself, it has nothing to do with independence. This is shown in the African case. In Nigeria, Nnoli argues, the origins of import substitution date back to the immediate post-war period (from about 1946), when the colonial system was still very much in place. It can thus be regarded as a form of industrialisation 'dictated by the changes that had taken place in the international division of labour within the world capitalist economy'.[18] This managed, proactive, form of import-substitution industrialisation (ISI), carried out by a dynamic multinational, is quite different from the kind of industrial development that had arisen during the crisis of the 1930s, when domestic capital in countries such as Egypt and Argentina had been forced by a weakening international economy to become more self-reliant.

But it is important to understand that import substitution also temporarily took a form in which it appeared to respect the national dimension. To understand why, we have to look at the specific historical stage in international capitalist development at which it occurred.

Critics of ultra-imperialism were correct in saying that there were limits to the organising capacities of capital, but they did not altogether have the right reasons for saying so. To a certain extent, it is true to say that capital is incapable of organising in such a way as to overcome competition, but there is also a sense in which it would not be profitable for capitalism to organise too much, as self-exploitation (Chayanov's term) does the job much better. Fortunately for capitalism, the accumulation structure tends to take on a life of its own, obliging economic actors spontaneously to seek niches within it.

This facet of capitalism, which erupted in full force in the new management systems around 1980, had been foreshadowed in a particular way in the post-Second World War environment. At that stage, globalisation had not reached a point where small economic actors could be integrated *directly* into the exploitative embrace of international capital, so the division of productive capacities was established primarily at a national level. It is in this context that import substitution as an apparently sovereign policy of apparently sovereign states must be seen; it was a peculiar, national form of self-exploitation, a temporary and transitional phase in North–South industrial relations.

Eventually, beyond internationalisation, there would be a new stage: globalisation. At this stage, specialisation would no longer be conducted primarily at the level of national economies, and economies in the South would begin to export cheap manufactured goods to the North, without much respect for national boundaries. As I have already argued in the discussion of imperialism, this had long been a latent tendency within capitalism. It directly benefited those sectors of capital which invested in this activity in the South, and, through the multiplier effect of the repatriated profits brought back by these companies, it indirectly stimulated the central economies. The companies manufacturing competing products in the North may have lost out, but globally the capitalist class would gain because the living costs of workers, and hence their wages, are held down. In the early stages of the industrial revolution this function had been performed by importing food and raw materials for textiles from the South; it was only the next logical step to import manufactured consumer goods.

The rationale which was eventually to justify 'export promotion', as it was called, was already in place. Trade theory had not remained static, and new elements, grafted on to the liberal foundations of the Ricardian model, appeared to address the problems of late developers, and brought trade theory back into line with the emerging concepts of 'development economics'. In the inter-war period, Heckscher and Ohlin had incorporated factors of production into trade theory, arguing that what gave countries their comparative advantage was the relative availability of capital and labour: each country would export the commodity which employed most intensively its relatively abundant factor. It was thus logical that industrial countries, which had plenty of capital, should specialise in capital-intensive sectors of the economy while less developed countries (LDC), with their cheap labour, should invest in labour-intensive activities.[19]

Given the strength of this argument, import substitution seemed, even at the time it was implemented, to be a step in the wrong direction. It seemed to reverse the main trend of capitalist development because it reduced the scope of the market and encouraged countries to gain greater self-reliance by consuming what they produced. But in a broader historical context it is clear that import substitution was a stepping stone towards post-national forms of exploitation. For this policy was adopted during the period of post-war reconstruction in the North, when industrial countries were developing their own consumer industries and following full-employment policies. The classic colonial exchange (extraction of raw materials and export of manufactures) had been only partially revolutionised, to the extent that capitalism was using cheap labour in the South to produce goods for the local markets. This policy fitted in with the complex political tasks of a transition from colonialism to neo-colonialism, when the centre had to cultivate an apparent respect for national aspirations. Under these conditions, import substitution was an effective tool for exploiting cheap local labour.

Nevertheless, I believe import substitution did have a flaw from capitalism's point of view. The problem was that if consumption of the product was local, wages would eventually have to rise to provide additional demand, and this would eventually contradict the whole assumption upon which internationalisation occurred, namely cheap labour. The developmental potential of the model was thus limited; it would work for a while, but would then have to be scrapped. And this is exactly what happened. At the end of the

1970s, the dominant forces in the world economy turned against import substitution as vigorously as they had once propagated it. The way forward was to find a way in which the product could be consumed in the North, for then there would be no limitation on the use of cheap labour in the South, and this is precisely what happened with the shift to export promotion.

Although imperialism theory undoubtedly shows that part of what happened could have been predicted, no one, in either centre or periphery, fully understood the long-term developmental logic of the systemic changes. Through a process of trial and error, in which initiatives from below were dissected and, where useful, co-opted, capitalism eventually discovered the way forward. In a sense, the accumulation process itself acted as a mechanism for doing this. But, as the long-term logic of the changes was not apparent at the time, ISI appeared much more conducive to national development than it really was, and was spontaneously adopted as policy by élites in the South. There was a separate logic for the élites' support for import substitution, and it is important to understand what this was.

It can best be understood against the background of the terms of trade issue: the theory of comparative advantage in its Ricardian form had suggested that the South might be in a stronger position to develop, since it could industrialise using its own raw materials, whereas the North could not replicate the natural conditions necessary for the production of many of the primary products that it had used to industrialise. But in practice none of the benefits of international specialisation accrued to the South. United Nations surveys in the late 1940s showed that terms of trade had been moving persistently against the developing countries and, in the period which immediately followed, that of the post-war boom, awareness that there was something wrong with trade theory increased: greater demand for primary products should have pushed up prices, but it did not. At the same time, productivity in the North was rising, which led to a bigger supply of manufactured goods, but this did not lead to a fall in world-market prices for the North's exports. Argentinian economist Raúl Prebisch noted that monopoly conditions in the manufacturing countries could have been partially responsible for this; and it should also be noted that there were monopolies that affected third-world exports, but in this case, they were on the side not of the producers but of the purchasers; in other words the Northern corporations which bought the raw materials could collaborate to keep the prices down.

Developing countries could respond by cutting off the international circuits of which the South was part, and in so doing begin to establish circuits within their economies: exports had created some domestic wealth, hence demand, which was fed by imports, and these could be replaced by domestic manufacturing.

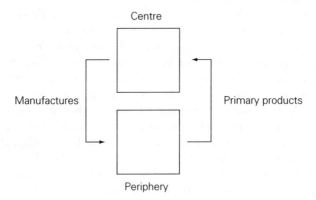

There is a certain reciprocity implied in this picture; that is, decline in the export of primary goods can be balanced by the rise of domestically produced industrial goods to replace imports. The idea of the model is to reduce both simultaneously so that the same cycle gradually takes over with the Southern economy.

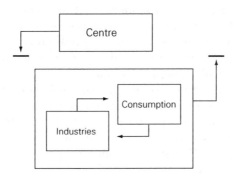

This model seems to fit in with the agenda of grassroots anti-colonialism, which aimed to break away from a situation where the South produced what it didn't consume and consumed what it didn't produce. But in practice, import substitution industrialisation was never capable of tapping into the grassroots. Fundamentally ISI's proponents took on board modernisation's assumption that only the official sector was respectable. There was never a genuine local basis among the élites for diverse, non-specialised economies; on the contrary, the whole way they defined development seemed dedicated to abolishing them.

Lacking a firm domestic basis at the grassroots, the Southern bourgeoisie was in a weak position to challenge the North in a power struggle. Once central capitalist countries began to realise that the way forward for them was growing interdependence on each other (on the basis of already established national economies whose boundaries could then gradually be dissolved), they closed ranks, and élite Southern national movements without a grassroots base were not strong enough to bludgeon their way in.

The question becomes clearer if we look concretely at the technology issue, which exposes the basic flaw in the assumptions of élite ISI strategies. A closed-economy stages theory assumes that developing countries are in a time-warp, going through the same processes as, say, eighteenth-century England, with presumably the same technology. But in reality, as Celso Furtado points out, for the South the competitor to be displaced by industrial-isation is 'not the artisan of low productivity but the highly efficient producer operating through the world market'.[20] Advanced technology has now become a commodity: its cost becomes an additional inflow, *not reciprocated by any equivalent outgoings*, unless additional primary products are exported, and to do this reinforces dependence. And even this is difficult, as monopolistic interests are unwilling to part with 'pure' technology. So often the technology is 'embodied' in the physical equipment needed in the production of consumer goods, which means that the apparent elimination of imports is illusory, for it leads to the situation described by Williams in his case-study of Nigeria: 'The development of neo-colonial capitalism substituted imports of inter-mediate and producer goods for imports of consumer goods. This con-solidates rather than undermines dependence on foreign suppliers, since production, as well as consumption, now depends on foreign imports.'[21] This equation can be made to balance only by an increase in the exports of primary products, which means that the viability of such models often depends on the market prices of the raw materials in question. In the case of Zambia, which is widely analysed as an example of the problems in ISI, growth was extraordinarily rapid up to the early 1970s, but the collapse of copper prices suddenly called into question the whole model.[22] To pay for capital goods imports, Zambia was selling copper at a loss on the world market by the mid-1970s.[23]

In reality what often happened was that Northern capital continued to control not only the technology but the actual production itself; and, if this was the case, what appeared to be import-substitution industries were really the last-stage assembly of kits. Tariff barriers protected these supposedly infant industries, but all this amounted to in practice was to give transnational capital an exclusive domestic market, so that they could pocket monopoly rents. The motor industry in parts of Africa is an example.[24] It is sometimes argued that this set-up actually inhibited indigenous capital-formation.

ISI is more consistent than export promotion, in the sense that, if production and the market are both internal, it is quite possible for all developing countries to be pursuing this policy at the same time. But this consistency was more apparent than real: countries had to bid for investment which transnational capital would obviously not spread around in a generalised way, and had to offer incentives, which undoubtedly came to constitute a new way of siphoning value from the South (in this sense nothing much changed with the shift to export promotion).

Typically, the privileges accorded to transnational capital went far beyond market protection. Even though the Ivory Coast is one of the more favourable cases, in the sense that development in some sense *did* happen (reflected in a significant migration of foreign labour into the country), foreign-owned industry was able to cream off a lot of the value created: in 1971, for example, European managers accounted for 4 per cent of the industrial workforce, but received 41 per cent of total industrial wages;[25] and the investment code, which encouraged foreign companies to invest, guaranteed their right to import all capital equipment and intermediate goods duty-free, and to repatriate unlimited profits. This soon led to more capital leaving the country than was newly invested in it, i.e. a reverse flow of resources or decapitalisation, which, according to the conventional definitions of economic growth, was perfectly compatible with a country recording high rates of expansion. Since, in practice, the sums did not add up, the only way of saving the model was to extend credit to the country; in this sense, the 'debt' problem was in-built into the post-war models of development. In the case of the Ivory Coast, the foreign debt had reached a total of US$14.125 billion by the late 1980s. Per head of population this amounted to US$1,261, as against US$793 for Brazil.[26]

Added to this are structural problems in the nature of domestic demand. Although ISI is apparently better than later doctrines because it assumes domestic consumption of domestic products, the practical difficulty is that the demand generated in the economy reflects prevailing class relations.

One could postulate a form of industrialisation linked to domestic *need* rather than demand, in other words a process that would lead to real development, but such industrialisation could not occur through displacing existing imports. For if ISI replaces existing imports, which by definition are consumed by an élite, the people who are not served by this tend to be further marginalised, even within the narrow limits of the genuine self-reproducing economy that is created.

There are two ways in which the development of a local industry merely to serve an élite hampers true development. First, it is problematical not just morally but in terms of feasibility: in the most successful cases, like Brazil, this model, implemented under prevailing class relations, is bound to come up against the problem of restricted demand (I will discuss this further in Chapter 10). Second, in the more typical case, the model does not even get to the point of exposing this limitation, because élite demand biases development into precisely those sectors where foreign producers are most difficult to displace. For development on this model bypasses not just the masses, but more specifically the rural world. In these circumstances, industrialisation, as Adedeji puts it, 'rather than constituting an engine for growth in Africa, tended to accentuate the dualistic nature of the African economy'.[27] This definition of dualism is worth thinking about. Conventionally, dualism views the traditional/rural world as a brake on industrialisation, but the reverse could actually be the case. The urban–industrial sector is not simply isolated from the rest of the economy (in Hans Singer's phrase, 'merely geographic') but can actually undermine it. Indeed, during the heyday of post-war development strategies, there was often a negative correlation between urban industrial growth and wider developmental goals. For instance, Nigeria's massive growth rate in the period of its second and third five-year plans was achieved against a background of stagnation in agriculture.[28] Rather than radiating benefits into the rural areas, as conventional economics suggests, the urban economy acts more like 'a whirlpool into which resources are inexorably drawn, and the whirlpool does not broaden out, but only grows deeper'.[29] As Naoroji's drain theory had already sensed, the centre–periphery relationship is internalised within the developing country. It could even be argued that the TNCs positively encourage indigenisation, for it favours the growth of a symbiosis between themselves, the local state, and the ruling class.

During this particular phase, when a replacement was being found for colonialism, some accumulation had to take place at a state level. But it had to be strictly limited: first, it could not call into question the country's peripheral status; and second, it had to reflect the particular set of circumstances in the international political and economic system at the time, and could therefore later be swept away by circumstances over which developing countries had no control. Specifically, the new *modus vivendi* between the centre and local state capitalists had to be peculiar to that precise phase of internationalisation that was occurring within a state-centric framework, and would logically disappear when the long cycle changed.

So the key problem face by imperialism at this stage was to permit a certain level of industrialisation in the periphery without allowing this to become autonomous. The very idea of permitting a 'safe' level of development in the periphery implies some way of managing one of the key features of imperialism – that is, the export of capital. But corporations could not be relied upon to operate very efficiently in this respect, so the centre looked for some sort of political control. It is here that we must examine the question of aid and the political influences over capital flows.

## Rationing the Transfer of Capital – Aid Policy

Capital is exported to the South not only for the classic imperialist reason that it permits manoeuvring between centre and periphery and thus acts as a safety valve for regulating social conflict at the centre (for labour would be in too strong a position if everything was invested there), but also because some form of dependent industrialisation has become increasingly necessary. The flow of capital, however, needs to be regulated to prevent the South from using the resources to catch up with the centre. At a simple level this could be done by limiting the quantity of investment.

Because the export of capital takes many different forms, it is difficult to keep tabs on it without some strategic overview. Eventually, international capital worked out the system by which the World Bank monitors both private and public capital flows to the South. This is to ensure, first, that development occurs only within the tightly controlled parameters of structural adjustment, and, second and more broadly, that political and social conditions for the global accumulation system are maintained. But before this arrangement was set up, there was a lot of trial and error, which is reflected in the history of aid policy.

Early approaches were comparatively crude. In the immediate post-war period, the United States espoused a grand conception of world order conducive to capital accumulation, and in accordance with this, it used aid in an overtly political way. The Cold War gave the United States considerable scope to draw up a strategy for harmonising two goals: on the one hand, the long-term order of the capitalist system and, on the other hand, the immediate profitability of transnationals. In the transitional post-war period, aid embodied the compromises we have already observed between multilateralism on the one hand and a *de facto* tolerance of bilateral neo-colonial relations on the other. The metropolitan countries were effectively allowed either to accumulate enough through their relations with ex-colonies to fund their repressive role in the Cold War division of labour, or to retain elements of the old bilateral special relationships. For example, France continued to purchase from its colonies some primary products at a relatively favourable price to encourage them to continue with a monocrop economy, and hence to go on supplying raw materials.[30] Aid was also used to help to establish a relationship by which ex-colonies would commit themselves to buying machinery from the former metropolitan power; this was the so-called 'tied' aid, earmarked for the purchase of particular equipment from the donor.

But there was also scope for a more innovative post-colonial form of funding, which could facilitate 'social engineering' to engender new élites. There was, however, always a contradiction, first between profit and social engineering, and second between the need for some development to undercut protest and the imperative to keep development under strict control.

This contradiction would become acute only where there was a net transfer of resources from the centre to the periphery. Otherwise, it was possible, at least in principle, to reconcile the conflicting demands by investment which simultaneously returned a profit and generated a certain social engineering as a spin off of a process that was fundamentally one of 'drain'. The classic form of this relationship has been well documented by Jalée.[31] This was behind the strategy, implemented during the Kennedy era, of targeting countries with a low per capita income, over half the money lent at the time going to India and Pakistan.[32] The exception, which was when there was a net injection of resources, occurred only as a result of the implementation of the strongpoint containment strategy. Results in South Vietnam, a large recipient, were ultimately disappointing, but the 'miracles' of South Korea and Taiwan owe quite a lot to this flow of capital. Elsewhere, the 'management of poverty' was the main policy determinant. There was not enough aid to permit real development, but enough, theoretically at least, to blunt class struggle.

From the South's point of view, the Cold War seemed to have a positive aspect, in that it offered opportunities for playing off one side against the other in the pursuit of better terms. But it must also be recognised that, with both superpowers competing to make a big impact rather than promote real development, 'the similarities between these two models, especially in the emphasis placed by both on capital formation in the development of large-scale manufacturing, might be more significant than the differences'.[33] It was the sort of aid which, for structural reasons, perpetuated dependency.

What was the rationale, from the point of view of élites, for welcoming aid or investment? They could of course have made a strong argument for aid as reparations,[34] on the grounds that all the wealth-generating capacity which by then existed in the North had been built on value plundered from the South. But the issue was hardly ever addressed in these terms; instead, the élites merely looked for a good business proposition.

There were three key aspects. First, the closed-economy model, characteristic of most development theories, did not provide the developing world with a totally satisfactory model. For, if strictly applied, 'stages' theory, according to which countries at an early stage of development are frozen in an eighteenth-century time-warp, does not permit developing countries to catch up with the North. But most developing countries want the gap to be narrowed rapidly. Brazil at the time of President Kubitschek in the 1950s had a slogan, 'fifty years in five',[35] which was fairly typical of thinking in the South at the time. Resources from abroad, it seemed, could fuel a fast rate of growth and allow the developing world to bridge the gap.

Second, if development is viewed as a business, then it seems reasonable to borrow, as all businesses borrow; and it makes sense for them to borrow if the value generated by the equipment purchased with the loan can be expected to exceed the rate of interest paid on the loan. And the fact that capital was at the time increasingly becoming internationalised could theoretically work to the advantage of the South. For the countries in the South had abundant labour but lacked capital; if they could obtain this missing factor of production from abroad, then they would be in an advantageous situation. From the angle of trade theory, it might enable them to escape from the situation where, on the assumption of immobile factors of production, they would be forced to specialise in commodities using cheap labour, tropical climate, and so on. It must be noted, however, that businesses have some form of limited liability, so it is generally easy for bankrupted individuals to start trading again. Their descendants are never held responsible for the mistakes of earlier generations. A country, however, cannot simply be liquidated and restarted under a different name, and development mistakes can mark a country for centuries.

Third, access to funds from abroad might provide the élites with a way out of a difficult dilemma. The investment necessary for successful import-substitution industrialisation would require a high rate of capital accumulation. But conventional wisdom in economics assumes that accumulation takes place at the expense of consumption, which would make it difficult to consume the products of the new industries. If funds were available from outside, it would be possible to invest without restricting consumption too much.

Élites understandably perceived existing aid policies as not only humiliating but also restrictive: they had to opt for a bilateral relationship; they were 'tied' to purchasing goods the industrial countries wanted to offload; and they got dragged into the Cold War. Since the reparations argument was never taken seriously, the next thing in these circumstances was to seek a form of capital with as few restrictions as possible. This pointed them in the direction of first giving multilateral institutions a greater role, and second having investment conducted according to business rather than political criteria. In practice, the two developments took place side by side, with the trend away from official aid and towards private capital particularly clear. In 1967, a World Bank commission reported that, although in the medium term industrial countries should implement the target of giving 0.7 per cent of their GDP in aid, the long-term future was for the developing countries to receive private investment and to have growing access to the capital markets.[36] During 1971–78 the share of private as opposed to public finance going to the developing world rose from 17 per cent to 39 per cent; a different estimate put it as high as 60 per cent in 1977. Whereas during the Kennedy period the North had sought to undercut the basic appeal of revolutionary politics in the more 'needy' areas, now profit rather than 'need' became the chief criterion. During 1971–75, the five countries taking the most loans in European financial markets were Mexico, Brazil, Indonesia, Algeria and Iran, who together accounted for 60 per cent of the total.[37] This general move towards business lending prepared the ground for the massive flux of speculative capital going to the developing world in the late 1970s.

This was accompanied by a large increase in multilateral lending, and it all happened with the connivance of Southern élites. In retrospect, it may well seem that the outcome was worse than the situation from which they were seeking to escape. The conditionality imposed by institutions such as the World Bank is far more restrictive than the restrictions imposed by bilateral lending, since it relates not just to specific projects but to the whole structure of the economy.

For a while it seemed that there might be a payoff for the South. For it began to appear that the development of the South was needed to solve the problems of the capitalist system as a whole. Once the post-war boom had dried up, capitalist growth declined in the 1970s. Some analysts believed that

the market in the North was becoming saturated, and that some transfer of
resources – not necessarily a direct infusion of funds, but a willingness to
accept a change in terms of trade favourable to the South – would have a
multiplier effect on the entire world economy. This was a persuasive argument,
as we will see in Chapter 6, but it was to be short-lived. What happened
instead was that the so-called NICs were exploited for short-term profit,
while at the same time, in the longer term, the machinery was created for a
new way of extracting accumulated value. It was the third-world 'debt' that
carried out this role, killing two birds with one stone: it allowed the North
to enjoy the value that was extracted, while ensuring that development in the
South did not become autonomous, as it might have done if the value had
been reinvested locally. But this did not happen for several years, and at the
time the future looked far more uncertain.

## Radical Nationalism in Search of Autonomous Development

The North could not completely achieve a limited and 'safe' model of
development for the South which it could readily manage; the question arose
as to whether élites in the South might take advantage of the weaknesses
within the scenario. Various factors could create the opportunity for such
radical nationalist approaches. The Cold War might encourage the West to
make concessions, particularly if the country in the South was flirting with
the Soviet model, which claimed that it could supply experience in managing
a planned economy. Radical development projects could channel the energies
of previous anti-colonial mass movements into safe forms that were not too
threatening to propertied classes. Or the existence of a seething mass movement could provide the West with an additional reason for valuing the local
élites who were containing it and for therefore giving them aid.

The state played a key role in the creation of such models. At one and
the same time it served as guarantor of a national project for which populations might make sacrifices (they would not do this just for entrepreneurs),
as the administrator of a planned economy, and as an authority that could
tell the Soviets what they wanted to hear, namely that there was a non-
capitalist path to development.

The state had considerable importance, given the value which it mediated
or controlled, and it used this to acquire its own autonomous sphere. But
what was the nature of its autonomy? The radical nationalists claimed that
the state embodied a supra-class national project in the interest of the general
public. But this is doubtful. More plausibly, as in the classic latecomer model,
the state might shield the development of a bourgeoisie. The problem here,
however, is that this could only happen through an international power-
struggle; since a fully fledged bourgeoisie would, by definition, not yet have
been developed, the state faced the very big responsibility of going it alone.

In practice this was very difficult. The enemy was highly organised in the form of corporate interests and, wherever necessary, the North could bring its own state machine into play as well. In Ghana, under Kwame Nkrumah in the late 1950s and early 1960s, the state got involved in a power struggle with TNCs. The key project was the Volta Dam, which was to provide abundant power for the energy-intensive process of turning local bauxite into alumina, and subsequently to form the basis of an independent process of industrialisation. But, as Ronald Graham has shown, the four big companies which dominated the world aluminium industry were brought together, through the personal intervention of US leaders Nixon and Kennedy, to ensure that Ghana did not establish a basis for independence. The corporations temporarily united into a single company, so they could negotiate from a position of strength. They won key concessions: the right to import bauxite from elsewhere, and to purchase further power regardless of Ghana's needs; the establishment of a special status for the joint company, enabling it to avoid most tax liabilities and transfer unlimited profits out of the country; licenses for the import of all the necessary equipment, and guarantees that protected the company against expropriation and allowed it to use whatever ships it wanted for all these transfers. In fact, the companies preferred to import bauxite from Australia and Jamaica for processing in Ghana and subsequent re-export, rather than expand facilities for mining Ghana's own bauxite which would have involved the risk of permitting Ghana to gain control over a single integrated production sector. The companies obtained the right to import alumina duty-free for 30 years, and negotiated a unit cost of electricity which was the cheapest in the world. The effect was one of 'eliminating, or at least dramatically reducing, the effect of any possible interposition of the nation state across the control relationship of vertical integration'.[38]

Ultimately, the Ghanaian state was not strong enough to sustain this kind of struggle, but the situation could be more favourable where there was already a significant basis for national capital. The case of Egypt is interesting here, because it had made several earlier attempts to develop, and in the inter-war period it had had some success with import substitution at a time when the dislocation of the world economy caused a kind of involuntary delinking of the South from the North. The nationalist coup of 1952 sought to push development much more decisively. But the international market for commodities was now expanding, and domestic capital was unwilling, spontaneously, to focus its investment in industry. The investment targets in the five-year industrial plan of 1957–61 were not fully achieved.[39] The state responded by nationalising key economic sectors, including half of industry, together with the whole of banking, insurance and the cotton trade. Since the Suez War of 1956, in response to Western hostility Egypt had been playing the Soviet card, and in particular it received Soviet backing for the regime's flagship project, the ecologically dubious Aswan High Dam.

To please the Soviet Union, the regime had increasingly presented its statist economic policies as socialist. With these policies, in particular the Soviet link-up, the bourgeoisie received, in Mahmoud Hussein's words, 'a provisional opportunity to flourish'.[40] But could this lead to something real, in terms of socio-economic development? As domestic class relations were closely linked to the international economy, the attempt to escape from raw-material dependency weakened to some extent the conservative landowning class. And industrialists had some success in processing cotton locally instead of exporting it raw.[41] It is unclear, however, whether all this really challenged the transnational agenda, since the decentralisation of processing tasks may fall within a logic ultimately orchestrated by the textile transnationals;[42] and the export of finished goods is notoriously difficult.[43]

With the radical models, the state could take action directly to influence class structure, and the classic area for action was land reform. In the Egyptian case, land reform certainly brought about change: the redistribution mainly favoured a middle stratum of peasants, with poor peasants sinking even lower, and it looked as if a rural bourgeoisie might be established.[44] Theoretically, they might invest in rural development, but the problem was that, according to the prevalent doctrines of accumulation, value would in practice be transferred from the rural to the urban sectors. An important mechanism of such transfers has always been to manipulate terms of trade to the detriment of agriculture. Abdel-Fadil thus refers to a 'double squeeze', meaning firstly transferring or requisitioning a proportion of rural produce for consumption in the cities, and secondly an 'expenditure squeeze' or enforced saving among the rural population.[45]

Despite this, there were dynamic elements within the indigenous capitalism that were waiting to burst through the shell of the state-centred model. But the problem was that they were heavily interlinked with the international economy. So when the state collapsed it did not leave behind independent capitalists; on the contrary, the nationalism vanished along with the state. In the Egyptian case the problem was compounded by hostile international political factors – Egypt had a heavy military expenditure, which constituted a substantial drain on resources and certainly reinforced dependency.[46] But militarism is not necessarily entirely something forced on Southern élites; they also often resort to it spontaneously, partly in order to pursue their dependent economic interests. In the Egyptian case, both the left critique[47] and Western academic analysis[48] seem to agree that the aim of the 1973 October War with Israel was not victory, which would have unleashed the mass movement, but a new relationship with Israel; Egypt's entrepreneurial stratum perceived this as a business opportunity.[49]

There is scope for a struggle to establish some local autonomy, but it is limited by the nature of the strata who conduct that struggle. The normal pattern is that central accumulation permits a small portion of value to accrue to local élites as a reward for their management of the economy within the prescribed parameters. They can at times bargain with the centre over the size of their portion, and this is presented as a national struggle. The radical version would be to fix the value in the nation (not just in the hands of élites); it would become an action of the 'national bourgeoisie', in the left terminology. But this begs the question of the nature of the nation. Very often the state substituted for a meaningful grassroots definition of the nation. The advantage was that a commandist state did not have to be built from scratch, for it was inherited from colonialism. It was a state whose purpose was to oversee accumulation in the interest of the centre. After independence, so the argument went, the 'centre' could be changed from the colonial metropolis to the indigenous urban–industrial sector. In this way, the accumulated surplus would be redirected to the cause of development; this was often the case, for example, with marketing boards for commodities, which the colonialists had used to squeeze the agricultural sector in their own interests, and the radicals claimed to use to squeeze the agricultural sector in the interest of development.

This state, which is not really differentiated from the colonial one, could itself become an object of struggle between rival groups. This was the case even with some radical movements which were explicitly directed against neo-colonialism. Rhetorically left-wing regimes such as the one that took power in Congo (Brazzaville) tended to equate revolution with a struggle of 'socialist elements' to occupy 'strategic' places in the state apparatus.[50] This is not to say that the mass movement was a pure fiction. In cases where there was a genuine mass movement behind independence, it formed a backdrop to struggles within the state machine, but still very much struggles between different groups over the value to which they had access through the state machinery. For example, in Algeria there was social change, both among workers and peasants. Although there was an objective basis for alliance between the two classes, there were also tensions, which groups among the leadership could exploit in their own interests.[51] The manoeuvrings of different élite segments occurred against the background of a real mass current, which different factions at times sought to enlist. The state occupied sectors where private capital was weak, with different fragments entering the state apparatus.[52] Sub-contracting to the private sector was an important way of linking state and private capital, via clans which may have a territorial basis.[53]

Given these problems, alternative, non-statist forms of development were considered in the search for a more consistent radical approach. In Tanzania, a form of socialism built upon traditional African co-operative systems was attempted. The strength of such an approach was that it broke away from the assumptions of conventional development economics. It realised that consistent capitalist circuits of reproduction, built within individual Southern economies through the same process which propelled development in the North, would probably not create dynamic entrepreneurs and innovative farmers but rather bureaucrats plus conservative landowners. Tanzanian leader Nyerere was perfectly justified in saying that 'third-world capitalism would have no choice except to co-operate with external capitalism, as a very junior partner'.[54] The orientation was, in the words of the Arusha Declaration (1967), that 'From now on we shall stand upright and walk forward on our feet rather than look at this problem [of development] upside down. Industries will come and money will come but their foundation is the people and their hard work, especially in agriculture.'[55] This is similar to the Gandhian idea that, in the relationship between the rural/village economy and the industrial one, 'the order of dependence will be reversed'.[56] More than this, though, objectively there was the realisation that the traditional economic systems had some kind of balance between 'high' economy and the grassroots economy. If central-type capitalism was unworkable, it said that an alternative viable economy would have to be pursued which functioned as a system. The traditional approach makes sense in this respect.

This analysis is fundamentally correct, but in practice the Tanzanian experience ran into a lot of problems. Obviously international capitalism had an interest in ensuring that this kind of initiative did not succeed. The economy also remained extroverted, confirming what Shivji cites as a law of under-development: divergence between domestic resource use and domestic demand;[57] and in general, the alienation produced by this situation made it difficult to mobilise the population behind any 'development' project.[58] But fundamentally, there is a problem with grassroots structures being designed from the top downwards; élites often have idealised views about what traditional peasant society should be. In practice, the government at first relied upon the traditional leaders to mobilise the people in its support, ignoring the fact that this policy threatened them; when this approach failed, it tried imposing social change from above, which also proved unsuccessful.[59] In today's circumstances, this solution could be approached in a different way, because there are many grassroots movements with their own impetus, so they would not have to be invented by élites.

More recently, statism has been undermined by the system of global accumulation itself. Bearing in mind how useful statism was to international capitalism, this may be puzzling. We have seen so far that not only the 'economy' – in the form of import-substitution models – but the state itself, the local élites and perhaps even the whole nation-building project were unwittingly part of a certain global regime of capital accumulation, the logic of which was not clear to those in the periphery (although this did not prevent peripheral countries from attempting to take advantage of possible openings within it). When the global regime changed, the peripheral structures could become redundant. Economically, there has been a shift away from the model where a locally-implanted industry served a local élite market, and where exploitative relations were conducted to a significant extent on a country-to-country level, to one where local industry serves export markets, mainly in the North. Politically, first the crisis and then the defeat of the Soviet model have been important elements. It means that it is no longer so necessary politically to appease nationalist sentiments or to 'invest in' friendly political structures. But Northern capitalism's triumphant dance on the grave of the statist models in the 1980s concealed problems which we will investigate later. By no means has the model of using a locally-accruing portion of value to fund a local mechanism of political repression (as ISI did) become outmoded; the demise of ISI leaves an awkward hole in the North's control mechanisms.

## Notes

1. For example, Rostow chaired a secret committee formulating anti-communist strategy during the 1950s, and later played an important role in the Vietnam War.

2. Cf. Aseniero 1985.

3. Rostow 1960, p. 277.

4. This is the so-called Harrod–Domar model, an influential part of development theory.

5. Later, obsessed by the need to compete with Communism, he went one better and spoke of 'beyond consumption'; in Rostow (1960), he accepts that the goal is similar to communism in placing the quality of life centre-stage once need has been fulfilled; but only capitalism could get there.

6. There were of course different nuances to development theory; the 'balanced growth' argument did include a demand element, but the ultimate implication was to simply add a further argument in favour of qualitatively massive rates of accumulation, since the multiplier would come into effect only in an economy that pushed several sectors at the same time. Thus, if one established a single factory making a single product, the rise in income of the workers would constitute demand, but obviously not all the demand would be for the single product; however, with a large number of factories making the whole range of goods, this limitation would not apply.

7. Lewis 1955, p. 182.

8. Lewis 1958, pp. 419–20.

9. This was formulated by the German economist Ernst Engel in the second half of the nineteenth century.

10. Griffin 1978, chapter 6 (the cited chapter was co-written with Azizur Rahman Khan).

11. I am using the term for convenience, since dependency is a well-known concept, although Amin would not identify himself with the term, preferring 'centre–periphery'.

12. See Amin 1978b, chapter 2.

13. Baran 1958, p. 76.

14. Baran 1973, p. 300.

15. It should be noted that another scenario is possible, in which the rate of profit averages itself out over the world economy as a whole, establishing itself higher than it would be simply on the basis of exploitation of relatively expensive Northern labour. I will discuss the more recent evidence for this in Chapter 10, but it is worth remarking here that, at a theoretical level, such a scenario would also be exploitative. This can be understood in the following way. The averaging-out of the rate of profit already happens within an individual 'complete' national economy. The real rate of profit in branches of production which are relatively labour-intensive would be higher, but if all the investment were to

flow into these branches it would penalise technical progress. In practice, therefore, investment evens itself out, in such a way that, in effect, the labour-intensive branches (where,
if insulated from the rest of the economy, the rate of profit would be higher than the
average) are subsidising the others. Within the capitalist class of a single country this is
not perceived as a problem. At a global level, on the other hand, if labour-intensive
countries were subsidising the rate of profit at the centre, there would be an obviously
exploitative relationship.

16. Foreman-Peck 1986, p. 147.

17. Quoted in Odle 1981, p. 35.

18. Nnoli 1981, p. 109.

19. It should be noted that this does not necessarily imply the pursuit of export-
promotion strategies by the cheap-labour countries, since free trade would also lead to
competition in the domestic market. However, the same argument can serve as a rationale
for such strategies, which is increasingly the case today. We will explore this point later.

20. Furtado 1976, p. 101.

21. Williams 1981, p. 46.

22. See Seidman 1979.

23. In 1964–69 copper cost on average 393 kwacha per tonne to produce, while the
price on the world market was K909. In 1975–79 the cost of production was K1,104 and
the market price was K1,095: Ncube *et al.* 1987, p. 127.

24. In Zambia, Fiat received an effective market monopoly in exchange for putting up
only 30 per cent of the capital, the remainder being supplied by the state. In Nigeria,
import licenses were imposed on cars under 2000 cc to protect factories set up by Peugeot
and Volkswagen, where the main components were supplied from Europe and merely
assembled locally. Cf. Seidman 1979; Williams 1981.

25. Alschuler 1988, p. 83.

26. Calculated from Banque Mondiale 1990, pp. 200, 240.

27. Adedeji 1984, p. 220.

28. In the second plan (1970–74), growth was targeted at 6.3% GDP and was actually
11%; in the third plan (1975–80) growth was targeted at 9.5% and was actually 6.5%. But
in both periods the growth rate of agriculture was negative; cf. Ayo 1988.

29. Weeks 1975, p. 92.

30. Amin 1973, p. 92 and tables on pp. 34–5.

31. Jalée 1969, p. 110.

32. Sampson 1981, p. 100.

33. White 1974, p. 209.

34. See, for example, APSP 1982.

35. Cf. Villaschi 1994.

36. It is interesting that no country except the Nordic states and Holland attempted to
attain this, and at the end of the 1980s the US figure was 0.2%! See Miller 1989.

37. Frank 1981, pp. 137–8.

38. Graham 1982, p. 181.

39. Hansen and Girgis 1965, p. 156.

40. Hussein 1971, p. 137.

41. See, for example, Izzeddin 1975.

42. See Clairmonte and Cavanagh 1981.

43. The Long Term Arrangement fostered by international capital (1962) limited the
access for finished textiles to Northern markets.

44. There was an upper limit of 100 feddans (about the same number of acres) for landholding introduced in the more radical stages of land reform in the early 1960s, but rich landowners were allowed to sell land over and above the ceiling; naturally those who could buy were the medium owners. So the real growth area was owners of 20–50 feddans. By 1965 they owned nearly one-third of total cultivated land, while about 50% of peasant families were poor or 'ruined' peasants with less than 2 feddans. Their lot didn't seem to improve with any reforms. Small peasants with 2–5 feddans constituted 25%, and eked out a subsistence living. See Abdel-Fadil 1975.

45. Abdel-Fadil 1975.

46. Cf. Zaalouk 1989. Savings constituted 13% of GDP in 1967, whereas in the years following the war they fell to 6%, while the balance of payments deficit rose from 3.35% of GDP in 1960–66 to 6.62% in the period following the war.

47. For example, Shoukri 1981.

48. For example Taylor 1982.

49. Cf. Kazzia 1979.

50. Wamba-dia-Wamba 1987, p. 105.

51. See Post 1979.

52. See Roberts 1983.

53. See Eteng 1981.

54. Meyns nd, p. 70.

55. Text in D. Cohen and Daniel 1981, p. 240.

56. Quoted in Ganguli 1977, p. 255.

57. Shivji 1976, p. 151.

58. Nnoli 1981, p. 115.

59. See Feldman 1975.

# 5

# The Socialist Challenge to Development

## Breaking with Capitalism – the Need for a Realistic Solution

Capitalism provokes resistance, and it constantly has to adjust to this, either crushing its enemies or co-opting acceptable facets of their struggles. But the form that the clash between capitalism and resistance takes changes across time. The period from the First World War to the 1980s was a particular stage in which the main resistance to capitalism appeared to be Communism as a *state* system. Historically, the emergence of the Communist state system coincided with the development of classic imperialism. Many on the left believed that imperialism would be the phase of capitalism's maturity and decline, so it seemed logical that it would be accompanied by the emergence and development of the system that would eventually succeed it.

Communism as a state system can be seen as the necessary prolongation of the mass movement; while spontaneous mass protests would always exist – and could force capitalism to adapt – there was still the need to create an alternative in a systemic sense, that is, something where all the economic and political elements fitted together and flourished in a self-reproducing way.

The big problem about shifting human development away from capitalism is how to begin. Because of uneven development, the openings occur in some areas before others, which allows capitalism to move in and suppress ruthlessly these new and vulnerable initiatives. This is where realism comes in. It has a lot of aspects: the search for allies, the use of tactics to prevent enemies from ganging up against the left, the building upwards from small reforms, and so on. But it would be fair to say that it always involves state power. Capitalism's main repressive mechanism is the military, economic and ideological power of the state. What Communism did was to turn this weapon against capitalism, erecting a shield, behind which, in a certain area of the globe, it was possible to evolve a *systemic* alternative to capitalism. Communism is not inherently statist; on the contrary, its objective in the long term was to move towards a system based on local communities. But without a strong state, such a system would never have got off the ground. To a limited extent, state power made possible an alternative course of development; it did so by partially isolating an area from the capitalist world so that grassroots initiatives could develop strong enough structural relationships with each other to liberate themselves partially from the constraints and limitations of having to grow within capitalism. Under conditions of a revolutionary state power, what emerges is not just a new phase of development in general, but, more specifically, a process of weaning society away from the ingrained habits of capitalism. Socialism becomes viewed as a transitional form of social organisation.

The above logic is very plausible, and major parts of the argument are probably correct. But there are two errors which mean that the extent to which the statist model can be the catalyst in defeating capitalism is exaggerated.

The more obvious of these errors refers to the assessment of the era: as I have already argued, it is a mistake to claim that no development of any kind occurs under imperialism. It can be argued that the period in question (the First World War to the 1980s) was one in which capitalism was grappling with the destructive elements revealed by classic imperialism. The two most important problems were the rivalry between heavily armed capitalist powers, and the difficulty of finding a new way of dominating the South without the costs of direct colonial rule. The period can be divided into two: first, a situation of impasse between the powers; second, the period from 1945 to the end of the 1970s, in which a solution had been found but needed to be worked out fully.

Both of these periods were, for different reasons, conducive to the growth of Communism as a state system. In fact, Communism could have taken greater advantage of its opportunities if it had realised that they stemmed from *temporary, not permanent*, changes in the international system, which could disappear in different circumstances.

I will return to the tactical implications of this, but first we should consider the second error. Although it is a mistake to neglect the developmental character of imperialism *within narrow economic parameters*, it is equally a mistake to neglect the deeper sense in which capitalism is not, *and perhaps never has been*, developmental: that is, its tendency to exhaust non-renewable resources.

It is essential that the communist movement, which claims to be the historical successor of the capitalist system and yet is condemned, for a certain time, to coexist with it, understands the importance of this question; its attitude towards the environment must play a key role in the forging of its identity.

Communism had a good basis for understanding the non-developmental character of capitalism from an ecological angle. Historical materialism argued that the starting point for development was humanity's ability to distance itself from nature, breaking the immediate identity with nature characteristic of early society.[1] So what does this mean for future development? The unilinear reading would be 'the more distant the better'. According to this simplistic view, Communism is an extension of capitalism's scientism and its struggle to master nature, and will be able to realise a potential for development which capitalism is unable to do because of its subordination to profit. But there is another interpretation: I would argue that, while it is correct that development hitherto has been a process by which mankind has separated itself from nature, this does not mean that this is a good thing, simply that it is a fact; while this must be the basis for future development, it does not imply more of the same. Through the negation of the negation, future development can seek to repair the breach. In fact, in a sense capitalism has taken things to a point where development cannot proceed along the same lines any longer; for example, capitalism's treatment of one crucial area – agriculture – has undermined the parameters of future development.[2] The contradictions that have arisen as humanity has distanced itself from nature have created pressures that, although unacknowledged, have helped to drive capitalism's own internal development. One of the main things for which capitalism has been condemned by the left is its susceptibility to crises. In a narrow sense, this could be seen to stem from the inefficient allocation of resources, something that could be resolved by socialist central planning. But this interpretation is superficial. As Perlman has shown in an important study, crises are to a significant extent the reflection of capitalism's ecological impasse.[3] Capitalism cannot escape from the fact that human society is embedded in an ecological system; the periodic structural crises of capitalism are an expression not just of economic contradictions (which could be resolved by inventing a new regime of accumulation), but of an ecological impasse which cannot ultimately be ignored.

In this sense, post-capitalist development cannot simply be seen as taking over where capitalism left off, but as correcting a wrong direction followed for many centuries. Communism has undoubted strengths in attempting such a task, for the aim of restoring the grassroots community is built into the very definition of communism. But in practice, there is a risk that competition with capitalism will lead communism merely to attempt to do the same things more efficiently. If this happens, the state will no longer be a shield to permit the growth of a radical alternative but will itself become the criterion for assessing the alternative, and eventually acquire its own momentum, becoming entrenched systemically within a self-reproducing set of social relations. This, of course, is what happened: the epitome is the Soviet system. We need to understand how this process worked, since it became a major part of the international system during the whole period up to the 1980s, and it allowed capitalism to cover up its own fundamental failings by claiming that the alternative did not work.

The origin of this problem is something very understandable, which would perhaps have been hard to avoid: since the radical state had to exist for some time, it naturally took on a role which was not just a 'shielding' one, but one of economic management. In order to understand how this happened, we need to look at the concept of 'socialism', viewed as an initial stage of communism or as a step in preparing for it. It can be seen from two angles:

THE ISSUE OF DISTRIBUTION  One of the fundamental issues of development and of economics in general is the difference between need and demand. Under capitalism, only demand is recognised; if people need something but cannot afford it, this has no economic significance, while at the same time there is demand for things like fossil fuels which in a more rational system should not be consumed. Resolving this dilemma could lead to a new and sustainable economic system.

But before this can happen, a transitional period is needed. In an advanced industrial country, wealth and productive potential exist but there is also poverty; the difference between the cost of subsistence and the actual output accrues to the capitalist, so there is no incentive to work *other than* the threat of poverty. Poverty, or the threat of it, thus takes on a functional role under capitalism (we will return to this issue in chapter 9), and this stands in the way of fully converting need into demand.

Now, under an alternative system of distribution, based on the unit of work performed, need could become demand. The state would have an economic role in planning production to meet a demand which did not yet exist strongly enough to make an impact in market terms, but which could be predicted on the basis of need.

This socialist system of distribution would be easier to establish in countries where capitalist development is relatively complete; but because international accumulation makes exploitation sharper in the periphery, it is here that opportunities have arisen for alternative systems. And these countries have frequently taken the second approach.

THE ISSUE OF DEVELOPMENT  Because capitalist development is incomplete, these countries have had to face the question of creating *forces* of production, rather than addressing distribution, and the state has tended to take on a classic latecomer role. The problem has been to define what is especially socialist about this, and to distinguish it from other forms of statism. This has not been an insoluble difficulty: socialist countries such as China have certainly worked out a path which, whatever criticisms can be made of it, is substantively different from the one followed by capitalist latecomer models. But this leads to the temptation to judge the success of socialism by its success in central planning. It should be noted that this relates in an interesting way to the violent character of the North–South contradiction: in the early stages it may have been necessary to adopt a form of war communism, which means that later the country should move on – seemingly retreat – to a less communistic structure in order to experiment with ways of organising a functioning social order.

## The International Context of Socialist Revolution

Socialist development has to be seen as an international issue. The problem is the relationship between the socialist *state* and the rest of the movement.

In principle, the relationship should be between the organised revolutionary movement and its own unstructured (but for that very reason more rich and diverse) basis. In this sense, the wider mass movement and Soviet state power should relate to each other as equals: one being an area where things can be tried out systemically, and the other being a source of initiatives and new ideas. The revolutionary movement loses something by becoming the establishment, the orthodoxy, and it is the mass movement in the rest of the world which provides the element of the unexpected, the innovations.

It was accepted in early debates in Russia that the main point of reference had to be 'the movement' in some wider sense; the difference of opinion was over how that movement should be defined, which in turn reflected differences in the analysis over what direction capitalist development as a whole was taking. Trotsky thought that revolution in one country could not be consolidated without revolution in the rest of the industrial world. Lenin sensed that the potential for revolutionary change was moving away from the industrial countries into those areas of the world which were more heavily exploited by imperialism. Imperialism would thus fall when the workers' struggle 'merges with the revolutionary onslaught of hundreds of millions of people who have hitherto stood beyond the pale of history, and have been regarded merely as the object of history'.[4] They would become the mainstream of development, from which capitalism had excluded them. While these were radically different views on the nature of the developing international capitalist political economy, there was agreement that the driving force behind international development was not the revolutionary state.

In practice, however, a hierarchy was established between the wider socialist movement and the socialist *state*, with the latter very much in command. So the statism of internal development was mirrored in the international sphere.

At first this was partly justified by the notion that it was the state that was demonstrating the practical success of socialism. But, step by step, the idea emerged that the state could also influence the international system itself in ways favourable to the wider revolutionary process.

In the period leading up to the Second World War, the international system was openly violent and structurally very weak, with such a destructive dynamic that it gained a momentum that threatened to destroy capitalism itself. In these circumstances, it not only made sense for the socialist state to take on a militaristic character, but also for it to play the game of power-politics in order to prevent its enemies ganging up against it. This is something that the Soviet leadership did with considerable skill: earlier than the capitalist leaders, it saw through Hitler's duplicity, and the eventual result of the Second World War was the establishment of a much larger group of socialist states.

But once the structure of the capitalist system became stronger, as was the case after the Second World War, profound problems arose from the Soviets' involvement with it. It is an old problem of traditional systems of international relations: how can one turn the weapons of an evil system against it, without being corrupted in the process?

The pre-Second World War experience misled the Soviet leadership about how easy it was to play the power-political game. Although they had to face immense threats and hardships, it could be said that in a *systemic* sense they had it easy, because of the weakness and lack of cohesion in the obsolete balance-of-power system which capitalism itself could no longer manage. But after the war, capitalism learned how to construct and manage a new kind of international system. This not only unified the capitalist world much more effectively, but also partly achieved this *by incorporating the socialist state itself*, giving the capitalist states something to unite against and to justify intervention in the third world. Soviet-style communism helped in this process by acquiring a tendency to use its hierarchy and monopoly within the revolutionary movement to stamp on any inconvenient and messy processes of mass struggle and innovation. This was useful to capitalism, particularly in getting it through the extremely complex period of the transition to post-colonialism.

In reality, the international system thus became a much more dangerous game for socialists to play, but this was far from the impression that was given. The very process whereby the socialist state was being co-opted into a systemic role which fundamentally served capitalism, created the *appearance* that it was continuing to play the game of international politics successfully. It had 'arrived', it had acquired recognition and apparent respect. It looked as though the socialist state was operating even more effectively than in the 1930s: then, it had simply exploited the system in a static sense to serve its security goals, but now it could adopt systemic ('milieu') goals, geared to influencing the development of the system itself. It seemed that, if socialism in the USSR could demonstrate economic success, the nature of the international relations system would gradually change, in a direction favourable to the emergence of socialism in other countries.

## The Soviet Union Seeks to Beat Capitalism at Its Own Game

Because capitalism and socialism were competing, and because socialism's success was essentially measured by what was going on in the Soviet Union, it was essential that the latter showed that it too could 'develop'. So, because of the way it conceived the international power struggle, the USSR got locked into a particular way of conceiving its internal model, which was essentially premised on doing the same things as capitalism, only better.

Slowly the qualitative content of socialism was lost sight of and capitalism itself, in the very act of its supposed negation, was affirmed as point of reference. This obviously encouraged a perception of socialism as a stage of development which in a sense carried on where capitalism left off: the idea became that socialist development was 'building on' capitalism in the sense that the latter had been authentically developmental, but had come to a dead end because of its internal contradictions, and was therefore ready to pass on the baton to a better system. According to this perspective, imperialism had created an impasse: it had uncovered certain trends of social development which were being held back in the reactionary and destructive imperialist system, but which, under an alternative system, could be freed to perform a useful role. The clearest example is monopoly. This is a bad thing under capitalism because, through the narrow pursuit of profit via accumulation, which is the very soul of capitalism and cannot be abolished while capitalism still exists, monopoly, with its massive power, intensified the destructive impact of capitalism on its human resources. Lenin made much of this: capitalist development pushes in the direction of greater organisation,[5] but since this is premised on competition, it results in conflict on an even larger scale. Socialism would have to sort this out, but as a reward, it could extract something useful for society, for itself: the concentration of power would be beneficial as an instrument of social transformation.

This line of argument is not altogether convincing, because monopoly (which is indeed a product of capitalist development) undermines the plurality upon which a new form of social creativity would have to be based. In a sense, the argument destroys the Marxist analysis of capitalism. In reality, the essential characteristic of capitalism is that it both destroys and develops at the same time. It is this unity of opposites which defines it. The key to the process is the parasitic nature of capital accumulation, which is both destructive and capable of development through a succession of (not pre-determined) structural changes. In one sense it has reached a dead end: it is not sustainable either ecologically or in the sense of the long-term repro-duction of human labour, for it consumes human and natural resources in such a way that they cannot be replenished. But within these limits it can establish circuits of accumulation which are self-reproducing, and if one of these runs out of steam it can find fresh solutions; for example, it showed that it could retreat from statism, even though, according to unilinear theories of capitalist development, statism constituted part of the historical antecedent to the socialist order. Marxism had already proved itself capable of analysing these new developments, but Soviet developmental theory blocked off this avenue by stating dogmatically that capitalism was obsolete because there existed an alternative.

There was also another risk: if successful, the socialist state could be a beacon of hope to movements elsewhere, by providing external support and by leading by example; but the danger was, if international capitalism suc-ceeded in making the socialist state experiment unsuccessful, it would drag down everything else with it. In fact, this failure was practically inevitable, because the competition was conducted on the terrain most favourable to capitalism.

To understand this, it is necessary to go back to the roots of the success of the Soviet model. In the inter-war period, Soviet socialism had been developing rapidly while capitalism was in an impasse, which made it appear easy to demonstrate socialism's superiority. At the same time, the extreme weakness of the capitalist *world* economy during this period (it had largely collapsed into protectionism as the crisis developed) meant that the difficulties of building socialism within an ambient capitalism could temporarily be ignored. But it is important to note that the apparent success of the Soviet model was premised on the fact that the two systems were at different stages. The Soviet economy was growing rapidly by pursuing very efficiently the tasks of a latecomer, building heavy industry and infrastructure; while capitalism, which had already completed this stage, was locked in a severe depression because of the extremely difficult (but not impossible) task of finding a transition towards consumer-goods production and a rising market. It was simply assumed that the basis for a solution to capitalism's crisis did not exist; or, to put it more specifically, that working-class *consumption* could not rise.[6] Capitalism had come to a dead end while socialism could for the moment push aside the problem of how it would itself realise the qualitative change to increased consumption. Capitalism's temporary loss of direction created the feeling that central planning was the next step in human social organisation. Even capitalists attempted to copy it from the Soviets (in Roosevelt's New Deal, and in Keynes' ideas). And the fact that capitalism had to resort to fascism was, after all, an admission of its impasse.

This, in effect, set the agenda. It was one which the Soviet Union continued to follow under quite different circumstances after the Second World War, when the image of it 'overtaking' capitalism could be sustained only by increasing self-deception. Rather than analysing what was happening to capitalism, the Soviet Union sought refuge in proclaiming its own superiority which, allegedly, would precipitate the decline of capitalism because people or countries would progressively desert it, like rats leaving a sinking ship.

## Subordinating International Struggles to the Development of the Soviet State

The success of the Soviet vision hinged on whether the economic aspect of international conflict could be separated from the politico-military one. Soviet analysts believed that the recognition by both superpowers of the dangers of nuclear confrontation would at the very least freeze military rivalry, and permit competition to channel itself into a purely economic dimension. Even more ambitiously, they thought it possible that the conflict itself would bring about a certain degree of collaboration in managing the international system. (Thus the period of most intense brinkmanship, the 1960s, was also the one when the ground-rules of superpower co-responsibility were worked out.) This led to what is known as '*détente*' (relaxation), a thawing of the early phase of the Cold War in which the two sides had not communicated at all. This change came about in the second half of the 1950s, and gives rise to what I see as a more useful concept for characterising the international system than the Cold War, namely a mutually accepted bipolarity. In political terms, international ideologues came to resemble one another. When the Soviet Union sent troops into Hungary in 1956, it justified it on the grounds that regional organisations were the primary level for resolving disputes,[7] just as the USA did when it intervened in Latin America. The Soviets encouraged the view that, given agreement between the two top decision-makers, 'there will be a solution of international problems on which the destinies of mankind depend'.[8] The very concept of two superpowers illustrates the way in which a common vocabulary was acquired.[9]

Ingrained in this perception from very early on was the idea that, since the international systemic balance determined the chances of success of all progressive movements, the latter had no option but to hitch themselves to the Soviet bandwagon. The success of liberation movements was attributed to 'the changes in the correlation of class forces on the world level in favour of democracy and socialism and to the detriment of imperialism. It is the result of an increase in the power of the USSR.'[10]

Implicit in this analysis is the perception that the Soviet leadership would prevent popular struggles from rocking the boat by becoming too messy and unpredictable. This introduces the possibility that international capitalism may have been *consciously* manipulating the Soviet system (as distinct from the spontaneous operation of systemic factors). America's *détente* overtures followed quite a devious strategic plan. Convened by Eisenhower's adviser on cold war strategy, Nelson Rockefeller, a secret panel chaired by W.W. Rostow met in 1955 to explore 'methods of exploiting Communist bloc vulnerabilities'. Having identified the disruption of the unity of the socialist camp as a key goal, it decided that the best way to achieve this was, in the words of a psychological warfare expert, to awaken Chinese fears of 'deals between alien westerners (e.g. "white men") at their expense'.[11] It was a complex strategy: the Soviet Union was wooed so that it could restrain China; and this, in turn, deliberately served to increase Chinese distrust.

It seems that manipulation of the Soviet Union went much further than it realised. It was programmed to act as a force for containing spontaneous mass movements, something which capitalism, at that time, had no way of achieving. Moreover, the Soviets' attempt to separate the military–political dimension from the economic was not really workable, simply because the military dimension was itself economic. The USA had indeed cut military expenditure in the 1950s,[12] but it rearmed heavily afterwards. The Soviet Union didn't have the economic resources to follow suit. Initially, Khrushchev tried to solve the problem by using nuclear weapons as a cheap substitute for conventional arms,[13] but the later forms of arms race were much more costly. The need to maintain the military stalemate, upon which Soviet theories of economic competition were based, in itself undermined the Soviets' chance of success in that competition because it absorbed too many economic resources.

The Soviets believed that the international system was developmental (in the sense that they thought it had the capacity to develop, making *détente* more firmly entrenched and shifting the distribution of power in its favour); but they did not consider capitalism to be developmental (in the sense of being able to develop under its own impetus) and indeed such a possibility was inconceivable, in that it would have led to the collapse of the whole ideological house of cards. So the Soviets were thrown back on an ingenious but ultimately futile argument: the idea that the Soviet Union had itself become the main force determining the development of the international system, in a sense even of capitalism itself! The argument involved the identification of three distinct stages in the 'general crisis' of capitalism. The first and second occurred under the influence of World Wars, but the third, coming about in the late 1950s, took place 'under conditions of competition and struggle between the two systems in peace-time and a change in the balance of power in favour of socialism'.[14] This was essential for political development: 'The change in the balance of forces of the two social systems constitutes a decisive factor in restructuring the system of international relations, because this balance is a key issue determining its very nature',[15] while Soviet policy became 'the leading and motivating force of the entire process of positive changes in international life'.[16]

It is hardly surprising that economic development in the South was also considered dependent on this relationship. Southern countries had the option of pursuing a 'non-capitalist road' (also called 'socialist orientation'):

> Newly independent countries are in this unique position due to the transitional character of our era, which pivots on the struggle of the two opposing systems. In the present era, national liberation revolutions can grow over into socialist revolutions. The objective prerequisite for this is the existence of the world system of socialism, which determines the main direction and the basic tendency of historical progress.[17]

Building socialism as a cosmic struggle against capitalism meant that socialism was forced to occupy the same economic terrain, and do better at it, its superiority being demonstrated by Soviet preponderance in industry: in 1980 socialist countries had 14 times the industrial production that they had had in 1950, capitalist countries only 3.8 times.[18]

## Repercussions of the Failure of Soviet Strategy

But the Soviet success could not be maintained: by the 1960s, the relationship had been reversed; capitalism was relatively dynamic, whereas the Soviet economy had excessive productive capacity and was beginning to stagnate. It could paper over this contradiction for a time by making a virtue out of what was, in fact, its economic weakness, namely the massive production of steel, means of production, machinery, and so on. The claim that the high level of production results not (as Western critics alleged) from restricting consumption but from the superiority of the socialist system[19] becomes a circular argument: since by definition the system is superior, the level at which it fixes the production of consumer goods must be the correct one.[20] What was really becoming evident was that the Soviet system was incapable of evolving away from a situation in which heavy industry came first and everything else was an afterthought.

Capitalism is supposed to be responsive to consumer choices, but this is largely a fiction: consumer 'preferences' are controlled by a culture which serves the big corporations and promotes what they want to sell. Socialism, for its part, should logically go much further in responding to demand, so that use values would gradually supplant commodities as a primary focus of economic rationale. But heavy industry was by now the bedrock of the Soviet economy, and the international dimension (the need to compete with the USA over figures for industrial production) served as a pretext for further strengthening this orientation. The slackening of growth rates from the late 1950s revealed a structural problem in the focus on heavy industry, but by then progressive forces in the rest of the world had become dependent on the interests promoting this orientation within the USSR; the internal system and the international context in which it was supposedly proving itself had become interlocked.

If the Soviet model of socialism had been developmental in the full sense, it would not only have been good at fulfilling the tasks of one particular stage of industrialisation, but would also have had the capacity to change direction when this became necessary. Although there were important debates about policy orientation from the 1960s onwards, much of the discussion concerned ways of going one better than capitalism in carrying forward the development process while overcoming its limitations, rather than of developing a qualitative challenge to the whole thrust of capitalist development and negating it in a dialectical sense.

The weakness of capitalism is supposed to be that the socialisation of production is mixed up with private appropriation of profits by rich economic interests; it is claimed that, if socialisation could be cut loose from this restriction, it would be free to develop. This argument seems to me dubious. Advanced capitalism is characterised by a highly centralised economic power, which is held in contradiction by the chaotic pressures of market forces. This means that the strong tendencies towards bureaucracy are held in check by the ability of the powerful economic interests to seek out innovatory forms of exploitation, and to collaborate with one another – or savagely eliminate one another – in doing so. If socialism merely leads to the abolition of the competitive aspect of capitalism, one would simply be left with a more exaggerated form of centralisation where bureaucracy would develop unchecked.

The solution would seem to be to allocate resources in a different way, which is better than the way the market does it. In an approach in some ways similar to one adopted by Western economists at the time, the Soviet economist Kantorovich tried to simulate the effect of the market in the process of calculating the optimum allocation of resources. The Soviet concept of a 'system of optimally functioning socialist economy' showed that they believed that economics could work out the best allocation of resources for any society; capitalism might be tending in this direction, but only socialism could realise it.[21]

There is a lot of sense in this; indeed it anticipated the way in which capitalism, through the use of information technologies (IT), would go beyond the market in organising production. But the full potential of this approach would have been realised only by breaking with the capitalist perception both of the market itself and of the basis of decisions within it. The capitalist economists argue that it is only the market that can bring together productive factors and demand. It is possible to criticise this argument within the scope of conventional economics, on the grounds that any endeavour is based on partial knowledge at the beginning, and that full knowledge can never be obtained prior to action.[22] But this criticism does not go far enough: demand is treated as given, whereas in reality it is manufactured, for in the capitalist pseudo-market demand is manipulated so that goods can be disposed of. It is also possible to criticise capitalism for failing to respond to need, and to argue that socialism, in contrast, could anticipate need and turn it into demand. But it is important to recognise that many of the demands generated by capitalism are not based on real needs. This does not mean that socialism would mean a step backwards to an earlier kind of society in which basic needs are met, for it would also permit the open-ended development of the human personality so that demand could be expanded to go beyond mere needs.[23] But it would not be like capitalism, in that this developmental process would not be driven by monopoly interests whose sole criterion for establishing demand is profit-maximisation. Similarly, the supply side of the economy could also reflect human creativity: the productive resources in an economy are not pre-established in a rigid way, but can be expanded by technological innovations from the actual producers. This is where popular regimes again become important, in that they can harness the corpus of people's knowledge, which has been built up historically.

It would be quite possible to have a new form of planning, using IT, which would incorporate these elements of innovation, but the criteria for the policy goals would not be determined by central bureaucrats.

The problem with the Soviet system was that its reform proposals were confined to a narrow terrain of conventional consumerism where, almost by definition, it could not compete with capitalism. Since this was not understood by Soviet planners, they had little option but to focus on heavy industry, which was the only area of the economy where they could compete successfully with capitalism. As Sapir predicted, this approach led to an authentic crisis of over-accumulation.[24] When eventually, in the Gorbachev period, the Soviet system could not continue in the old way and had to recognise the accumulation crisis, the planners at last admitted that the set-up had reached its limits: Aganbegyan recognised (empirically though not theoretically) that there had been 'unprecedented stagnation and crisis' in 1979–82 when the Soviet Union had smelted more than twice as much steel as the USA and produced more metal than the whole of Western Europe, most of which had been channelled into an excessive number of machines, such as tractors which state enterprises were forced to purchase.[25] It was a crisis of a given accumulation structure, but it was identified as a crisis of socialism as a whole; and once this happened, the only way out appeared to be the introduction of the capitalist market.

But the sudden collapse of the Soviet system was in fact due less to an intellectual conviction in the role of the market than to the interests of the élites actually taking the decisions. It seems a paradox that it was the bureaucrats themselves who pushed things towards the market, but there is an explanation, which is that in almost all cases the supposedly free market benefits those who already control the resources. The change was sudden because there was a flip-over point when the bureaucrats abruptly switched from trying to maintain the system to maintaining their own entrenched position within a new one.

## The International Significance of Chinese Socialism

China is significant because it challenged important parts of the Soviet orthodoxy outlined above. During this period, the South was the cutting edge of the battle. International capitalism naturally wants to destroy anyone who asserts the possibility of an alternative, so development was inseparable from war, making it somewhat pointless to speculate what the experience of countries like Nicaragua, Vietnam, Grenada, Cuba or Mozambique would have been under peaceful circumstances. While the experience of constant threat made these countries sceptical about Soviet notions of peaceful transition, their vulnerability to imperialism meant that they could not afford to antagonise the Soviet ally. China, on the other hand, was big enough to make it dangerous to attack, so it was able to pursue a strategy different not only from the capitalist development agenda, but also from Soviet-style communism.

The periphery is characterised by the incompleteness of its capitalism. Indeed, we are still waiting for proof that full capitalist development is a possibility in the South (save hypothetically in a very few special cases), as it remains a persuasive argument that only socialism can develop the South at all. This makes revolution more likely, but it needs to be a socialism of a new kind. Socialism was supposed to be development from capitalism, but as capitalism itself was never fully established in the first place, socialism itself has to be rethought. In a sense, the incompleteness of capitalism could be an advantage because it means there are still-functioning grassroots structures in the South which could form the basis of an alternative social system. But it also means that parts of the capitalist development process have to be carried out in a controlled way under socialist leadership. In particular, it becomes necessary to create the basis for industrialisation using the usual parameters of balancing out accumulation and consumption. An abstract model of socialism starts with a wide circulation of commodities and then gradually shifts to things being produced for their usefulness, rather than for their exchange value. But in the periphery, the problem arises in a special form: the commodities are produced for external consumption. So it may be necessary to allow the market to rise domestically first, in a sense using quasi-capitalist market forces to overcome the higher degree of alienation involved in extroverted economies. So the abolition of the commodity economy can only come later, by a circuitous route. From this angle, social change might be slower.

For these reasons, a peripheral revolutionary movement has both to affirm the positive nature of some of what is stigmatised as 'backwardness', and to recognise realistically that the domestic market must be allowed to mature and that this will take time.

The Chinese experience illustrates that this could be done. A strong element of self-reliance emerged in the Chinese model, which reflected the way popular anti-colonial movements had always wanted to break the predatory link with the external economy. The Chinese Communists, for example, traced their roots back to the nineteenth-century Taiping movement, which, they said, had done this.

## Qualitative Elements in the Chinese Model

Central to the Chinese socialist model was the idea of balanced development in which not everything was subordinated to industry, particularly heavy industry. Industrialisation was still the goal, but it was believed that this goal could be achieved more efficiently by a circuitous route. As Mao Zedong said,

> There are now two possible approaches to our development of heavy industry: one is to develop agriculture and light industry less, and the other is to develop them more. In the long run, the first approach will lead to a smaller and slower development of heavy industry, or at least will put it on a less solid foundation, and when the over-all account is added up a few decades hence, it will not prove to have paid. The second approach will lead to a greater and faster

development of heavy industry and, since it ensures the livelihood of the people, it will lay a more solid foundation for the development of heavy industry.[26]

This is a far more subtle line of reasoning than is contained in most contemporary development theory, whether Western or Soviet. At a superficial level, its distinctiveness lies in allowing for production to meet people's basic needs, so that economic growth contains a demand element. But at a deeper level, the Chinese approach views people as an active element in the equation. This is something that mainstream development theories have only recently begun to recognise, and even now, it is just because they have woken up to the possibility of exploiting such initiatives.

This approach opens up a number of creative perspectives on the development issue. At the most obvious level, it shows that investment in human resources is compatible with accumulation. It is for example economically logical to invest in health. China's community health workers (with elementary training in diagnosis, immunisation, education, simple treatment, and liaison with the qualified medical sector) provide an interesting illustration.[27] This form of investment in health goes beyond basic needs in the direction of empowerment. At this level, human resource investment is not just compatible with accumulation, but even becomes it; it liberates human creativity, so that the resources available to national planners are no longer finite. Amin rightly speaks of 'the accumulation of hundreds of thousands of tiny improvements, at a low cost in investment terms'.[28] There is also a sense in which consumption by the collective economy, of machinery for example, is itself a form of accumulation, in that productive resources are being built up.

When this consumption/accumulation takes place in the rural economy (which was largely the case), it becomes possible to escape from the assumption that development is equivalent to urbanisation. If the countryside is where things are happening economically, there is no reason for migrating to the cities.

This is an ecologically innovative solution from two angles. First, productivity can increase (and thus labour be shed) in the agricultural sector without population being physically displaced from the countryside because they can be absorbed in local industries, sideline production, and so on. Second, the policy of 'take agriculture as the base and industry as the leading factor' implies a planning approach in which industrial growth can respond to agriculture's demand for its products and to the amount of foodstuffs agriculture can make available to feed urban workers, and so on. Bettelheim made the striking observation that in taking the varying cycles of agricultural production and consumption as its 'base', the economy begins to follow the rhythms of the natural world, which are necessarily not wholly predictable.[29] This also implies breaking with the aspect of the central planning model which aspired to master and subdue nature.

The balance between the urban and rural economies can be adjusted through the pricing structure. In China, rural–urban (agricultural–industrial) terms of trade were maintained at a level far more favourable to the former than in other developing countries. But is this a distortion? The point is that the international accumulation system introduces the real distortions, since world market differentials reflect the amount of labour which is 'socially necessary' as a product under the most advanced conditions, that is, those prevailing in the industrial countries. These differentials tend to be reflected in the domestic terms of trade inside countries of the South, so that the farmer does not receive a fair price for the labour expended in goods produced under much more labour-intensive conditions. This makes it difficult for farmers to accumulate enough to raise their productivity eventually. What the socialist state was doing was not imposing an artificial and invented set of differentials, but shielding the local economy from the distorting effects of the world market so that realistic differentials could be established. China not only maintained a differential favourable to agriculture but in fact accentuated it.[30] And the adjustment of prices to stimulate agriculture in no way undermined the growth of industry.[31]

It is possible to maintain relatively favourable terms of trade for agriculture only if the urban population remains relatively small. In effect, under this model, the state subsidises urban consumption of rural products. If there is a large urban population, this puts too much strain on the state budget. Recent IMF policies, which have sought to increase incentives to the farmer while simultaneously cutting food subsidies, in countries where urbanisation is much higher than in China, have come up against an impasse. In China's case, the increase of urbanisation, from 19 per cent of the population in 1960 to a projected 35 per cent in 2000,[32] is fairly low in comparison with most developing countries; it is particularly modest given the structural transformations in terms of industrial growth during that period.

Chinese planners also attempted to achieve an interesting element of balance within industry, between large-scale urban industries – where the technology and hence productivity would be relatively advanced – and small-scale, more labour-intensive industries in small towns, which were still partly linked with the rural economy. It was possible to achieve a high level of co-operation between the two sectors, for example the equipment in the more advanced sector did not have to be written off but could be handed down to local factories.[33]

As productivity differed widely in industry (that is, between small-scale local industry and more advanced urban industry), prices were averaged out over the economy as a whole, and then distributed unevenly between specific sectors. So production goods were sold at a cheap average price and consumption goods at a very high price. The overall differential between industry and agriculture thus probably reflected productivities realistically enough, but the structure between sectors was used to promote factors favouring certain kinds of industry, that is, those conducive to the growth of productivity in the rural sector (tractors, fertilisers) above the growth of consumption.

Liberal economists today defend the dual economy in the capitalist countries under the name of flexibility, while denying it to socialist countries under the accusation of protecting inefficient industries. It can, however, be very effective. This element of dualism makes it possible to conceive of a socialist application of the new management systems, in other words, subcontracting from the modern economy to the small-scale economy in a non-exploitative way. The Chinese model had a good record from this point of view, having always valued indigenous technology, and initiatives from the producers themselves. What is seen in the West as the new concept of technology-blending has been known about for a long time in China. It was the basis for a totally new approach to the division of labour, which at the same time anticipates and transcends the capitalist management revolution of the 1980s. Although initially focused around production goods consumed by local units, this approach would certainly be adaptable to individual consumer goods.

One key question was whether or not it would be possible to develop the Maoist system of non-exploitative dualism in economic structures ('walking on two legs') so as to take on board new technology. Initially, China missed the boat, which could have led to the same over-accumulation situation as that faced by the Soviets. But the Chinese system was ultimately strong enough to encompass change. In this sense, it was more authentically developmental than the Soviet system.

The problem of changing any system – and the capitalist economy has faced the same problem – is that, if the system is functioning coherently and is developmental within its own framework, it is difficult for planners to take the initiative to change, because the different parts all have a stable relationship with each other, and the *whole* pattern of relationships has to be changed, which is a big step. One of the major achievements of the economic structure built during the Mao period was that, after his death in 1976, it proved capable of changing without a major dislocation.

The transition within the Chinese model was realised by successfully addressing two major problems which could have proved fatal had they been neglected, but were instead transformed into a source of strength.

First, it was difficult for the existing system to accommodate individual consumption. The consumption that did exist was overwhelmingly collective. In the rural areas, the communes (into which the rural population was organised) could buy machinery, fertiliser, and so on, but the bureaucracy with which they were run meant that people often failed to identify this sort of consumption as an improvement in their personal conditions. If people had felt they were benefiting from the system, they would have wanted to stay in the countryside, but as this was not the case, the authorities had to maintain fairly strong *administrative* measures to prevent rural–urban migration. The basic problem was that consumer goods were very expensive. This stemmed from a form of scarcity which could only have arisen in a centralised economy: prices in terms of labour and materials involved should logically have been much lower, but the planners wanted to restrict supply. They thought that collective consumption and investment in human resources was possible, but that individual consumption would have restricted accumulation too much. They therefore restricted the supply of consumer goods by keeping prices artificially high. This does not necessarily mean that the collective structures needed to be abandoned in order for individual consumption to rise. But it remains true that the Maoist system, which had successfully built heavy industry and infrastructure, had an ingrained tendency to restrict consumption, in the sense that 'an acceleration in the rate of growth of national income usually served to accelerate the rate of accumulation so that consumption growth was slower than that of national income'.[34]

In addition to these domestic factors in explaining the Chinese transition, there was also the international context. Mao always thought of China developing in the thick of the complex struggles of the international political economy, and did not want to fence the country in, but a certain degree of autarky had been forced on China by the US blockade. China's response had been to forge close links with the Soviet Union, but this both restricted China's ability to construct its own development model, and meant that, when the Soviet relationship collapsed, China became somewhat isolated again for a while. This began to change with the ending of the US blockade at the beginning of the 1970s. This in itself created a mixture of problems and opportunities. On the negative side, globalisation made it difficult to fence China off from the consumer culture of the world market, and this had political repercussions in promoting rollback against socialism, as well as bringing to China the economic demands of the accumulation structure of the time. But on the positive side, there were also openings for China in the new international context, such as the Northern demand for cheap manufactures. Realising that a bold change of course was required, the Chinese leadership was able to find a way of exploring the positive openings in the international context to help to resolve an internal problem, namely that of finding a way to increase consumption without limiting investment too much.

Although the Chinese leadership successfully addressed some of the main problems, and managed to turn them into something positive, there was one problem which was not confronted, namely the institutional focus of decision-making. Although the post-Mao reform decentralised decision-making by giving far greater economic autonomy to actors such as provinces and firms, it failed to introduce democratic reforms in the sense of allowing independent mass organisations to act as a check on the various élite institutions. In industrial terms, the leadership created economic actors which worked independently of it to seek out niches in the world economy, and are in some ways probably different from the classic capitalist economic actors. In agriculture, the political economy that emerged from the reforms is of a new kind, in that the atomised peasant households which emerged after the dismantling of co-operative structures are insulated to a considerable extent from the international market, and aren't squeezed in the interests of industrial accumulation. But the new actors are still élite ones, part of the official society, albeit of a new type.

This failure to allow the development of independent grassroots movements closes off an important avenue for developing human resources and demand in a new way, one which would give greater play to the qualitative aspects of socialism. It is an issue which was anticipated by Lenin in his writings on the trade union movement under socialism, when he said there should be scope for people to organise independently of the state.

Paradoxically, a socialist model where the state monopolises much of the political space may be better equipped to suppress 'new social movements' than the capitalists are. Just because it was so successful in many respects, the model adopted during the Mao period generated a powerful homogenising force. Women as objects were in some sense liberated by it, as the commune structures allowed for new facilities, such as collective childcare, but the model did not allow them to develop their independent initiative within a system which remained fundamentally patriarchal, so women as subjects remained oppressed. The strong emphasis on unity in policy terms undermined, at the level of both minority nationalities and local initiatives, the plurality which is an essential requirement for future development. The model claimed to respond to grassroots initiatives, but only those approved at the centre were allowed to continue, and there was no possibility of a lot of different initiatives being pursued at the same time. Paradoxically, the Cultural Revolution may have made it even more difficult to pursue local initiatives, as concrete *economic* discussions were considered bourgeois. Struggles over what the party line was to be were conducted in a very abstract way, and not linked to any analysis of the Chinese economy and society. Nor was 'capitalism' criticised as it really existed, that is according to the centre–periphery model. In this way, local decision-making (which the Cultural Revolution was supposed to facilitate) was deprived of any economic basis. These weaknesses will probably prove a major restriction on the future development of the Chinese experience.

## Notes

1. 'the identity of nature and man appears in such a way that the restricted relation of men to nature determines their restricted relation to one another, and their restricted relation to one another determines men's restricted relation to nature, just because nature is as yet hardly modified historically', Marx and Engels 1969, pp. 32–3.

2. Cf. Marx 1965, pp. 998–9.

3. Perlman 1987.

4. Lenin 1965, p. 232.

5. 'Capitalism in its imperialist stage leads right up to the most comprehensive socializa-

tion of production; it, so to speak, drags the capitalists, against their will and consciousness, into some sort of new social order', Lenin 1970, p. 25; see also p. 43.

6. See Day 1981, p. 267.

7. Cf. Remington 1971.

8. Gromyko 1964, p. 30.

9. Cf., for example, Franck and Weisband 1971.

10. Quoted in Light 1988, p. 267.

11. Chang 1990, p. 151.

12. Cf. Kolko 1969b, pp. 41–3.

13. Cf. Kolkovitz 1967.

14. Nikitin 1983, p. 201.

15. Kapchenko 1975.

16. *Kommunist* no. 14, 1975.

17. Solodovnikov and Bogoslovsky 1975, p. 88.

18. Nikitin 1983, p. 203.

19. Smirnov 1981, p. 304.

20. This appears, in effect, to be the argument in USSR 1957, p. 671.

21. Cf. Sutela 1991, chapter 2.

22. Roland 1989.

23. Cf. Meister 1994.

24. Sapir 1980.

25. Aganbegyan 1988, pp. 3, 35.

26. Mao Zedong 1977, p. 286.

27. Cf. Weigel 1989, p. 39.

28. Amin 1981, p. 58.

29. Bettelheim 1965.

30. State purchase prices for agricultural products rose 57.4% between 1950 and 1963 (61.4% for cereals), while retail prices of industrial goods sold by the state in the countryside rose by 13.7%; Bettelheim 1965, p. 129.

31. Figures given by Thomas Rawski show that in the period 1952–78 the proportion of agriculture in GDP shrank from 45.7% to 25.2% (growth rate 3.4% p.a.), and the proportion of industry rose from 27.4% to 52.1% (growth rate 9.4%); the proportion of services actually shrank from 24.8% to 17.4%. The growth rate for GDP per capita during this period was 3.8% per annum; in Amin 1981, p. 40.

32. United Nations Development Programme 1996, p. 176.

33. Cf. Tissier 1976.

34. Ghose 1984, pp. 268, 260–1. The figures cited in this source show that by 1978 45% of farmland was irrigated, 49% was machine-ploughed, and 89 kg of fertiliser was used per hectare. Particularly after 1965 when the commune structure was stabilised and production restored to 1957 level, progress was rapid. Tractor-ploughing expanded at an annual rate of 7.7%.

# 6

# The Third World Challenge

The fundamental problem faced by the South is external, that is, exploitation by the economic power centres in the North, but this expresses itself internally. This is partly a question of economic structure – for example, the cultivation of cash crops instead of goods for domestic consumption. But this in turn is embedded in social structure, for it can reinforce the unequal ownership of resources, as élites may be satisfied by selling goods on the international market without wanting either to raise domestic demand or to produce the goods which could meet that demand.

While it was impossible to separate in a meaningful way the international and domestic facets of dependency, there was an argument for a campaign to target specifically the international aspect. International dependency had an economic dimension, which we have discussed in earlier chapters, but also political repercussions. International systems functioned only for the benefit of the powerful. Among the dominant states, each sought to maximise its own power but, because they were all doing this, they understood each other, and sought a 'balance of power' which meant that they could avoid tearing each other apart while they were exploiting everyone else. It was clear that the independence of a large number of new states would pose a challenge to this whole system. This became a burning issue in the 1950s when the independence movement acquired an unstoppable momentum. The force of the mass movements was propelling élites in the colonial and semi-colonial countries to demand a change in the existing power structure. It was evident that such a movement could potentially unite different social classes, which in its way would have just as revolutionary an impact as the domestic class struggle because it would highlight the *racial* element in capitalism expressed in the economic and political exclusion implied by the North–South divide.

## Unity as a Weapon in Challenging the Systemic Constraints on Third-World Development

Two issues can clarify the impact of the mass movement at this time. First, the term 'third world'. This idea was put forward in the early 1950s by a European, Alfred Sauvy. The analogy is with the history of the French

Revolution when the Third Estate (the common people) had no scope for realising their interests through or within the system, and could do so only by destroying it. Through the term, he expressed the white world's fear that the mass movement in the South might do something similar. The term expressed a real risk, and it gradually came to be used by the oppressed themselves.

Second, at a major historical event, the Bandung Conference of 1955, the then independent Asian and African countries came together to put forward their own proposals for the international system. The Conference unquestionably expressed a common consciousness that had arisen in the popular movements and had been pushed by them on to the agenda of the élites. It showed that the peoples of the South had taken some important steps towards overturning externally imposed definitions about themselves, their place in the international system, and the nature of that system itself.

The élites in the South had a dual character. Because they came from the oppressed peoples of colour who had been excluded from the system, they were not dehumanised to the same extent as the oppressors in the North. It is impossible not to be excited about the breath of fresh air they brought to the international system which until then had been dominated by cynical power-politics. But the élites in the South were not averse to practising some power-politics on their own account, for their relationship to the North was ambiguous. There is a sense in which they were saying to the white world that the only way they could prevent Sauvy's nightmare from coming true was to make moderate concessions and give them a voice within the power-centres of international relations.

Ultimately, this attempt to change the international system failed. The North would not accept the idea that things could be done differently and that humanity could advance through solidarity rather than through the struggle in which only the fittest survived. Instead, the North did everything it could to drag the third world states down to their level, and it has to be admitted, surveying the situation today, that it was quite successful in this task. So much so, indeed, that the dominant powers today are reaping the results of the evil they sowed in the form of an extremely unstable environment which they themselves can no longer control. I will examine the implications in Chapter 12.

It is interesting to speculate whether, given the fact that the system refused to accept reform, the prediction underlying the original formulation of the third world concept will come true. It must be said that the analogy with the French Revolution is somewhat stereotyped. If the third world rises up in revolution, it will not simply be a question of people waving pikes, because the multifaceted movement behind the uprising – indigenous peoples, women's groups and environmental movements – will not necessarily do things in this way. But in the last analysis the prediction is probably true, and in some sense the mass movement will have to tear the capitalist system apart.

Originally, third-worldism had a radical connotation, in that it signified the unity of revolutionary grassroots forces (represented by people like Che Guevara), and promoted the idea of an eventual revolutionary solution. But it also accepted that different social forces would have to unite, so that they could advance step by step to bring about structural change. The big danger the movement faced was that if it focused on international structural issues, the Southern élites would divert attention away from domestic contradictions, but it was perhaps a risk that had to be accepted. The mass national liberation movement was in the process of achieving statehood, and the existence of these new states in themselves implied a challenge to the international system; the third world movement would have been stupid not to try to push the change through to its logical conclusion.

## Is It Possible to Achieve Change by Working within the System?

There were three key elements of novelty in the third world movement, which was conceived as a movement of cross-class unity aiming to change the international system. First, there was the idea that, whatever the differences in size, geographical location and so on, developing countries shared a common identity and a common cause. Unity was their main weapon in fighting for change. Second, by targeting the system the movement broke with the assumption that 'underdevelopment' was 'their problem'. Instead, it identified the problem as unjust structures at a world level, structures which had a historical dimension. Though it was an élite, bourgeois movement, its platform was, from this angle, revolutionary: even large sections of the European left had refused to admit this dimension. Third, the movement promoted the idea that the particular interests of the most oppressed sections are also the general interests of humanity. It said that, although the dehumanisation of the system affected everyone, the *force* pushing change could come only from the oppressed. The movement sought to face the international community with its collective responsibilities, with the need to make choices about humanity's destiny, saying that the very notion of community implied questioning the narrow focus on selfish national interests which had hitherto dominated international relations.

It is interesting that Sauvy's model implied that the North would have an interest in accepting *some* change. The *Pax Americana* of 1945 had changed almost nothing about big power dominance, though it involved some change in the internal working of the big powers, but a post-colonial system, which was now becoming inevitable, would in some sense imply a new system of international relations, and it was possible that, if the momentum for change was allowed to accelerate, the industrial powers would end up conceding more than they would ideally like. The Southern élites defended a concept which eventually, in the 1970s, was given a title – 'the democratisation of international relations'. It is important to recognise the limits of this definition of democratisation: it meant that smaller states would have an equal voice within a system composed of state-actors, not that the masses would have a direct say on international issues (foreign policy is traditionally one of the most élitist areas of politics). Even with this limitation, though, the campaign was quite revolutionary because it targeted the racial exclusionism of a world system which would be terrified at the idea of recognising African statesmen as equals.

The idea of working within the international system in order to change it appeared plausible because of an important new development – the creation of potentially democratic international institutions. The UN instituted majority voting (by a two-thirds majority on non-procedural matters). This did not initially worry the Americans because the Cold War enabled them to control enough votes, and the General Assembly was even a convenient tool in neutralising the Soviet veto in the Security Council. But this could change; as more states became independent, developing countries would eventually constitute a majority – which is exactly what happened soon after the beginning of the 1970s when US dominance ended; it was graphically illustrated by the collapse of their policy of excluding the People's Republic of China from the UN.

There was an argument for saying that the idea of working through the UN was a dangerous illusion, which would dissipate energies that could be used elsewhere for changing the world. For example, the Indonesian leader, Sukarno, who had called the Bandung Conference, thought that the 'old declining forces' (OLDEFOS) should be left to rot, together with their institutions, and that efforts should be concentrated on bringing together in a new organisation, outside the UN, the elements of vitality in the world system, the new emerging forces (NEFOS). But Sukarno's advice was ignored and, instead, an attempt was made by the developing nations to capture and use the official structures. With hindsight, it can be seen today that the strategy failed: the NEFOS are more divided and difficult to group together than they were in the 1960s, at least at a state level (they also exist at a grassroots level, a point I will address later), and the UN is more than ever entrenched as a tool of the rich and powerful. So perhaps Sukarno was right. There is, however, a strong argument for saying that the experience of attempting to capture and reform the system – which was what the developing world attempted in the new international economic order (NIEO) – was a necessary learning process. It would be tragic if the lessons from the NIEO's failure were not seriously taken on board, because there is certainly no point in having illusions a second time round. This is precisely why the history of the NIEO project is interesting and instructive.

The attempt began in the early 1960s. The UN had launched a development decade in 1960, but it was defined without consulting the interested parties, the developing countries themselves. It was a Kennedy-style attempt to encourage a veneer of development to undercut the appeal of revolutionary Cuba, which had become America's pet obsession. Developing countries needed to counter this manipulated agenda by making their own input. A conference of their own economics experts at Cairo in 1962 called for the holding of a United Nations Conference on Trade and Development (UNC-TAD). This conference was eventually held in 1964, and, rather than being a one-off event, it became an institution in its own right.

In order to realise the possibility of change, developing countries had to be united. They constituted themselves into the Group of 77 (the number of developing countries at the beginning of UNCTAD, though it soon included more than 100 out of the roughly 150 states which existed at that time). It functioned as a major pressure group within the UN, usually managing to formulate common goals, and eventually drawing up a common programme for a New International Economic Order. The significance of this should not be underestimated. Whether or not the developing countries were ultimately successful in changing international relations as a whole – and, on the whole, they were not – the experience of the Group of 77 does at least show that within their own subsystem it was possible to conduct international relations in a different way, based on consensus rather than conflict. In most cases, they gave precedence to 'milieu' goals, that is, goals for transforming the system itself, rather than favouring narrow policies premised on maximising their individual national interests within the existing system. Through a careful use of divisive tactics, the global capitalist interests, with the willing connivance of some third-world élites (who could, for example, hope to gain something for themselves by applying conventional power politics at a regional level), eventually managed to destroy the collective approach, but the historical experience of the movement still shows that international relations (IR) can be conducted differently. In some respects, this revolution in the form of IR was as significant as the actual content of what the developing countries were putting forward.

## Targeting Terms of Trade and Commodity Prices

It was the content of the proposals, however, that was largely responsible for the eventual fate of the movement. So what systemic goals was it trying to achieve?

To understand third world demands, it should be noted that Latin America soon came into the movement, to complement the Asian–African focus arising from Bandung, and immediately exercised a strong influence because the Economic Commission for Latin America (ECLA) had been thinking about the systemic issues for some time. Raúl Prebisch, who became the first head of UNCTAD, already had systematic views about the kind of changes which would benefit developing countries. His views, reflected in his report, had considerable support at the time.[1]

The campaigns of the early period focused on two key demands. The first called for a redistribution of value based on a change in the terms of trade for commodities. It was formulated in such a way so as to allow space for an accommodation with the North. A model could be designed that, while allowing the South greater rewards, would also include incentives for the North by enlarging the markets for Northern manufactures, and by ensuring that the social benefits would strengthen the basis for a dependent local bourgeoisie which would ensure the wider interests of accumulation. I will raise some issues relevant to this question in examining the concepts of global Keynesianism later in this chapter, but as a generalisation it has to be said that on the whole the North rejected this overture; it preferred to forgo the advantages that it offered, in the interests of preserving its access to cheap raw materials. Attempts were made to address the issue through agreements on specific commodities. Some agreements were negotiated in the 1960s on coffee, sugar and tin (they were soon followed by others on tea, cocoa and sisal). But there was little concrete success. Such price changes as there were reflected US policy rather than the actions of the third world.[2]

The second demand was for greater access for Southern manufactures to Northern markets. It was certainly in principle possible for the North to co-opt this demand, and indeed it could be argued that it fitted in with the long-term development needs of international capitalism. I will investigate the theoretical basis for this in Chapter 10. But in the 1960s the North was not prepared to take this step. It was still wedded to full employment policies, and could not afford to stop manufacturing for its own market. The South asked for a generalised system of preferences (GSP) in their favour, and this demand for lower tariffs was obviously only a means to the end of increasing their market share. By and large, industrial countries blocked this fundamental change by imposing quotas.[3]

So, in effect, both sets of demands were rejected. The weakness of the strategy was the weakness of the bourgeois aspect of ECLA, the assumption that unequal relations could be sorted out by attacking the issue of trade. The strategy proved ineffective in narrowing the gap; the per capita GDP of developing countries as a percentage of that in the industrial countries in fact decreased from 8.5 per cent in 1960 to 8.3 per cent in 1975.[4]

But the North–South issue changed in the 1970s. The real reason for the change was that the old system was moving into crisis, but it looked as if it had been caused by an improvement in the position of the South in the balance of forces. Since, temporarily, the third world held the high ground, it was able to put forward new ideas which soon became known as the project for a new international economic order.

As they had a majority in the UN, the third world movement could dictate the agenda as long as it retained its unity. It was an exciting prospect, but there was a problem: while the developing countries could pass any resolutions they wanted, the rich countries controlled the UN's finances. Even so, there was reason for believing that maybe the North would be unable to halt the process of change, for the world economy was in any case moving into crisis at this time and no one, apart from the South, had a clear vision of where it should go. What further helped the South was that Keynesianism was still the dominant philosophy at that time, and it recognised the possibility of different solutions to a given set of economic circumstances. Democratic debate could thus determine what solution would be adopted.

## A Broader Challenge to the System: The New International Economic Order

The NIEO idea went beyond the early demands over access to markets and commodity prices, and began to address the more fundamental issues of ownership and control. It argued that developing countries needed to emphasise their *own* ownership, in other words their sovereignty over their own resources (with the right to nationalisation, and to campaign for an exclusive economic zone in the sea, and so on). It also began to question the enormous concentration of economic power in the hands of transnational corporations, and to monitor the operations of the TNCs. It argued that, in order to counter this organised monopoly power, the South should itself get organised, and it supported the creation of primary producers' organisations.

It also raised important questions over how the Southern countries organised their co-operation between themselves and their dialogue with the North. The first should be a precondition for the second, in the sense that the South could hope to bring about a negotiated solution to its problems only if it was strong and negotiated with the North from a position of strength. This concern led to the creation of new concepts such as economic co-operation among developing countries (ECDC), technical co-operation among developing countries (TCDC), the whole crowned by the concept of collective self-reliance (CSR). In 1977 the Group of 77 drew up the Arusha Programme for Collective Self-Reliance. This recommended the setting up of joint marketing ventures and said that mechanisms should be found for building on the complementarities among Southern economies, as well as for exchanging technology. UNCTAD studies of TNCs showed that production, consumption, finance, pricing, marketing, transport and distribution on the world market were largely controlled by the industrial countries, and that a vicious circle helped to maintain this situation: 'CSR strategies, if successfully implemented, could help reduce these external controls, but by the same token, the existence of the controls constitutes a constraint on the implementation of CSR strategies'.[5] It was argued that a way out of this vicious circle would be to pursue complementarities between groups of developing countries so that costs and benefits of different economic activities could be distributed evenly. What is interesting in all this is the new approach to international decision-making: 'The most important contribution by ECDC and TCDC was to add substance to the political co-operation reflected in the Group of 77.[6]

A concrete embodiment of CSR was the experiments in regional organisation, which took on a new, radical content in the 1970s. The was particularly strong in Latin America, where, for example, the Latin American economic system (Sela) was set up to co-ordinate different regional groups, and a real clash developed with the US over policy in the latter's 'backyard'. Amazingly, even the Organisation of American States (OAS), which had always been considered to be under the thumb of the USA, became an arena of struggle in the second half of the 1970s over the role of the TNCs. Demands were articulated which included the principle of respect for sovereignty over natural resources, so that TNCs should be subject to national policies of economic development and contribute to carrying these out, should supply relevant information to the host country, should 'conduct their operations in a manner that results in a net receipt of financial resources for the host country', should contribute to indigenous scientific and technological development and should refrain from restrictive commercial practices.[7]

The underlying strategy in the call for a North–South dialogue was to brandish the threat of rebellion from disaffected lower orders, as contained in Sauvy's original third world idea, and then to offer a Keynesian type of solution to it. It was correctly perceived that 'the economic malaise in the international economic system is not a phenomenon of a cyclical nature but a symptom of underlying structural maladjustment'.[8] And it was argued that 'The developed world as a whole no longer has any pretext to shirk its responsibility, nor to allow itself to fail to recognise the fundamentally indivisible nature of world prosperity.'[9] The NIEO thus demanded 'a new set of relationships based on mutual interests and mutual respect, and a fairer sharing of power and decision-making between states'.[10] Its proposal received encouragement from Northern groups such as the Brandt Commission, a think-tank of political leaders, which accepted that 'Many individual societies have settled their inner conflicts by accommodation, to protect the weak and to promote principles of justice, becoming stronger as a result. The world too can become stronger by becoming a just and humane society.'[11]

But there was also a second, more concrete facet to global Keynesianism. This in effect brings together two elements: product cycle theory and the notion of escaping from stagnation through increasing mass demand. The measures recommended included the relocation from the North of industries in which developing countries enjoyed a particular advantage, such as textiles, considered a labour-intensive industry characteristic of the early stage of industrialisation. It was argued that, if the South was allowed to get wealthier, this would benefit the North, which could switch to high-technology goods and export them to the third world.

This looked plausible. The problem was that the North was in effect working towards its own version of a new international economic order, the details of which we will examine in the following chapters. At this time, it was certainly not as clearly formulated as the South's NIEO project, but one thing was certain: it did not involve any sharing of decision-making, restraints on corporate interests, etc. The North seemed to be negotiating, but these were really the sort of negotiations colonisers employed with indigenous peoples when they were not yet strong enough to impose a genocidal solution – they were buying time.

The South itself did not take CSR seriously, so it could not negotiate from a position of strength. An example is the oil issue. OPEC gave a big boost to the third world through its assertiveness around the time of the 1973 war in the Middle East, but it missed a crucial opportunity with the money it earned through oil exports. There was some recycling of petroleum money into development projects, for example via the OPEC Special Fund, which gave 20-year interest-free loans,[12] and Venezuela financed coffee stockpiling. But by and large, most of the income was invested in the industrial countries, which, by a strange logic, even managed to make things worse for the developing world, as much of the money was lent back by Northern bankers, thereby fuelling the build-up of the third-world 'debt'. Eventually, developing countries had to recognise, in the words of the Havana Non-Aligned Summit (1979) that 'no real progress has been achieved because of the absence of genuine political will on the part of a large majority of developed countries to engage in meaningful negotiation'.[13] But by then it was too late.

Although temporarily in disarray, the North clearly had greater underlying strength than the Southern élites perceived. At an objective level, the accumulation juggernaut (inherently premised on the centre–periphery relationship) prevailed not only within one structure of the IPE, but also over the process of transition to a new one. This objective process was helped on its way by deliberate policy initiatives from the rich, particularly ones orchestrated by the United States. At the Nairobi UNCTAD meeting in 1976, developing countries were organised and the North divided. The USA argued for the industrial countries to rebuild urgently their unity,[14] but this was not enough; the North also needed to undermine the unity of the democratic forces in the South. It developed the idea of hitting troublesome developing countries with punitive trade legislation, and at a Senate Finance Subcommittee meeting in 1976, Henry Kissinger openly proposed that bilateral relations with LDCs would in the future have to take account of how each country behaved in international meetings, particularly how it voted on certain key issues.[15] In practice, this amounted to buying votes in the UN so as to undermine the NEFOS' takeover attempt. This led eventually to an attack not only on the role of Southern countries within international institutions, but also on the institutions themselves.

What became the make-or-break issue for the NIEO was a scheme known as the Integrated Programme of Commodities. The expressed aims of this scheme included establishing a level of commodity prices fair to both sides, raising export earnings of producers, maintaining the competitiveness of commodities with respect to synthetic products, helping producers to diversify away from excessive dependence on primary-product export, and assisting them to process primary products. In 1976, UNCTAD began to discuss concrete measures with respect to a number of key products.[16] Negotiations for the programme began in 1976, and at that time developing countries rightly stated that action on this question was a matter of urgency. It was at this stage that the rich countries began to stall the process. Initial negotiations dragged on for four years, and it was 1980 before Articles of Agreement were finally adopted (the fund was to have a capital of US$470m plus voluntary contributions of US$280m). For it to come into force, however, it had to be ratified by 90 countries and to have raised two-thirds of the necessary capital. The deadline was 1982, but by then the conditions had not been met, and the deadline had to be extended. Throughout this process the USA refused to ratify the programme, which was the main reason why the necessary capital was not raised and why many other countries also did not bother to ratify the scheme. In fact it was only in June 1989 that the Fund finally came into existence, thirteen years after the original statement of its urgency. These tactics had effectively stalled the process until the impetus was lost.

The objective behind the programme was to make an input into *how* the international economy was to be restructured. By the end of the 1980s it was too late; by then the economy had been restructured, and the programme proved ineffective in a climate now totally hostile to any attempt to influence human destiny. In fact the industrial countries' agenda, marshalled under the banner of the new ideology of neo-liberalism and Reaganomics, decisively ditched the Keynesian premises upon which the North–South dialogue was based, and by as early as the first half of the 1980s, at the unsuccessful meeting of UNCTAD VI at Belgrade in 1983, it was clear that the opportunity for a consciously-managed, humane restructuring of the international system had basically been lost.

But when all allowances have been made for the North's scheming, there were fundamental weaknesses in the way Southern élites framed their projects.

## The Deception of the North–South Dialogue – Why the Movement Failed

The élites were seeking a more favourable division with the North, something which was in principle possible since the degree of exploitation is not fixed by any iron law. But, from a wider ecological perspective, this was already questionable. In essence, the élites were calling for a larger share in value, which was produced by socio-economic structures which themselves undermined the basis for a deep-going development. The regimes were debating with central capital over who was to appropriate that value, but did not call into question the structures which produced it. The very models which were being enthusiastically promoted by the élites as a path to self-reliance had an in-built tendency to disempower popular economic initiative and to siphon away wealth from agriculture. No alteration in the *international* division of value could change this. Under conventional development theory, accumulation could occur only as a product of the exploitation of the natural world and of people.

However, if we accept the élites' demand within its own narrow economic terms, its validity is still questionable. A useful issue to raise at this point is the question of 'rents'. As Amin says, the peripheral bourgeoisie claims a fee on the raw materials extracted from its countries.[17] Rents should accrue to the possessors of resources for which there is a demand. Because capitalism is essentially international, the rent first accrued to the colonial powers, and historically, where it was an object of struggle, this was waged between rival groups of exploiters. Now, it seemed that the apparent new distribution of power associated with the transition to neo-colonialism might change this. In practice, if the Southern élites obtained a share of rents it would probably take the form of a stipend for providing a useful service to central capital, but this would not be impossible. One form of rents would be to pay them to the economic actors which possessed monopolies, but as Chibuzo Nwoke has plausibly argued, it was illusory to think the South was strong enough to achieve this.[18] But there are other forms of rent. As Mohsen Massarat points out, in the case of minerals (but not in the case of industry, for example), prices are determined within limits by the worst conditions of production, which leaves a substantial profit to be pocketed by whoever produces them in the best conditions, as in the case of petroleum in the Middle East.[19] Earlier, it was the colonialists (and the companies which flourished under their protection), who got this windfall profit, and with decolonisation, modern TNCs simply stepped into their shoes; in effect, comparative natural advantage became subsumed as part of the internal profit-calculations of the TNCs. In the post-colonial situation, it seemed that the local state could now become an independent player, and with co-ordination and the use of international institutions, Southern élites might be able to reinforce one another in the attempt to appropriate this rent.

But this simplistic idea of seeking a bigger slice in some cake did not take account of the realities: the problem was that the portion of value under contention was *already deeply embedded within a well-established and recurring accumulation structure*. Far from being prepared to dish out more value like a portion of cake at a tea-party, the North would resort to war if there was a serious effort by the South to increase its share. What would be the nature of this war? Some of the academic debate is a sterile confrontation of two one-sided positions: Massarat thinks the struggle is conducted directly between classes (without any centre–periphery dimension at a national level[20]) whereas

Nwoke proposes a model where the countries relate to one another effectively *as classes*. Neither model is adequate. What is needed is a model that appreciates the interaction between both dimensions of struggle. It is supposed to be a national struggle, but effectively the Southern élites are saying to the centre that they will keep the lid on the 'dirty' mass movement below, the mass assault on the white power structure which so terrified Sauvy, if they are allowed to accumulate locally. The accumulation would be conducted at an apparently national level; in practice, it would take the form of national-*capitalist* development, which alone would allow the élites to begin to function as true classes.

But there is a problem in this scenario: an important aspect of the international structural crisis (which was beginning in the 1970s but whose outlines were not yet clear) was the crisis of the prevalent development models in the South. The added value (in the form of rents) could never be permanently prised away from the North *unless it could be embedded in some viable new local accumulation structure*. But the social basis of such a model was lacking. The postwar development model had assumed that some of the benefit of working people's exploitation would be distributed back to them once take-off occurred; but by the end of the early post-independence period, this assumption was wearing thin. This gravely undermined the prospects for the kind of national unity necessary to wage a successful redistribution war against the North.

Without this unity, the Southern élites could only devote whatever advantages they managed to gain from the NIEO campaign into papering over the cracks in the *old* development models (or send the money abroad). The problem was that this model was soon to be swept away, along with the global accumulation system of which it formed a subordinate part.

The internal systems that constituted the basis of external dependency were also the basis of the élites' power. Inevitably, the movement for a South-centred model of development would reveal the link between international dependence and *domestic* systems, and in making this link the social, cultural and economic basis of neo-colonialism would be called into question. Élites fixed the NIEO agenda precisely to prevent this happening, and at its worst, it degenerated into an empty anti-imperialist rhetoric which merely diverted attention away from these issues. This was very prevalent in Africa, and it even had the effect of discrediting all anti-imperialist discourse, leaving people vulnerable in the face of the subsequent ideological offensive of the IMF.

Despite these limitations, the NIEO movement was a significant historic event, an attempt at democratic revolution at the international-system level. The refusal of international capitalism to compromise in any meaningful way was eloquent testimony to the realities of the system, and in this sense, the defeat of the movement was positive because it taught a powerful lesson.

Although the official NIEO movement has been fragmented, new grassroots forces have emerged out of the ruins, and these undoubtedly possess a systemic dimension. There is also a new, if limited, élite movement which could attempt to exploit the fact that the current accumulation structure is heavily dependent on manufactured exports from the South. The relationship between these two currents will be explored in subsequent chapters.

## Notes

1. See, for example, Jones 1983.

2. A short-lived coffee price-rise did indeed occur, but this was essentially permitted by the USA as a temporary measure to compensate Latin American governments for the embargo on Cuba. On the other hand, sugar prices fell when the USA expanded beet production, again as part of its strategy to pressurise Cuba.

3. Nabudere 1979.

4. Mitra and Werde-Bruniger 1984, p. 38.

5. O'Neill 1980, pp. 48–9.

6. United Nations 1979.

7. Organisation of American States 1978, p. 47.

8. Declaration of the Colombo Non-Aligned Bureau meeting, 1979, quoted in Singham and Hune 1986, p. 201.

9. Non-Aligned Movement, Colombo Conference (1976), Economic Declaration, in *Nouvel Ordre international et Non-alignement – Recueil de Documents*, 1982, pp. 203–4.

10. UNCTAD 1979, p. 1.

11. Brandt Commission 1980, p. 33.

12. See *Le Monde diplomatique*, September 1979.

13. Quoted in Singham and Hune 1986, p. 228.

14. *Le Monde*, 5 June 1976.

15. *Le Monde*, 1–2 February 1976.

16. These included bananas, bauxite, cocoa, coffee, copper, cotton and yarn, hard fibres, iron, jute, manganese, meat, phosphates, rubber, sugar, tea, timber, tin and vegetable oils.

17. Amin 1978b, Chapter 6.

18. See Nwoke 1987.

19. Massarat 1980.

20. Ibid., p. 47.

# 7

# Realities Overlooked – Women's Labour and Nature

## Capitalism is Not a Purely Monetary System

The relationship between 'pure' capitalism and a shadowy area behind it is an underlying theme of the whole of this study. In this chapter, I will attempt to bring this issue more into the foreground, to gain greater understanding of the process of change in long cycles in the international economy. Although I will focus on the 1970s, I hope to provide theoretical insights that will be of value for understanding the major changes of the present period.

To recapitulate, I have defined the 'pure' capitalist economy as one where all inputs are remunerated. It was one of Marx's major achievements to show that exploitation could still occur even when labour was being paid at its true value. Since as a result capital could accumulate on the basis of exploitation, it looked as though the capitalist economy could be a self-contained arena of reproduction.

But a closer look shows that there are indispensable external conditions, without which this apparently self-contained reproduction will not work. Raw materials and cash crops must be plundered from the third world without accounting for their real human and ecological costs or allowing for the reproduction of the human and ecological factors involved in producing them. Similarly, without unremunerated household labour, it would be impossible to provide labour for the monetary economy. The argument that the 'family wage' *includes* the cost of reproduction does not in any way detract from the fact that unremunerated labour is taking place.

We can therefore speak of a relationship between two different 'areas' of the economy. The term 'area' should be used in a dual sense: literally, to refer to a geographical division between centre and periphery where there are tangible boundaries; and conceptually, to refer to the exploitation of households, racially defined groups, and, to some extent, the informal economy as a whole (since hidden exploitation can occur in the geographical centre as well as the periphery).

Dependency theory uncovered part of this relationship, essentially the

racial capitalism that exists between the North and the South. It showed that
so-called modernisation recasts, in a purely exploitative form, those aspects
of traditional relationships that ensure that labour is reproduced in such a
way that capitalism does not have to bear the full economic costs. This is the
fundamental reason why development can normally proceed without undermining the centre–periphery division. A major theme of this book is to
explore the continuing relevance of this point. But dependency theory fails
to provide a framework for understanding the questions of gender and
environment, which is why I intend to focus on these issues in the present
chapter. In the last analysis, the centre–periphery relationship cannot fully be
understood unless we see it as part of something bigger – the whole category
of inputs into the sphere of 'pure' capitalist reproduction, whose full costs
are not borne by the capitalist system.

In this section I will consider how the role of unremunerated inputs
(other than those expressed in the centre–periphery division in the most
obvious sense) is affected by the restructuring of capitalism. I will first
consider women's labour as part of the unremunerated reproduction of
human labour; and then consider how the environment has been used as a
non-monetarised source of natural resources. Taking the case of the food
system, I will finally consider how, in concrete terms, the social and natural-
resource issues are interlinked.

## Women's Unremunerated Labour

Women's labour has always served capitalism in a dual sense: by generating
immediate profit, and by opening up ways forward for eventual structural
change. Women's work is centred in the non-monetary household sphere, but
when required it can partially be integrated into the formal sphere. When this
happens, women can still be super-exploited for two reasons: their 'official'
work is still influenced by gender-ascriptive roles originating from the household sphere; and they can be paid less because their labour is regarded as
occurring only provisionally (or partially) in the monetary economy. Recently,
the concept of flexibility, which originally arose with reference to women's
work, was extended and became a central plank of the restructuring which
occurred at the beginning of the 1980s.

Mainstream economics in the post-war period stubbornly refused to
recognise the importance of women's labour. All their non-remunerated work
was excluded from the calculations of national wealth, made according to
the definition of gross national product.[1] Statistically, women were considered
inactive economically (an absurdity given the work they really did).[2] Since the
orthodox definition of development was in effect the *growth* of GNP,[3] women
were considered irrelevant to it. From a sociological point of view, women
were guilty by association of possessing many of the 'primitive' and 'un-
disciplined' characteristics ascribed to the traditional sector; they were blamed

for holding backward values, inimical to modernisation;[4] and for being inadequately socialised as citizens.[5] At best sidelined by the development process and at worst regarded as its enemy, women often found that the more development there was, the worse their relative position became; for example, some studies found that, 'women's participation in the agricultural sector is inversely proportional to regional development'.[6] A UN Food and Agriculture Organisation (FAO) study said that women made up 80 per cent of food producers in some African countries, but received only 2–10 per cent of 'extension contacts' (technical assistance).[7] Land reform programmes were male-biased, and failed to take into account women's rights under traditional ownership structures;[8] so even supposedly radical changes actually made the distribution of power more unfavourable to women.

Now, there are two problems in this approach, from capitalism's point of view. First, if development itself is regarded as a form of exploitation, the more women are marginalised, the less their labour can be exploited to its full potential. And second, since women are effectively the basis of the family structure through which labour is reproduced, if they are exploited beyond certain limits, there is a risk that the whole system will collapse and future exploitation will be jeopardised. Since the 1970s, capitalism has been attempting to come to grips with these two problems: there have been some promising new initiatives (from an exploitative point of view) on the first of these questions, but their effectiveness is being partly undermined by the intractability of the second problem.

The fundamental dilemma is that the partial monetarisation of the periphery meant employing men in commercial agriculture or industry, leaving women with the responsibility for providing all the labour which used to be performed by them *and by men* under the old gender-based division of labour. This is the basic reason for the recent trend for women to become the family head. In India, the poorer a household is, the more likely it is to be headed by a woman.[9] By the late 1970s, 30 per cent of households in the third world were headed by a woman.[10] In Africa, women head 20–50 per cent of households, depending on the region.[11] Societies, it would seem, are becoming matrifocal once again.[12] Moreover, women have to exist within the interstices of the capitalist economy, as well as in their traditional role. Even the man's wage is often being recycled by the woman through the informal economy.[13] And the working day is not infinitely expandable: according to an Economic Commission on Africa (ECA) survey, African women were already, in the mid-1970s, spending 15 hours a day working.[14]

The conflict between squeezing out the maximum profit now and conserving the social basis for future exploitation (of men as well as women) has always been a tricky problem in capitalism. It has been possible, within the centre, to maintain some sort of balance between the two. As representative of the long-term interests of capital accumulation, the state, by passing Factory Acts, forced the employers to sacrifice short-term profit. But there is no equivalent of the state at an international level. It could be argued that the international system is capable of producing 'regimes' in the special sense employed in international relations theory, that is, bodies which do not have coercive power exactly, but whose rules are observed because participants find them useful. In a sense, the World Bank perceives itself in this role. By taking on board the issue of women's 'empowerment', it is trying to limit present exploitation in the interests of future exploitation. I will discuss the issue of regimes, and specifically the World Bank's role, in later chapters, but on the specific question of women's conditions, there is very little evidence that the World Bank's policy will work. The General Agreement on Tariffs and Trade (GATT) works as a regime (its rules have been observed even when they could not strictly be enforced) because it provides *immediate* payoffs in terms of expanding the value of capital. But the argument that profits must be sacrificed in order to build the social infrastructure to ensure long-term profitability, almost always falls on deaf ears.

## Feminisation of the Workforce and the Search for a New Basis of Exploitation

It is clear that capitalism has led to the super-exploitation of women. This would not offer much consolation if it had only meant heightened misery and oppression, but fortunately it has also provoked resistance. And capitalism has become aware that if it completely ignores or suppresses this resistance, it might become more and more radical, eventually turning into a movement for self-reliance and perhaps even the nucleus of a possible new social order. So the system has seen the need to provide a safe outlet for this protest, even creating the conditions for part of the protest movement to be co-opted. Women are pushing to the forefront issues which had previously been ignored, which gives capitalism a chance to take a new look at the issue of women's labour, and perhaps to find fresh ways of exploiting it.

This helps to explain why the 1970s were characterised by initiatives from international institutions, notably the UN, which inaugurated a UN Women's Decade from 1975 to 1985. It was a chance to look at where capitalism was going. It was clear that there was a crisis, and gender relations might well be a component in its resolution.

It might be possible to develop a kind of Keynesianism for the gender issue, that is, to bring women more into the monetary economy so that their increased consumption acted as a boost to capitalist development. In the late 1970s, Carmen Diana Deere argued that there was a strong case for bringing women into the labour market and for turning into commodities goods and services in the household sphere so as to provide an expanded market.[15] This line of development did not mean that household tasks would be carried out *socially*, because goods and services would be delivered to the individual household, but it would allow consumption to rise. This could be considered a gender equivalent to the global Keynesianism model put forward with respect to North–South relations.

But this is not what capitalism actually did. It was only in the North that women became more 'active' in the sense recognised by official statistics (that is, in mainstream remunerated employment). The percentage of women defined as economically active rose markedly in the industrialised countries between 1970 and 1990 (from 38 per cent to 50 per cent in North America), although segregation according to employment in areas determined by gender roles was probably still strong.[16] In the South however, the formal economic activity of women stagnated or declined – the only exceptions being North Africa and West Asia (the Middle East), where it was historically very low, and Latin America.[17] Even in Southeast Asia it declined.[18] The number of women employed directly by TNC subsidiaries is much smaller than is often assumed, even in Asia.[19]

This does not mean that women's labour is less important in the current phase of the IPE, but simply that the exploitation of women still occurs predominantly outside the official monetary sphere. Fundamentally, women's labour has not been 'modernised' in the sense of abolishing the old determinants, but the old forms of exploitation have been supplemented by new ones. In effect, an attempt to 'empower' women (which means developing their initiative enough to make it easier to exploit them) has been grafted on top of basically unchanged relationships. If we are to judge from the experience of the most 'advanced' countries in Asia, economic development is not (as a unilinear developmentalist model might suppose) *positively* related to a lessening of inequality. For instance, a crucial part of the Japanese model was a particular way of exploiting the labour of young women before marriage.[20] This was not a hangover from the past because, with the new management systems, it became the future of capitalism, a future which was shaped by the impure nature of the systems which were reproduced and expanded through the nature of capitalist development itself.

Of all countries for which statistics of women's average earnings as a percentage of men's are available, the two where the percentage is lowest are Japan (52 per cent) and South Korea (50 per cent).[21] In some newly industrialising countries, to undervalue women's labour is equivalent to undervaluing them as human beings, and it becomes a human rights issue. In the case of India, girls are consistently more undernourished than boys. The ratio of females to males has been falling, with several Indian states recording about nine females or less for every ten males.[22] This suggests that girl babies are dying from neglect, a trend which is reinforced by actual infanticide and sex-determined abortions (of which 78,000 were carried out in India during a five-year period[23]); it all adds up to a 10 per cent shortfall in what would be expected to be the female population. So women are subjected to an attack which reduces their physical numbers, but, as with immigrants in the North, this onslaught does not mean they are less important to the economy than the men; on the contrary, they are perhaps even more important, but the attack reinforces their subordinate role.

The importance of women's role in the current phase of the IPE can be understood better if we look at the difference between two definitions of the cyclical development of capitalism. Let us look first at the business cycle, which brings periodic ups and downs to the economy, and is a persistent problem for capitalism. I will expand on this issue in the next two chapters, but the point to be stressed here is that Keynesianism only postponed the problem through massive quantitative growth.

Since the restructuring of the 1970s, cyclical fluctuations in employment have become the norm once again and a way has to be found to manage this. The response has been 'flexibility'. On the one hand this is a determination borrowed from women and applied more widely; on the other hand, women are themselves the most important single component of the flexible workforce. They are flexible not only in the sense of being considered easy to dump when there is a downturn, but also because they have apparently been less effective in building the defensive strategies employed by trade-unionism, which contemporary capitalism wants to abolish.

The current phase thus includes two contradictory (both exploitative) ways of dealing with women's labour: on the one hand, the 'feminisation of the workforce', and on the other, its exclusion. In the past, with mainly men employed, it was men who tended to lose their jobs during a downturn, and the system actually appeared less sexist than during periods of growth.[24] This is no longer the case: as there are more women in the mainstream economy, they are the ones who most often lose their jobs during the downturn of the business cycle, in effect providing a handy form of 'ballast' to permit adjustments to be made without too much disruption.

But now we must look at the changes that are occurring within the other cyclical development, the development of the long cycle. For the growing reliance on 'flexible' labour had created an increasing role for the informal economy, which has meant in its turn an increase in women's effective role despite their apparent marginalisation.

The relationship between these contradictory trends is partly governed by the succession of business cycles which unfold *within* the overall long cycle, but partly also by the North–South divide. The 'feminisation' of the official economy is more focused in the North, partly because consumption is also focused there; women's monetary income is helpful to capitalism in the North because they can be sold things, while in the South this is not the case. Maria Mies' concept of housewifisation is correct in emphasising the growing importance of ascribed roles,[25] but the criticism that it is Eurocentric[26] has some force, since conditions are never homogenised between centre and periphery.

Ever since flexibility has been generalised across the economy, it has become less specific to women, while some of the characteristics of the informal economy have been allowed to 'leak' into the official world. This raises the question of whether the lines of demarcation between the 'formal' and 'informal' economies are becoming fudged. Obviously, the immediate result has been to exploit women – and in the process, also men – more efficiently. But it remains true that capitalism carries out fundamental restructuring at a cost: it will never be as straightforward to enforce gender divisions as it was in the past.

## Capitalism's Ambiguous Stance on Scarce Resources

Alongside unremunerated human labour, the other main source of inputs whose real costs are ignored by conventional capitalist economics is the environment. Capitalism's calculations are based exclusively on monetary cost. If resources are available for a low economic cost – water, raw materials obtained for practically nothing by manipulating terms of trade with the third world, and so on – they will eventually be used up. If waste products can be dumped without economic cost, they will be dumped. Such processes fund capital accumulation without capitalists having to take responsibility for their long-term impact.

Although for the most part capitalism shows little concern for the way it consumes these resources, it is intermittently fearful of the natural world. The gloomy side of the capitalist discourse is typified in the 'Malthusian' perspective (after the British economist Malthus, writing around the beginning of the nineteenth century, who predicted an uncontrollable population explosion). The relationship between these two outlooks is influenced in a complex way by social conflict.

As well as articulating capitalism's optimistic self-image, the notion of progress associated with the French Revolution also enabled radicals to argue that poverty was caused by exploitation, and that scarcity was caused by the wastefulness of ruling classes who monopolised the ownership and benefits of resources. Malthusianism attacked the idea of progress – perceived as threatening from the standpoint of the ruling order – by asserting that there was an absolute contradiction between population and finite natural resources *independent of social system.*[27] This is not a genuine ecological discourse because it neglects the extent to which today's species are a product of interaction with human development, and the fact that population has been a dynamic factor pushing societies to higher levels of economic organisation.

But in its static and pessimistic form, Malthusianism did not accommodate capitalist development (and it is interesting to note that Malthus was for this reason also anti-colonialist). This is because exploitative systems, such as capitalism, also need to develop – in their own terms, to 'progress' – which could not be envisaged within the constraints of Malthusianism. Imperialism clearly needed, at the ideological level, a concept of national development behind which different social strata could unite.

This problem was conceptually resolved in the nineteenth century by the addition of social Darwinism to Malthusianism. It was stated that, under conditions of scarce resources, development would be possible for some nations by denying it for other peoples or 'races'. More upbeat than pure Malthusianism, it provided justification for both the colonial seizure of resources from the oppressed peoples, and the frantic competition among the colonial powers to see who could monopolise most of them. There could not be a 'place in the sun' for everyone. In the words of early twentieth-century racial-Darwinist Karl Pearson, the nation would develop 'chiefly by way of war with inferior races, and, with equal races, by the struggle for trade-routes and for the sources of raw materials and of food supply'.[28] These assumptions provided the hidden basis for the whole structure of IR, at least until the Second World War.

As a doctrine of development it is fundamentally false, because the driving force is presumed to be biological, and the importance of social structure and culture as mechanisms of adaptation is denied. However, social-Darwinism contains an important truth which capitalism has been seeking to gloss over ever since: that there is no scope for all countries simultaneously to pursue a form of development (capitalism) which is inherently wasteful of resources and damaging in its pollution; and that the established powers only make sure that *they* get the resources, by restricting the development of the periphery.

Such frankness leaves capitalism vulnerable in the handling of its relations with the South. It openly pronounces the conflict to be a war, a fight to the death without any scope for the harmonisation of interest between oppressor and oppressed. The nineteenth-century English racist Robert Knox, for example, said, 'It is a war of extermination – inscribed on each banner is a death's head and no surrender; one or the other must fall.'[29] This discourse made it impossible to have any global or planetary definition of human identity, as well as making impossible any kind of North–South 'dialogue' with indigenous élites *even of a purely tactical kind*. As a result, it could actually encourage national liberation movements, because it showed them that they had nothing to lose by a fight to the death.

As it soon became apparent that liberation movements could not be suppressed without co-opting élites, these truths became extremely dangerous. So a new assimilationism emerged, represented by the ideology of growth and Rostow's stages theory, with its promise of unlimited growth for an unlimited number of actors, all doing exactly the same thing as the USA at the same time. It only meant abandoning any reference to resource constraints, and dropping one of the most important planks of establishment ideology, Malthusianism.[30] In effect, to facilitate the transition to neo-colonialism, the system made promises it could not possibly fulfil.

The idea of limitless growth was so absurd that it could not be maintained in the long term. The cracks in the theory began to appear at the end of the

1960s and beginning of the 1970s. It was the period leading up to the structural crisis, a crisis which surfaced first in ideological form. Many valid questions were asked about where capitalism was heading, with the formulation, for instance, of the notion of 'post-industrial' society. Scientific understanding of the environment was also increasing in a process which was eventually to raise public opinion about the linked problems of the hole in the ozone layer, the greenhouse effect, the destruction of rain forests, and so on. But once the structural crisis began to move towards a resolution based exclusively on continued profitability, these important questions were swept away, at least for the moment.

## The South Menaced by the 'Limits to Growth'

One of the most important factors pushing for a rethink was the South's campaign for a new international economic order. The previous period of linear growth in the industrialised countries had raised demand for commodities and encouraged the producers to seek monopoly rents. The threat to the North had been particularly evident in the 'energy crisis' of 1973, which had encouraged the NIEO campaign to improve terms of trade, and to assert sovereignty over resources. Southern struggles were not expressed clearly in environmentalist terminology, but the implication was that if the countries who had the resources asserted their sovereignty over them, this would reduce wasteful consumption. Colonisers have always depicted other peoples' sovereignty as a retrograde step because it stands in the way of opening up resources to 'common' use. But the South had a strong case for arguing that the consolidation of the state in the developing world was a necessary step in moving towards a planetary identity, a genuine assertion of a 'common concern' in approaching the future organisation of the world's socio-economic system. The threat of a redistribution of power in the South's favour prompted capitalism to rethink its earlier position and to call into question the status of 'growth' as an article of faith.

At this point it becomes interesting to consider the relationship between the pseudo-free market, and organised capitalism. Ideologically, the most important rationale for capitalism has always been the free market. Yet it is precisely here that capitalism is on the weakest ground ecologically: even if one accepts that the key assumption of the free market – that the greater good will automatically emerge from the pursuit of individual acts maximising short-term interest – is valid in terms of the monetary economy, it is hardly plausible in a wider, ecological sense.

Another defence of capitalism, which its own apologists dare not offer, is, in reality, more convincing: that the real basis of contemporary capitalism is not the free market at all, but rather the large organised interests, such as transnational corporations, which could theoretically operate in a more strategic way.

From this angle, I would argue that ultra-imperialism, if it really existed, would have to have an ecological dimension. It is interesting here to look at Lenin's argument against the existence of ultra-imperialism. Lenin argued that, whether or not the 'good' aspects of the market ever existed in an ideal sense, by the time we have reached the monopoly stage, all that is left is the chaotic aspects, which reproduce themselves at a higher level under the auspices of the giant corporations. The question we may ask is: who can take advantage of this chaos? Although (very hypothetically) industrial capital might have an interest in conserving the resources it needs for the future, it is now ruled by finance capital, which is inherently much more geared to the short-term. Ultra-imperialism is therefore unlikely to exist in the sense of a capitalism able to take long-term conservationist decisions. The actual developments in the recent phase of capitalist development would strengthen the ecological critique of ultra-imperialism in a new and sharper form: far from concerning itself with the environment, finance capital today is speculating on the future prices of primary products, which means it could just as well benefit from the depletion of natural resources as from their conservation.

Apart from the role of the corporations, organised capital also has a statist aspect. But the whole character of the Keynesian period encouraged the state to promote the most harmful aspects of the 'growth' orientation. As Waring has shown, the way in which economic indicators, such as GDP statistics, are drawn up means that environmental destruction is viewed as a form of economic activity, hence desirable, while conservation, by not producing an 'output' does not contribute to growth.[31]

In the long term, these factors stand in the way of capitalism developing an organised approach to the environmental issue. But this has become apparent only recently. The late 1960s and early 1970s was an unusual period, for the structural problem of continued accumulation had become apparent, while the neo-liberal solution had not emerged. In these circumstances, capitalism briefly appeared capable of a long-term, strategic perspective.

Given the global nature of the environmental problem, the logical forum for formulating a strategic response would be international institutions; and a conference, held in Paris in 1968, duly inaugurated the Man and the Biosphere programme, which was followed in 1972 by a UN Conference on the Human Environment at Stockholm. This started a trend for big conferences that continued to the Earth Summit of 1992 and up to the present. But a strategic response required not only a new institutional framework, but also a new conception of development itself. Could capitalism produce the structures to do this? At first, it seemed as if it might: the Club of Rome, a think-tank of capitalist economists and industrialists, headed by a management consultant who worked with Fiat and Olivetti, was set up in 1968. At its behest, computer experts, working at the Massachusetts Institute of Technology and funded by Volkswagen, came up with models encompassing the following five factors: population, agricultural production, natural resources, industrial production and pollution. In 1972, the Club of Rome published a report with the historic title *The Limits to Growth*. Asserting that on present trends it would be impossible for the world economy to grow for more than another 100 years, the report said that an attempt should be made to 'establish a condition of ecological and economic stability that is sustainable far into the future. The state of global equilibrium could be designed so that the basic material needs of each person on earth are satisfied and each person has an equal opportunity to realise his individual human potential.'[32]

This reflected a fundamental rethinking of development theory. The vocabulary used in the report belonged to a different world from Rostowism: sustainability, steady-state economics, systems theory (systems acquire mechanisms for maintaining their stability and compensating for disruption, but if the equilibrium is lost, it is difficult to re-establish). Key new concepts, such as the basic needs idea, and capability-building as a goal of development, were foreshadowed in this new vocabulary.

It appeared progressive and humanistic, but there was a threatening subtext. For the report hinted that the Rostowite promise – that developing countries could, by rapid growth, close the gap with the North – was untenable. The new concept of steady-state economics would eventually undermine the vision of take-off. When this is taken into consideration, the basic needs idea, together with associated concepts such as intermediate technology and 'small is beautiful', started to look like ideas for limiting the South's ambitions, rather than proposals for empowerment.

If the South was denied frantic growth, Rostow-style, so it could close the gap from below, the only way for it to catch up would be if the powerful interests in the industrial countries reduced their consumption of scarce resources, so that a common conception of 'basic needs' could be defined at a planetary level. But there was no evidence whatsoever of this happening; it became all too obvious that environmentalism was serving as a way of holding back developing countries. This discredited environmentalism, and eventually, the concept of 'newly industrialising countries' (NICs) emerged as a new version of social-Darwinism. It fits in quite well with the imperialist version of Malthusianism, in that it propagates the survival of the fittest, but it is certainly not in any sense conservationist.

This does not mean that, from the perspective of the South, sustainability, empowerment and so on are bad ideas in themselves, but the question is who defines the agenda. It is perfectly possible to have a radical position which distances itself from the neo-Malthusianism of *The Limits to Growth*, without falling back into Rostowism. The lines of demarcation were not always clearly drawn, and the argument that science can sort anything out resurfaced in contemporary criticisms of *The Limits to Growth*. It was argued, for instance, that the limits were not absolute but reflected the application of technology to the wrong things – for example, 50 per cent of R&D was going on military objectives and only 2 per cent on agricultural, industrial and environmental problems facing developing countries.[33] The argument is progressive as far as it goes, but, as we will see later, even agriculture-oriented R&D can serve the imperatives of capitalism, which are accumulation benefiting the centre, and political dominance. A more consistently radical position would be to argue for a different kind of development. One way would be for the South to use its own human resources to provide a sound basis on which to assimilate technology. In this way, it becomes possible to attack the rigid neo-Malthusian position while still being environmentalist; one can argue that resources are flexible (no absolute limits) because of human creativity, but a social form of using them must be found which respects the commitment to symbiosis with the natural world that is charac-teristic of traditional systems. Basic needs and intermediate technology take on a different, less restrictive sense if they are used to mean restoring the link between what is produced and what is consumed, between technology and popular culture. Expressed intellectually in the 1970s in the work of people like Malcolm Caldwell, Johan Galtung and Ignacy Sachs, the real objective force of this perspective is its embodiment in grassroots movements.

Malthusianism has taken on a contemporary form. Not only has population been rising much more rapidly than before,[34] but the increase is also unevenly spread – being concentrated in the developing world. As a result, it has been insidiously suggested that the problem of deteriorating resources is thus developing countries' fault. The argument is wrong for a number of reasons. First of all, resource use is concentrated in the area where population growth is lowest, that is, the industrial world, which regularly accounts for 85 per cent of the world's energy consumption.[35] Per capita energy consumption in China was recently only one-thirteenth of that in the USA.[36] Second, it can be argued that it is the plunder of resources which is causing the population rise, rather than the other way round, in the sense that population growth is a reflection of incomplete development: the old functioning traditional systems, which limited population to the level the land could support and gave women the power to control their fertility, have been disrupted, but without being replaced by full-scale capitalism, where, as in the industrial countries, the state would provide a safety-net to replace the support mechan-isms of the family. The household has emerged as the crucial unit and, in a situation of general poverty, it measures its economic strength in the number of productive workers it contains. There is therefore a strong incentive to have more children.

This analysis suggests that the way to address environment/resource problems would be to attack the structural inequalities in the system which prevent developing countries from holding on to their resources and investing them in their own development. The argument is not fully satisfactory – since it is questionable whether a generalised *capitalist* development is possible – but at least it knocks neo-Malthusianism on the head.

For a while, as we saw in the last chapter, it looked as though élites in the

South would be able to influence official society through the international institutions. Although probably motivated by the desire to appropriate rents, their campaign to raise raw-material prices could still have arrived at the right result for the wrong reasons: if prices rise, consumption should fall and substitution be encouraged. But the South's campaign was destroyed by central capitalism.

What has happened since then is a curious paradox. On the one hand, the new environmentally conscious development discourse has continued, typified by the Bruntland Report,[37] published in 1987. In it, sustainability was placed in a socio-economic rather than a physical context. Caused by the limitations of social organisation, poverty was seen as a central problem, and these social limitations were seen as the main constraint, rather than limits of finite resources. This approach is to be warmly welcomed, but what has happened in practice has been very different. The industrial countries have been primarily concerned with their own security (in the sense of stable conditions for capital accumulation). Measures to encourage energy savings (for example, speed limits) have not been retained in the long term. Instead, there has been an attempt to force energy prices down, part of which was the contingency plan to invade the Gulf. The use of new technology to provide substitutes for traditional raw materials – which, in the abstract, is a progressive thing – has mainly served in practice to undermine the South's bargaining power, to keep the prices of raw materials low, and thus effectively to encourage their consumption. Further action by international institutions, in which the main actors are governments, has proved disappointing. Little was achieved in either the UN Conference on Environment and Development (UNCED – 'Earth Summit'), held in Brazil in June 1992, or the later Kyoto conference on limiting carbon emissions.

The conceptual and practical changes in capitalist development since the beginning of the 1980s have not helped. The growth of environmental consciousness coincided with the decline of Keynesian 'managed economy' approaches to capitalism, and once statism had been rejected, the pretence had to be maintained that environmental issues could be managed through the free market. This is something that those defending extreme *laissez-faire* have always maintained. At a famous debate in Chicago in the 1950s, attended by Friedman and other leading liberals, R.H. Coase won them over to an even more liberal position by asserting that earlier liberals, such as Pigou, were wrong in saying that environmental issues were an exception and had to be handled by the state. Instead, said Coase, the state should simply create rights (either to pollute or to avoid pollution) which could be bought and sold. The optimum level of welfare would be arrived at through the market, according to the value that economic actors placed on either continuing to produce while polluting, or stopping production.[38] This seemed to be a reduction of liberalism to the absurd, until the United States, with a supposedly ecologically conscious administration, came up with something very similar as a basis for the Kyoto conference on carbon emissions in 1997. At the same time, there is a contradiction at the heart of the term 'global'. What is called globalisation has weakened the existing states, but it has done this in the name of *laissez-faire* and has therefore made it difficult for environmentalists to prevail with their own ecological definition of globalisation.

With the increasing inability of the official world to find solutions, new forces have come through, as reflected in the grassroots activity around the Earth Summit and subsequently. Grassroots movements are environmentally aware because environmental issues affect the reality of their day-to-day struggle. This opens up the possibility of a new environmentalism, an issue which I will address in Chapter 14.

## The Contradictions in Capitalism's Claim to Modernise Agriculture

If the Uruguay Round of GATT is anything to go by, agriculture has been a leading-edge industry in recent years. In one sense, this is a reversion to the early period of industrialisation, when agriculture was also at the leading edge of technology. But the parameters have also changed: in the early days agricultural development was assessed in terms of the support it gave to industry, because an increase in agricultural productivity was necessary to support the growing number of workers not producing their own food. But today, agriculture has increasingly become part of industry, serving as an area of accumulation in its own right. Capitalism develops by breaking up those aspects of old natural economies that have survived until the present and then reorganising them on commercial lines. Food production presents many opportunities for commercialisation: marketing, the introduction of new crops, brand identities, and so on And it is in itself interesting that direct accumulation is increasingly targeting agriculture today. It suggests that the industrial basis of accumulation may be insufficient.

The land is the basis of capitalist development in a social as well as an economic sense, for the land question underlies the international political economy. Land was the fundamental issue in colonial struggles, but in general poor peasants did not improve their tenure on their land with decolonisation. Instead they had to face a mixture of old-style landlordism, pressure from transnational corporations, and the disruption caused by developments such as commercial land speculation by local élites.

The land reform issue is in the first place one of ownership, but it also affects the deeper issues of conservation and land *use*. If ordinary people gained control of their land, they might start practising subsistence agriculture, cultivating food rather than cash crops.

Orthodox modernisers would be suspicious of this move, as they are of subsistence agriculture in general. It is indeed true that small landowners tend to find it difficult to accumulate enough to make the investment in productivity which is an indispensable condition for industrialisation. These problems would need to be addressed, probably through a form of co-operativisation which did not act as a mask for bureaucracy and for the exploitation of the rural economy by the urban. But in the light of post-war experience, it looks as though it would have been better for the national economies if producers had owned the land; for what in fact happened – large-scale agriculture, the global food system, the development of scientific methods, and so on – are all manipulated by the global accumulation system in the interests of Northern capital. In the early industrial revolution, as I argued in Chapter 1, knowledge was expropriated from the direct producers and turned into a way of oppressing them, but this was done within a national context. More recently, this has been done at an international level, so oppression does not even carry the consolation that it facilitates national systems of capital accumulation.

The power relations in this post-war set-up are embedded in relationships which at first sight appear economistic and technical, but they are very hard to shift, precisely because they embody, in a disguised form, the more fundamental issues of environmental degradation and cultural alienation. A good way to understand this will be to examine the concept of productivity.

There are two forms of exploitation: of people and of resources. In capitalism's calculations the notion of productivity links the two. In the global political economy of agriculture, value, derived from the natural world, circulates, alongside political influence based on the control of that value. Countries are supposed to specialise in products that they can produce with less labour: the South because of so-called natural advantage, the North because heavy investment has enabled huge amounts of agricultural goods to be produced with a small outlay in wages. The population engaged directly in Northern agriculture is very small – hence productivity is high – but its significance within the economy is much larger than this would imply. Taking into account inputs into agriculture, marketing and processing, the farm-related sector of industrial countries may comprise 30–40 per cent of GDP.[39]

This helps to explain, in narrow economic terms, why the economies in the North are coherent, and those in the South are not. In the former, the different parts fit together: increasing agricultural productivity makes it possible to feed the urban population, whose rising demand becomes the incentive for further investment. It is the *social* balance of forces which makes this coherence possible. But in the South, these social conditions are missing. Though it often appears as if it is industry that is blocking development, there is a strong case for arguing that, at a deeper level, the problem lies with agriculture.

To understand how this happens, we must look at the role played by Southern agriculture in the relationship with the North. The international accumulation system not only reinforces the disparity between the North and the South, but makes it *self-reproducing*. Gradually, the North began to export staple foods to the South, inhibiting their development in the South. Whereas in the mid-1930s the North was a net importer from the South, by 1978 it was the developing countries (Asia and Africa) which had become importers of 65 million tons of cereals.[40] Imported cereals have pushed out staples that have traditionally been produced domestically, such as durum wheat in the Maghreb and maize in Mexico. And the agricultural products which the South manages to export are governed by the rules on the world commodities market, over which the South has no control (coffee, for example, had become the second most valuable commodity after oil by the beginning of the 1980s).[41] The North, in contrast, can use the dominance of its agricultural exports to obtain political and economic benefit.

This situation was probably the result of two processes that had arisen independently and had then converged: on the one hand, cash crops were being grown in the South on land which earlier would have been used for food; and on the other hand, in the North, the original rationale of increasing food productivity to feed the local urban population had been replaced by one of treating food production as a major field for capital accumulation in its own right. In the earlier period, the USA had notoriously destroyed food surpluses, and then effectively subsidised farmers not to produce, but eventually the food surplus became part of the self-reproducing circuits of capital accumulation, and acquired its own momentum. Although to some extent the Northern economies have become rivals in the field of food exports, this is not something the South can take advantage of; in the Uruguay Round of GATT, for example, the South was out-manoeuvred and the final outcome was a system which has strengthened the industrial countries' collective dominance over the food system.

But a more subtle interaction also exists between the internal structures of Northern and Southern economies. The productivity gap between the two is immense: according to UN statistics from the late 1970s, the number of workers per million US dollars of capital in the top industrial countries was four; in the poorer LDCs it was 1,563.[42] This difference in productivities makes it impossible for the South to close the gap with the North. The mechanism for this has been explained by Samir Amin: agricultural prices tend to be determined by the level of productivity in the North, but unless Southern farmers obtain prices which reflect the amount of labour they put in, they will never be able to accumulate enough capital to make their own agriculture more productive.

## The Environmental Critique of Agricultural Productivity

It is important to understand these dangers hidden within the conventional calculation of productivity, but we need to proceed further in the argument, and to do this we have to introduce an ecological dimension. According to the conventional economistic definitions, the only determinants of productivity are capital and labour, for conventional economics ignores inputs from the natural world. But, in practice, the latter can be increased in a non-sustainable way to provide an apparent rise in efficiency which is not really efficient in terms of the rational use of resources. Indeed, there is a huge stimulus to produce unnaturally cheap food in order to reduce consumption costs (since people can subsist on lower wages) and hence increase the rate of profit.

One way of showing what is going on is to compare the calorific content of the crops that are produced with the calories used up in the processes that produce them. For the most favourable of traditional crops, cassava, the output:input ratio is as high as 60:1. But industrial countries' agriculture includes huge energy inputs from fertiliser, fuel for machinery, processing, canning, transportation, refrigeration, cooking and so on, and the figure is often negative. In the US food industry, the calorific output:input ratio in 1940 was only 1:5 (that is, inputs were five times as great as output) and by 1970 it had deteriorated further to 1:10.[43] Returns are clearly diminishing. The case of fertiliser illustrates this well: increasingly large applications are needed for a decreasing improvement. Holland uses fertiliser at the extremely high rate of 300 kg per hectare. Japan consumes more fertiliser than the whole of Latin America.[44] Resources such as phosphates or oil are drawn in at an insubstantial cost (neither reflecting the full value of the rents, nor that of the labour used to extract them) to make agriculture *seem* more efficient. A less obvious, but interesting, example of this phenomenon relates to the meat industry, and is highlighted by Malcolm Caldwell's phrase, 'protein imperialism'. Animals consume 10 times as much plant protein as they produce meat protein (in the case of beef, 21 times).[45] Grain converted to meat loses 75–90 per cent of its calories and 65–90 per cent of its protein.[46] According to FAO figures for 1978, animal feed accounted for 36 per cent of the total world consumption of cereals and for 61 per cent of the world consumption of maize.[47] The total cereal deficit of the Sahel countries during the famine of 1973 was 1 million tonnes, which was only 0.25 per cent of the amount of grain fed to animals in the industrial countries in the same year.[48] A significant quantity of animal feed takes the form of high-quality protein imported from the South (fish meal, oilseeds, etc.).

So productivity in the conventional definition of producing more with less labour is increasing while efficiency in real terms is declining; there can be little doubt that the two phenomena are linked.

## The 'Green Revolution' and the Convergence of Politics and Business

The plundering of these inputs from the natural world (not fully counted in the official, monetary economy) has become part of the process of accumulation on a world scale. It involves a power game, in which economic and political elements stake their claims. Even though the food system has become an out-of-control juggernaut – an example of the alienation arising from capital accumulation – it is still partly the result of a strategy formulated by political and business interests.

There was an East–West dimension. With the beginning of large-scale petroleum exploitation in Siberia in 1972, the Soviet Union earned hard currency. It could relax its tough controls on the peasantry, through which it had extracted food for the towns, and start to buy food on the world market instead.[49] But in the politics of food the North–South dimension is far more important. The North began to use its monopoly of food production as a leverage against independence, having become aware that surpluses could buy control, perhaps even more effectively than invasions and CIA coups. In 1973, the US Secretary of State, Henry Kissinger, declared that food in US hands was a more powerful weapon than the H-bomb.[50]

It seemed evident that the next step for the North was to entrench this food monopoly through the argument of comparative costs: the North would farm food grain, and developing countries focus increasingly on cash crops like coffee or sugar. This indeed formed one strand in US policy.[51]

But there were risks in such a strategy, and it is here that we should consider what is known as the Green Revolution, a typical instance of politics–business convergence. The business community wanted to make money by involving themselves not just in dependent industrialisation, but in agriculture in the third world. The kind of 'scientific' methods that had been used in the North to increase productivity at the expense of the natural world could also be used in the South – with even less concern for the environmental impact, but with heightened concern for retaining control over core technology. Such a development would increase the efficiency of cash-crop production. It would also lead to a rise in food production in the South, but this was acceptable, since technological dominance would more than make up for the weakening of the North's monopoly on staple food.

This economic argument converged with a political argument for increasing food production in the South. US policy during the Kennedy era understood that Western interests should not just rely on isolated dictators for their protection, but needed some broader social stratum that would be dependent on Western technology and economic culture. Given the predominantly rural character of societies in the South, such a stratum would need an agricultural basis. This could be achieved by enriching them through cash-crop production, but there was another solution. Since social unrest is associated with hunger, an expansion in food production would at the same time consolidate a faithful élite and defuse protest. So, provided the new agriculture was high-tech, Northern interests could simultaneously draw rents from the technology and ensure that greater food self-sufficiency was not translated into greater effective autonomy. Moreover, raising food productivity would both block the demand for radical land-reform, and mean that land would not have to be withdrawn from the cultivation of cash crops. It is not surprising that the Green Revolution appeared an ideal solution.

The origins of the Green Revolution go back to the foundation in Mexico in 1943 of the research institution CIMMYT, which was set up by Rockefeller and was linked to Standard Oil, a big manufacturer of artificial fertilisers. Subsequently, the Ford Foundation (Ford being a major manufacturer of tractors) set up academies for rural development at Peshawar (West Pakistan) and Comilla (East Pakistan) in 1959, and then the International Rice Research Institute in the Philippines in 1963. The agenda was thus controlled by Northern corporations, and designed to sell the commodities they wanted to offload. The experiments conducted in these institutions led to the introduction of high-yielding varieties (HYVs). These were heavily promoted by multinational interests, by the US administration and by international bodies; during the 1970s, 120 of the largest TNCs in fields such as chemical fertilisers, pesticides, farm machinery, seed production and food processing, set up a joint programme with the UN Food and Agriculture Organisation (FAO).[52]

The apparent success of the venture was remarkable in certain areas, mainly in Asia. Rice production doubled in the Philippines and there were spectacular increases in Indonesia and Pakistan as well. It appeared superficially that the economic preconditions of development were being created. After all, successful industrialisation in the North had been accompanied or preceded by a technical revolution in agriculture, which was the precondition for feeding a growing urban population.

But the analogy is not accurate. Any form of technological revolution under capitalism serves the interest of capital accumulation rather than realising the objective of actually feeding the people. In the case of the agricultural revolution in the early stages of existing industrial powers, the need to feed people coincided with the demands of nationalism, but in the contemporary international context this is not the case. The accumulation interests are now international, the historical background is one of dependency, and the rise of agricultural productivity occurs against the background of this dependency, and serves to entrench it. In effect what happened was that Northern dominance over food exports was retained, but the instrument for this dominance was partially displaced; instead of just sending food to the South, the North also gave an increasing role to technological dominance.

This had an important economic impact, because technological monopoly secures substantial monopoly rents. As an illustration of the primary imperative of accumulation, new plants were developed in response to the North's selling requirements, rather than to local development needs. As Warnock has pointed out, there was no compelling reason, from a farming point of view, to develop plants to use a lot of fertiliser (they could have been bred to make the best use of sunlight, for example); it was commercial logic that drove the research.[53] It is estimated that a new strain of plant costs US$2m to produce, while a new pesticide costs US$40m; this shows why it is more profitable to adapt the former to the latter than the other way round.[54] The new technology demanded a substantial transfer of value through the purchase of inputs. Fertiliser imports, for example, became a significant drain on Southern countries' resources.[55]

These economic factors probably constitute the immediate motivation behind the Green Revolution, but there was also a strong element of pure power relations. It is common to contrast 'bad' militaristic science with 'good' agricultural science, and to argue that R&D should be switched from military to development ends, but it must be remembered that in terms of the North–South power struggle, the 'good' agricultural R&D can also be a weapon.

However, the most important negative effect of the Green Revolution was social, for it was only the rich peasants who could afford to pay for its inputs.

The politico-business alliance behind the Revolution had two key objectives: to build a middle stratum through social engineering, and to sell expensive products to those who could afford them. Both tended to increase polarisation through the policy euphemistically called 'building on the best', that is, channelling more resources to those farmers who were supposed to be progressive and exemplary. Although this appeared forward-looking, there was a conservative undercurrent: it strengthened the existing landed interests, which was the class most opposed to land reform. In India, the landowners welcomed the Green Revolution with open arms for precisely this reason.[56] By the end of the 1970s, the poorest half of the rural population in Bihar owned just under 4 per cent of the land, which was less than it had owned 25 years earlier.[57] In East Pakistan/Bangladesh, the strategy pioneered in Comilla was adopted in 1970 as the basis for a nationwide Integrated Rural Development Programme, presented as a programme of progressive agricultural change. Before the Programme, 14 per cent of the farmers were landless; by 1960 this figure had grown to 17 per cent; and by 1977, after the 'Big Push' for green development had been undertaken, the proportion had risen to 32 per cent. If one includes families with less than 0.2 ha. (which is virtually landless) the figure is 53 per cent. And of those families with land, 78 per cent possessed less than 0.8 ha., which is scarcely enough to support them. Although laws theoretically limited landholding to 13.35 ha., in fact 90 per cent of land was in the hands of farmers with bigger plots.[58] The study of one state in Mexico shows that the number of landless peasants grew over the 1960–70 period.[59] It is a similar picture in Indonesia, where even casual labourers lost their jobs.[60] It should be noted that peasants' indebtedness is an important and underpublicised aspect of the third world debt crisis. Using the case of the Philippines, Swasti Mitter points out that the new landless poor were absorbed into the global capitalist economy in other exploitative relationships.[61] Polarisation thus increased without the counterpart of a constructive form of accumulation.

The result was growing malnutrition, caused, in reality, by the lack of purchasing power – in conventional economic terms, the lack of demand – rather than by deficiencies in production, and this in turn meant that there was no incentive to invest further in staple food production for domestic consumption: 'there is ample evidence that failure to provide a food "surplus" for an expanding urban or industrial population has resulted more from lack of market incentive than from inadequacy of farming methods'.[62] However, there was a demand – an exogenous one – for cash crops, whether traditional ones like groundnuts and cocoa, or increasingly 'non-traditional' crops like out-of-season vegetables for consumption in the North.

Any form of accumulation involves inputs which are not part of the economic sphere at all, such as materials from the natural world and un-remunerated human labour. This is the hidden cost of accumulation. The worst of the hidden costs tend to be transplanted into the third world, without the latter obtaining the 'benefit' of a locally fixed accumulation which could fuel independent capitalist development. This is why the problem of depletion is most serious there, in terms of both the ecology and human resources.

Some environmentalists argue that the environmental issue is so serious that it has to be given priority over class politics. This is wrong simply because it is capitalism that is the problem. But it would be equally wrong to say that the environment is a long-term issue which can be dealt with later, once the political conditions have been created, for grassroots move-ments are making it an immediate issue, and they are precisely the really existing forces which can challenge the system. At the most fundamental level of exploitation, accumulation is conducted not in a pure monetary form but by excluding groups of people from the official world and then exploiting them more intensely. This puts them in the same predicament as the environment, so it is not surprising that a rapprochement has occurred.

## Notes

1. D'Onofrio-Flores and Pfafflin 1982, p. 62.
2. Cf., for example, Latin American and Caribbean Women's Collective 1980.
3. Aseniero 1985.
4. Cf., for example, Saffioti 1978.
5. Dennis 1987.
6. Tadesse 1982.
7. United Nations 1991, p. 91.
8. Cf. Sen and Grown 1987, p. 34.
9. Cf. Agarwal, Bina 'Neither Sustenance nor Sustainability', in Agarwal 1988.
10. Ward 1984, p. 32.
11. Rau 1991, p. 170.
12. See the data referred to by Pine 1982.

13. A survey in Kinshasa in the 1970s showed that many male wage-earners handed over a significant proportion of their monthly wage to their wives to buy something like smoked fish, which was then resold; see Cutrufelli 1983, p. 105.

14. Cutrufelli 1983, p. 90.

15. Deere 1979, p. 142.

16. In one study in the USA in the 1980s, only 10% of workers were in jobs which included both men and women; cf. United Nations 1991, p. 87.

17. We can assume that Latin America is special because of the growth of the service sector there, itself a reflection of the existence of a parasitic bourgeoisie linked to transnational capital.

18. United Nations 1991, p. 84.

19. Cf. Benaria 1989.

20. See Patrick 1976.

21. United Nations 1991, p. 89.

22. Agarwal 1988, p. 90.

23. Shiva 1988, p. 119.

24. See Niem 1980.

25. Mies 1986.

26. This point is made by Potts 1990, but the argumentation and basis of the critique are not clearly established.

27. The way Malthusian arguments about resources were used against the Left made it very problematic for the latter to work out its own environmental position, tending instead to fall back on the argument that science would solve all problems once private ownership of resources was removed.

28. Quoted in Hayes 1973, p. 24.

29. Knox 1862, pp. 244–5.

30. Another important determinant of the new ideological configuration is that opinion in the industrial world saw labour shortage as the main constraint. This was already so with Keynes, despite unemployment in the 1930s, and such a perception became even more pronounced in the post-war boom. In France, immigrants were desperately sought after. This climate was not conducive to Malthusian ideas. The corollary of this is that in those countries where a labour surplus prevailed, i.e. the LDCs, this was seen as the major favourable condition for development, as in the Lewis model.

31. Waring 1989.

32. Meadows 1972, p. 24.

33. Cole 1973, p. 11.

34. The parameters are that a 2% increase in world population means the figure doubles every 35 years, and this is just what happened: in the period 1950–87, population doubled from 2.5 to 5 billion. In the early 1980s the UN began to work on the assumption that population will stabilise by 2100 at 11 billion, so the challenge would be the doubling of population between the beginning of the 1990s and 2050 to about 10 billion; cf. *Le Monde diplomatique*, May 1990.

35. Warnock 1987, p. 34.

36. Environmental Information Center, Tokyo 1994, Statistical Appendix, p. 20.

37. Bruntland 1987.

38. An interesting, sympathetic account of this debate can be found in Eatwell 1987, in the entry under R.H. Coase.

39. Blakie and Brookfield 1987, p. 227.

40. Castro 1983, p. 106.

41. Dinham and Hines 1983, p. 51.

42. Cole and Miles 1984, p. 145.

43. Cf. Glaeser and Phillips-Howard 1987, pp. 130–1, for these figures. According to the same source, studies of rice and vegetable farming in Hong Kong in the 1930s by traditional methods showed an ER of 24.4, whereas by 1971, using modern methods, it had sunk to around 1.

44. Dumont and Cohen 1980, pp. 134, 129–30.

45. Caldwell 1977, p. 103.

46. Warnock 1987, p. 137.

47. Castro 1983, p. 98.

48. Dumont and Cohen 1980, p. 138.

49. Cf. Medvedev 1992.

50. Quoted in Linear 1985, p. 23; cf. also a number of quotations along similar lines in Frank 1981, p. 63.

51. See the discussion in Sen and Grown 1987, pp. 52ff.

52. For the latter programme, cf. Linear 1985. He particularly focuses on a critique of the management of a campaign against the tse-tse fly which began in 1974.

53. Warnock 1987, p. 39.

54. See Brac de la Perière 1990.

55. In 1967–77 the Philippines increased imports of fertilisers from 208,000 to 735,000 tonnes, while in Sri Lanka fertiliser prices rose by 250% in 1974–75; see Delpeuch 1985.

56. Cf., for example, Agarwal 1988, p. 96.

57. Cf. Dumont and Cohen 1980, p. 73.

58. Buchholz 1984.

59. Cited in Delpeuch 1985.

60. Scott 1986.

61. Mitter 1986, p. 36.

62. Morgan 1978, p. 26.

# 8

# New Technologies and New
# Management Systems to the Rescue?

## The Role of Technology in Periodically Reinventing
## Capitalism

Development occurs in qualitative leaps, and it is important to see why. If we speak of capital accumulation as a 'system' this means, using the term precisely, that the different parts (economic, technological, cultural, military, and so on) fit together as a coherent whole. The system is stable over a period of time if it can adjust to absorb any distortions, but at crucial points blockages occur and the whole structure has to change. Such a change occurred at the end of the 1970s, and at the time of writing we are probably approaching another of these moments.

Not all changes of system follow the same pattern. In 1945 the blockage preventing change was swept away by a major shift in international politics. At the end of the 1970s, alterations in the technological management system played a crucial role. A new set of practices rapidly became generalised across capitalism. Electronics were introduced at all levels of the economy, from trading and banking to the organisation of production itself, and to marketing. New techniques, such as lasers, fibre optics and genetic engineering were adopted. Because of these changes the human element had to be handled in new ways. The emphasis shifted away from mass production and the factory system organised around this, to the 'Japanese' management system and its techniques for dealing both with people and production itself, which involved far more subcontracting, and much tighter controls over stocks.

In 1945, two factors had facilitated change: war had undermined the existing framework, making it easier to begin afresh; and there was a hegemonic power with the ability to impose at least partially a blueprint for the whole society. These conditions were lacking in the 1970s. In 1945, a conscious decision was taken to effect change, and special initiatives, such as the Marshall Plan and the creation of the Bretton Woods institutions, were undertaken to achieve it. At the end of the 1970s, in contrast, the change gradually emerged as the result of many different decisions made by a large number of actors.

In seeking to explain what happened in the 1970s, it is necessary to avoid the twin dangers of, on the one hand, endowing systems themselves with volition, and on the other hand, conspiracy theories. This is easier to do if we have an understanding of alienation. Value is the product of human labour power which has been sold (the material sense of alienation). The accumulation process into which the labour is drawn takes on a life of its own and becomes more real than the material act which originally produced it (the ideological aspect of alienation). A change in system comes about through trial-and-error experimentation by the decision-makers, who are increasingly institutionalised, and whose only criterion for accepting or rejecting an innovation is whether or not it is good for accumulation. It is thus the accumulation system (and not the market) which acts as a communications mechanism between the different effective actors, and it is in this way that the different elements of a new structure 'find' each other. The eventual mix in the new structure is the result of this exploratory process; it does not exist as a predetermined or ideal form that is waiting to be discovered. Nevertheless, it is not a random process, since development must make sense in terms of resolving the contradictions of the existing set-up.

Economic theory, whether establishment or radical, acknowledges a difference between individual decisions and aggregate trends. The technology issue is one of the best illustrations of this point. Businesses innovate because individuals are competing to increase profit by outproducing rivals. As more investment goes into technology, the investment in labour (which has to be exploited in order to make a profit) shrinks as a proportion of the total capital outlay, and the rate of profit declines. As capitalism seeks to maximise profit, this trend *is not the one capitalism would choose if it had a strategic overview of its interests.*

This picture changes with the arrival of imperialism and the introduction of oligopoly and the economic role of the state. It is now possible for the individual capitalist to take decisions that are at least in some sense strategic. So, paradoxically, as the organising power of capitalism increases (since it is no longer at the mercy of forces generated by its aggregate trends) its dynamism may decline, because the pursuit of profit can now lead to a policy of limiting technical innovation.

It is, however, possible to envisage a strategic choice in favour of technical change under certain conditions. I do not believe that this comes about through 'grand' strategy in the sense of leaping immediately to what might be, according to a theoretical formulation of capitalism's long-term interests, an ideal outcome. Instead, the logic of capital accumulation leads to a series of intermediate stages in which the decisions still have a lower-level strategic character, but need to make sense in terms of immediate profitability. The motivation is not, in a narrow sense, economic, but rather social. Change is not the result of an intellectual understanding that a given structure has in some abstract sense become 'out of date'; instead, it is produced by the struggles which it can no longer contain. To be viable, a new structure should be able not only to repress such struggles more effectively, but also to co-opt their acceptable aspects into its own vocabulary.

But first, in what sense had the existing accumulation system become out of date by the 1970s?

## Why a Technological Revolution Made Sense in the 1970s

Accumulation can take two fundamental forms: firstly, money capital, and secondly, fixed capital (embodied in machinery and so on). Both forms may be affected by 'over-accumulation'. In the case of fixed capital, this happens when there is no scope left for the expansion of the old industries. Industries affected in the 1970s were those which had constituted the growth-poles of the former accumulation model. Particularly significant was the contraction in demand for steel, since steel-consuming sectors, such as car manufacturing, consumer goods and the construction industry, had been the growth sectors of the old model. So the structural weakness of demand for steel reflected, in Yachir's words, 'the crisis of the accumulation model on which the world capitalist economy was based since the War'.[1]

The manufacturers' initial reponse to the crisis made the situation worse, for, in an attempt to counterbalance shrinking profits through economies of scale, they increased productive capacity in what were already doomed sectors. This was the case with the US chemicals industry, where 'because of the several-year-long planning and construction period for new chemical plants, large-scale state-of-the-art plants, designed to achieve economies of scale and maintain or increase market share, continued to be brought on line even when company officials recognised that demand had fallen'.[2] Once investors become aware of the over-accumulation in fixed capital, they stop putting their money into creating even more productive capacity, and this, in its turn, leads to over-accumulation of money capital.[3]

The economy is in crisis. And there is now a very good reason for revolutionising both the products and the way they are produced, for only a new range of products will provide a new outlet for investment.

Imperialism theory had cast doubt on the idea that capitalism would be affected in an absolute sense by underconsumption, that is by some inability to expand reproduction within its own frontiers. But I would argue that it is perfectly possible for a form of underconsumption to arise at times of structural crisis. It is expressed in a surplus of money capital which is in fact the reflection of over-accumulation of fixed capital: because there is too much productive capacity, or the wrong sort of productive capacity, the money cannot be invested profitably.

I will consider first a single-country model of what was happening in the 1970s. According to this model, the problem can be summarised in the following way: within Northern economies, capital's immediate problem was a combination of, on the one hand, over-accumulation in physical productive capacity of old industries which were not going anywhere, and on the other, the favourable bargaining position of metropolitan labour under conditions of full employment.

Within this framework, the solution would be: first, to create new products so as to remove the structural stagnancy of physically embodied accumulation; and second, to introduce labour-saving technology that would destroy labour security, and thus pave the way for a return to profitability. However, capital is incapable of moving directly to implement this solution. Kozo Uno has produced a model which can help us in part to understand the indirect route that is taken.[4] During a growth phase, capital can accumulate 'extensively' by drawing in more and more labour, and the working class can bring about a rise in the value of labour power.[5] However, once this phase of extensive accumulation is completed, there is an opportunity to revolutionise the production process itself in order to reconstitute the reserve army. What happens in practice, according to this model, is that a rise in wages and the value of labour power brings about a fall in the rate of profit, and capital is then temporarily withdrawn from circulation, producing the symptoms of crisis. In the ensuing depression there is an opportunity for revolutionising the production process, thus renewing the basis for the existence of a reserve of unemployed. This reserve in fact already exists because of what seems to be a merely cyclical downturn, but, in fact, the unemployment has now become structural, and the process of extensive accumulation begins anew.

This model is useful up to a point in illuminating what happened in the North. It helps to explain why the unemployment which the new technology serves to create must nevertheless be allowed to arise before the introduction of this technology. It makes it clear that, if it were not for this tortuous route, the resistance from labour would be difficult to overcome. And it also shows how low-level strategic choices by capital indirectly result in a much more radical system-change.

There is, however, another dimension, which this model does not address: in the concrete situation of the end of the 1970s, the technical and managerial features of the new long cycle are such that, *however fully it develops its potential*, this is unlikely to be expressed in full employment. Before examining this, however, we must first expand our frame of reference by incorporating the North–South dimension. The indirect nature of the transition between long cycles will now appear under a new light.

## Illusions of Developing Countries During the Transition to the New Structure of Global Accumulation

Part of the capital that leaked away from productive investment in the North in the 1970s flowed to the South (we will examine what happened to the other part in a moment). In the period 1960–73 the growth of direct investment to developing countries had been slower than that to developed countries, and the trend became even more marked after 1968. However, the trend suddenly reversed in the period 1973–78,[6] with proportionally more direct investment going to developing countries. It would be simplistic to create an image of disgruntled Northern investors pulling cash directly out of local industries and putting it into the South. It was more a case of new capital markets fuelled from a number of sources. But the fact remains that this investment would have occurred in the North if the conditions there had been attractive, but they were not, so the South temporarily benefited.

There was a great increase in the purchase of 'turnkey' (complete) industrial plant by Southern would-be developers. To say that the North was offloading its surplus money capital and using it to finance the sales of its unwanted embodied capital (industrial plant) would again be an over-simplification, but nevertheless the underlying point is true. Quite simply, the capital was turned into loans to finance the purchase by the South of plant that was surplus to requirements in the capitalist countries and was implicitly outdated (in terms of the technological evolution of the productive process which was about to occur as a result of the structural impasse in the capitalist system).

At the time, however, it seemed that the new frontier of development was shifting to the LDCs. It appeared that the trend which had, as we saw, characterised the Keynesian era overall, whereby the industrial countries invested mainly in each other, had come to an end.

Although the solution was neat, in the sense of being coherent and self-reinforcing from central capital's point of view, it was not orchestrated through a grand plan (for example, decisions to lend money by financial institutions were notoriously haphazard). So there *was* a risk of it getting out of hand, particularly since capital flows coincided with a militant third-world movement. But this could be countered by controlling technology. So in addition to the domestic argument I have just outlined, there was a North–South argument in favour of re-technologising the North. If it could reassert its technological dominance, the North would once again be in the favourable position of having to invest in the South only when it was advantageous to do so.

Earlier 'product cycle' theories had implied that complete industries – such as textiles and footwear, historically associated with early 'stages' in industrial development – could be handed down to the South, like cast-off clothes to poor relatives. This is very much like the optimistic reading of imperialism, which implies that it just cannot help spreading. Often attributed to Raymond Vernon, product-cycle theory was anticipated to some extent by Japanese thinking, and the Japanese certainly developed a version of the theory which was particularly relevant to the Asian NIC experience. A good example is the writing of Kojima in the late 1970s.[7] He put forward the following cycle: first, an industrialised country carves out a niche for a product which it exports; then it seeks to use foreign direct investment (FDI) as a way of producing abroad for local markets, and then the technology is standardised. So a developing country which began by importing the product is then able to produce it domestically for its own market; at a particular point, the developing country is able to build comparative advantage on the basis of its factor proportions (i.e. cheap labour), so that it can then export the product to the country which originated the process; by then, however, that country will have undertaken the necessary structural adjustment to enable it to switch to producing something else.[8]

It should be noted that this theory establishes a rationale for the notorious concept of structural adjustment, in that it allows for the dismantling of trade barriers in the South and suggests that industries where the South enjoys 'comparative advantage' will emerge. However, IMF–World Bank efforts to sweeten the pill of structural adjustment by suggesting that it will by itself lead to technology-diffusion are quite specious. The Japanese idea of technology-diffusion is definitely not premised on *laissez-faire*; it is very much a doctrine for managing the international economy, expressed strategically in the flying-geese idea, which means *deliberately* hiving off industries to the South as the advanced countries move on to a higher level. At the beginning of the 1970s, Japanese officials were preaching this to the rest of the industrial world. For example, the Vice-Minister in charge of international trade and industry declared to an OECD meeting in 1970 that it was logical for an advanced country to abandon step-by-step some of its sectors to other countries as its own industry became more sophisticated.[9]

Clearly, this argument is, first and foremost, a way of defending Japanese interests. Even at this level, though, its logic is questionable, particularly when one comes to consider the difficult relationship between the product cycle on the one hand, and long cycles of the capitalist economy on the other. Before we can consider this, however, we need to realise that there is a crucial weakness in product-cycle theory in general; namely, the assumption that *complete industries* would be transferred to the South.

It was not difficult for the North to prevent this dangerous new development, because new technology suddenly came up with a way out, but it is important to recognise that the pressures behind the search for a solution were political. Opinion in the North had become worried about deindustrialisation. This was used as a convenient way of uniting different classes behind patriotic slogans. The US trade union federation AFL–CIO alleged in 1973 that 'The multinational has not only declared war on the jobs of American workers, but on the traditional concept of Americanism.'[10] Once the new technology arrived at the end of the decade, political leaders found they could play the patriotic card in a different way: they claimed that, as long as the working class accepted the new technology (with everything this implied in terms of losing the positions they had painstakingly negotiated within the old management systems), it would be possible to avoid deindustrialisation. Shortly after President Mitterrand's election in France, his adviser on industrial policy said in an interview: 'You can make shoes in old factories using out-of-date machines and traditional methods. Or you can use computer design, advanced numerical-controlled machine tools and modern methods. If you do the latter you can be competitive in France.'[11] This is obviously a serious rebuttal of the flying geese theory, with its idea that whole industries could migrate to the third world.

In some respects, it is perfectly true that Northern capitalism was investing to re-technologise the old industries in order to hang on to them, and since this combined with the goal of smashing working-class organisation, the attractiveness for capital is clear. Britain witnessed a massive investment in new technology in the textiles industry in the period after the recession of 1980–81, when there were huge job losses. In 1983–88, £5 billion was invested in new equipment.[12]

The result was that not only did the North not lose these industries – which, according to product-cycle theory should have gone to the South – but the leakage of capital was also stemmed since it was now possible to invest in the industrial countries again. So, in two complementary ways, the 'spreading' scenario was suddenly halted.

It should be emphasised that this does not imply a reversion to nationalistic or closed-economy solutions, since a major feature that emerged during this period was the growing interdependence of the North as a whole. Different studies confirm a significant rise in 'intra-core' investment (that is, investment between the core countries) in the 1980s.[13] Even Japan, which had pioneered the 'flying geese' model of shifting industries to the South, switched investment to the North during this period. Japan sent 57 per cent of its direct investments to developing countries in 1975, but only 33 per cent in 1986, and by 1988 almost half of Japanese investment went to the USA.[14] I will explore the implications of this for North-North relations later. The point to emphasise here is that the temporary 'underconsumption' associated with the crisis proper was reversed in the 1980s.

But, although there is some truth in this 'bringing it all back home' scenario, it does not give an accurate overall picture. Although the North avoided losing *complete* industries, it was quite happy to send *part* of an industry to the third world. What was crucial was to hang on to the controlling part of the productive process and export the rest.

Empirically, TNCs would naturally seek to do this.[15] But we have to understand the strategy's basis in theoretical terms. The key concept in industrial organisation is the division of labour. From the early period of industrial capitalism it was perceived, at a national-economy level, that cheaper labour – for example according to gender determinations – should be used for certain parts of the productive process. In their important analysis (written prior to the restructuring of the early 1980s), Fröbel, Heinrichs and Kreye trace this principle to the nineteenth-century English writer Babbage, before arguing that the post-1945 era created conditions for the same thing to happen at an international level, which it did at the beginning of the 1960s.[16]

This means that, instead of industries existing as self-contained entities (which could be recycled to other countries) they can be fragmented, and only the labour-intensive parts of them exported to the South. Following this line of argument, I believe that, with the new set of conditions that came in at the end of the 1970s – the new technology plus the ending of the Keynesian full-employment regime in the North – internationalisation took a further leap, which was the final nail in the coffin of the product-cycle idea. Let me explain.

Despite the continuity, the new technology and management systems that were introduced at the end of the 1970s were not merely a prolongation of earlier trends; there was a major qualitative element. In a way, imperialism had until then been treating the South as a sort of safety valve, which could be used to stop the centre itself from developing in unpredictable ways. In the period of classic imperialism, this safety valve took the form of the export of capital. In a more modern phase of imperialism, this was supplemented by the export of productive capacity.

Although the export of productive capacity was a radical change – capitalism was finally breaking away from the old mercantilist approach of deliberately restricting colonial industrialisation – it still had (in its 1960s–70s form) a conservative aspect, in that it made it possible to retain an older form of exploitation: if profits could still be realised on the basis of abundant, under-remunerated labour in the South, capital could avoid the uncertainties of a technical revolution which would destabilise the Keynesian full-employment regime in the North.

## Towards a 'New International Division of Labour'?

But in the late 1970s the North–South relationship began to operate in a new way: it now acted to stimulate technical innovation, rather than to prevent it. Part of the reason for this change was the TNCs' determination to undermine the third-world élites' strategy of using producers' organisations to force a new share-out of profit that was more favourable to them. So the TNCs began to look for new technological substitutes for the old commodities, as with the use of fibre optics instead of copper in some applications, and the synthetic replacement for cocoa butter. But more fundamentally, the new technology became a way of keeping overall control of industry in the North's hands. This could be achieved, firstly, if those parts of a given process in which there is a higher technological component remained in the North; and secondly, if the communications aspects of the new technology permitted the orchestration of a global productive process to the North's advantage.

While the 'new international division of labour' theory performed a valuable service, notably in revealing the weaknesses of the product-cycle idea, we must beware of assuming that capitalism has in any general sense gradually become more international. It was international from the beginning:

notably, the racial divisions in the international economy were established in the early period of capitalism, in the sense that the capitalist firm always exploits labour from groups of people which are seen by society as 'inferior'. The notion of an 'original racism' within capitalism is of course compatible with the idea of progress within capitalist development, according to which it gradually becomes purer. It is possible, as Greenberg has attempted, to classify the different images of how the capitalist firm addresses the 'race' issue:[17] the 'optimistic' view associated with 'modernisation' is that, while capital is not philanthropic, the very pursuit of profit will oblige businesses to sweep away irrational barriers which stand in the way of maximising profit. An intermediate assumption is that, even though in an ideal world businesses would behave in the above manner, in the real world they 'accommodate' to existing stratifications. The third image sees 'racial' elements as fundamental to capitalism.

Now, in a broad sense, my argument is closest to the third of these propositions, but this does not mean that the racism within capitalism cannot change; on the contrary, it can 'develop' so that new ways of exploiting the out-groups are found. The weakness of the Fröbel model is that it neglects this long-term historical dimension for the stratification of labour. In its more recent phases, capital is 'modernised' not in the sense that it progressively removes the old labour divisions, but that it finds new technical ways of exploiting them.

## The Capitalist Firm: Growing or Shrinking?

My earlier argument implies the existence of three sets of boundaries within the capitalist IPE: first, there are the boundaries of the 'national' economy (though different developmental strategies relate to these in positive or negative ways, they are always an important point of reference); second is the North–South 'colour line'; and the third is the frontier between the formal (monetarised, waged) economy and its informal hinterland.

Firms have evolved in such a way that they can take advantage of this terrain, manoeuvring across the different boundaries in such a way as to maximise economic benefit. Under imperialism a new phase of concentration began through which firms swept more and more activity under their direct control. If the development of capitalism were straightforwardly unilinear, concentration and monopoly would simply increase. But this has not been the case. What we have seen instead is an increasing concentration in the effective power of corporations without a concomitant growth in their size. There are two aspects to this.

THE DESTRUCTIVE PROCESS IN RESISTING CONCENTRATION   By the end of the 1970s, firms had got locked into a downward spiral: measures to combat the falling rate of profit - increasing the mass of profit through economies of scale - had stimulated concentration, which in turn had strength-ened monopoly, thereby inhibiting the competition that normally drives technical innovation. The result, it seemed, would be a stagnant economy with over-accumulation of fixed capital, low profitability and little innovatory change. There was clearly a conflict between the developmental logic of capitalism and the interests of accumulation, and the question was how this conflict could be resolved. Not all the contradictions within capitalism *can* be resolved, but in this case a solution was found. It worked as follows.

During this period, speculative capital had become increasingly important relative to industrial, and this began to limit the process of concentration. Conventionally, company takeovers are instruments for *increasing* concentration, but in this period they had in fact the opposite effect. Speculative capital launched raids (hostile takeovers) to dismember companies. It raised huge amounts in 'junk bonds' to smash conglomerates, dispose of the pieces and realise a rapid return.[18] This peculiar phenomenon was possible because of the over-accumulated money capital built up during the crisis: although some of it had been absorbed by the North re-investing in its own productive base in the 1980s, a lot was also channelled into fuelling an essentially destructive process.

Predators preyed on the vulnerable in this Darwinian struggle for survival. Although these raids were dominant during a relatively short period, they had a permanent impact, in that they favoured parasitic capital, which was rewarded not just by direct profits and high interest rates, but by social pacts that brought them a larger share of consumption. The effects are still visible today.

THE CONSTRUCTIVE ELEMENT: A NEW STRATEGY FOR THE FIRM
The second aspect is the more positive, in that capitalism made a conscious decision to advance into new areas of industrial organisation, in which 'leaner' firms could be more efficient. From the standpoint of capitalist profitability, the shrinking firm is a creative and forward-looking strategy.

Establishment free-market economics regards the firm as a negation of the market: 'the distinguishing mark of the firm is the supercession of the price mechanism', and the firm will grow 'until the marginal costs of the rational organisation of production overtake the marginal benefits of elimin-ating the market'.[19]

This is partly useful and partly confusing. The useful aspect is that it points us towards considering the possibility that there is a theoretical optimum size for the firm. Imperialism theory implies that the firm grows because crises enable bigger companies to absorb or eliminate rivals. This would acquire a momentum of its own which is unlikely to respect any optimal limitations, and capitalism would suffer as a result. If it were possible to resolve this by cutting the size down again, an efficiency gain would result. Part of this process was the result of an objective force – the impact of speculative capital – referred to above, but there was also a subjective element, a new philosophy of the firm.

But at this point the free-market-based theory of firms ceases to be helpful. The reality is not a spontaneously existing universe of floating free-market actors which begins as soon as we step outside the firm. On the contrary, control over the area beyond the boundary of formal organisation is every bit as important as control over what happens within it. The market is itself organised, even 'manufactured'. The crucial thing is to exploit labour without paying its full cost, which can mean shifting work to a sector where many of the conditions of production are treated as the individual responsibility of the workers themselves.

We are now much closer to a realistic, concrete model. The optimum size of the firm is not static, because it depends on the firm's ability to organise the productive process. And the organisation of the productive process is conducted not only within the firm but also outside it. The management decisions are influenced in a crucial way by the state of technology. It may seem on the surface as if a process is being organised, but fundamentally what is occurring is the organisation of labour. It would be a mistake to assume that more sophisticated means of control would serve the purpose of helping the firm to become larger. If this were the case, increases in management efficiency would be positively related to an increase in the size of the firm. But often the exact opposite is the case. The main efficiency gains may be made by exploiting the informal/peripheral economy, and if this is so, it would be an admission of defeat to carry on with a large firm, an admission that technological/management development was not yet strong enough to exploit informal workers and that the firm only knew how to operate by making itself fully responsible for a large number of workers. Once the technological conditions were right, an expansion of the exploitative tentacles of transnational capital would be perfectly compatible with the shrinkage of the formal firm, indeed would probably require it.

The essence of the new economic system is that it takes hold of the core–periphery distinction (which had always existed in terms of 'racially' and gender-determined labour) and generalises this in a much more structured form by encouraging the formation – in the outer space beyond the firm – of a constellation of small firms or self-employed individuals which are not its direct responsibility.

There is a political aspect to all this. Traditionally, the large corporation controlled several workforces and could use divide-and-rule tactics, and it has been argued that this was a major factor in the original dynamic that led to TNC formation.[20] However, the divide-and-rule potential of playing off the core firm against the informal periphery is probably even greater. The old dualities now serve as pattern for a much wider informalisation of labour, and traditional working-class structures, generally blind to 'race'–gender impurities, are ill-equipped to meet the challenge.[21]

There are risks for capital, too. It extricated itself from the crisis by generalising the informal economy and extending it to a range of workers outside the traditional gender and 'race' determinations. As a result, the old divisions have become confused, which could create problems in the future. For the moment, however, there are vast new openings for profitability. In order to tap these, a new management doctrine has been elaborated. I will now consider in more detail how this relates to labour.

## A New Approach to Controlling Labour

The immediate logic propelling companies to adopt a new way of managing labour can be summarised as follows.

Under the traditional system of production-line manufacturing, alienation and full employment came together as a dangerous cocktail. Strikes could bring production to a halt, and even boredom often gave rise to informal sabotage. The dangers of the old system meant that companies had good reason to look for a change in organisation. This was the 'negative' stimulus.

But there was also a 'positive' stimulus. The post-war system had been so radical in some respects that it had been able to be lazy in others. On the management front, for instance, it had simply carried forward earlier American practices. Because of the inherent weaknesses of those practices, there was a tremendous potential for innovation. Let me explain why.

Capitalism has always developed its organisation of industry by means of a division of labour at various levels. One of the most basic is the division within the workplace. American management theory, particularly that associated with Frederick W. Taylor in the last years of the nineteenth century, claimed to take this to a new peak, to the status of a science in its own right. Under the Taylor system, the division of labour was developed to the point of monitoring the precise way in which the worker carried out highly fragmented and monotonous tasks. Its specific technological basis was the production line, with tasks laid out along it.

Although the Taylor system claimed to be more efficient in some abstract sense, its main advantage, as Braverman has pointed out, was that it exploited labour more effectively.[22] While this point is valid, Braverman's critique is inadequate, for, by claiming that scientific *management* is unscientific, it assumes that the rest of production technology is scientific, in the sense of being pure and neutral. The feminist critique of science has shown this to be untrue.[23] Even with respect to basic research, the appearance of being scientific is a reflection of the attempt by industrial (capitalist) society to dispense with humanity's links with nature. Under capitalism, this form of alienation is probably the fundamental precondition for technology to become 'rational', that is, subjectless. So 'rationality' is defined so as to exclude any goal other than accumulation itself. It is a way of appropriating knowledge from the direct producers and placing it in a realm to which they can have no access, thereby facilitating control over their labour. In this sense Taylorist management (which attempts to place control even of the worker's own gestures in the hands of a specialist staff) should not be seen as a misleading attempt to appropriate the 'scientific' label, but as a logical (and in its own terms legitimate) extension of the whole industrial–capitalist approach to science. Thus the technology of production itself and management technique itself have to be seen as two closely related parts of a whole.

Taylorism seems to be the end-point of a historical development whereby labour becomes progressively more mechanical, more severed from the conscious element. So where can the organisation of labour go from here?

To understand the next step, it is necessary to understand that the most fundamental trend within labour organisation under capitalism has not been the mechanisation of labour, but rather its homogenisation. It might at first sight appear that the division of labour would lead to increasing specialisation, but clearly this is not the case. Instead, labour becomes uniform, indeterminate, able to be applied to any task. Thus far, the critique of Braverman by Bahr is helpful.[24]

Now, in a certain sense the Taylor system, which in its caricature form has a worker monotonously repeating the same task, is a barrier in the way of the further uniformisation of labour. A flexible system, on the other hand, would permit the realisation of the potential of indeterminate human labour in a new way. So the crushing of shopfloor initiative, which seems an inexorable, unilinear trend, is no longer the way forward for capitalism. It becomes clear that, on the contrary, a flexible system which allows for initiative can exploit the human potential in a much more comprehensive way than Taylorism permitted.

But we also have to go further than the critics of Braverman, and scrutinise the assumption of homogenisation. A form of capitalist development which, by making labour uniform, frees people from the personal determinants of servitude (colour, sex), might provide a positive side to alienation! But this does not happen, for the formation of abstract equivalents operates only within the boundary of 'pure', core capitalism. The Taylorist factory system always co-existed with more 'primitive' forms of production.[25] This is true even within the industrial countries (women's labour in the service sector, the construction industry), but even more so in the South, where labour-intensive methods had already been actively promoted through the 'development' models examined earlier in the book.

The problem was that, for the more 'primitive' forms of production to be properly exploited, the core needed to be organised effectively. By the 1970s Taylorism was becoming inefficient for this purpose. An alternative did not have to be invented from scratch, however. Some American management specialists had already recognised the alienating and initiative-suppressing features of Taylorism, and their ideas, ignored at home, were influential in Japan.

At this stage, a change in management can be regarded as the logical next step forward for capitalism. The innovations occurred in Japan because at the time it was at the leading edge of capitalist development.[26] But the new approach could not become generalised while Taylorism was integrated into a mutually interdependent system of international political economy, since it was impossible to ditch one part of the system while the whole was still functioning. However, when a structural crisis erupted, all capitalist interests were forced to rethink the whole system.

Although this explanation is useful up to a point, it is nevertheless insufficient, as it tends to imply some unilinear evolution towards 'higher' forms of management. Before we can take the next step in the argument, we need to look carefully at the role of Japan.

## Japan's Role in the Structural Shift

The 'Japanese' system was built on a mode of social–industrial organisation which, in fact, had always been significantly different from Taylorism. The influence of society over the core workforce was all-pervading. Market relations even penetrated the factory. Those within the core firm were subjected to a special form of workplace-based social control: privileged to be part of the core, they did not want to lose this status and sink into the underprivileged mass who worked in insecure conditions and provided low-cost inputs into the main productive process. These patterns obviously existed in other capitalist countries, but they were less systematic, particularly when the majority of the workers were nationals of the country they were working in. These conditions had allowed Japan to develop a far more flexible mode of social–industrial organisation: in the 1980s, 46 per cent of Japanese industrial workers were employed in small factories with less than 50 workers. Workers in small factories earned much less: people employed in enterprises with 1–9 workers earned 33.8 per cent of the wage of workers in the largest companies, and those in enterprises of 10–49 workers earned 54.8 per cent.[27] The social provisions in the larger companies would make the effective difference even larger.

The crucial characteristic of this system is the way large firms subcontract smaller ones. According to one study, Toyota alone has 47,000 small firms working for it.[28] Moreover, the subcontracting system is itself hierarchised: according to another study, the production system of each automobile manufacturer involves on average 171 firms in the first layer, 4,700 in the second layer and 31,600 in the third.[29]

The Japanese 'tradition' is in fact a fairly recent invention,[30] and it is interesting to see how it arose. In contrast with Europe, where feudalism had to be destroyed to permit a new system to emerge, nineteenth-century Japan had to confront an already present world capitalism which was restricting its development. An effective defensive measure was to strengthen tradition, and in the process reinvent it. Thus elements of feudalism – paternalism, hierarchy – were incorporated into the new model.

Throughout its evolution, really-existing capitalism has always contained elements of 'impurity', which play an essential role. This does not occur through a linear succession of phases. At different stages, capitalism has had different mixes of old and new exploitation, for at a crisis point capitalism is just as likely to dredge some strategies out of the past as it is to invent something 'modern'. Just as an element of slavery was useful at one stage in capitalist history, so hierarchy is useful today, and Japan was in a strong position to serve as a jumping-off point for the incorporation of these hierarchical elements into modern capitalist systems elsewhere. The specificities of Japan's historical legacy came together with Japan's status as the most dynamic capitalist country to produce the 'Japanese model'. Once the conditions were in place, the new system coalesced quite rapidly around some internationalised 'best practice'.

The restructuring of the capitalist centre is the crucial issue in the IPE, not because the main source of profit is necessarily there, but because, if the centre is weak, there might be openings for Southern national strategies to draw some kind of monopoly rents for their cheap labour. It thus becomes important to capture part of the core–periphery relationship within the centre. The way found to achieve this was to make the market itself the mediator of hierarchical relationships. In this way, the liberalising face of capitalism, which was supposed to have abolished servitude, has emerged as a key way of entrenching it.

## Seeking to Avoid the Falling Rate of Profit

The model outlined earlier, according to which capital simply introduces new technology in order to be able to accumulate extensively without putting labour in a favourable position, fails to reflect the qualitative nature of the technology in question.

The postwar Keynesian long cycle was wedded to 'full employment' as an integrated solution to the twin problems of, first, dealing with left-wing movements motivated by poverty and unemployment, and, second, generating a mass market to propel the conversion of capitalism away from its heavy-industrial/infrastructural phase, into one of consumer production. But this model, with its full employment, inhibited technical innovation, and in this sense a systemic imperative reinforced the more obvious effect of oligopoly. It was important to find an alternative systemic imperative which could override this effect. In a sense, 'pure' research, and above all the arms industry, kept up the impetus of technical innovation which mainstream industry failed to provide. All the 'raw materials' of a technological revolution were therefore waiting in the wings. It could not be introduced as a single variable, since long cycles reflect a mutual systemic 'understanding' between several parameters.

The technological revolution could occur only when conditions were ripe for systemic change which could permanently replace labour.

Subjectively, the rate of profit provided an important focus. Establishment studies in America showed that it was falling, and in the official propaganda the problem was presented as one of 'productivity'.[31] At first sight this seems strange, because measures to increase productivity (whereby a single worker would use more equipment) would further decrease the rate of profit. It is true that, at a strategic level, it is also important to consider the balance of class power: the advantages to capital of the labour insecurity resulting from structural unemployment cannot be measured simply in economistic terms, and the right-wing Northern governments of the 1980s acted politically in this sense. However, this does not fully explain why individual capitalist companies took the decision to introduce the technological revolution. To understand this, the specificity of the new technology must be considered.

The more obvious aspect is that new technology could offset the rate-of-profit decline by permitting savings on fixed capital. The new systems replace the simple pursuit of economies of scale with a strategy whereby the size of 'batches' is determined by a trade-off between economies of scale and the diseconomies caused by a lot of capital being tied up in stocks. This requires the use of information technology in monitoring stocks and linking them up with orders.[32] At the same time, machines wear out less slowly (for sensors can capture information and use this to modify feed rate, reducing wear and thus depreciation). Even more important is the adaptability of the machines themselves; as they can be programmed to carry out different tasks, they need not be written off when production lines change. Once again, this development has been implied within capitalism for some time,[33] but its implementation required not only microprocessors, but a whole complex of socio-political factors.

This is the aspect of technological change which would be most readily admitted by capital itself: it reinforces the idea of technological determinism which seemingly reduces the scope for human decisions. But although the above argument is, within its limitations, true, it also masks a much more important aspect: technology's role in controlling labour. The term 'means of production' conjures up an image of expensive machines. This is partly accurate (robotics etc.), but an important aspect of IT within the new means of production is its role in controlling labour. Software does not have the same relation to productive technique as pure science: it is a new intermediate level specifically applied to the management and control of production. It commoditises the thinking element of the productive system far more than was possible under any earlier regime, the value attributed to it reflecting not just the labour going into training the IT specialist, but the labour which, thanks to the software, the latter now has the power to control.

## 'Flexibility' and the Control of Labour

The developmental significance of flexibility is enormous: it shows that capitalism recognises that its strength lies precisely in its non-linearity. But capitalism needs to conceal the fact that it has borrowed elements from the past. The trick is amalgamating the technological and human aspects, to present something called 'flexibility' as an unstoppable objective trend to which everything human should be subordinated.

The term 'flexibility' means one thing to workers in the core firm, and another to those in the informal economy outside it. In the first case, which we will now examine in some detail, it is functional, meaning that people are expected to be adaptable to different tasks. Under this heading, multi-skilling can be viewed as a further extension of the conversion of concrete into abstract labour, detached from a specific product. At the same time, the Taylorist distinction between the thinking process and the task of labour is apparently dissolved. Workers are themselves given 'responsibility', notably for quality control, which is shifted to the sphere of production itself.

The new systems pay apparent respect to initiative. Theoretically, this is a good solution for capitalism, because it unleashes new potential for profitability, by both exploiting the thinking element in labour and countering the alienation characteristic of Taylorism. However, the real effectiveness of this is questionable. Workers often approach corporate culture, such as the training they are given in problem-solving techniques, in a cynical and minimalist spirit. The demoralisation that comes from the threat of redundancy probably outweighs the theoretical possibility that alienation may be reduced through increased scope for initiative. What in practice happens is that the new systems become most effective as control mechanisms. The new systems are in their own way just as restricting as Taylorism. The old production-line system is replaced by the policing of time. In the Just In Time (JIT) system, goods are produced or circulated around the factory at exactly the moment they are needed.[34] This is presented as a rational control over materials, but in reality it controls the workforce in a new way.

'Flexibility' is also used to break down the demarcation between jobs, defended by the unions, which leaves management in control of the allocation of tasks and promotion criteria. With the introduction of flexibility, the old union structures have been subjected to a massive attack. What has replaced them is a system which, according to some studies, was created not in response to a strictly productive rationale, but to construct 'good workers'. A study of women workers in the Irish electronics industry (where certain aspects of 'Japanese' techniques are applied by US firms) revealed the existence of a vast number of supervisory staff who cannot be considered functional in production terms, but instead serve firstly to 'evaluate' workers, and secondly to provide a justification for a number of superior levels into which they can aspire eventually to be integrated.[35] The prospect of promotion perhaps provides an intra-firm equivalent of the illusion of social mobility characteristic of 'democratic' capitalism.

The desire of capitalists to undermine unions is nothing new, and the apparently more 'democratic' organisation of the firm is simply the most recent strategy for doing this.[36] But by abandoning that aspect of union power which, under the old dispensation, was functional to capitalism itself, the new system represents a radical change in a deeper sense. The existence of a 'parallel' economy is a well-established part of European industrial economies,[37] but the basis of this dualism was typically a core organised around institutionalised union power. During the former long cycle, the corporate role of unions was viewed by many analysts as the blueprint for its future for the clear economic reason that it allowed for more favourable solutions to the trade-off between employment, inflation and real incomes than would have been possible under conditions of decentralised bargaining. Analysts are now having to rethink these assumptions,[38] since today's dominant ideology (monetarism) denies the need for such a trade-off.

Apart from discovering new sources of value in exploiting the core workforce in a new way, the challenge for capitalism is to consolidate the core strongly enough, so that the falling rate of profit can be offset by finding a new way of exploiting labour-intensive production in other areas of the economy. Within the workforce outside the core, we therefore come to the second form of flexibility, which is numerical: people can be thrown into the wilderness or recruited back into jobs according to the state of orders. Less-skilled and marginal workers tend to be laid off according to fluctuations in demand, and in the US women suffer most from this.[39]

The core workforce itself is privileged, but has to accept a strong discipline or risk losing this status. Given the situation of structural unemployment in the centre, it is possible to screen applicants, not so much for their formal qualifications as for their attitude. When it set up a new plant in Britain (at Burnside in Derbyshire), Toyota had 20,000 applications for 400 posts. The selection procedure stretched over six months, with candidates being assessed for their commitment, orientation, behaviour, and so on, for sixteen hours.[40] And there are always plenty of applicants. In January 1995, an unconfirmed rumour that General Motors would be taking on new workers at its factory in Toronto in Canada led to a modern 'gold rush', with about 15,000 people arriving, some from all over the country and many spending the night outside in temperatures of 20 degrees below zero.[41] This desperation is a product of the perceived impermeability of the boundary between formal and informal economies. It looks very much like a contemporary expression of the boundary between official society and those excluded from it.

In a certain sense the imperative to deploy and discard labour is nothing new. As Cohen points out, some economists were already recommending this during the Keynesian period.[42] But it is important to realise that capitalism cannot pick and mix strategies. The Keynesian solution was a coherent whole, with high consumption of undifferentiated products, a particular factory system to suit, and a political set-up in which labour movements built their strategies on the expectation of transforming some of the benefits of increasing productivity into added consumer power. Before labour flexibility could be introduced, the whole system had to change.

## Notes

1. Yachir 1988, p. 13.

2. Baily and Chakrabarti 1988, pp. 60–62.

3. If an expanded volume of capital produces a smaller surplus than it did in the previous cycle, this could be seen as leading to an overproduction of capital itself; cf. 'The Current Crisis, a Crisis for Over-Production of Capital', *Social Relations* (Milan) March 1992.

4. See Uno 1977, especially pp. 53, 88.

5. It is worth noting that Sweezy speaks simply of the rise of wages in this context (Sweezy 1968), but it would be better to speak of the value of labour power; this is historically determined and thus poses more of a threat to the system in the sense that, once established, it would have a certain historical tenacity and resistance to being clawed back by employers.

6. Marcussen and Torp 1982, p. 25.

7. The Japanese form of product-cycle theory is closely related to the issue of regional integration, of which Kojima himself was an influential advocate. We will take up this aspect of the question in the next chapter.

8. Kojima 1977.

9. Quoted in Mureau 1989, p. 127.

10. Quoted in Portes and Walton 1981, p. 149.

11. Quoted in Benson and Lloyd 1983, p. 122.

12. *Independent,* 25 February 1990.

13. Cf. Ikeda 1996, p. 49.

14. *Le Monde diplomatique*, November 1988.

15. Cf. for example, Clairmonte 1986.

16. Fröbel *et al.* 1980.

17. Cf. Greenberg 1980. While the models are well described, the substantive analysis is less useful, since this author proceeds in a rather mechanical way by dealing with the dimension within particular countries in isolation from other factors.

18. The most spectacular of these, the raid by Kohlberg, Kravis and Roberts on R.J. Reynolds and Nabisco, involved US$28 billion in junk bonds; for details of this, see Kolko 1988, pp. 76, 69.

19. Hymer 1990, pp. 10–11.

20. Cf., for example, Cowling and Sugden 1987.

21. The discourse about 'post-Fordism', though it obviously contains an element of truth, also reflects the standpoint of an orthodox labour movement suddenly waking up to an impure/informal element in capitalism that had always been there, but which they ignored.

22. Braverman 1974.

23. Cf., for example, Harding 1986.

24. Cf. Bahr 1980.

25. Robin Cohen has correctly pinpointed this at an empirical level, but needs to situate this analysis within a coherent model of capitalism and its evolution across phases.

26. According to some American theories, which we will discuss later, it had been able to focus R&D on consumer rather than military projects.

27. Oliver and Wilkinson 1988, p. 25.

28. Sumiya 1989, p. 120.

29. Dickens 1991, p. 24.

30. Cf. Takashi 1993.

31. In the United States, the rate of profit had fallen in all sectors since 1965. In 1973–79 it fell 1.85%, before stabilising itself more or less (without rising) in the period 1979–86; see Baily and Chakrabarti 1988, p. 3.

32. In a deeper sense, it may be that economies of scale are less important, as the costs of manufacturing itself shrink in proportion to R&D, distribution etc.; cf. Doz 1987.

33. Such an approach is implicit in the punched card system used in Jacquard looms, and certainly in numerically controlled machines of the 1950s.

34. The system known as Kanban is a form of JIT pioneered by Toyota, according to which components are circulated in response to specific demand.

35. Murray and Wickham 1985.

36. Thus Nissan in Britain brought worker representatives on to the company council, but by-passed the collective power of the unions by ensuring that these were not union delegates; see Dickens 1988.

37. For example in Italy nearly a quarter of manufacturing output was estimated to come from the underground or unorganised sector during the 1980s; cf. Mitter 1989, p. 21.

38. Cf., for example, Schmitter 1990.

39. Cf. Grunwald and Flamm 1985, p. 223.

40. *Guardian*, 17 December 1992.

41. *Independent*, 12 January 1995.

42. R. Cohen 1987, p. 117.

# 9

# The Role of the Capitalist Centre within the Current Phase of the International Political Economy

## Why Capitalism Re-invented the Free Market

Capitalist development as a whole was redefined after the crisis of the 1970s. One of the most important aspects was the way the capitalist centre re-organised itself so as to be able to dictate the agenda of the new period.

As I argued in the previous chapter, the shift to a new structural regime has to be explained in terms of the accommodation of the interests of many key actors, since, unlike in 1945, there was no hegemonic power or war-induced clean slate. Nevertheless economic and political leaders, including those who controlled the media, intellectuals and think-tanks co-ordinated their actions at a strategic level, at least to a certain extent. The purpose was to project a coherent vision of capitalist development to replace the old ideologies, including Keynesianism and development economics.

The fundamental ideological premise of the new developmental vision is the free market. The success of this principle would be judged not just by how accurate it was in describing reality, but also by how false it was. By this I mean that capitalist ideology needs to distort reality and to conceal the realities of exploitative relationships, in order to defuse the solidarity mechanisms of the oppressed. But it must also create the norms or identities which determine the role of the actors within the new accumulation system, and from this angle it is not enough simply to create any sort of confusion, for the distortions must seem to reflect reality and must actually serve the real needs of the new system, which requires, for instance, that economic actors be scattered and self-exploiting. The idea of the free market satisfied these different demands in the following ways.

HIDING NEW AND OLD STRUCTURES OF DOMINANCE The free market helped deflect attention away from reality, which was firstly that monopolies and speculative capital really controlled the economy, and secondly, that within a refurbished structure of domination, it was still a white-power system, despite the assertion of equal opportunity and of 'united colours'.

UNDERMINING SOLIDARITY MECHANISMS An apparent culture of opportunity was created which, in exchange for a largely fictitious promise of individual betterment, undermined solidarity movements in the third world and elsewhere.

ENCOURAGING THE CREATION OF FREE-FLOATING ECONOMIC ACTORS In the absence of solidarity mechanisms, the new hierarchical, subcontracting economy isolated countries at the international level, and individuals at the national level. In this respect, liberalism responds to the shrinking size of the firm and the rise of subcontracting relations by creating what appears to be a market, but is in reality a new form of monopoly control without direct management.

DESTROYING THE SENSE OF AN ALTERNATIVE SOCIAL PROJECT The new period put an end to the Keynesian era's shamefaced tendency to pay tribute to Soviet-style communism by plagiarising the tools of central planning. Formally, the 'end of ideology' occurred only in the post-Cold War period, but liberalism's inherent refusal to tolerate alternatives was visible to some farsighted observers in the late 1970s, long before Reagan.[1]

DESTROYING THE NOTION OF A DEBATE OVER THE LARGE-SCALE ORIENTATION OF SOCIETY Keynes had recognised that there were different equilibria into which a system could settle, opening the possibility at moments of change of a social debate to decide which was the most desirable form for the new society. This was the first such structural change in post-industrial society in which the sharing-out of work to make possible increased leisure was an issue, while the NIEO movement sought to raise the debate over development to an international level. But capitalism, determined to retain sole control of the agenda, nipped all discussion in the bud.

FINDING A MARKET FOR THE PRODUCTS OF THE NEW PRODUCTIVE SYSTEM What appears to be a choice between commodities replaces the choice between social projects. Products seem differentiated, particularly as they come from small production runs, but in reality they consist of the same components assembled in slightly different ways, which is what the new management systems require. This creates the impression that people can escape from the grey uniformity of the big agglomerations of the old solidarity systems. The state in its interventionist role is blamed for the alienation which people experience, deflecting attention away from its real cause – capital accumulation. Ironically, it is precisely the state in this role which could have stimulated debates about possible uses of the state to counteract the unbridled dominance of capital accumulation.

## A Failure of Strategic Vision

But there is something missing in all this. Keynesianism in its time had responded to similar demands; it had worked at an ideological level by creating the idea of a neutral state; and it had worked economically by creating a mass market for the kind of products capitalism wanted to sell. But it had done one thing further: it had provided capitalism itself with a strategic vision. Even though neo-liberalism was fairly effective in creating a new ideology and in moulding consumers, it may be seriously deficient in this respect.

Neo-liberalism makes some claim to provide both 'big' philosophical ideas and, with monetarism, a guide to the day-to-day conduct of the economy. But the new orthodoxy is by no means consistent. It is a hotch-potch of a number of arguments of which the following are typical:

RIGHT-WING STRUCTURALISM  This can be seen in the work of Friedrich von Hayek, an anti-communist ideologue from the 1930s who was resurrected by Thatcherism. Structuralism holds that powerful structures emerge which give significance to individual acts, even though those who are performing these acts are not conscious of this. Left-wing analysts would view this as alienating and oppressive, but for the right 'spontaneous order' is sacrosanct: 'Any desire we may have concerning the particular position of individual elements, or the relations between particular individuals or groups, could not be satisfied without upsetting the overall order.'[2] Language, a key issue in structuralism, is used as an analogy to explain the role of money, which is seen as providing the currency for communication in human economic life, which is the role played by language in society in general.[3] The all-encompassing role played by money in the overall structure emerges only through individual micro-level transactions where there is no consciousness of the grand design that emerges out of them. An international relations version of this approach was put forward at the end of the 1970s by Waltz, who draws his fundamental analogies from the field of micro-economics.[4]

THE POST-MODERN VIEW THAT FOCUSES ON DIFFERENCES RATHER THAN AGGLOMERATIONS  The predominant current in contemporary liberalism is, however, deeply hostile to structuralism, perhaps because the latter shares some concerns with the left. Modern establishment thinking prefers to ignore the left, rather than lending it credibility by attacking it, as Hayek did. The trend known as post-modernism denies the validity of large-scale generalisations about history. A representative of the old school of anti-communists, such as Walt Rostow, who specialised in propagating right-wing historical generalisations, suddenly found himself left out in the cold by the new orthodoxy, and responded with a virulent counter-attack, which makes interesting reading.[5]

TECHNOLOGICAL DETERMINISM Here the argument is that technological developments have an autonomous and decisive role in the development of society, so social organisation must either fit in efficiently with new technology, or fail. This strengthened the feeling that the new management systems had a historical inevitability, as well as leading to the view that government is a purely technical affair without room for fundamental debates about orientations.

These different elements do not really cohere at an intellectual level. A technological determinist like Toffler,[6] is clearly a 'grand' normative theorist of the kind post-modernism is supposed not to like. There is a contradiction between a writer like Daniel Bell, who had been arguing for some time that the term 'mass society' was never accurate,[7] and someone like Toffler, who implicitly believes that it was once but has now been superseded.

The theoreticians agree in practical terms on the negative agenda of beating down popular movements: all would, for different reasons, condemn labour struggles, whether as a distortion of market forces, a futile attempt to improve upon 'spontaneous order', an imposition of uniformity on really-disparate individuals and interest groups, or a barrier to technical progress. But can they provide any positive guidance to capitalism itself?

Monetarism is more of a political tool than a tool of practical economics. It is supposed to address the problem of moving capitalism into a new, steady-state phase, anticipating the 'end of history'. As we saw earlier, there was a real problem with Keynesianism, which did not explain what would happen once full employment was attained, or, more specifically, how it would handle the business cycle. In the 1950s, Milton Friedman addressed these questions without openly attacking Keynesianism, arguing that American business cycles were associated with fluctuations in money supply. He was widely interpreted as saying that the latter was the cause of the former.[8] Behind this apparently technical argument, there was a philosophical point which secretly challenged the basis of Keynesianism: it was argued that economic decisions must be depoliticised, insulated from any political pressures to increase spending at a particular time (the modern expression of this is to hand over decision-making power to the central banks). And, in a deeper sense, this argument ties in with the wider philosophical assumption that any action to better the human condition will actually make the situation worse.

Unemployment becomes inevitable. Since there is said to be friction in a market system, as not all the elements communicate smoothly with each other, there is, in the best possible circumstances, a 'natural' rate of unemployment. Any attempt to intervene to create full employment would mean committing the heresy of assuming that one can do better than the market, and would fail. In this way, whatever the rate of unemployment is at any particular time is presented as natural, just as oppressive conditions have always been presented as natural. The hidden agenda was always to transfer resources to capital. Hayek even admitted this long ago, with the justification that it makes investment possible.[9] Abandoning the goal of full employment simply provides an apparently neutral and technical argument for doing the same thing. The decline of inflation was in reality no more than a spin-off from these measures to transfer more power to capital: once they were in place, corporate interests no longer found it necessary to sustain their profits by means of oligopolistic price rises. The practical impact in the fight against inflation of limiting the money supply was quite insignificant, which severely dents monetarism's credentials.

## Is the New System Socially Coherent?

It makes sense to break down organised labour and solidarity as a *transitional* strategy, but the crucial question is whether the North can establish a coherent accumulation dynamic. There are two aspects: the strictly economic (whether or not the products which capitalism needs to sell are being consumed) and the social (whether enough people identify with the system; whether there is enough social control).

It is useful to begin by considering what Keynesianism really represented. A simplistic 'stages' model would imply a general progression away from the inequality characteristic of early industrial society, but, as Townsend's argument suggests, what really happened was that the social strata important for the consolidation of a given accumulation regime were rewarded by being permitted to consume.[10] Experience in other industrial countries seems to confirm that, while there were short phases in which income distribution became more equal, there was not the smooth progression to greater equality which a unilinear stages model would imply.[11] In the United States, the rise of average incomes readily co-existed with increased polarisation, and in fact it seems that with growth in the extremes of poverty and wealth the segment which corresponded to the average became less and less representative.[12] The 'Great Society' of the 1960s was geared more to defusing social protest for political motives than to really integrating the poor into the economy. What happened instead was that more was spent on handouts.

In this way, the 1960s provided an experience which could be used by neo-liberalism, and there is more continuity between the two periods than there seems at first sight. The new post-Keynesian political economy also seeks to reward new social groups which support it and, just as with Keynesianism, it makes sense to get these groups to consume the products they make.

In many ways, the new structure appears to work. Since mass production is no longer the basis of the physical accumulation system, consumption need not necessarily suffer if full employment is abandoned. A narrower, more segmented market can still consume the goods.

This is consistent with the marginalisation of a fairly substantial section of the population, squeezed between the decline of free services and the anti-inflation policies which benefit only those with incomes. With marginalisation, capitalism has to pay the apparently heavy financial cost of providing welfare, but this is offset by two hidden advantages: first, the financial problem can itself be used as justification for further reductions in the benefit system overall, with the excuse of targeting the most needy; second, and more important, the marginalised actually provide a vital service to capitalism (well worth the cost of maintaining their bare subsistence) by hovering as a threat over the rest of the population, persuading many of them to accept any job going. With this are created the essential conditions for a cheap-labour, flexible economy in the North, which spans the marginalised (who are forced to work under the worst conditions in a semi-legal way to eke out benefits) and many of those employed in insecure conditions in the formal economy. It is important to the North to have this kind of economy within its frontiers, for it means that the South cannot extract monopoly rents for its cheap labour and bad working conditions.

But although the system is functional, it is vulnerable in some ways, particularly if compared with the earlier system. Corporatism, which gave the organised, official labour movement a role within the mechanisms of social control, was a very sophisticated defence mechanism for capital. In the narrow economic sense, it was based on the assumption that a relationship existed between unemployment and inflation, and informed bargaining took place over the trade-off between the two. In a broader sense, it gave at least the appearance of being able to debate different social projects. The social costs of scrapping this may be much higher than the economic ones, and there are real problems in generating a sense of identity within a society when the state – and even the nation – are under attack from the new economic forces. The extreme right may thrive in a climate of marginalisation and nostalgia for the old identities. This is why the EU, which tends to be more concerned about social coherence, has put forward the Social Chapter.

Internationally, too, the stages theory of development had a powerful unifying effect, in that it told the South that if it tightened its belt for a generation, it would be rewarded with high mass consumption. It suggested that inequality might increase in the early period of industrialisation to make possible the accumulation necessary for creating heavy industry and infrastructure, but that with the transition to more consumer-based industries, inequality would decrease. The Kuznets model, which asserted this, appeared plausible.[13] It made it possible to tell the South that what they thought was imperialist exploitation was really simply the transition from one stage to another. But now, with the rise of neo-liberalism, there is no obvious replacement for stages theory. Inequality is rising again in the promised land of post-industrial society. It is now clear that mass purchasing power only increased provisionally under Keynesianism because capitalism needed a market for its mass production. The South might well ask whether what was gained was worth the sacrifice.

These contradictions are only latent at the moment, but they could rapidly become acute, particularly since the current accumulation regime is likely soon to enter its downward phase. If what happened in the late 1960s is a guide, even while the economic structure is functioning coherently, cracks are likely to appear in the social fabric.

## The International Dimension of the New Control Agenda

It was not enough for the new form of accumulation to create a viable basis within the individual capitalist economies; it also needed to organise the international system. And here, too, there were difficulties.

Part of the success of the post-1945 system, from a capitalist point of view, had been its ability to realise two major changes: it transcended great-power rivalry in favour of international regimes, and it effected the transition to neo-colonialism. But it was the very success of the system in carrying out these tasks that helps to explain why such an excellent system both could and must be changed.

I will deal with this issue from an international systems perspective in Chapter 12. The relevant issue at this point is the North–North aspect of the system.

A basic lesson to be learnt from centre–periphery analysis is that central economies dominate because they are 'complete'. This statement helps explain both the abiding relevance of centre–periphery theory and why it needs to be changed to describe the current situation. The classic formulation assumed that the central capitalist economies were individually complete. This accurately described a temporary feature, a Listian vestige which was not fundamentally challenged by the post-1945 order (although the tendencies that it unleashed ultimately implied such a challenge), because the preponderantly economic role of the state was maintained, in some respects even strengthened.

The current political economy, however, threatens to make completeness impossible at the level of the individual country. And this, in turn, begins to challenge something that has always played a very important role for capitalism, namely nationalism. We have just seen how the nation, as an idea, has been eroded internally by the collapse of corporatism and solidarity. This is being reinforced by an external attack, as growing interdependence, together with the collapse of the state's economic role, begins to 'rationalise' over-lapping economic sectors across the capitalist world as a whole, bringing them into a single international structure.

## The Trend towards Interdependence, and against Economic Nationalism

Perhaps the easiest part of the new agenda was trampling on the South; what was difficult was redefining capitalist development once it began to outstrip the familiar terrain of state-centricity.

In the 1970s the new sense of direction that capitalism needed was supplied by a new internationalised élite that was beginning to acquire a common vocabulary. This was adequate for the transitional period, when a new system was created, which began to unleash new forces, notably corporate interests without definite national loyalties, and speculative finance capital. But once these forces had become dominant, there was no vision of how to channel them. To some extent the globalisation process had, in fact, been conducted according to the old conventional policies associated with the state-centric system. But this may be misleading: although the institutions of the 1970s (G7, the European Council, and so on) seem to have strengthened statist decision-making power, they may also be steering capitalist development into uncharted territory.

According to conventional IR theory (for example, neo-realism) the problem is the ending of US hegemony. But this is not the real issue: post-hegemony can be, and is being, handled within the context of a fairly structured regime guaranteeing the collective hegemony of the North. In this sense, what is happening is not inter-imperialist rivalry of the old type, but rather an attempt at maintaining the United States in its crucial role as gendarme, but in such a way that the costs and benefits to the other actors are taken into account.

At a deeper level, the problem is that in the past these efforts to create an equilibrium have been between capitalist countries, each of which was relatively 'complete' and coherent in the sense of containing a self-related system of machine-building, consumer industry, consumption, food production and technology. Now capitalism is faced with a new contradiction between, on the one hand, the economic dimension of capital that is becoming globalised (partly through the new management systems, partly through its growing speculative–parasitic aspect), and, on the other, the state, which still operates as an instrument of organisation and repression.

This problem has existed as a latent possibility since the days of classic imperialism, but it was temporarily resolved when corporate interests reached an accommodation with the state, by which they used it for their own purposes but respected it as a major economic force. In the post-Second World War system, the new economic interdependence within the North was of a peculiar kind: it was not the interdependence predicted by Ricardo, premised on specialisation, but was rather the 'Volkswagen-for-Renault', the exchange of goods from the same branch of production with different brand identitities. It was thus possible to reconcile two apparently mutually exclusive goals: on the one hand the rise of interdependence, which was essential in order to overcome the internecine conflict of classic imperialism and to create a unified Northern persona *vis-à-vis* the South, and on the other hand the maintenance of complete economies, containing all the major sectors, at the level of the individual country.

This was reinforced by another factor: the development of a new role for the state in the post-war era. Some kind of transition from the Listian era was probably needed, and Keynesianism made a crucial contribution by providing it. Far from undermining the state's traditional economic role, it sanctified while at the same time 'civilising' the state, converting it from the ultra-selfish organ that had created at an international level the anarchy it had abolished internally, into a tool of management capable of delivering the goal of full employment in the domestic economy in a way which did not exclude international co-operation. In France, for example, a consensus emerged between different political forces over the importance of having nationalised industries in key sectors, while in Germany state companies had holdings in many private corporations. In the United States, the state played the extraordinarily important role of placing military orders in key areas of the private sector. Japan used its Ministry of International Trade and Industry (MITI) to plan both industrial production and trade in an integrated way. In addition, all governments resorted to strategies such as regional aid, employment subsidies, export credits, tax concessions, tied 'aid' to developing countries, direct government involvement in the negotiation of major contracts, and the funding of R&D, with spin-offs for the private sector. The state consolidated its role and in some respects may even have expanded it.

However, the surplus capacity engendered by several separate entities in different countries, which were all seeking to maintain complete economies, must have contributed to the over-accumulation which eventually exhausted the post-war long cycle. Internationalisation offered the only solution. In this sense, those defending 'less state' in the economy were looking for a more efficient allocation of resources within the central capitalist economy as a whole, while at the same time believing that greater interdependence among the Northern economies would cement their cohesion as a bloc *vis-à-vis* the rest of the world. But this created a problem. The maintenance of 'complete' economic systems in individual countries had given them their Northern 'status' in contrast with the South. If they did not retain this basis for their domination at an individual level, how could it be maintained collectively? Indeed, it proved difficult for the North to eliminate surplus capacity and promote interdependence without undermining its status. But a balance was achieved through a very complex relationship which contained elements of both a resurgent nationalism and globalisation.

## The Trend to Restore Nationalism

Britain was one of the first nations to abolish national capitalism. The argument behind the decision to destroy an identifiably national industry was that it would, through the low pay it could then pay its workers, gain a comparative advantage in the field of labour conditions and thus attract a big influx of the newly internationalised investment capital. Some Asian companies, lured by the access they would acquire to the whole European market, have invested in Britain. But the British model has clear weaknesses: it is dangerously dependent on the health of Asian economies, for instance. And this has encouraged the opposite trend, of economic nationalism, in other countries in the North.

I have already argued that one of the key problems for imperialism is to prevent the South becoming the main industrial power at the expense of the North, and this issue will be discussed more fully in the next chapter. But the threat came not just from the South; there were factors within the Northern economy itself that were encouraging de-industrialisation. Influential US analysts expressed concern in the 1980s that savings were not being invested in domestic industry.[14] For some time, the USA had been becoming increasingly an agricultural economy; it has been argued that, in the late 1970s, only exports of corn and soybeans averted a balance-of-payments crisis.[15] This was humiliating for a once-great industrial exporter. To some extent the USA tried to make the best of this new role, which led to a long-running squabble with the EC, in which both sides poured massive subsidies into agriculture.[16] But the long-term solution was to look for ways of safeguarding industrial power. The US government invested heavily first in projects such as Very High Speed Integrated Circuits,[17] and later, in the 1980s, in High Definition TV (using military funding, under the excuse of creating guidance systems for tanks).[18] But some overall theoretical view of development was needed to underpin the new strategy. What happened was that, alongside pure free-market economics, which was sold to the general public and to the third world, the establishment created a kind of parallel economics which tried to incorporate some elements of the real world.

The central premise of this new thinking was that, since markets were obviously not really free, the effective decisions were those taken by the powerful actors (corporations and states), and their decisions were strategic. There was no point pretending it was a system of pure economic actors, even if one believed that in an ideal world such a system would be better. It was recognised that, in fact, the economic actors made their own comparative advantage.[19] This meant learning from Japan where decision-making at the strategic level was most fully developed, with, for example, monthly meetings of huge networks, each of which brought together the heads of several of the major companies, and which in turn patronised factions within the ruling party.[20] It was also recognised that to be successful, strategic decisions had to take into account social factors as well as purely economic ones. This branch of the new economics is avowedly Listian, and claims that List's discussion of 'mental capital' foreshadowed the concept of 'intellectual capital' widely used today.[21] Here again, the role model is Japan, where the state was concerned not so much with providing industry with crude protectionism as with stimulating production experience.[22] 'The essence of comparative advantage', it is argued, 'is not static factor endowment or natural resources, but a dynamic technological or efficiency edge'.[23] Such an approach is even more relevant today where, as Simai points out, the rapidity of technological change and the role of advanced information technologies nullify what used to be thought of as the 'advantage of the latecomer'.[24]

The North was learning from Japan in order to use this knowledge against it, for it was concerned that the leading edge of capitalist development, and with it the main productive investment, was leaking to Asia. To some extent Japan's status as honorary Aryan could be seen as provisional, in that the white world could gang up against it if it became too threatening.

## Is Speculative Capital out of Control?

One aspect of the de-industrialisation problem within the central capitalist world was thus the perceived risk that the balance of power was shifting to the disadvantage of some capitalist powers. But there was also another way in which the problem could be perceived: irrespective of the relationship between national economies, industrial capital as a whole in the North had lost ground to speculative capital. By making it possible to invest in the real economy again, the technological revolution should have put an end to the situation in which over-accumulated capital was desperately seeking an outlet. But in practice, though there was once again heavy demand for capital, much of it was leaking from the real economy into speculation. The junk bond phenomenon was part of this: it may have helped by liquidating conglomerates, but it also had the disadvantage of rewarding speculative capital very highly.

Speculation was also encouraged by several other factors, which reinforced each other. First, the rise of the 'futures' market: created originally because economic interests (including producers) sought to hedge against the risk of fluctuations in the price of raw materials, it quickly took on a life of its own and contributed strikingly to the increasing rewards of speculative capital. Second, the decline of the real economy in the USA had for a long time been masked by the printing of money to cover the balance of payments deficit, and these funds (largely unsupported by anything substantial) came to constitute the Eurodollar market. Reinforced by the introduction of new technology into investment and banking, this market really took off in the 1980s. Third, attempts to create a post-hegemonic currency system (following the withdrawal of the dollar as the mainstay of a system of fixed exchange rates) turned currency speculation into a major area of activity in its own right. Fourth, since the highest profits were now made in speculative areas like futures and currency trading, the banks – which earlier would have been funding industrial companies – devoted increasing resources to these activities. Fifth, the industrial–productive sector itself became drawn into the speculative economy, as major corporations began to hedge against the risk of losses by speculating on currency markets.

Some figures highlight the scale of the problem. The Eurodollar market, where financial institutions borrow from and lend to one another, was estimated in the mid-1980s to have an annual turnover of US$75,000 billion, or about twenty-five times the volume of world trade. Foreign exchange transactions (in which the speculative buying and selling of currencies takes place) amounted to US$35,000 billion.[25] At the end of the decade it was estimated that, while the total annual amount of merchandise traded world-wide was running at US$2,500 billion, the volume of foreign exchange traded amounted to an average of US$500 billion per day.[26] These developments show that alienated labour (that is, value seeking ways of expanding itself) was moving into a dimension far beyond the old partnership with the state.

But in the United States it was the state itself that was indirectly en-couraging the move into speculation. The arms race – which eventually destroyed the Soviet system by forcing it to withdraw resources from con-sumption just when the new consumer ideology was at its most appealing – was financed by vast deficits. At the same time, consumption itself was being encouraged by American policies, which has led neo-Keynesians – with ironic humour – to hail the Reagan administration, with its policies of massive government spending, budget deficits, and consumption boom, as a confirmed exponent of their ideas.[27] America was not producing enough to fuel this consumption boom, so goods as well as capital were imported from other industrial countries, which led to an increase in the US trade deficit as well. By 1986 the US was running a budget deficit of US$220 billion and a trade deficit of US$140 billion. Foreign investments, which plugged the budget shortfall, expanded from US$500 billion in 1980 to US$1,300 billion at the end of 1986.[28]

This situation was beneficial for the other industrial countries because it provided them with a market. At the end of the 1980s, the US domestic market still accounted for about half of the combined market of the seven major industrialised countries, even though by then US output had declined markedly. During the Reagan period, US consumption grew by a remarkable 23 per cent, as against 8 per cent in West Germany, for example; by the late 1980s, it amounted to US$2,700 trillion.[29] So within its own frontiers the industrial world had found a way to get rid of its products as well as of its over-accumulated capital.

There is the risk, however, that if speculative finance capital becomes preponderant, it can accentuate the de-industrialisation process. In Britain, for example, the weight of the City is pushing the economy in this direction.[30] Can state intervention be used to counteract this threat?

Here we come to an interesting paradox. In order to strengthen the 'real economy' (that is, the productive economy) in the balance of power with finance capital, the state has to give in to its demands, removing, if necessary, restrictions on the growth of monopoly. It used to be the state which, by regulating monopolies, provided the only guarantee for the continued exist-ence of some semblance of a free market. But now the era of neo-liberalism, which was supposed to mark the triumph of the free market, actually signified its demise. In 1982, the Assistant Attorney-General of the United States remarked that 'mergers are a very, very healthy phenomenon of the capital markets and should not be interfered with except in exceptional circumstances'.[31] The EC/EU had been more cautious, mounting a regional level of defence of the industrial economy by permitting capital to carry out only the 'right' kind of mergers. There are numerous instances of the Community itself acting directly to co-ordinate the actions of the main Europe-based TNCs,[32] as with the attempt at united action by Thomson, Phillips and Bosch, with the direct encouragement of the EEC, to challenge the Japanese to battle over High Definition TV.[33] These measures can be seen partly as an attempt to defend European companies against their rivals (although they have not been at all successful in stopping European TNCs from linking up with Japanese ones), but at another level they are clearly intended to help companies to channel investment into industrial rather than speculative activities.

The capitalist powers as a group have probably realised that (from a politico-military angle as well as an economic one) they need the United States as the central agent of their collective dominance. While the Bretton Woods system of fixed exchange rates was still in force, the USA was permitted to maintain trade deficits and cover these by printing money. But although in one sense this looks like privileged treatment for America, it also undermined the US manufacturing base. With the end of the fixed exchange-rate system, it should have been possible to sort this out. At first, this seemed to be the case. The Japanese yen, which had been pegged at 360 to the dollar under the Bretton Woods system, rose to 175 by 1978. But all this ended with the accession to power of Reagan in 1980. With Reaganomics, the high interest rates necessary for the deficit-based consumption boom had the dual effect of increasing once again the value of the dollar and further damaging industrial development, so it was imports that benefited from the increase in consumption. Japan's trade surplus with the USA soared from US$7.5 billion in 1980 to about US$52 billion in 1987.[34] The markets were so ineffective in reducing the US trade deficit that action by the Group of Five was necessary in 1985 to engineer a rise in the value of the yen.

In response to the strong yen, Japanese industrialists made a strategic shift in their policies, increasing the internationalisation of production so that they would not have to export goods from the strong-currency home base.[35] But if this had been the full story, Japan would still today be the most dynamic force on the world economy, which it is not. Something else was happening. As Itoh pointed out, if the Japanese economy had still been growing at its pre-crisis rate, Japanese companies would have had ample investment opportunities at home and would not have been attracted to higher interest rates in the USA.[36] So foreign investment may be a sign not of dynamism, but of failure to absorb capital at home.[37]

At the same time, it is clear that capital has become more internationalised, speculative, divorced from loyalty either to the real economy or to national roots. This raises very complex problems. One effect of the high degree of internationalisation of speculative capital is that the market does not now act to redress structural problems as it did in the past (by, for instance, encouraging capital to move from one sector to another to compensate for the weaknesses revealed in balance of trade deficit). Instead, the market today accentuates the difficulties, as speculators bet on an unfavourable outcome for a country when it is in difficulties, which pushes the country further in that direction, thus creating the anticipated result. Moreover, it is not just the direct currency speculators who gain from this, but also those who lend money to a government in difficulties so that it can support its currency.[38] The formation of the EU was presented as a once-and-for-all opportunity to stand up to the destructive forces of this new economy before they had wrought too much damage. For this reason, the Maastricht Treaty insisted on making union 'irreversible'.[39]

Let us sum up. The imperialist phase of capitalist development unleashed all the forces visible today. Some have developed in a qualitatively stronger way, in particular the growth of finance capital through the internationalisation of currency and commodity markets. Early imperialism attempted to maintain these forces in a balanced relationship with national economies, but the competitiveness this entailed was so destructive that it became untenable. The far-reaching changes of 1945 moved capitalism onto a developmental path which put an end to the old internecine destructiveness, but it did so in a way which temporarily strengthened the managerial role of the state. This meant that the full implications of the changes that started with imperialism were delayed and started to work their way through only in the 1980s.

The growing weakness of the centre is reflected in the unpredictability of capital unleashed from the tutelage of economic management at a state level. But if the centre becomes weaker, does this mean the centre–periphery relationship becomes weaker too? For the moment, no. For there are several mechanisms for making sure that the worst impact of the current changes falls on the South, and the new forms of capital still operate, as the old ones did, to siphon value out of the South. But when the present accumulation structure begins to fall apart – which is sure to happen soon or (depending on how we interpret the events of the late 1990s), may already be happening – the North's ability to protect itself from damage could also be undermined.

It is the North alone that is trying to find a political mechanism for regulating the flows of capital around the world. The decision-making process behind the Multilateral Agreement on Investment (MAI) of the late 1990s illustrates this (even though, in the wake of the Asian crisis, the future of this initiative looks uncertain). It is obvious that, in the short term, it has been the South which has suffered most, but it is also becoming clear that the basis of the new era of Northern joint hegemony, established at the end of the 1970s, was itself riddled with contradictions, and that these will become increasingly obvious over the next few years.

## Notes

1. Cf. *Le Monde diplomatique*, 'Le Libéralisme contre les Libertés', Paris, (Le Monde) nd.

2. Hayek 1973, p. 42.

3. It is worth remarking that this analogy is very questionable. Money is by definition homogenised rather than plural, and the uniformity it expresses conceals the social differentiation which is associated with its dominance; language on the other hand, interestingly and accurately encapsulates social differentiation in the form of plurality of cultures and social classes, which express themselves differently.

4. See Waltz 1979.

5. Cf. Rostow 1984.

6. Toffler 1980.

7. Bell 1965.

8. The reasoning is that there has been a tendency towards pro-cyclical increase in money supply, in the sense that banks will pump more money into the economy at times when demand is high, in order to prevent interest rates going up; obviously, expectations of default would also be lower. While the assertion that if money is in large supply its value will decline (and hence the prices of goods measured in it will rise) is tautological, the deduction is logically wrong since the causality could be the other way round, or both could be caused by some third factor.

9. Cf. Hayek 1939.

10. Townsend 1979, p. 116.

11. Some research suggests that inequality in the USA increased between 1959 and 1968, while in France it probably increased from 1956 to 1962, and then declined up to 1971; cf. Cole and Miles 1984, p. 19.

12. Between 1960 and 1975 the percentage of those close to the actual average, i.e. earning between 80% and 120% of the average income, fell from 35.9% to 27.8%. The percentages of those earning above 120% and below 80% both increased; cf. Ginzberg 1986, p. 26.

13. For an assessment of this model, see, for example, Rubinstein 1986.

14. See, for example, Grunwald and Flamm 1985.

15. See Portes and Walton 1981, Chapter 5.

16. There were big increases in US subsidies from 1977 and especially from 1982, so that by 1986–87 both blocs were putting about 0.6% of GDP into this. In America's case this amounted to over US$25 billion in 1986; cf. Zietz and Valdes 1988, pp. 18–19.

17. Hart 1990, p. 108.

18. This work was subsequently cut back by the Bush administration in 1990.

19. See especially Borrus *et al.* 1988.

20. The six big entities are Mitsubishi (including shipbuilding, chemicals, steel, artificial fibres, automobiles and oil), Mitsui (chemicals and shipbuilding, plus Japan Steel, Toyota and Toshiba), Sumitomo (chemicals, metal industries, plus the Nippon Electrical Company), Fuji (Nissan, Hitachi, Canon etc.), Dai-ichi (Ashahi Chemicals, Steel, Isuzu motors, Fujitsu, C. Itoh and Company), and Sanwa (steel, shipbuilding, Daihatsu Motors, Sharp); see Sumiya 1989.

21. Freeman 1989.

22. See Motoshige Itoh 1990.

23. Thurlow 1985, p. 250.

24. Simai 1990, p. 124.

25. Kakabadse 1987, p. 40.

26. Hartland-Thunberg 1990, p. 76.

27. Stewart 1986 is an example.

28. George 1988, p. 26.

29. *Le Monde diplomatique*, 'Le Libéralisme contre les Libertés', Paris, (Le Monde) nd.

30. Thus, the financial sector has grown as a share of national output, while the industrial sector has decreased, and the two have almost crossed. Manufacturing hardly increased its output following the 1979–81 recession and shrank from 28.4% to 22.2% of national output between 1979 and 1989, whereas finance rose from 11.6% to 19.8% over the same period; *Independent* (Business), 16 September 1990.

31. Quoted in Clairmonte 1986, p. 150.

32. For example, the Eureka initiative to bring together industry and research establishments, the JESSI programme dealing with electronic components, or PROMETHEUS dealing with passenger vehicles.

33. *Le Monde*, 17 January 1990.

34. Makoto Itoh 1990, p. 201.

35. See Dickens 1991, p. 32.

36. Makoto Itoh 1990.

37. This restates, in a way, Krugman's idea about the Asian NICs, which we will consider in the next chapter.

38. Britain would appear to have spent £30 billion trying to support the pound in the period leading up to its disappearance from the Exchange Rate Mechanism in September 1992, £23 billion of which was borrowed from other central banks; *Guardian*, 27 February 1993.

39. Maastricht Treaty, Protocol on Transition to the Third Stage of Economic and Monetary Union.

# 10

# From Periphery to Centre?
# The Newly Industrialising Country
# (NIC) Strategy

## A Change in Development Paradigms

Countries of the South face rapidly changing external circumstances, while the theories which tell them how they should adapt to this reality have also changed drastically over recent years. Development theory has acquired a split personality and is sending out confusing mixed messages. Whereas one part of it talks about empowerment, sustainability and the role of women, another speaks in reverential terms of the newly industrialising countries (NICs) as supposed success stories to be emulated. The contradiction between the two discourses is evident: one of the most successful NICs – Taiwan – is an eco-disaster, and another – South Korea – exploits women in the informal economy, and so on. We need to understand this contradiction if we are to understand the role allocated to developing countries by the capitalist system within the current phase. In later chapters I will consider the 'humanistic' facet of the development discourse, which may in fact be much more exploitative than it seems. In the present chapter, I will address the NIC question. Of the two discourses, this is the more concrete. Whereas empowerment remains largely hypothetical, NICs do at least represent some real change – changes in the physical structure of production, its location, the social groups which are rewarded by access to consumption, the growth of élite techno-cultures, and so on. But what has really changed may not necessarily correspond to what is supposed to change, according to development theories. The crucial issue is to discover what benefits NIC development brings to global capitalism.

I will argue that objectively the NIC phenomenon creates structures, presented under the guise of national development models, which act as local nodes for the global accumulation process. This is the function which has emerged for them as part of the restructuring of capital accumulation. The NIC theory is a distorted reflection of this reality, which it generalises into a model, making it sound more autonomous than it really is. But while the ideal type of NIC development may be a disguised form of dependence, it is also possible that some parts of the South could take advantage of weaknesses in the North's control mechanisms and gain some degree of real autonomy.

## Why Might NIC-style Development be Useful for Global Capital Accumulation?

In some sense, the issue is as old as imperialism: there is a real risk that industrial development may occur in Asia, and the art of imperialism is to turn this risk into a benefit, in such a way that the mechanisms for limiting development in the South become mechanisms of accumulation for the centre. The interesting paradox is that, while some features of early twentieth-century imperialism, such as the irreconcilable contention between the great powers, have faded away, other of its more profound features, which were then visible only as latent tendencies, have only now been able to come to fruition.[1] In this sense, NIC development can be considered one of the strongest indications that we are still in the era of imperialism.

The key issue is the development of *rentier* capitalism.[2] Lenin devoted a lengthy section of *Imperialism, the Highest Stage of Capitalism* to what proved to be a highly prophetic discussion of this issue,[3] but it is interesting to look at the earlier work of Hobson, upon which Lenin partly drew. Hobson's work clearly expresses the racial dimension in imperialism which it was not polite to talk about among the communist tradition typified by Lenin. Hobson's view of imperialism strongly reflects the way in which capitalism was both infatuated with Asia and afraid of it, with the associated fear of the 'decline of the West'. In some sense capitalist development cannot bypass Asia, but the Euro-American world must not succumb to the temptation of getting Asians to do all the manufacturing and simply living off the profits. The result could be an international system where 'the white races, discarding labour in its more arduous forms, live as a sort of world-aristocracy by the exploitation of the "lower races" while they hand over the policing of the world more and more to members of these same races';[4] and this could lead to 'some terrible *débâcle* in which revolted slave races may trample down their parasitic and degenerate white masters'.[5]

How can this *débâcle* be avoided? I believe there are two sets of conditions. Only one of these was directly addressed by imperialism theory: the need for the industrial powers to co-operate to impose a world strategic agenda that is favourable to them. The problem of managing Asian development, specifically the incorporation of China into the international division of labour, can thus encourage what Hobson calls a 'federation of the Western States'. This condition is fulfilled today in the unified structure that lies behind the OECD, the G7, the EU, the World Bank and IMF, and most recently the WTO. I have discussed this issue economically in the previous chapter, and will take up some of the more political aspects in Chapter 12.

But there is also a second condition: some structure within countries of the South which can permit development to proceed in a 'safe' way. The old state-centric development model of ISI does not provide this structure, because it mainly arose in response to the demands of transition from old-style colonialism. What is needed is a new kind of model, a sort of genetically engineered development organism with the autonomy gene removed, which can safely be unleashed to propagate itself, without ever threatening central capital. The NIC/export promotion model is the answer.

Empirically, the 1980s appear to have witnessed a shift of manufacturing away from Western Europe and the USA in the direction of Asia, and within Asia itself, away from Japan.[6] It looks like a move towards *rentier* capitalism. And the question becomes: how can the centre simultaneously control this new development and profit from it?

There are two key questions that need to be answered: first, what is the impact of this *rentier* capitalism on accumulation within the North? And second, does it affect the availability of the South as an area where Northern capital can be deployed? Though these goals are broadly in harmony, which is why the current regime of accumulation functions as a coherent whole, there are also contradictions that will become increasingly apparent.

THE EFFECT OF NIC DEVELOPMENT ON ACCUMULATION IN THE NORTH   The effect on accumulation within the North is as follows: if people can buy cheap manufactured consumer goods (sports shoes, electronic goods, toys etc.) their cost of living can be kept down, so employers do not have to pay such high wages and can therefore maintain the profitability of their own productive system. Ideologically, the availability of new consumer goods is meant to breed contentment and distract attention away from the big social issues. At the same time, there is an element of threat: the spectre of Asia, which would have to be invented if it did not exist, forces trades unions to accept flexible working practices beneficial to capital.

NICS AS AREAS FOR INVESTMENT   In some sense, capital is processed by the NICs, which act like some carefully designed enzyme beavering away in the interest of accumulation. Statistically, this is not straightforward to describe, since different sources define the categories in different ways (or, frequently, do not explain them clearly). However, I will briefly present some indicators which, taken together, give an idea of the overall trends.

As we have seen, the history of capital flows to the NICs can be summarised as follows: firstly, in the 1970s a great deal of capital flowed to some developing countries, to profit from the tail-end of the old development strategies, such as the sale of 'turnkey' equipment. But then, in the early 1980s, with the emergence of the new model of accumulation, capital began to be invested in the North again. What has been happening more recently? Statistics from a European Commission think-tank provide strong evidence of the

North–North pattern of capital flows becoming more dominant throughout the 1980s, whereas less developed countries attracted 55 per cent of global capital flows (excluding capital from international institutions) in 1980, their share had dropped to only 2 per cent in 1990.[7] As no definition is given for 'less developed countries', this reduction may be partly the result of certain countries no longer being perceived as 'less developed'; but what it does at least show is that capital was not interested in developing any new NICs.

But there is also some evidence of a third phase, beginning in the early 1990s, when capital flows to the South increased again. Developing countries' share in net aggregate long-term resource-flows seems to have increased markedly in the early 1990s; in 1994 they received a private capital flow of US$173 billion, which is estimated to have been as high as 75 per cent of total resource-flows in that year.[8] According to a different estimate, private capital flows to developing countries quadrupled in the period 1991–93.[9] But the form of the capital changed. Instead of loans – which would be profitable only in the form of interest repayments (and interest repayments were proving increasingly unpredictable) – Northern investment switched during the 1980s to direct investment in the ownership of productive capacity. The share of foreign direct investment and equity acquisition within North–South finance flows increased from less than 10 per cent in 1981 to 25 per cent in 1991.[10]

The North was highly selective in the countries it chose for these resources, targeting a handful of NICs which seemed promising as relays in the global accumulation process, and virtually ignoring the rest of the South. This resulted in a highly differentiated economic performance in the countries of the South: the so-called 'dynamic Asian economies' accounted for 45 per cent of all manufactured exports from developing countries in 1988,[11] while the share of the 102 poorest countries in world manufacturing exports fell from 7.9 per cent in 1980 to 1.4 per cent in 1990.[12] So it appears uneven development is alive and well. In Asia, the promising NICs – Indonesia, South Korea, the Philippines, Thailand and Malaysia – received US$93 billion of private investment in the period 1996–97.[13]

This form of investment has strengthened the supply of cheap manufactured goods which the North needs, while ensuring that, through the returns on the investment, the benefit of the cheap labour is taken out by the North and not allowed to remain in the South where it might further a truly autonomous development. The North has been encouraged to invest in the NICs by an important mechanism: a higher rate of profit. Although, as I argued earlier, an equalised rate of profit would itself be exploitative, the evidence seems to point to exploitation through *different* rates of profit. A recent study asserts that 'there is virtually no evidence of an increased tendency towards profit rate equalisation over the post-war period',[14] and this is extremely interesting given the fact that there has indisputably been an increased tendency to capital mobility. The reason why such capital mobility made no impact on the rate of profit can only be the differential in the value of labour (ultimately, in the value placed on human life) between centre and periphery, which is consolidated by the colour line. This line is increasingly transparent to international capital (with the collapse of statist policies which sought to impose restrictions) which can thereby appropriate the added value created by undervalued Southern labour. Empirically, it appears that equity investment in developing countries yielded a substantially higher rate of return than in the USA, for example.[15] So this international influence on the rate of profit supplements the beneficial effect of NIC development on the rate of profit within Northern economies.

On this basis, it is justifiable to say that international capital develops symbiotically with the NICs. Indeed, given the fact that certain critical thresholds are involved in accumulation (Rostow was right in talking about such a threshold; it was his practical application of the idea which was wrong), there may be an argument that a certain rate of Asian NIC growth is a necessary condition for the continued growth of capital accumulation in the North. It is interesting that some futurological scenarios, including one from an official British government source,[16] predict catastrophe if Asian NIC growth-rate falls below a critical point. While we should be wary of making a catastrophist reading of the recent Asian crisis in the immediate term, the NICs' symbiotic role poses very difficult longer-term questions.

While it is clear that central capital can benefit from NIC development, one important question remains: how can it be controlled? Part of the answer has, in fact, already been supplied, for if the relationship is leading to accumulation in the North, then the value transferred to the North is being lost to the South, inhibiting the possibility of locally-centred accumulation. But dependency theory already recognised that this kind of answer is not sufficient: it is necessary to look at the structural, social effects of the relationship within the South. The task is to see what form these take under contemporary conditions. Before considering the economic issues, I will briefly address the ideological ones.

## Why the NIC Idea Appeals to Élites

The evidence about what is really going on strongly suggests that the phenomenon of the NIC is highly selective. Yet the ideological dimension is felt throughout the developing world, spreading beyond those who have a realistic possibility of becoming NICs. Even the large areas of the South which, realistically, central capital will never view other than as a passive reservoir of cash crops or raw materials, might be reconciled with the system if it seemingly opens up an avenue for advancement.

The fundamental ideological role of the NIC phenomenon is to promote a culture of individual advancement in order to defuse the third world movement. The unity of developing countries in Asia, Africa and Latin America had exposed the different value placed on life in the South and the

North, and challenged the system of double values. Sauvy's concept of the 'third world' reflected the white world's fear of a destructive 'mass society' with no stake in the system. In particular, the third world movement achieved two things: it showed that developing countries must advance together, in solidarity; and it targeted the system, arguing that humans could act consciously to improve the system in which they live. Both these ideas have always been dangerous to exploitative systems. For this reason one of the most important goals of the neo-liberal phase of capitalism has been to attack third-worldism as a movement.[17] The NIC idea helps to fragment the third world into different categories – NICs, developing countries, least developed countries, and so on – which are supposed to have different interests. It is simply divide and rule.

Why do Southern élites fall for this? Paulo Freire's ideas on class relations are helpful here: rather than thinking of becoming free from oppression, it is easier to think of becoming the oppressor.[18] Instead of minuscule gains diluted among the many, it is better to take the small chance of a massive gain. This is how lotteries work, and in effect NIC development is a lottery. The reasoning is fallacious, in the sense that the gains from a change in the system would not be diluted by being shared among the beneficiaries, but, as Freire would say, it requires stepping outside the bounds of the current ideology to realise this.

But of course, the NIC model would not catch on if it did not contain some element of truth. And what is true in the model is something that imperialism theory and dependency theory have always recognised, namely uneven development. It is paradoxical that at a time when mainstream theory keeps repeating (in order to stop people studying them) that dependency and imperialism are no longer of any relevance, such an important part of those theories has implicitly been confirmed in the NIC model. This is a step forward in terms of realism compared to earlier right-wing models, such as the one formulated by Rostow, which implied that every nation on earth could pursue American-style growth simultaneously. Only the perceived threat of communism made the system invest in such nonsense. With the new NIC theories, the unstated (but inescapable) corollary is that most countries never will develop, and in terms of the orthodox capitalist 'growth' models, this is unquestionably true.

If something of value for the South exists within the NIC idea, it could only amount to a recipe for using uneven development rather than being used by it. Not surprisingly, NIC theory has not handed the oppressed a workable model for doing so, and it would scarcely be in the interest of the centre to do so. For, even though the NIC model implicitly acknowledges uneven development, it does not use the concept in the same rich way as it is employed in the imperialism–dependency perspective. In particular, it refuses to recognise the dialectic between internal and international aspects,[19] and ignores the fundamental problem which dependency has always pinpointed, namely that uneven development occurs not only at an international level. The same phenomenon of unevenness which, occuring between countries, is supposed to create opportunities for would-be NICs, also operates within their economies to undermine the practical possibility of such opportunities leading to real development. Many of the problems highlighted by the earlier radical critique of the old development theory – for example that the extroverted port economy acts as a parasite on the rest, making it extremely hard to develop in a truly coherent way – are still in evidence. Any unconsidered, simplistic strategy attempted by an NIC to use uneven development as a springboard for autonomous development would carry this danger within it like a time-bomb.

Still, the world economy has moved on. Although the mainstream may have no interest in handing out a workable blueprint, it is still worth asking whether the South could today on its own account build a viable strategy for taking advantage of uneven development. Let us make the attempt, on the assumption that the strategy is being worked out by an enlightened decision-maker with no particular social interests to defend. It is important, first of all, to see the context within which the NIC model emerged.

Import substitution industrialisation (ISI) was, in its day, presented as a strategy for the South to gain autonomy, but in practice it became part of a wider logic of capital accumulation which ultimately served the North. How was this allowed to happen? According to the conventional critique of ISI, its main problem was that the industries it established were protected, hence backward by world standards. Although the establishment stops short at this point, we could take the critique further.

CONSCIOUSLY EXPLOITING THE 'ADVANTAGE' OF CHEAP LABOUR
From this point of view, ISI's weakness was that it did not consciously pursue the advantage of cheap labour. On the contrary, it claimed to be using the other, Ricardian, aspect of advantage, the so-called natural advantage, to promote development: it planned to seek external markets for its primary products, then use the wealth generated by these exports to constitute a domestic market, which would initially be fed by imports and then by the products that domestic industry itself would manufacture. But this is not, in fact, what happened. What really occurred with so-called industrialisation was that foreign transnational capital exploited local labour while accessing protected domestic markets. Foreign capital was able to appropriate the *accumulated* value generated by this labour (which should theoretically have served to launch national development), while the countries had to continue exporting raw materials to bridge the gap. This brings us to one of the advantages of the idea of export promotion within the NIC model: as it is based on a strategy in which cheap labour is consciously used, it contains fewer illusions, which perhaps means that there is more chance for some of the value to be pocketed locally.

AN INTERNATIONALISED VERSION OF THE 'STAGES' IDEA As we have seen, the 'stages' theory had two weaknesses: first, ISI was premised on a world economy which was developing through the incremental addition of state-centric building blocks, an image which even by then was already outdated; second, the orthodox version of 'stages' theory meant permanently lagging behind, and missing out on the advanced technologies (particularly those characterising the qualitative shifts of long cycles), which is very serious, as it is the advanced technologies which create the *controlling* power within the IPE. For these reasons, even in its heyday ISI was outdated; and this is doubly true in the post-1970s situation, where the IPE has apparently transcended the 'national' dimension, even before this dimension has really been built in the South.

The above reasoning shows that decision-makers in the South were well advised to be seeking a model more adapted to contemporary realities, one which recognised – and perhaps even anticipated – the trend to increasing internationalisation, seeing it as the context within which it had to build competitive industries which conformed to advanced world standards. For some countries, export promotion seemed to be the answer.

There is, however, one fundamental reason why it is difficult to make this model work in practice. My simplified presentation so far has implied a confrontation between two conflicting NIC strategies: one that acted almost as a conspiracy to create conditions for capital accumulation on behalf of the North, and the other, which was formulated by class-neutral decision-makers keen to promote real development in the South. But obviously this black-and-white picture is not accurate; what happened, in fact, was that the new strategy emerged by trial and error through an interplay of interests on both sides. Once the new accommodation had acquired a certain stability, the NIC idea could be invented as a model and propagated consciously.

It is important now to understand the social basis for the emergence of what eventually became the NIC model.

## The Social Basis of the Transition to Export Promotion

Development of any sort is always accompanied by shifts in the balance of power within élites. The history of compromises between landlords and industrialists in England is just one example. But the difference in the South is that élites are closely bound up with the world economy. At watersheds in development they naturally seek to maintain their own class interests and in practice their strategies to do this are often harmonised with the needs of international capital.

The earlier post-war decades in the South were typically characterised by some degree of consensus across the classes behind development goals. But there were still conflicts of class interest, and in these circumstances élites would naturally seek outside backing in defence of their own interests. When labour movements campaigned for better conditions, the ruling classes could find support in the development theory approved by the international establishment, which argued, for example, that militancy would damage development by raising the price of labour as a factor of production.[20] In this way, élites kept their class status, and international capital was guaranteed cheap labour.

However, once import substitution had gained a certain momentum, a turning point was reached. Most developing countries never reached this point. Of those that did, it is interesting to consider the case of Brazil, which, without involving the special external factors that affected Asia (which will be examined later), provides a good illustration of the kind of social basis that emerged for the new export strategy.

It is interesting to specify the moment at which this turning point, or watershed, is reached: in a model premised mainly on internal demand, development will run out of steam at a certain point if only the ruling classes are consuming; but in order to broaden consumption, there has to be a redistribution, not just of wealth but of class power, and this is incompatible with the capitalist system. It would also have been incompatible with the capitalist system for the North to have increased consumption through a redistribution of class power. But for the North there was a way out: the proceeds of external exploitation enabled the ruling class to maintain or even improve its position relative to labour while domestic consumption grew. In the South, there was no such solution. This impasse was the basis for the emergence of export promotion as a compromise solution between the two sets of élites, because growth is no longer premised on domestic demand. Export promotion enabled development of a kind to proceed without the balance of class forces having to change.

Brazil had been relatively favoured by post-war uneven development. Some right-wing economists come close to admitting that the reason for this was racial: countries such as Argentina and Chile, with European identity, were by-passed because they aspired to a European-style collective bargaining,[21] but Brazil was permitted to develop as long as its largely black labour was kept in a third-world state of subjection. An attempt by left-wingers in Brazil in the early 1960s at development by expanded demand from below was crushed by a repressive military coup in 1964.

With hindsight the logic of this change becomes clear: a transition to export promotion, whereby growth will be premised on external rather than internal demand, and redistribution of wealth will never need to occur. Eventually the IMF can take over from the old development economics and invent new reasons for holding consumption down, such as the need for resources to be diverted to the export sector to pay the foreign 'debt'. Once such a logic has been strongly enough established, it will be quite possible to introduce democracy on the assumption that whoever wins elections would have to follow the same policy. But this result could not be arrived at directly.

Instead, it was necessary to have an intermediate period characterised by an important element in the NIC saga, namely the supposedly nationalistic dictatorship. 'Authoritarianism', it is said, can provide the conditions for a strong development strategy, because of its strength in channelling accumulation into key projects, in breaking the resistance of conservative social strata, and in embodying a project about which there is an implicit national consensus. Certain authoritarian set-ups can indeed generate consensus for a time because they bring rapid change and it looks as though the conditions are being created to end poverty. In Brazil, where 72 per cent of equity capital in the machinery sector was foreign-owned in the early 1960s, by 1979 this had sunk to only 36.5 per cent; by then the state itself held as much equity in industry as did all foreign capital. At its height in the early 1970s, the public sector generated half of the GDP. The excitement generated by these apparent possibilities spread abroad to produce the idea of the 'end of the third world'.[22]

The 'end of the third world' idea raises an issue which is implicit in a lot of the export promotion policy, namely that the North will somehow 'accidentally' develop the South while trying to make a profit out of it. But there is a conceptual flaw: the centre–periphery division has existed from the earliest days of capitalism, and, predating mature capitalism, it is embedded in the circuits of accumulation without apparently being in any way attenuated by whatever structural changes occur subsequently. It is this which nullifies not only the simplistic ideas of an inherently 'spreading' late capitalism put forward by people such as Bill Warren, but ultimately also the more intelligent attempts of someone such as Palloix[23] to construct a radical critique of imperialism which denies the centre-periphery dimension, presenting capital accumulation as a single process which is always creating uneven development anew. I believe, on the contrary, that the uneven development which is constantly created in ultra-modern forms is the embodiment of a more ancient substratum – the centre–periphery division or colour line.

Alongside this international dominance – and providing the basis for it – is another reason why it is not really the end of the third world: extremes of poverty and oppression are still there within the apparently developing countries. This is what makes development 'safe' from the North's point of view. The convergence of interests occurs not between domestic social forces (as one would expect in the case of a unified national development crusade), but rather between domestic élites on the one hand – who want to maintain existing class differentials and hence to limit consumption – and foreign capital on the other, which wants cheap manufactured imports in order to reduce the cost of its own labour. By denying the redistribution of wealth, development does not simply preserve the existing distribution, but tends to make it worse: polarisation occurs as part of economic growth,[24] and eventually it turns into marginalisation. Since mass demand is no longer required for growth, those who do not play a role in production are considered to have no economic value, hence no value as people. This underlies the statement of the minister responsible for Brazil's 1970s economic strategy that 'I can only work for 60 per cent of the population; the other 40 per cent are no concern of mine'.[25] It is therefore unlikely that the country will unite behind a 'national' economic strategy. Industrialisation could be a battle-front in the North–South war – the casualties are certainly there in military proportions,[26] but what is missing is an agreed definition of 'national interest' Ultimately, working people engaged in production for export do not identify with their product as the embodiment of a meaningful collective strategy, because the divergence between resource use and consumption is inherently alienating.[27]

The assumption of supply-side economics that accumulated wealth will necessarily be translated into growth is simplistic, but even if we take it at face value, there is little to suggest that such growth can be reliably 'fixed' in the South. Much of the accumulated value which arises from past growth is siphoned off directly to the North – in the form of profits on investments or 'debt' repayments; and, out of the portion which local élites do manage to appropriate, some often ends up fuelling growth in the North by an indirect route. Even in a simplified model of an economy open only to trade, if local capitalists consume imported goods, this leads to 'growth' in the centre. But since the economy is open not just to trade but to the flow of capital, investment too can 'leak' out to the North. When this happens, important segments of the bourgeoisie become detached from the local economy and form part of the globalised one.[28] The World Bank estimated capital flight at 32.3 per cent of developing countries' GDP in 1993;[29] and its officials blamed local élites for their 'irresponsibility', refusing to see that their action is only a logical response to the conditions created by the centre–periphery division.

In the longer term, this situation could mean that the grassroots could put forward a new rationale for raising local consumption. They could defend their case, not only with reference to the traditional argument of conventional economics (consumption overcomes the constraints on growth at a macro-economic level by increasing demand) but by turning to a new economics which argues that, by linking production and consumption within local communities, it is possible to 'fix' the value which might otherwise be sucked out into the global accumulation process. I will return to this in Chapter 14.

But for the moment, the situation is safe for the centre, because polar-isation within Southern societies makes it practically impossible to implement what seem to be obvious strategies of resistance. The focus of these strategies could be 'debt', since it pinpoints the transfer of value in a very tangible form. In Latin America's case this was massive[30], and as the global accumu-lation system is interdependent, developing countries would have leverage for threatening to bring the whole structure crashing down. Certain elements in the Brazilian élite were urging a militant stance on debt around 1986, but it came to nothing for social reasons. Quite simply, polarisation has made it impossible to develop the national solidarity needed for such a struggle. And in the last analysis the élites use the IMF as a convenient scapegoat: they can implement policies that defend their class position while blaming them on someone else.

Though in the short term social dislocation means that the North can safely extract value from the South, this same factor may have the opposite result in the longer term. If a serious social crisis erupts, social marginalisation may become self-reinforcing, in the sense that both central and local investment will tend to flee (local capitalists may even be more volatile than the central ones, since the latter have a firm base within relatively stable Northern economies and can therefore afford to take more risks). Societal cohesion could then collapse to a point where it would be very difficult to reconstitute. It is already clear that it is not possible indefinitely to ignore the 40 per cent, who can quickly become 60 per cent or more. Capital accumulation is becoming unsustainable in a human sense, in that the current pattern of accumulation is undermining the reproduction of the labour which needs to be exploited as a basis for future accumulation. The number of Brazilian 'street children' has been put as high as 12 million.[31] The more far-sighted functionaries of international organisations are conscious that the basis of future profitability is being eroded at a world level, and would like to intervene to make the world safe for future generations of exploiters by rebuilding the 'social' element, but, given the short-term pressures for profitability, there is little chance of this happening. Even a fundamental restructuring of the accumulation system would not solve this problem, which has for many years been embedded within the NIC models, waiting to explode.

Before we can look at prospects for the NIC model within global capitalism, we must look more closely at the Asian experience, without which the NIC idea could never have established itself, fallaciously, as a viable global trend.

## The Special Circumstances of Asia, as Spearhead of the NIC Trend

Certain special factors have enabled Asian NICs to accumulate locally some of the value created by their cheap labour, and in some cases, temporarily at least, to avoid the extremes of polarisation. Basically, the causes are political. The Cold War made it important to have local capitalism well established in the key area for 'containment', particularly in that part of divided countries (such as Taiwan and South Korea) that had remained capitalist; this was, of course, to make sure that capitalism compared favourably with communism. When the USA became desperate to disentangle itself from Vietnam, it was another opportunity for another set of right-wing countries, including Indonesia, to develop.

At the most superficial level, these countries were simply given huge amounts of money.[32] But far more importantly, they were permitted to do certain things which no other developing country would have been allowed to do. There are two key aspects.

COMBINING EXPORT PROMOTION WITH PROTECTION OF THE DOMESTIC ECONOMY  This was rarely permitted, only in exceptional circumstances to a few honorary Aryans. And it is evident that almost anyone could develop a country if they were permitted these conditions. If generalised, such a policy would lead to the collapse of the open world economy (Ricardo's critique of mercantilism is correct on this point).

A STRATEGY WHICH CONFLICTS WITH 'NORMAL' DEVELOPMENT ECONOMICS  This strategy, which was the one commonly employed by the Asian NICs, gave a key role to the state. The establishment claims that NICs were successful because they did things differently from the way proposed by mainstream post-war development economics. This is in a way correct, but for the opposite reason to the one alleged: the NICs departed from the mainstream not at the free-market end of the spectrum, as is often claimed, but at the other end. They showed that the role of the state need not merely be to protect certain industries or to promote exports. It can also perform functions like planning; it can own key sectors, create social infrastructure, and serve as a focus for ideologies and identities. They gave the state not merely a quantitatively greater role (which would not have solved anything), but in some respects a qualitatively different role too: it impinges into the forbidden zone of political economy inhabited by List, where real-economy considerations replace abstract principles. Yet, by an ideological sleight of hand, the supposed NIC experience is used as an excuse to force Africa to implement a model of such reduced state spending that education is massacred in order to transfer resources to the cultivation of out-of-season vegetables for Northern supermarkets.

If politics explains why a few Asian NICs were allowed to get away with such anomalous policies, it is still important to understand at an economic level what international opportunities they were able to grasp. And it is against this background that we should consider another factor – the evolution of the international political economy.

It is recognised that the centre's relationship to the periphery includes two motions, backwash and spreading. These terms should not necessarily be equated with 'bad' and 'good'. 'Spreading' means breaking up traditional structures, which can be 'bad', but it can also mean the growth of local capitalism, which, from the standpoint of our current argument, is something 'good'.

It is often asserted that the NIC experience disproves dependency theory, but I would argue the opposite. A widely quoted definition of dependency by Dos Santos asserts that the dependent country's economy is 'conditioned by the development and expansion of another economy', that the dependent country can expand and be self-sustaining only as a reflection of the expansion of the dominant countries, 'which may have either a positive or a negative effect upon their immediate development'.[33] Asian development strongly confirms this proposition. This becomes clear if we look at the considerable work on dependency theory that has been done precisely in South Korea, including work exploring the limitations of the Korean model which the mainstream has chosen to ignore. Kim Young-ho, for example, considers the backwash-spreading dichotomy against the background of a local dichotomy between 'progressive' and traditional elements.[34] Where the most favourable of each of the two variables coincide, development could occur, although the development of 'semi-development' is the more likely outcome.[35]

An interesting point now arises: there were two imperatives, first the political one, part of the Cold War, to permit some autonomous capitalism to exist in Asia, and second the economic one, to encourage the manufacture of cheap consumer goods. How can we conceptualise the relationship between the two? I have already noted that within an individual country's political economy, capitalism 'rewards' those segments which are useful to it politically by allowing them to become the chosen ones to fulfill the economic tasks necessary for capital accumulation.[36] It can be hypothesised that this would occur internationally as well. In the domestic context the rewards primarily take the form of consumption, but in the international context they could take the form of production.

The two imperatives are therefore harmonious in principle, but this does not necessarily mean that they are smoothly enmeshed in practice; this would require a master-plan of which imperialism is incapable. What happened in practice was that NIC élites were able to take advantage of a situation of disarray in the industrial world. Although Dos Santos spoke of the expansion of the centre acting to 'spread' development, it is also possible that circumstances of crisis and confusion in the centre can be propitious. There are two significant ways in which this happened.

THE CRISIS OF OVER-ACCUMULATION IN THE OLD INDUSTRIES IN THE CENTRE This occurred during the difficult period of adjustment at the beginning of the new long cycle, before the North could restructure in such a way as to confirm its dominance on a new basis. To some extent NIC élites were able to act as independent agents, 'in spite of' their masters. The shipbuilding industry was an example, for Asia apparently managed to 'grab' it during this period. But even here, it is by no means certain that a Northern counter-attack will not eventually take place.[37] It is clear, however, that shipbuilding played a 'launching' role for Asian economy in general during this period.[38]

THE CHANGE IN INVESTMENT PATTERNS IN THE 1980S The NICs faced problems once the restructuring of the North had begun in earnest. But there were also openings (particularly caused by relations among the industrial powers) of which they could take advantage. My earlier discussion of the new technology drew attention to a 'bringing it all back home' scenario in which capital was once again absorbed within the North (in a mixture of industrial re-investment and speculation). Part of this same tendency was a movement of Japanese capital away from the developing world and into other industrial countries. There is evidence that the growth of automation in the industrial powers in the early 1980s was directly linked to the decrease of Japanese investment in the Asia–Pacific region, which freed up resources for hi-tech investment in the North.[39] But these difficulties for the NICs were offset by some positive developments. The huge government borrowing during the Reagan period kept the dollar at unrealistically high levels, which meant both that US companies began to invest increasingly abroad in pursuit of low-cost production bases, and that exports to the United States received a boost. The percentage of Asian NIC exports going to the USA rose from 25 per cent in 1980 to 40 per cent in 1984.[40]

Another development – which once again confirmed the dependency model – occurred in response to further changes within the industrial world. Hitherto, the Japanese had been allowed to maintain an undervalued currency: this helped them to export industrial goods, and Americans feared that the USA would become de-industrialised as a result. In the second half of the 1980s, to counter this, the USA and Europe ganged up to force Japan to raise the value of the yen – it doubled in value against the dollar in the period 1985–88. The response was a huge increase in Japanese investment abroad, as companies sought a base from which they could export. In the second half of the 1980s Japanese companies invested nearly US$600 billion in manufacturing projects abroad.[41] Much of the investment was in other industrial countries, but Asian NICs undoubtedly derived some positive fallout. It should be remarked in this context that, although it looks as though NIC élites were 'grabbing' these opportunities, they were to a large extent being used. Japan had a definite strategic agenda in expanding its management system away from co-location within the home base, as I will show in Chapter 13.

The circumstances that allowed the NICs to develop were very temporary, which illustrates once again that development in the dependent countries is the result of (reversible) external conditions. It does not indicate that countries in the North have permanently accepted Asian development.

## The Optimistic Vision of Export Processing

Foreign investment was by definition an external factor, but NIC élites were not passively waiting for it, but taking active measures to attract it. In this sense, their strategies once again created the openings which central accumulation was able to adjust to. An important example is the strategy of export processing zones (EPZs).

The strategy is an interesting one because, as with export promotion in general, if one examines it theoretically, and ignores class interests, it seems quite ingenious. As I argued earlier, one of the problems the South faced in attempting to turn uneven development to its advantage was that the latter exists within countries, not just between them. In a way, the EPZ idea tries to latch on to this problem and turn it into something positive. Let us look at the thinking behind the EPZ strategy.

In practice, a large part of the supposedly nationalistic NIC approach consisted in handing central capital what it wanted – cheap labour, lack of environmental safeguards, and so on – in a conveniently packaged form. The idea was that capital would rush to seize the bait and could thus be encouraged, almost against its will, to spread. Eventually, some of the benefit could be recouped in the interest of local accumulation. What the EPZ idea did was look at the extroverted port sector – correctly identified by dependency theory as a problem because of its lack of articulation with the rest of the economy – and try to turn it into something useful. The assumption was that external capital could be fenced off into a closed area, and be regulated in a very different way from the rest of the economy. Such an attempt at turning dualism into an advantage eclipsed the Lewis theory in its ingenuity.

Unlike the old development theories, the EPZ idea was propagated by *institutions*, a significant sign of the times. But even more significant, UNCTAD played an important part in its propagation. Taiwan set up an EPZ in 1965, followed by Mexico, Brazil, the Philippines and India, and an UNCTAD report of 1972 synthesised these experiences and encouraged other countries to follow. By the mid-1980s, 84 zones existed in 37 developing countries, with many more under construction.[42] I have been arguing so far that UNCTAD and GATT represented opposing agendas, the former pinpointing structural inequalities, the latter naïvely supportive of the free market. But UNCTAD was after all an institution of élites, and they were excited by the prospects of export promotion. UNCTAD and GATT collaborated in jointly managing the International Trade Centre, which strongly encouraged such schemes.[43] So in a sense the tactics of export promotion grew out of the same élites which had produced the NIEO. This is hardly surprising: rather like the Soviet bureaucrats in the late 1980s, they had milked the old system for what they could get while preparing to maximise their interests within the new one.

Although the EPZ idea has spanned two eras – that of the old development theory, and the neo-liberal era – it has not remained unchanged. To understand in a deep way what has altered, we have to look at the relationship between mobile capital and mobile labour. Under the *Gastarbeiter* model it is the labour which migrates to where the capital is. In this way, central capital can theoretically avoid the long-term reproduction costs of labour, which are met in the country from which the workers originate and to which they are expected to return. However, in the real world it is often difficult to prevent people settling. EPZs are a solution: by exploiting labour in its country of origin, the centre avoids the problem of it settling in the North. Mexico is an interesting case. There used to be systematic schemes (such as the 'Bracero programme'[44]) for exporting Mexican labour to the USA; the Mexican workers should have returned, but in practice many settled, and US capitalism became unhappy at having to meet their reproduction costs.[45] This is the background against which we should consider the Mexican version of export processing, known as *maquila*, a term with feudal resonances.[46] The *maquila*, being based in Mexico, had the advantage (for the USA) of getting Mexico to pay for the reproduction costs of labour, but there was seemingly a compensating advantage for Mexico: the state, which allowed the foreign capital in, could use its authority to enforce national development priorities. To some extent, this was done in the 1970s: US corporations were not permitted to set up wholly-owned subsidiaries but could only operate directly, and they were forced to export 80 per cent of what they produced,[47] which left most of the domestic market for local capitalists.

But there was a flaw in this procedure: because of the dependent nature of the classes which it represented, the state could be captured from within. And this happened in Mexico in the 1980s: using the 'debt' as a lever, foreign capital was able to change the rules and to take over whatever productive capacity it wanted, using the so-called 'debt–equity swap', by which foreign debt papers were exchanged for equity in a productive company. This is a very interesting innovation in capital accumulation: accumulation cannot indefinitely continue to be wholly extractive, so there must be a way of converting the passive liability represented by 'debt' into an active participation in productive capacity which can guarantee the basis of a *future* expansion of value. This ties in with the trend noted earlier, for investment to move increasingly into buying equity in local businesses.

If the state no longer acts as counterweight against foreign capital (as has increasingly been the case with the weakening of the Southern state), it is no longer easy for the South to maintain some wider concept of national development priorities within which to circumscribe and contain the export-processing sector, as was the case in the original EPZ formulation. Instead, export processing becomes the national interest which it had previously been supposed, as something separate and external, to serve. Sri Lanka's Public Security Ordinance of 1992 made it an offence, punishable by a minimum of 10 years imprisonment, to publish or circulate documents detrimental to the export promotion drive.[48] A law of this kind cannot simply be justified in a positivist sense (as an expression of the will of the sovereign power), for, if it is to be regarded as legitimate, there must be an underlying consensus that this is a national goal. But it is difficult to see the real basis for such a consensus. The 'stages' model carried a fairly plausible vision of a future stage of 'national' development when the benefits would eventually be shared. This is missing in the new models.

It may be that a 'new' EPZ phase began in the 1980s, when it had to be accepted that conventional statism had been abandoned, and élites sought to make a virtue of this, by playing the game of globalisation to the full, and cornering some of the factors of production which they could supply more cheaply. Economic growth in its own right became the goal, which is reflected in a terminological shift towards speaking of 'Newly Industrialising *Economies*',[49] which implicitly questions the classic NIC social-Darwinist model according to which the effective units are countries.

Although this appears as a step backwards, it has to be admitted that the 'old' EPZ strategy, with its naïve 'spreading' vision of imperialism, had an inherent and critical weakness which was bound to come through eventually: if spreading occurs because of the existence of cheap, peripheralised labour, there is nothing to stop capitalism 'spreading' from one country to another in pursuit of better conditions. In fact, as can be readily shown, such a danger would arise precisely when development seemed to be working. The only reason why foreign investment targeted such enclaves was the fact that the rest of the economy remained underdeveloped, so that family structures, traditional agriculture, and so on enabled labour power to be purchased below its true value. If dualism was reduced and wages increased, the attraction would be removed. Research has shown that Malaysia lost about 40,000 jobs in the 1980s, simply because transnational investment moved to places where wages were still lower.[50]

The only way to prevent this was to build up gradually the level of skills and infrastructure, so that international capital continued to invest, this time in higher value-added activities which did not depend purely on cheap labour. Even so, highly skilled labour in the periphery is very cheap by central capitalist standards.

## Practical Pitfalls of Export Processing

This strategy for keeping the EPZs atractive for foreign capital is all very well in theory, but in practice it is full of pitfalls. The following are the main problems that had to be faced.

DIFFICULTY OF GETTING COMPLETE INDUSTRIES I discussed product cycles and the new international division of labour in Chapter 9. A new set of circumstances arose in the 1980s, which stemmed directly from these developments.

Since the Fröbel model was put forward, the new technology and management systems have created a whole new range of options for fragmenting the process of production. While vertical integration still exists within the classic TNC, many experiments with post-Fordism have occurred in the centre–periphery context. A study of the ICI paints division[51] suggests that hiving-off batch production to the periphery can permit a firm to make enough profit to delay modernising the centre (where change is costly in terms of fixed capital investment and social relations). But – and this is more important – the product-cycle assumption has been called into question from a different angle. Product-cycles have become so much shorter that some products never have a chance to 'mature', while at the same time apparently mature sectors can be revitalised by the introduction of new technology. A case study of Black and Decker's 1980 restructuring shows that the company integrated vertically in the high-tech sector of chucks and gears, while building up a large catalogue of apparently different tools simply by combining various components (switches, bearings etc.) in different ways. This resulted in a massive demand for standard components, enabling the company to make bulk purchases on the world market.[52] In the motor industry (a key area of power in the IPE), the 1980s witnessed a move by trans-nationals (AC Delco, GKN, Lucas) to strengthen their control over the production of components through restructuring.[53]

As technology replaces labour, it becomes less important to invest in areas where labour is cheap. This is most obvious in the high-tech sector, which gives us a new insight into the limitations experienced by apparently successful models of the South Korean variety. As the corporate head of the South Korean electronics industry put it in 1980,

> the manufacturing costs of a television set in Korea and that of the US are practically comparable to each other. Rapid advancement of industrial techno-logy is eliminating labour-intensive portions of the electronics industry; this tends to make it harder for Korea to earn enough foreign currency to import expensive new technology.[54]

But this same problem is also visible in industries which are not at all high-tech, in other words the ones which used to be considered low-level entry-points for developing countries. Textiles are a case in point. The NIEO project was based on the idea of the product-cycle where the product was a unified entity, so that entire industries could be relocated into Southern economies. The 'new international division of labour' meant that this was already dubious even at the time of maximum NIEO optimism.[55] And new technology has rendered this idea even less workable. Today basic parts can be cut in a highly automated central process, using computers, laser, and so on, and then assembled through a kind of putting-out process.[56]

In the jeans industry, for instance, automatic looms are capable of weaving 760 metres of denim per minute.[57] This requires massive investment, and the cost of the labour wielding the machinery becomes more or less irrelevant. The point, however, is not to eliminate sweatshop exploitation, but rather to develop it further, while ensuring that the South cannot recoup the value generated by the comparative advantage of cheap labour. The North can offset the danger of becoming a pure *rentier* by controlling the high-tech aspects of industry, but it also has to deal with the secondary risk that the South might be able to extract monopoly rents from its cheap labour, and to prevent this, industrial countries also have to cultivate their own informal/sweatshop economy. This leads to a huge diversity in the level of technology used. Los Angeles County, an important jeans producer, combines the highest and lowest technology levels in the USA. A single jeans manufacturer in that area was found to employ 500 different subcontractors.[58]

It is important to note that, while the EPZ phenomenon can be considered an alternative to labour migration – because it permits Northern capital to exploit labour *in situ* where its reproduction costs do not have to be met – there is still a need for very cheap labour in the North, which, paradoxically, anti-immigration policies provide: they guarantee a supply of clandestine workers who can be exploited beyond the usual norms and are excluded from welfare provision. Labour migration, which continues despite being banned, does not undermine the difference between the two rates of profit, because clandestine workers yield a third-world rate of profit even when they are exploited within the North.

So perhaps product cycles in the old form are dead. Even Vernon, whose theories remained in a Rostowite time-warp of discrete national economies, had to recognise, in a World Bank-sponsored report of the late 1980s, that the industries where the South enjoys greatest comparative advantage through cheap labour, such as textiles and footwear, were under considerable pressure to upgrade to advanced machinery in order to remain competitive.[59] In fact, it may be that global products are tending to acquire global prices, determined by socially necessary labour-time, that is, the labour required in the most technologically advanced production system. This means that labour-intensive products competing in the same markets get undervalued in comparison. If the South sticks by its 'comparative advantage' there is an exchange of unequal values. The only way of countering this increased exploitation is for the South to get control of the technology. But this is very problematical.

THE CONTROL OF TECHNOLOGY ITSELF    Clearly, IT is a crucial aspect of control in the current development of the international division of labour, opening the way to a global network for orchestrating a productive process.[60] Measures to hold on to control over hardware are one example. In the statist phase of Brazilian development, the Secretaria Especial de Informatica (SEI) exercised overall control of the sector, dividing the industry into mainframe and smaller computers, with the latter reserved for domestic (mixed public and private) control. This led to some successes.[61] At the same time, the computer industry at a product-identity level is firmly controlled by the North. How independent the Brazilian industry became is open to debate.[62] But even if we assume that statism scored some successes in this department, this only strengthened the resolve of the giants of the computer industry to prevent this happening again. Attempts by the residual statist policies to impose indigenisation rules were strongly resisted. Mexico tried to insist on having a majority shareholding in foreign computer subsidiaries, and Apple and Hewlett-Packard set up companies where they held only 49 per cent. But in 1985 IBM forced the Mexican government to permit it to set up a 100-per-cent-owned subsidiary, whereupon the other two companies converted their subsidiaries to 100 per cent ownership as well.[63] There was a similar attempt in Indonesia, where the Indonesian government planned to get a 51 per cent holding in joint ventures within 10 years. Its success was mainly limited to low-technology projects. When it wanted the American National Semiconductor Corporation to set up a plant in Bandung, it had to allow it to have 100 per cent ownership.[64]

The battle over control of software has been just as fierce. The US authorities have not hesitated to step in to defend the interests of their software houses, using economic reprisals in unrelated areas to attack countries of the South that have tried to gain independence. In 1985 the Americans accused Brazil of 'unreasonable protection' over the rights of authors of software. Negotiations dragged on until 1988, when Brazil was forced to modify its own copyright laws under threat of reprisals. South Korea was forced to make a similar climbdown in 1986.[65] As I will argue later, the USA attempted to use the intellectual property issue in the Uruguay Round of GATT to extend its domestic protectionism in this field.

BRAND IDENTITIES Another element – brand identities – has gained crucial importance in recent years. Much of the new world order rests not on pure economics/management but on the manipulation of identities: the product determines the identity of the person who consumes it, so the creation of brands and consumer identities is as important as the manufacture of the products themselves. In cases like the sports shoe industry or the 'badging' of laptop computers, the marketing company is often not involved at all in the manufacturing process.

It is hard to overestimate the importance of this dimension. It is the element that Hobson was unable to predict – the magic weapon that enables the North to gain the benefits of *rentier* imperialism while avoiding the dangers. In the past, industries such as footwear were given as examples where the South enjoyed an advantage, since production tended to be small-scale and competition was on price; but the phenomenon of trainers has changed all this, not only because of the technology used in the manufacture but above all because of the importance of brand identities. By controlling these, the centre can appropriate all the value while the actual work is done elsewhere.

In the export promotion context, any viable industry in the South has to create global products, and this is difficult. The problems are seen in Malaysia's flagship project, the Proton car: technologically a Mitsubishi, the US attempted to include it within the restricted quota of imports it allocates to Japanese cars, something that both Japan and Malaysia tried to deny. But Malaysia still needed the Japanese brand to sell the car: when it marketed it in Britain it used the slogan 'Japanese technology plus Malaysian "value" – that is, cheap labour. All attempts to 'use' the global economy are circumscribed by this problem of brand identities.

## Can the Post-National Dimension of Political Economy be Used to the South's Advantage?

The question now arises whether it is possible for the South to make creative use of the post-national dimension of the current international political economy. The global information system is undoubtedly chaotic, with many different actors trying to impose conflicting agendas.[66] This probably means that the current system will never be controlled by anything resembling the ultra-imperialist command centre of the old world economy. This means, hypothetically at least, that if the new technology has not helped capital to get better organised, there could be some openings in this chaos for élites in the South to use to their advantage.

There are two major problems with such an assumption. First, even if the IPE is not likely to become ultra-imperialist – if we define this as a form of organisation which can avoid crisis – it can still be highly organised at the level of corporations controlling subcontracting to make sure the core technology is not lost.

Second, the element of chaos within the system has a negative side to it which threatens to outweigh all the hypothetical advantages that developing countries might gain from it: facilitated by the new technology, financial speculators can use the chaos in their own interest. Although this undermines ultra-imperialism, it can also be very damaging to NICs, as I shall show.

If we understand dependency in a really dialectical way, it is not a one-way process. Even though the centre occupies the dominant position within this relationship, social groups in the centre and the periphery develop in a mutually related way, as they explore openings in the global accumulation process. In this sense, the development of exploratory strategies in the South is not only a possibility but a necessary part of the overall picture.

It is probably true that access to the information side of the new technology is becoming more open to some developing countries. The classic example of 'spreading' technology is the way software authoring has increasingly been subcontracted to India in recent years. An ambitious government in the South can use this greater access as a springboard for hardware development. Malaysia recently planned a sort of internationalised cyber-city, with the objective of attracting the internationalised élite to the prospect of Malaysian-financed and assembled products. It proclaimed: 'Component manufacturing can be done in China, on machines programmed in Japan, with software written in India.'[67]

The premise behind this proposal is the idea that a national economy is a thing of the past, and that development has to be situated in an entirely different dimension. But this implies an acceptance of the demise of anything identifiable as social solidarity within a given country. Indeed, such an acceptance is in fact implied in the idea behind the subcontracting of software authoring to India: it is precisely the massive difference in living standards between the élite and the masses which enables central capital, for a comparatively small investment, to offer the new techno-élite a very high status relative to the rest of their society.[68]

The 'flexibility' of the new economic systems makes it possible for small Southern capitalists to develop the strategy of inserting themselves directly in the global structure. They can, for example, use textiles as a springboard but then avoid being trapped at that level by using creatively the disruption of the product-cycle situation to hop from one industrial process to another. Through a succession of investment cycles, they might be able gradually to accumulate value in this way. The actors who evolve to fill this role would fill niches which, to extend the Darwinian image, the powerful brutes of the world economy (transnationals etc.) are too cumbersome to reach.

The term 'guerrilla capitalism' has been coined to describe a new strategy developed by overseas Chinese businesses. As described by Lam and Lee, the 'Chinese' strategy is to create a system of small firms with mutually interlocking ownership which to some extent share information and resources. The firms bid boldly for contracts even if they cannot fulfil them, and then subcontract part of the work, so that, in a departure from the classic capitalist model, the loser in the bidding also derives some benefit. In practice, a company may own only one major piece of machinery, which is clearly insufficient by itself for completing any contract.[69] The scheme became possible because the cost of robotisation, which was initially very high because of the R&D it embodied, fell quite heavily, making the technology accessible to small companies. The Chinese got the idea from Japan, where, at the beginning of the 1980s, small companies were equipped with multi-function robots.[70] The Chinese realised that it was possible, even if you were small, to own a small amount of sophisticated equipment, provided it could be used flexibly: for example, a stamping machine for making automobile parts can be switched over to making computer casings if that is where the demand happens to arise at a particular time. It is crucial to Lam and Lee's model that the firms remain small, either by a process by which managers of family firms leave to set up business on their own (as in Hong Kong and Singapore), or, as in Taiwan, firms send off managers to set up a new company in which the original company retains an equity interest.

How can we conceptualise this theoretically? It must be placed within the overall analytical framework of the centre–periphery theory. The minority of establishment economists who deal with real-world issues in international trade have emphasised the existence of monopoly, but I would take this one step further and say that there are small actors who can survive within the world of monopoly. The difference between the new small capital and the small capital described in a traditional Marxist analysis is that the latter was a relic of a pre-monopoly era whereas the former has evolved specifically in the context of the monopoly era and is adapted to survival within it. International relations theory would correctly recognise actors who adapt themselves to a post-statist environment, but we can understand how they behave only if we place them in the centre–periphery context. This is simply because what underlies it all is the exigencies of capital accumulation and its development across time. Accumulation regimes do not develop according to any conspiracy or grand design, but through a process where, just as small capital seeks to adapt to large capital, large capital in its turn adapts by incorporating examples of initiative and 'entrepreneurship' within its profit-making system.

The appearance of autonomy is falsely cultivated by neo-liberal supply-side economics. Thus Chowdhury and Islam's narrow and economistic study of NICs cites the fact that NIC development did not apparently respond to a pre-existing demand;[71] thus, by implication, they suggest that NIC entrepreneurs took the initiative, without any outside stimulus. But this glosses over two crucial points: first, the contemporary economy is not driven by conventionally defined consumer demand, but rather by marketing strategies. While there is scope for small Southern entrepreneurs, combining high-tech and low-tech elements, to respond to openings in the international economy, this does not mean that they are participating in the strategic elaboration of the culture which creates Northern consumer demand, nor of course in the fundamental R&D which creates the technology. Second, with the current international division of labour, demand today is not for finished products but for components and assembly work. In this respect, the South's role remains passive.

The above analysis shows that there are indeed profound changes occurring in North–South relations. Since dependency is the background against which these changes are occurring, it can be assumed that they will lead to new forms of dependency. At the same time, although there is no overall (ultra-imperialist) structure imposing a grand design, it is evident that there are only a limited number of concrete openings which permit the South to take advantage of the chaos.

Despite this, it is possible that the élites in the South will be able to elaborate a new strategy which will influence the development of the global accumulation structure in the immediate future, particularly as capitalism will have to introduce profound changes in the coming period. Even if in principle these changes will lead to a new form of dependency, they nevertheless remain inherently unpredictable.

## China's Example for a Strategic Campaign by
## Southern Élites

I will now sketch out some aspects of such a strategy. In doing so, I will use China as a case study: my purpose is not to carry out a detailed examination of Chinese policy but rather to attempt to isolate the main elements in a possible Southern élite assault upon the world economy. The Chinese case is significant for the following reasons:

First, partly because of its size, China may be able to develop a Southern strategy which, although it is unlikely to be successful in bringing about a fundamental redistribution of power, could very well disrupt the global accumulation system, forcing international capitalism to carry out a major restructuring from a position of weakness, which would have very unpredictable results. More specifically, China could act as a catalyst for forcing the North to allow part of the accumulated value to be 'fixed' in some more deep-going local development.

Second, the Chinese leadership has always been sophisticated in the strategies and tactics it has developed with a view to exercising initiative within the international system, and not just responding passively to it. The traditional Chinese dialectical view of using the strength of your adversary in order to overcome him, and of operating from a standpoint of a higher moral order within a world of savage internecine conflict,[72] appears very suited for developing strategies for operating within a capitalist world economy, in a sense behind enemy lines.

Third, there is an important element of mass consumption in the Chinese model. The 'turn outward' conducted by the Chinese leadership at the end of the 1970s was based upon the groundwork successfully established by the Maoist model earlier. This does not mean that the contemporary Chinese system should be considered a continuation of the earlier mass movement, since the policies I am describing were undoubtedly formulated by an élite and in many ways bypassed the grassroots. However, despite this, it is still true that the social system in China could not have been produced by conventional development models. The rural economy has been far less underprivileged than in conventional models, and following the post-Mao changes whose domestic basis I mentioned in Chapter 5, consumption in the rural areas has risen dramatically.

Before discussing the role of consumption within a new Southern élite development strategy, it is necessary to discuss in a more general form some of the issues around consumption.

So far I have argued that the switch to export promotion was achieved by denying domestic consumption. This is certainly the main trend, and it explains at a fundamental level how internal and international class relations are interconnected, for Southern countries are indeed prevented from consuming what they themselves produce. But we should also recognise that there is an element within Northern capital which needs the South to consume products which the North produces. There are two main aspects, and I shall look first at the most obvious, which applies to some extent to all the NICs.

CONSUMPTION BY THE PROCESS OF DEVELOPMENT ITSELF NIC development consumes production goods supplied by the North, traditionally heavy industrial products. There is still a heavy industry which needs to export to the South. In fact, the armaments industry is as important as ever, and the NICs are major consumers. While there are significant political dangers in the arms race (I will examine these in Chapter 12), at least from an economic point of view it is 'safe' for the North, because it consumes hardware without increasing the South's productive capacity. But there has also been a change in the definition of production goods. The contemporary economy witnesses the growing importance of an intangible sort of goods which can yield a continuing profit to the industrial world without any new investment in raw materials or (beyond the initial development costs) in labour: the best example is patents, where, once the original R&D costs have been absorbed, any new market brings what virtually amounts to pure profit.

If these goods are to be bought, the local economy must accumulate enough to buy them. Logically (in terms of conventional economics), this would have to be achieved by limiting consumption at a mass level. But this is in contradiction with another of the aspirations of central capital:

INDIVIDUAL CONSUMPTION There has been some expansion in the export of mass consumption goods from the North. As with production goods, there has been a subtle change in the composition of these goods: increasingly they contain a heavy element of brand identities, such as music, soft drinks, communications and cigarettes, along with the advertising that makes people consume these things, which is also an industry in its own right. The industries that produce these goods are dependent on an expansion in the mass market that consumes them. And mass consumer industries serve global capital not only economically but ideologically: since the end of the Cold War, consumer culture has been practically the only possible unifying factor. Even though this form of consumption in itself creates a new form of dependency, it is also true that the North's awareness that it needs this consumption in the South might make it tactically possible to play off the element of Northern capital which needs Southern consumption against the element that wants to squeeze out every drop of value.

While the demand of pure exploitation makes it difficult for international capital to create such a model (since it lacks the strategic vision enabling it to forgo immediate profit), it can adapt to one that already exists: China. And this, in turn, gives China some bargaining power.

The most obvious precedent for a country seeking to exploit these kind of factors was Russia in the period immediately after the Revolution. Russia was seeking its own societal goals, but could only realise these through exploiting whatever openings might arise within a still-developmental capitalism.[73] Later, the Soviet leadership abandoned this approach in favour of building an entirely distinct and self-encapsulated IPE to challenge capitalism as something external to itself. The Chinese, however, had always been sceptical about this:[74] autarky was not voluntary but forced on China by the American blockade. Deng Xiaoping's post-1978 reforms led to both an important discussion on the nature of the capitalist IPE,[75] and in particular to a re-examination of Soviet debates on these questions.[76] Once again, an attempt was made to create a theoretical perspective with which to analyse openings within a developing capitalist political economy.[77] Like the early Soviets, the Chinese have never seen a contradiction between developing long-term socialist goals and applying political realism in the immediate term; on the contrary, the latter is seen as an indispensable basis for the former.[78]

But in one important way the Chinese leadership also went beyond mere passive accommodation with capitalism: for not only did they believe that they must take account of a developmental capitalist IPE, as an external factor, in furthering their societal goals, they also – and more importantly – maintained that they must influence the direction of the development of the international economy if they wanted to attain their goals. They therefore developed a twofold strategy, of interest-maximisation within the current system and of the pursuit of the milieu goal of aiming to change the system itself as a condition for future development. It was for this reason that the Chinese continued to uphold third-worldism even when it went out of fashion. And they went further: they refused to accept the conventional view that adoption of the NIC path means an abandonment of third-worldism (indeed this is one of the main reasons for the establishment propagating the NIC idea).

This is not to claim that the 'Chinese path' is necessarily progressive from a grassroots angle; decision-making is perhaps as centralised in China as in other NICs. But the point I am making is simply that China is a special case, in which importance has been given to social values, first because of the wide spread of consumption and second because of the role of the state as a powerful bargaining force *vis-à-vis* international capitalism. These factors could have a positive impact on the balance of accumulation between the centre and the periphery, and they can only be developed on the basis of a strategic reading of development at an IPE level.

Even though there was quite a lot of continuity in these general orientations between the Mao and Deng eras, there were also important changes after 1978. Before that, China had condemned capitalism in blanket terms, which made it difficult to analyse the developmental aspects of capitalism as a basis for China's strategy; a political campaign at the beginning of the 1970s had even criticised those who advocated making 'electronics as the core' of China's own industrialisation.[79] When at around the same time the US blockade collapsed, China began importing turnkey industrial facilities in exchange for raw material exports, particularly petroleum exported to Japan. If China had persisted with this it would have had to face the same problems as the other would-be NICs: the supposed symbol of independence – heavy industry – would itself have become the basis of a new dependency. In a similar fashion, in the period immediately before the 1978 reforms, China was registering a phenomenal rate of accumulation,[80] which was necessarily beginning to restrict consumption. It was clear that much had to change if China was to embark on the kind of industrial development that would promote the virtuous circle of growth with rising mass consumption, in contrast to conventional NIC development which promoted growth with polarisation.

What was needed was the kind of change which the Soviet model ultimately failed to achieve. At a theoretical level, what was required was to switch the emphasis away from heavy industry to consumer industries. This would mean that accumulation would no longer be necessary at the previous rate, so that demand could then rise, which would simultaneously provide the new industries with a market and build social consensus. But the practical problems of management in attaining this goal were immense. At the time, the technology necessary for economic development was advancing rapidly, which meant that the large investment required for the new industries was threatening to curtail the consumption upon which they were premised. But China found a solution, which will be summarised here. Although the elements of this solution are peculiar to China in their specific form, they also form a useful checklist of what is needed in the model for a 'strong' Southern élite strategy.

IMPORTING TECHNOLOGY ITSELF   The key was to import technology itself, rather than technology embodied in physical plant. Guidelines promulgated in 1982 stipulated that contracts should not restrict China's own R&D, nor restrict the possibility of China making innovations with respect to imported technique nor the possibility of using the technology after the expiry of the contract. At the same time, the technology had to be guaranteed appropriate to China's needs, could not be tied to the purchase of equipment, and had to leave China free to use other suppliers. The supplier also had to guarantee to provide information on any improvements or modifications.[81] One way of China gaining such concessions was by dangling the bait of its huge domestic market in front of the faction of international capital which wanted to sell goods to the developing world.

GAINING ACCESS TO INTERNATIONAL FINANCE   World Bank funds and private funding approved by World Bank guidelines have helped China, not only in providing finance for infrastructural projects, but in damping down an 'overheated' economy without sacrificing long-term growth. There is a contradiction in international capitalism's attitude which China has been able to exploit. On the one hand, capitalism can force policies of an open economy upon China as a condition for the latter's access to finance, or as a condition for it joining the GATT/WTO. Leverage can be used against the surviving elements of socialist economy: for example, the GATT has argued that it has to be able to verify accusations of dumping (selling goods in foreign markets below the cost of production), that in a non-market economy it cannot determine the real costs of production, and so, as a condition of membership, China has to dismantle the state element. But on the other hand – and here lies the contradiction – the collapse of the state would weaken the country's cohesion, and jeopardise the social basis for consumption, thus undermining China's attractiveness as a market. Moreover, China's strong government, which effectively controls the territory, appears increasingly attractive at a time when post-Cold War forces are threatening to bring civil wars, the exodus of refugees, and so on. (I will discuss these issues in Chapter 12.) Interestingly, the recent tendency in World Bank thinking to recognise the importance of such things as social cohesion and the need to reduce income disparities, which is leading it, implicitly, to recognise the role of the state in guaranteeing these things, has been visible for several years in its analysis of China.[82]

EXPORTING THINGS TO PAY FOR TECHNOLOGY IMPORTS   The decline of petroleum prices in the first half of the 1980s forced some developing countries to increase exports in order to maintain a constant level of income, but China was able to take the contrary course of action, and to decide in 1986 to export less. Petroleum shrank from 25 per cent of its exports in 1985 to only 7 per cent in 1988.[83] As a result, the deficit in China's bilateral trade with Japan grew rapidly for a couple of years to reach more than US$5 billion in 1986.[84] China was, however, able to make adjustments to eliminate the deficit:[85] instead of raw material exports, China switched to the export of cheap industrial goods. During 1987–90, its exports of manufactured goods to OECD countries at least doubled, while those of Hong Kong, South Korea, Singapore and Taiwan were static or declined.[86]

Both inward investment and the injection of value created by Chinese labour into the global accumulation system made China vulnerable to the danger of dependency. The purpose of foreign investment is to appropriate the value generated by the cheap labour. When it decided to set up a Jeep plant in China, American Motors cited the fact that wages would be US$0.60 per hour, as compared to US$20.00 in the USA, and claimed that, although the chairman of the subsidiary would be Chinese, 'basically, we will run the plant'.[87] But the danger of being dragged into a dependent relationship can be countered in various ways. The obvious tool for this is the state, but in contemporary circumstances it would not be sufficient on its own. The solution could be an alliance between the state and small capital. Case studies show that subcontracting by centrally managed factories to local ones is common. This may mean that the new management systems can be used in a non-exploitative way to ensure a significant 'social' component within the political economy (as Lenin had attempted to do with the Taylor system in his time). When the Chinese formulated their version of EPZs, called Special Economic Zones (SEZs), they attempted to analyse these from a class point of view, which involved re-examining the issues of Russian revolutionary history, notably the period of the New Economic Policy in the 1920s. There are various forms that an alliance could take: it could be an alliance with large-scale capitalism to transcend rapidly the small-producer economy (as in post-revolutionary Russia), or alternatively an alliance with small capital against bureaucratic capital. One influential faction defended the 'social formation' argument, seeing SEZs as 'socio-economic structures with a variety of economic components of which state capitalism is primary'.[88] Behind the debate there was almost a sense of 'luring' capitalism into the country. This could lead to a new and complex stage of class/national struggle, which would partly occur within the boundaries of a state which identifies itself as socialist. The definitions adopted in this debate were not, in my view, adequate; but even so, the strategy of the state harnessing the new small capital, which has adapted itself to survive under conditions of international monopoly, makes sense. Within this strategy, part of the role of the state would be to ensure that the value generated by the small capital would feed into a genuine development project.

MOBILISING THE DIASPORA  The alliance with small capital was essentially a class issue, within national boundaries. But there was also an international dimension to China's strategy for escaping dependency: to mobilise investment from Chinese living outside the PRC. Historically, most of the investment in coastal 'Special Economic Zones' has actually come from Chinese living abroad. In the early 1990s, the US$10 billion invested by Hong Kong capitalists alone accounted for 60 per cent of total foreign direct investment in China (interestingly, this sum was exceeded by the PRC's own investment in Hong Kong).[89] The osmosis between Taiwanese capital and the mainland was such that the Taiwanese regime found itself obliged to try to limit the scale of the funds moving into the mainland, since the funds available for its own investment programme were drying up. From the national angle, this can be seen as comparable with the idea that Marcus Garvey put forward for Africa: to harness the wealth and knowhow which diasporas have acquired within the international capitalist economy in order to build the country of origin.

FINDING SAVINGS DOMESTICALLY  China found another source of savings by modifying policy in response to its appreciation of the international political scene, carried out within the long-cycle perspective. During the Mao period, it had been necessary to disperse industry in remote areas to guard against the threat of invasion.[90] As this had been extremely costly, it was possible to make important savings by changing the policy. It was also possible to reduce military expenditure in real terms during the decade 1979–89.[91] Particularly significant was the decision to switch plants originally used for the production of arms to manufacture consumer goods. It was a low-cost option for increasing the supply of consumer goods while maintaining a residual defence capacity which could be reactivated if necessary. By 1990, 80 per cent of the production of factories run by the defence ministries was of civilian consumer goods.[92]

While it is certainly the case that at an economistic level the Chinese approach might be able to accommodate popular pressure to raise remuneration, this is quite different from an effective popular influence over development strategy. If it is to become a genuine mass movement for development, the Chinese model will require a much deeper definition of popular participation than it presently allows. The paradox is that, because of its socialist credentials as a movement which undoubtedly originated in a genuine mass struggle, the Communist Party of China is well placed to suppress any spontaneous grassroots movements and popular protests. It is possible that China will evolve in the direction of some meaningful definition of pluralism – not pluralism in the sense of competing élite political groups, but of grassroots movements. For the moment, however, it may be wiser to see China as an élite movement, but as the strongest and most purposeful of today's élite movements. It is possible to envisage a scenario where it could act as a catalyst for the creation of a wider Southern élite movement which – without in itself furthering development in a human sense – might disturb the accumulation dynamic in the international system and thereby create conditions favourable for a mass campaign of the poor. I will expand on this argument in the final part of this work.

### The Limitations on the Asian NIC Model, and the Crisis of the Late 1990s

In the recent period, NICs have increasingly exposed their limitations. The most obvious conclusion is that this leaves the industrial world in a stronger position. It is even possible that the Asian crisis of the late 1990s was engineered in such a way as to realise the objective pinpointed by Hobson – of ensuring that Asian development did not get out of hand.

But for this analysis to be correct, the North must be able to extract its own economies from the trouble, and this is by no means self-evident. Some major structural crisis of the whole accumulation system is bound to occur within the next decade or so. If it so happens that the Asian crisis was the precursor of this, then the North could find itself in a position of strategic weakness. The crisis has already extended beyond what are conventionally seen as NICs. It has begun to embroil Japan, which did not recover from the problems of the 1980s to the same extent as the US. Economic weaknesses, such as over-extended bank loans secured on the basis of over-valued real estate, are festering remnants of the artificial boom economy of the 1980s which undermine Japan's ability to re-galvanise the Asian economy today. Russia has also been sucked into the economic maelstrom, leaving a huge expanse of disorder across Eurasia, the supposed new frontier of investment capital. In these circumstances, the industrial world could be obliged to make sacrifices to shore up certain NICs in order to prevent the destruction their collapse would cause. This could in turn place some cards in the hands of the NICs, though whether their élites would be steadfast enough to use them to the full is another question.

There are thus two conflicting deductions we could draw: on the one hand, it could be argued that the balance of power has shifted in favour of the Euro-American business world, consolidating the colour line, removing the spectre of the 'decline of the West' and making it easier for imperialism to keep Asian development under control; or, on the other hand, it could be argued that, given the interdependence of international capital with the NICs, the crisis will seriously undermine the whole system of capital accumulation. But these viewpoints are not as incompatible as they seem; one or the other may predominate at particular phases of the crisis.

If the crisis came as a shock to the establishment, this is only because it had for a long time been fooling itself. It had cultivated a naïvely optimistic scenario: it saw NIC development as a sort of escalator, with South Korea at the top and others, such as Indonesia and Malaysia, firmly on their way up. As they vacated spaces at the bottom, other countries could step on. This analysis seemed to combine the virtues of an up-to-date 'stages' theory (whose point of reference was firmly contemporary, in contrast with the questionable historical analogies of the Rostow model) with elements of both the product-cycle and flying geese models.

But this standpoint has always had fatal flaws. Part of the difficulty is political. Even if we accept what it says about Korea, it does not explain what will happen to countries like Indonesia and Malaysia which had traded on anti-communism to get concessions. Unless we assume that their development has become, in Dos Santos' phrase, 'self-expanding', and has thus broken free from the capacity of the North to trample on it, it is questionable whether or not it will be able to survive the end of the Cold War and the re-definition of US policy on economic lines. It is all a question of how many honorary Aryans the system can tolerate.

But there is also a more fundamental economic flaw which calls into question even the 'best case' (South Korea). It becomes evident if we look at issues like indebtedness. Until the crisis broke out in 1997, the full scale of the dependence of Asian NIC development on foreign indebtedness was somehow obscured. But it is now apparent that internal borrowing in South Korea was heavily reliant on the availability of external capital. Domestic banks would lend money without any normal business considerations because they knew that external funds would cover the gap. It has become clear that the peripheral economies are self-expanding only in so far as they absorb finance from outside. In late 1997, South Korea was discovered to have an external debt of US$110 billion,[93] which served as backing for an internal debt accrued by Korean companies that amounted to a staggering US$323 billion.[94] In all, it can be seen that the NICs and the international credit system had acquired a symbiotic relationship one to the other.

But theoretical issues, too, had been swept under the carpet. It is true that individuals within the economics establishment had made a critique of the Korean model. In particular, Paul Krugman had argued that initial growth-rates had reflected the use of non-renewable inputs. He said that the Asian models had mobilised these very effectively, but that ultimately they would prove no better than the Soviet model in generating long-term growth, which could only come from increases in efficiency, which means, ultimately, from new ideas. From this angle, the fact that Asian NICs are now exporting capital can be considered a reflection not of their dynamism, but of diminishing returns at home.[95] From the viewpoint of the North, this analysis is reassuring in relation to the problem raised by Hobson, for it suggests that as long as the ideas are safely in Euro-American hands, Asia will not become genuinely autonomous. But this analysis raises another issue which cannot be answered so readily: was it correct, ideologically as well as financially, to invest so heavily in a model whose future was so dubious?

Krugman's analysis was somewhat economistic, and the question of the NIC model not being self-expanding has to be understood in a social as well as an economic sense. But other authors added a social dimension to the critique of pre-crisis South Korea. Bello and Rosenfeld were right to point out that, while the regime of Park Chung-hee which dominated South Korea in the 1960s and 1970s could force the privileged class to pull in the same direction, it is by no means certain that this created a dynamic, self-sustaining élite social structure which could survive once the authoritarianism was removed.[96] Taking these different elements together, it was hardly possible for global capital to claim that it had not been warned.

But the illusion that all was fine was maintained nevertheless. It was necessary to admit South Korea to the OECD (the club of industrialised states) to demonstrate that international development is a 'career open to talents'. If no countries ever succeeded, there would be no point in all the other developing countries making the sacrifices. If the inner weakness of the NIC model had been revealed, there was the risk that the whole edifice of export promotion and structural adjustment would collapse like a pack of cards and with it the local basis for global capital accumulation. But there was also a risk in *not* admitting the weakness, in that global capital could become seriously exposed by shoring up the NICs beyond a point where it was rational to do so. By and large the establishment observed the first of these imperatives.

As long as local growth and global accumulation were both going ahead, the economic and ideological aspects were in harmony. But once the crisis began, this neat concordance fell apart. Investment in NICs was still justified from an ideological point of view (as a way of prolonging the illusion) but from a strictly economic angle, the NICs suddenly appeared as a 'sink', which absorbed capital to no immediate purpose.

The different pre-crisis critiques of the NIC model generally agreed that the NICs lacked real technological autonomy. Indeed, the Asian countries' lack of autonomy had been cruelly exposed in the second half of the 1980s, with the Cold War waning. Reprisals against Asian exports sharply increased in Europe in the period 1985–88 and a computer price war, launched by the big American companies in 1991, led to a wave of bankruptcies in Korea and Taiwan. The Korean company that won the top award in 1990 for computer exports went bust in the following year![97] It was clear that, without technological independence in practical terms, the writing was already on the wall for the Asian NICs.

This was in an important sense the background to the crisis which broke out in the late 1990s, so why was the impact delayed? It could be argued that this was part of a strategic master-plan and that investment in component production and assembly in the NICs was still yielding a profit. But it is questionable whether capital is in fact capable of behaving so strategically. It seems much more convincing to argue that investment and speculative capital had taken on an autonomy of its own, and not even the capitalist powers were able to control it.

The international system of credit must, in fact, take much of the blame for artificially prolonging the NIC models in the face of their structural weakness. Credit has never been regulated since the advent of the Bretton Woods system.[98] Far from helping to resolve the crisis, speculative capital seems to have played the crucial role in accentuating the weakness of the models once the crisis had begun. Speculative capital has increasingly taken on its own momentum, a process which has accelerated very rapidly in recent years. It has been estimated that whereas in 1975 80 per cent of foreign exchange transactions were to do with the real economy (buying commodities or goods, investing, and so on), by the late 1990s this had shrunk to 2.5 per cent, the remaining 97.5 per cent being speculative.[99] In practice, it is difficult to maintain the distinction between 'good' industrial capital and 'bad' speculative capital, as banks and TNCs increasingly indulge in speculation as a hedging activity. Indeed, speculation has taken over as the main mechanism of realising capital accumulation. And speculative capital may have an interest in exposing the myths which other sections of capital would like to sustain; one of the most obvious ways in which this happens is by speculators moving against the value of the currencies of the NICs. Once this has happened, credit also dries up.

If capitalism were governed by strategy, capitalist interests would perhaps have decided either not to sustain the NICs with such thoughtless injections of credit in the first place, or not to undermine them so suddenly once the crisis had begun. But reality again shows how far we are from ultra-imperialism. During a crisis, different facets of capital often pull in different directions. And it is awareness of the profound lack of concordance between the different forms of capital which almost certainly lies behind some of the more catastrophist pronouncements of establishment spokesmen. The World Bank's chief economist said that the Asian crisis 'reminds us of the risks that private capital poses for all countries'.[100] Japan's deputy finance minister said that it was not really an Asian crisis but a 'global crisis of capitalism'.[101] The problem is that if the NIC economies do not, in some limited sense, develop, it will become impossible to continue using them as a basis for speculation. And if speculation ends abruptly, the whole credit system will be undermined and equity investment will also be damaged. There will be no basis for future accumulation.

So the North is now trying to insulate itself from the effects of the crisis. The European Commission said that 'economic recovery is now pulled by internal demand, which has replaced external demand as the chief motor of growth'.[102] This is partly true in that an NIEO-style global Keynesian model of growth, propelled by rising Southern mass demand, has clearly been rejected. Instead, it is being firmly stated that the North is the main market, and the NICs are dependent *on this*: 'The US market still plays the role of the centre of Asian industrial dynamism around which Asia's export-driven growth has been organised', and even the idea that this could eventually change, with Asia consuming its own product, excites considerable scepticism.[103] It is argued that if Northern economies can remain healthy, despite decreasing demand in the South, and if their good health is the condition for continued NIC growth, then maybe there is a way out of the crisis.

There are other signs, such as the currency question, that the industrial countries are still in control, or at least want to appear that they are. Until the crisis, Asian NIC currencies were pegged to the US dollar. This did not hamper their export competitiveness unduly because the value of the dollar was falling relative to other currencies. But the peg effectively helped to maintain some of the value generated by the cheap labour within the countries that produced the labour: it prevented the parities from fully reflecting the lower value of labour (ultimately, the lower value of human life) determined by the colour line – as has happened with the devaluations imposed by SAPs on Africa. Now that the NICs have been forced to devalue, it will be far cheaper to buy local companies and to hire local labour, which will significantly increase the rate of profit for the North. Some of the US business press have been openly rejoicing over the fact that, in compensation for the value lost by those sectors of capital which need to export to the NICs, multinational companies will get Asian labour much cheaper.[104] The valuation of American companies and, in fact, the health of the US economy itself is strongly influenced by the level of profits they can extract from Asia.[105] This shows that international capitalism does not fundamentally fear Asian exports. But there is a hidden problem, analogous to the one encountered in ISI, namely that the acquisition of advanced industrial capacity (upon which export success is based) is conditional on the import of technology and intermediate goods. These imports used to be funded indirectly by external credit, but now devaluation has increased the cost of these inputs. And of course, the cheap industrial goods imported from Asia by the North have become even cheaper; again, US economic circles welcome this as a way of reducing inflation, but what it really signifies is that the rate of profit has improved, at the expense of NIC labour.

So there is considerable cause for celebration in the North, but it is easy to see why much of this optimism may be misplaced. First, although the North is not wholly dependent on selling products to the NICs, it still needs two things from them: to import their products in order to keep up the rate of profit, and to expand the value of Northern capital by drawing in the value generated by the cheap labour used in making those products. Second, in the past, local élite interests guaranteed the reproduction of local structures, as there was a certain accommodation with central capitalist interests that enabled them to accumulate enough to do this task. This equilibrium has now been disturbed, and the reproduction of the South's structures is now increasingly problematical.

This issue is fundamentally social, in that some appearance of local accumulation is a minimum condition for the maintenance of social cohesion. In the absence of consumption in the South, the only basis for national identity at present is the promise that development is proceeding along lines which will eventually allow, or even require, consumption to rise. Growth made it possible to create the illusion of a unified movement which brought together different classes and ethnic groups – even though, in a case like Indonesia, this was so unconvincing that the set-up could collapse with only a small push. And when economies collapse there is the risk of famine, the exodus of refugees, competition between countries over scarce resources, military conflicts, with the firing of missiles at each other, and so on. All this adds up to a strong case for the North to relax part of its exploitation. It is against this background that we find not only the World Bank but even the IMF trying to take the long-term view and play at ultra-imperialism. What are their chances of success?

There are two kinds of crisis: ones that occur *within* the existing regime of accumulation, and others that are a crisis *of* that regime, which could only be resolved by changing it fundamentally. The two perspectives merge into one another, in the sense that any phenomenon receives its character from the contradictory forces within it. They achieve a kind of harmony but retain the element of antagonism, functioning simultaneously as determinants of the thing and as forces for change. Capitalism's present objective is to shore up the existing system, but in my view, this can only be a short-term solution, since IMF intervention in support of NIC economies is bound to siphon credit out of other areas of the IPE. The money pledged to Indonesia and Thailand – a sum far in excess of the amount permitted under IMF rules – seriously depleted the IMF's funds. In all, the packages arranged by the IMF for South Korea, Thailand, Indonesia and the Philippines amounted to US$113 billion. It came from a variety of sources, but US$41 billion was the IMF's own money. It has been estimated that this left only US$40–45 billion in the IMF's reserves, so, faced with the probability of other crises in the future, it has been forced to raise another huge sum: US$287 billion.[106] The sums involved are so large that they would seriously affect capital accumulation if so much value was tied up without immediately reproducing itself in an expanded form. In 1998 the IMF was already having a lot of trouble in getting the USA to stump up an extra US$14.5 billion.

There has never been a Marshall Plan for the South. Historically, the North has only been prepared to sanction for very short periods a scheme by which short-term profitability is sacrificed for long-term economic and politico-ideological goals. This is precisely the reason why the money was formerly focused in key areas, such as the so-called miracles of South Korea and Taiwan, where the ideological conflict was very evident. But today the Cold War is over. Even Russia, suffering the repercussions of the Asian crisis, is placing major demands on this 'fund'. It is hard to see where all the money can come from.

In a deeper sense, we can probably say that the crisis of the late 1990s is a precursor of a crisis of (rather than within) the accumulation regime. To be resolved, it will require drastic action, since the whole accumulation system (in the North as well) will be called into question. It will only be resolved by changing everything, but the dominant interests are not ready for this yet. Moreover, a major structural crisis is never expressed in the international economic system alone, but in the prevalent internal development models as well. In the 1970s, it was the whole of import substitution, the 'stages' and two-sector model in the South and Keynesianism in the North, which were suddenly called into question. There is every likelihood that the current crisis will not be resolved simply by patching up the existing semi-statist export-oriented models of the NICs. Instead, the entire model will be challenged, and at the moment no one knows what will emerge from the process of transformation.

Given the vulnerability of the world economy and the resistance that many capitalist forces are showing to the idea of a total restructuring, the question arises whether the NICs could turn their very weakness into a source of strength and threaten to tear the whole system down, as a basis for gaining concessions. It is true that a similar opening was wasted in the 'debt' crisis of the early 1980s, but in some ways international capitalism was stronger at that time, since it was exploring the potential of a new long cycle rather than wrestling with one already in decline.

I believe that it would be logical at this moment for the South to develop a strategy to exploit the current situation. Perhaps under pressure from below, élites might well press for concessions which, although not incompatible with international capitalism as a whole, would be incompatible with the current regime. It is unlikely that this will become a basis for effective 'spreading', but it is possible that it could precipitate the crisis in the current accumulation regime. The role of China in this will be crucial.

As we have seen in earlier chapters, there have been times when capitalism seemed to be in a structural impasse, but eventually it found a way out of the crisis. This suggests that this time too we should be sceptical of catastrophist visions of capitalist crisis and collapse. However, this is true only in narrow economic terms. For what is problematic for capitalism is guaranteeing the future basis of its development, and it is far from certain that here capitalism has found a viable way forward. In a deeper sense, the crisis is socio-ecological, in that it lies in the sphere of the non-reproducible resources – both ecological and human – consumed as part of capital accumulation. From this angle, the problem will not be affected by the transition to a new accumulation regime. As Indonesia shows, the social and ecological aspects of the crisis coincide. In this sense, the future must lie not with élite NIC movements but with grassroots forces which address the fundamental socio-ecological issues. The upsurge of such forces is in fact an expression of the acuteness of the contradictions which in this case are related to the crisis not just of a particular accumulation regime, but of capitalism as a whole.

Even if we accept that, in narrow economic terms, the transition to a new regime of accumulation is possible, it is clear that it will take place under extremely disruptive circumstances, possibly exacerbated by a Chinese-led Southern élite strategy aiming at maximising concessions from the restructuring. This will provide important external conditions for the rise of grassroots movements in other parts of the South that will seek to promote an agenda of radical system-change.

## Notes

1. The two sides of the contradiction are related, in that it was partly the surviving great-power rivalry which prevented the realisation of these tendencies earlier.

2. The term *rentier* refers to people (by extension, nations) who live entirely on the income from investments, and don't do any work of their own.

3. Lenin 1970, Chapter 8.

4. Hobson 1938, p. 195. Given the growth of militarism in the South, this latter statement is quite far-sighted.

5. Ibid., p. 230.

6. cf. Ikeda 1996.

7. Petrella 1996, pp. 70–71.

8. Khanna 1996.

9. Cook and Kirkpatrick 1995, p. 10.

10. Ibid., p. 20.

11. Ikeda 1996, p. 55.

12. Petrella 1996, p. 79.

13. *Observer*, 8 March 1998.

14. Epstein 1996, p. 215.

15. Khanna 1996.

16. Cf. *New Statesman*, 18 July 1997, p. 13.

17. The journal *Le Monde diplomatique* made this point in a far-sighted way in its collection of articles published as *Le Libéralisme contre les Libertés*.

18. Freire 1972, p. 22.

19. In mainstream theory, to the extent that internal dislocation is recognised (in the theory of dualism, or 'two-sector' models like that of Lewis), this is separated from the international aspect.

20. Cf. R.S. Eckhaus, 'The Factor–Proportions Problem in Underdeveloped Areas', in Agarwala and Singh 1958.

21. Cf., for example, Lambert, Denis-Clair, *19 Amériques latines – Déclins et Décollages*, (Paris: Economica, 1984).

22. See, for example, Harris 1987; the following statistics are taken from that source, p. 83.

23. Palloix 1975.

24. This can be glimpsed using admittedly unreliable statistics. Brazil had successfully overhauled India for example, but this was reflected in a relative deterioration of the living standards of ordinary people. In 1983 the poorest 40% received 8.1% of national income (India 20.4%) Banque Mondiale, *Le Développement dans le Monde* 1990, pp. 258–9.

25. Quoted in Roddick *et al.*, 1988, p. 130.

26. In one year in the early 1970s there were 13,000 fatal (35 per day) and 50,000 permanently disabling industrial accidents in Brazil; Frank 1981, p. 12.

27. Cf. Okwudiba Nnoli, 'A Short History of Nigerian Underdevelopment' in Nnoli (ed.) 1981.

28. See Ghai and Hewitt de Alcantara 1991, p. 27.

29. Cf. Cook and Kirkpatrick 1995, p. 22.

30. Over a ten-year period ending in 1993, Latin America as a whole paid US$296 billion in interest on the 'debt', while during same period the 'debt' itself increased from US$242 to US$429. In Brazil's case US$112 billion was paid, while the 'debt' almost doubled to US$120 billion; *Guardian*, 8 February 1993.

31. *Keesings Record of World Events*, May 1990.

32. See White 1974, pp. 202ff.

33. Dos Santos 1970, p. 231; the definition is reproduced from an earlier article by Dos Santos published in 1968.

34. I would not accept the tendency to equate traditional elements with backwardness, which is to be found within the dominant discourse of 'modernisation'; if there is any truth in it, it is only because such elements are in reality truncated structures of class dominance, which are themselves generally reinforced by the centre–periphery relationship. Just as spreading is not necessarily good, tradition is not necessarily bad.

35. Kim Young-Ho 1987, p. 184.

36. This theory develops some of the sociological insights of Peter Townsend; see Townsend 1979.

37. Indeed, in early 1994, after the conclusion of the GATT Uruguay Round, the United States launched a vigorous interventionist campaign to hold on to its own shipbuilding industry.

38. It has the characteristics of a labour-intensive process without economies of scale, with a high skill factor and significant linkages to other economic sectors in the country where it is sited; cf. Mureau 1989.

39. Rada 1985, p. 575.

40. Qi Luo and Howe 1993, p. 747.

41. Hill and Lee 1994, p. 298.

42. For a survey of this history, see Crane 1990.

43. Cf. Hoekman and Kostecki 1995, p. 53.

44. See Cohen 1991, Chapter 4.

45. California has, for example, witnessed intense political agitation over the social costs of education etc. of latino working people.

46. The term is derived from a feudal practice, in which those who do the actual processing work are entitled to retain a proportion of the product.

47. Castel 1988.

48. Hettiarachchy 1992, p. 7.

49. Although immediately this term reflects the ambiguous international status of Hong Kong and Taiwan, at a deeper level it is highly symptomatic of a switch away from the 'country' as a point of reference.

50. Benaria 1989.

51. See Clarke 1986.

52. Lehnerd 1987, pp. 59–62.

53. See Foreman-Peck 1986, p. 147.

54. Quoted in Rada 1985, p. 575.

55. The more general points suggested by the Fröbel model, that this began well before the emergence of the new management systems, are confirmed in this case by Clairmonte and Cavanagh 1981, Chapters 1–2.

56. Cf. an officially commissioned report prepared in France about the future of the textile industry, which employs the term 'artisanat industriel'; Le Monde 6 december 1989.

57. Baily and Chakrabarti 1988, p. 65.

58. Gereffi 1993, p. 65.

59. Vernon 1989, p. 26.

60. It is interesting to note that the nineteenth-century English management theorist Babbage, on whose works a lot of the Fröbel model is based, was also the pioneer of computing.

61. See Preston 1987.

62. Schwartzman 1988.

63. Cf. Castel 1988, p. 191.

64. Cf. Taylor and Thrift 1992, p. 122.

65. Raghavan 1990, p. 73.

66. Cf. Simons 1987.

67. Malaysian premier, Mahathir Mohamad, quoted in the Guardian, 22 March 1997.

68. Cf. Srinivas 1998.

69. Lam and Lee 1992.

70. Cf. Bell 1984, p. 57.

71. Chowdhury and Islam 1993.

72. Cf. Cleary 1988.

73. Cf. Day 1981.

74. Cf. Friedman 1979.

75. Cf. Shambaugh 1991.

76. Cf. Rozman 1987.

77. Cf. Brugger and Kelly 1990.

78. I am grateful to Jaspal Singh for emphasising this point.

79. This critique is referred to (approvingly!) in Tissier 1976, p. 111.

80. I argued earlier that this rate had been excessive in the 1950s, and attempts were made to reduce it in the 1960s. However accumulation escalated again with the four modernisations programme. Since 1970 the rate of accumulation had been over 30%, and by 1978 had escalated to 36.5% (see B. Reynolds, 'China in the International Economy' in H. Harding (ed.), *China's Foreign Relations in the 1980s*, p. 77). This was far in excess of the rate which had appalled Bettelheim in the context of the Leap Forward.

81. Simon 1984, p. 303.

82. Cf., for example, Sheahan 1986.

83. Naughton 1994.

84. Liao 1984, p. 251; Whiting 1989, p. 93.

85. It is significant that Japan accounted for only about 15% of foreign investment in China in the late 1980s; cf. Nester 1992, p. 141.

86. Yeats 1991, p. 12.

87. Quoted in Cumings 1984, p. 247.

88. Crane 1990, p. 42.

89. Yahuda 1993.

90. See Naughton 1991.

91. Most of the increase in 1992 was apparently absorbed in a one-off purchase of military aircraft as part of a barter deal with the USSR; see Bin Yu 1993.

92. Folta 1992, p. 123.

93. *Financial Times*, 25 November 1997.

94. *Le Monde*, 20 November 1997.

95. Krugman 1994; Krugman is much more effective in debunking Japan and the 'tigers' than he is with the case of China.

96. Bello and Rosenfeld 1990.

97. Liu 1996, pp. 149, 151.

98. Cf. Altvater 1992.

99. Lietaer 1997.

100. *Guardian*, 25 March 1998.

101. Quoted in Golub 1998.

102. *Le Monde*, 26 November 1997.

103. Berri and Ozawa 1997.

104. Cf., for example, *Fortune*, 27 October 1997, p. 139.

105. Cf. *Time*, 3 November 1997.

106. *The Times*, 13 January 1998.

# 11

# Permanent Subordination? Structural Adjustment as Control

Structural adjustment is a concept developed over a number of years by the World Bank and IMF – but acquiring particular importance since the 1980s under the impact of the 'debt' situation – whereby countries are forced to change their whole economic structures in accordance with a philosophy imposed from outside. Nominally, the prescribed policies seek an efficient form of management by emphasising market forces. But I will argue that, in the last analysis, structural adjustment really signifies making the internal structures of the South conform to the dictates of the international system of capital accumulation.

To understand this, we can borrow from structuralism a perspective which sees certain phenomena as having a function, without implying that it is completely purposive, still less conspiratorial. The World Bank does not necessarily start from a subjective desire to promote exploitation. The point is simply that for them the system is 'given', it cannot be altered or improved, so one can only conform as best as possible to it. The system is, in the last analysis, driven by capital accumulation. From this it follows that the internal structures of countries must be designed to conform to its dictates.

The liberal critique of structural adjustment programmes (SAPs) often assumes they are wildly mistaken, but this is to forget that SAPs are not really there to help countries develop, but to integrate them into the system of the self-expansion of capital. If they make the people poorer, this could be a sign that they are doing a very good job.

But we should be wary of giving SAPs more praise than they deserve. The international capitalist system is riddled with contradictions. Objectively, SAPs seek to ride the tiger of these contradictions, using them creatively as far as possible, but in practice more often than not they tie themselves in knots. In this chapter, I will try to show both how SAPs serve the needs of capital accumulation, and the contradictions which could bring about their downfall.

The fundamental contradiction centres around the problem of short-term profit versus the long-term conditions (economic – the reproduction of

labour – and socio-political) for future exploitation. This contradiction can
be seen under two aspects. First, the general problem raised by Rosa Luxemburg's contribution to imperialism theory: is capital accumulation renewing
itself or merely exhausting its own basis? Second, the aspect specific to the
changeover of long cycles. The change of long cycles happened around 1980
which was just when SAPs came in, and this is not a coincidence. They
helped to design the Southern component of this change, using the 'debt' as
a lever to break resistance to the demands of the new accumulation system.
But this still leaves a big question: SAPs may have been good at destroying
the old, but this does not mean they could provide a basis for a stable self-
reproducing set-up even within the confines of the current accumulation
regime.

## The Historical Significance of Structural Adjustment – the Institutionalisation of Control

The use of international institutions to issue orders to the South is an
innovation. Colonial exploitation was carried out by individual powers; oc-
casionally they collaborated (for example, over China) but this was not
institutionalised. Decolonisation inaugurated a second phase, which involved
an apparent recognition of the autonomy of the Southern entities as countries.
This provided a cost-effective substitute for old-style colonialism, in which
indigenous élites did the governing and countries were integrated into the
international division of labour through the kind of state-level dependent
industrialisation promoted by ISI models. By paying lip service to the notion
of building complete national economies in the South, these models harmonised in a rough-and-ready way the political demands of transition to neo-
colonialism with the specific forms of economic activity needed by central
capital at that time. Retrospectively, it can be seen that the global economy
at that time was not sufficiently developed for economic actors to be integrated
directly into it, so accumulation could be realised only through the intermediary
of identifiable national economies.

Structural adjustment coincided with the transition to a third phase of
North–South relations where this constraint is transcended. I will call it
post-neo-colonialism. The Bretton Woods institutions found themselves cast
in the role of enforcers of this change. A key problem in the 1970s was that
the third world movement was putting forward a definition of 'structural'
which was very threatening to the dominant interests; for example, according
to this radical definition of 'structural', when a developing country suffered
deficits, this was often a reflection of the 'drain' of resources to the North.
This subversive definition had to be destroyed, and who better to do this
than the World Bank and IMF? Historically, their policies had always been
based on a narrow, apparently purely technical definition of the term 'structural', according to which, if countries have a trade deficit or their currency

is under attack, this implies that they have not discovered the right niches in the world market. Within this framework, it makes sense for the support they receive – whether in the form of short-term finance to maintain the currency, or long-term aid to actual development projects – to be conditional on their adopting structural measures to ensure resources will find their way to the sectors which are competitive. This spurious continuity with the original orientation of Bretton Woods, which was to maintain monetary stability as a basis for free trade, hides the real reason why global capitalist institutions stepped in to police Southern societies directly. The new discourse completely rejected NIEO-style demands to change the system itself, so policy was reduced to a question of 'adapting' a country in the South to fit into the system by creating local conditions (for example, reducing interference from local bureaucrats) so that capital could find its way without hindrance to the most promising sectors.

Although the link between SAPs and the change in long cycles is important, it does not provide a complete picture. In reality, the World Bank's role in developing countries began earlier. In this sense, structural adjustment was merely the expression at a particular moment of a longer-term imperative, which began with the dismantling of old-style colonialism and will probably continue after the demise of SAPs. This imperative is the need to find some social basis for a multilateral dominance over the South.

## The Grand Design of Social Engineering and Its Failures

Many critical works on the World Bank cite its early head Eugene Black saying that World Bank aid serves US business interests. This is often taken at face value, but we should understand the hidden subtext: the reason Black said this was because he needed to sell the idea of the new institution to business! Then as now business had to be convinced that it was necessary to make an investment in the socio-political basis of long-term exploitation at the expense of short-term profit. From the beginning, this was the World Bank's vocation. Its structural role was further developed under the leadership of Robert McNamara, who took over the job in 1968. At the beginning of the 1960s, he had been President of the Ford Motor Corporation, and then became Defense Secretary during the escalation of the Vietnam War. His business experience had convinced him that it was necessary to make the world safe for multinationals, but Vietnam had showed him that this could not be done by military means alone. What was needed was a pre-emptive, proactive approach that, through social engineering, would achieve two goals: first, give élites some developmental incentive to align with the West, and second, mitigate – or, better still, appear to mitigate – the poverty which encouraged revolution.

The first of these imperatives is reflected in World Bank analysis in the late 1970s, which claimed that newly industrialising countries (NICs) were moving from low-tech to high-tech industries, leaving room for other LDCs to take their place, a process which it said the bank should be actively promoting. As many as 30 countries were identified as good candidates for 'promotion'. This was the original reasoning behind structural adjustment loans (SALs).[1] It was, in effect, a Rostowite model that was being applied, with the idea that the Bank could push countries across the threshold of take-off. The second imperative is reflected in a 1977 document, where the World Bank took over the 'basic needs' ideas then emerging in the development debate, and argued that it was necessary to look for ways 'in which basic human needs can be met earlier in the development process'.[2]

It can be argued that together these two elements responded to the needs of capitalism at that time, but this is not to say that they are compatible. To try to graft a basic needs approach on to the stages theory is not consistent with Rostowism, because it would mean that accumulation would have to be restricted, and Rostow had never promised rewards here and now. Was it possible to square the circle? Logically, this would require significant injections of funds from the North, in order to invest in the poor without curtailing accumulation.

While success stories were clearly needed, it was never likely that capitalism would accept such an injection of funds, particularly as it was being suggested that as many as 30 countries should benefit. A counter-attack was launched against this sort of global 'Great Society' agenda. It was part of an ideological fightback which eventually became dominant, at least in the consolidation phase of the new long cycle, that is, under Reaganomics.

It took the form of a concerted attack upon both aid and, more generally, development economics as a whole. American P.T. Bauer led an early onslaught on the grounds that aid inhibited Southern peoples from developing 'the faculties, attitudes and institutions favourable to material progress'. Their traditional society, he said, already encouraged an 'unquestioning acceptance of the nature of things', which aid would only entrench.[3] This was an argument against any Marshall Plan-type social engineering which would involve large-scale investment. The Marshall Plan itself was all right, according to Bauer – and interestingly so was aid to Israel – because 'The populations already possessed the faculties and motivations appropriate to successful development.'[4] This was only a whisker away from arguing that you were doing the South a favour by exploiting it!

For all its crude racism, this argument could, interestingly, be twisted to fit in with a 1980s-style post-modern pseudo anti-racism, on the grounds that traditional development economics patronised peoples of the South because it made an exception of them. This struck a chord among a segment of Southern élites who were prepared to connive in the destruction of the national-economy models which previously guaranteed their own status because they saw a chance rapidly to consolidate their status within the international economy. An example was Deepak Lal, who argued that 'The hallmark of much of development economics has been a paternalistic denial that the poor and ill-educated masses of the Third World could respond rationally, as either consumers or producers, to changes in relative prices.'[5] This was very much a 'united colours' approach which in substance consolidated the racial divide by denying the South the special measures that it needed to attack the institutional poverty embedded in the world system.

The shift to Reaganomics sanctified the repudiation of large-scale aid. By and large, the World Bank and IMF fell into line: they attacked the third-world state in general, but were prepared to break their own guidelines to shore up a particular government if this suited Reagan. Huge transfusions of aid went to Sudan in the period 1978–1984, and in 1984 Reagan even paid off Sudan's arrears with the IMF out of US public funds.[6] The IMF took on an increasing role, which serves as a convenient excuse for the World Bank to fall in behind an essentially short-termist policy geared around the supposed rectification of balance of payments problems. In this sense, the division of labour between the two institutions was like that between two policemen interrogating a suspect: the nasty cop (the IMF) was overtly brutal and overbearing, the other (the World Bank) was friendly, concerned about the well-being of the suspect's family, and critical of his colleague, telling you he really had your interests at heart when he cajoled you into signing the paper (the SAP).

But this alignment only papered over a fundamental contradiction. Reaganomics was an ideology appropriate to smashing resistance, but it had no real capability for building something new. The proactive, interventionist trend survived in the World Bank, which in a sense became a true 'regime' (a quasi-independent actor) of international capitalism, distancing itself when sections of the US establishment veered towards either pure repression or isolation (most right-wing American populists hate the World Bank).

But can structural adjustment be more successful than Reaganomics in generating something with a more positive content?

## In Search of a Positive Content for Structural Adjustment

While there is certainly a tendency for the Bretton Woods institutions to take on an autonomous role as representatives of global capital (independent of the individual states of the North) their scope has been constantly limited by the amount of resources which the capitalist interests are prepared to abstain from grabbing from the South. Within these limitations, is there enough room for them to find a new, post-McNamara economic equation to secure the long-term future of exploitation without sacrificing short-term profit?

I will attempt to construct the basis of such a solution; its logic is inherent in the system of capital accumulation itself, and it is not necessarily articulated subjectively by the institutions themselves.

FUNDING CHANGE FROM THE DEBRIS OF THE STATE  Structural changes can be funded in a low-cost way (that is, without a significant North–South transfer of funds) by generating resources from the smashed-up Southern state. Some of these resources would certainly be grabbed by the North, but enough could be left to fund the long-term basis of a new accumulation system.

A NEW FORM OF COMMAND ECONOMY  There is an element of a new kind of planning inherent in SAPs. Neo-liberalism constantly asserts that a command economy is less efficient than the market, but this is just propaganda to undermine the possibility of a social dialogue about what such planning could achieve. The problem for international capitalism is not economic planning *per se*, but the fact that, if this is done by the state, the latter will tend to become a repository of a significant amount of value which the exploiters cannot lay their hands on directly. But if the allocation of resources were to be directed by a sort of plan orchestrated by international institutions, there could be efficiency gains without these risks. At the most ambitious, this could be a sort of ultra-imperialism conducted not by firms but by institutions.

THE ORGANISING POWER OF THE NEW MANAGEMENT SYSTEMS  The basis for the new system could be the new management systems, towards which the institutions could direct the endeavours of developing countries. The 'debt' would give them added leverage in asserting this dictatorial power. The interests of international capitalism could now be addressed directly, as it would no longer be necessary to waste time, as in the days of ISI, by paying lip service to nationalism.

A DELIBERATE FORM OF UNEVEN DEVELOPMENT  As both imperialism theory and dependency theory noted, uneven development is a crucial aspect of modern capitalist development. This means developing particular sectors or geographical areas within the South so that they can serve the needs of central capital, without individual economies progressing so far towards an effective national development that they threaten the North–South colour line. So far this has happened spontaneously, but if it were planned, it might be more efficient.

Concrete cases can show how these different elements can come together in practice. For a long while, when World Bank policies were not applied generally in the South,[7] the Philippines served as a guinea pig, and at the beginning of the 1980s it became a showcase for Structural Adjustment Loans. An IBRD industrial survey mission in 1980 recommended that Filipino companies should switch to subcontracting for the manufacture of components for machinery, appliances, transport and electrical equipment. Kodak, General Motors, Singer, General Electric and Siemens were among the companies involved in this scheme.[8] The shift to new orientations was evident in Africa too, particularly in the 1981 IBRD 'Berg Report', *Accelerated Development in Sub-Saharan Africa – an Agenda for Action*, which can be considered a blueprint for structural adjustment. Its policies too fitted in well with the new global management philosophies, for it strongly emphasised the need for *flexibility*, the lack of which had allegedly prevented the 'diversification [of African economies] into products with rapidly growing markets'.[9] The uneven development aspect was reflected in the World Bank's recommendation that Africa should focus not so much on industry, but rather on 'non-traditional' cash crops; these would be welcomed by the increasingly powerful Northern supermarket chains.

How can countries be forced to export? Since what has emerged today is a form of post-neo-colonial direct rule, it is not surprising if there are some similarities with colonialism. In the colonial days, the local community was made subservient to the international capitalist one by introducing taxes; in order to pay these, families had to switch to cultivating cash crops. The modern equivalent is the 'debt', which forces countries to sell their output rather than consume it. In this way the debt crisis fitted in neatly with the overall picture.

Despite this, however, I believe there is a convincing argument for saying that structural adjustment was more effective in destroying the old set-up than in creating anything to replace it.

## The New Social Engineering Undermined by the Profit Motive

The problem raised by Rosa Luxemburg is still relevant: is accumulation really self-regenerating or does it depend on liquidating a non-renewable 'fuel'? This is a kind of ecological perspective applied to economics itself. Today this issue crops up in a new way with respect to the state. The liquidation of the state certainly makes sense in terms of the *transition*. But is the accumulation system solidly enough based to survive when there is nothing left to break up?

There would be no problem if the only call upon the resources freed by smashing the national development model was for the restructuring of Southern society into a new stable format conducive to global accumulation. But most of the new value has in fact already been appropriated by the North, and I believe that the role this value has played has been actually structural. After all, the industrial countries were undergoing their own structural adjustment at the time, which involved massive investment in new industries. The question arises as to whether this could have been funded purely by domestic accumulation. This seems unlikely, particularly as the 1980s were a period of immense *consumption*, which was also necessary to provide the new industries with a market. Historically, there has been a tendency for global capitalism, at times of big industrial regeneration, to fund the restructuring through a massive exploitation of the South – one example is the massive quantity of bullion taken from India in the eighteenth century. Is it pure coincidence, then, that the industrial restructuring of the 1980s was accompanied by a huge resource influx from the South, linked to 'debt' repayment? I think not. In fact, I believe there was a high degree of interdependence between, on the one hand, the mechanisms of investment in the North, and, on the other, the extraction of value from the South via the 'debt'. Capital (which in the 1970s had been going to fund NIC projects) was at that time brought back to the North, particularly to cover the increasing American deficits (which among other things promoted the consumption which generated the demand for new industrial sectors). The deficits led to high interest rates, which helped to attract the capital back. At the same time as it found capital drying up, the South suddenly faced a massively higher 'debt' because of the higher interest rates, which meant that it could pay only the interest and not repay the capital. In an important sense, the international institutions came to fulfil the role of an official receiver who keeps a bankrupt company ticking over for creditors to squeeze whatever they can out of it. It becomes difficult to carry out large-scale social engin-eering in these circumstances.

It should be noted that the costs incurred by Northern capitalism in the changeover of long cycles were not simply the economic costs of investing in new industries, but also political ones. In order to destroy the Soviet sphere, the North had to invest heavily in the arms race, which forced the Soviet Union to divert resources away from consumption into military expend-iture. This would pay for itself economically in the long term because, once socialism was destroyed, it would be possible to economise on 'investment in the poor' on the assumption that revolution would be less likely if there was no external support for radical movements. But the immediate costs of the arms race were immense, and in an indirect way the South footed the bill: interest rates shot up as the US administration strove to attract the necessary capital, and the amount developing countries spent on 'debt' servicing increased accordingly.

More specifically, it was not the South as *countries* who made the sacrifices, but the popular masses within them. Empirically, export promotion in the South has been funded by diverting resources away from consumption. It is the North–South divide itself which makes it possible for the Southern countries to *neglect* consumption. At the centre, capitalism has to juggle between the search for profit (which implies driving down wages) and the need for the product to be consumed. This provides a framework within which, as Amin has pointed out, metropolitan labour movements have been able to obtain gains for their labour commensurate with the increase in labour productivity.[10] One of the characteristics of the 'Fordist' regime of accumu-lation at the centre was 'the continual adjustment of mass consumption to rises in productivity'[11], and the same feature is still present in a different form in the current set-up in the centre, since the product still has to be consumed. But there is no reason why in the South, where industrial production is geared to exports, gains in productivity should lead to wage rises. In the peripheral context, 'local labour in producing countries represents only a cost of production and not a purchasing power value necessary for realisation, the product being destined for external markets'.[12]

Moreover, it is only a small step from neglecting consumption to actually transferring resources from it. This is in effect what SAPs do. In these circumstances, all the talk about human development sounds suspiciously like telling people to be content with their simple pleasures.

The pretext for bleeding resources from consumption is that excessive consumption leads to demand for imports, which creates a need for foreign exchange, thus weakening the balance of payments situation. So consumption must be curtailed, initially by a demand-oriented 'shock'. It is seen as necessary to reduce the amount of resources going to bureaucracies and urban workers, to free up money for those sectors which are competitive internationally, and have been starved by previous *dirigiste* policies. To some extent austerity policies are also used to decrease domestic demand for domestically produced goods, which are then free to be exported. This is known euphemistically as 'disabsorption'. The SAP scenario assumes that this initial shock will be temporary, part of the process of getting the supply side back in shape. But often, in fact, it becomes ingrained as part of the mutually reinforcing features of the new accumulation structure.

At its most simplistic, liberal economists argue that if some sectors of the economy are benefiting, then eventually the poor will benefit too, because the money will be invested and increase economic activity. Years ago Keynes discredited this assertion, but today, the right-wing backlash of the 1980s has censored his ideas and returned to the crudest form of trickle-down. The paradox is that, while the World Bank has distanced itself from trickle-down as an explanatory model within a country, it has retained it at a global level, for it claims that increasing wealth in the North will pull the South into development, either through increases in investment or demand, an assumption that is even less plausible.

There is an explanation for this paradox. What the World Bank has done is to pinch from radicals like Griffin the view that poverty is a constraint on development and cleverly transform it into a right-wing policy. So the SAPs have developed an anti-poverty rhetoric which certainly does not weaken local élites in general, who are still the necessary intermediaries for the North's agenda, but may serve to attack those structural forms of the concentration of wealth which constitute a blockage in the South's response to the demands of the global system. According to the old modernisation strategies, it was rent-seeking feudalists who were diverting resources away from development. Structural Adjustment says that it is the state and urban interests. The hidden agenda is that, by removing the state, all areas of the Southern economy would now be subordinated directly to the global system, and thus be able to respond more efficiently to the new opportunities. This strategy takes different forms in different areas. In Africa, it is the 'urban bias' that is attacked, because Africa has been selected to produce mainly cash-crops, as opposed to industrial exports, so it is the rural producers who have to be encouraged. But in one way or another, the overall trend is always for resources to be channelled into those sectors which serve international rent-seekers, that is, 'debt' repayment and export promotion.

It might seems that, as resources are being channelled into promising export sectors, there may be a risk that some countries in the South might really develop independently. In fact, preventing this is one of the North's lesser worries.

## Avoiding the Risk of Effective Take-off

It has happened before that creditors from the North have taken direct control over the victim's finances, for example with the Ottoman Public Debt Administration in the nineteenth century, and the extraction of reparations from Germany after the First World War. But these were unsophisticated in comparison with structural adjustment, which can treat 'debt' repayment as part of an interlocking regime of North–South relations. I will give a few examples of how this happens.

'DEBT' ENSURES THAT THERE WILL NOT BE LOCAL ACCUMULATION The 'debt' guarantees, in straightforward fashion, that the value generated by export promotion will not fund local development. Export earnings effectively simply become debt repayment.[13] In remarkable fashion, the North has its cake and eats it too.

WITHOUT STATISM, A 'HARD' EXPORT PROMOTION STRATEGY IS IMPOSSIBLE It is possible for a country in the South to make use of any 'comparative advantage' it gains from its cheap labour only if it can draw up a national strategy – for example for targeting foreign markets and wiping out domestic and foreign competitors within them so that the value which was initially squeezed out of the exporting country's domestic economy (to enable goods to be exported cheaply) can be recovered subsequently by raising the selling price. By undermining the state, SAPs ensure that export promotion will be 'safe' (that is, it will not subvert the North–South divide).

WITH MANY EXPORTERS, IT IS IMPOSSIBLE TO RAISE PRICES The generalisation of export promotion puts the sellers (the South) in a weak position, making it impossible to improve terms of trade as had been attempted in the days of the NIEO campaign. The obvious question becomes:

'how many of the developing countries can realistically be expected to export their way out of the debt trap when essentially the same advice is given to all of them – i.e. to promote exports?'[14] In effect, competition among them ensures that the exchange of value will remain uneven, to the advantage of the North. But, and this is the interesting point, *there is no corresponding competition among sources of finance*, making it hard for the South to bargain for better terms in funding: 'There has been a tendency for bilateral donors to follow this trend towards conditionality, some riding the back of the Fund and the Bank, others pursuing it more actively, like for instance the United States.'[15] In effect, this trend towards greater conditionality applies to investment capital too: while capital is increasingly free to move – and to play off one would-be recipient against another – it presents a united front to developing countries in demanding that approval by the IMF is a necessary condition for investment. Earlier, developing countries had argued in favour of aid being administered multilaterally because this seemed preferable to the more obvious domination implied in bilateral aid. But it is now clear that the multilateral situation is even worse, for the conditionality imposed by SAPs is more stringent than earlier forms of 'tying'.

DEVELOPMENT CANNOT OPERATE AS A NORMAL CAPITALIST 'BUSINESS' If we view development as a business, it is clearly not absurd *per se* to borrow; capitalism could not work without it. The decision may involve calculating whether interest rates will stay low, whether there will be a market for what you produce, whether expected sources of income will keep up with debt repayments, and whether the equipment you buy is appropriate in terms of the average level of technology in the branch in question over the expected time-horizon. In a normal business context, the external factors which determine the success of enterprises are influenced by state policies which can be assumed to be broadly supportive of capitalist endeavours. In the international context, this is not at all true. Both the cyclical and structural activities of the world economic institutions take as their only point of reference the global system of capital accumulation. On a very few occasions, countries may be shored up (as happened to Indonesia in the recent period), but this is because it is thought that their collapse would shake the whole system. By and large, the countries of the South are regarded as subordinate and left to their own devices.

Even if the above safeguards fail to operate, it is hard to see how any value could be 'fixed' locally and turned into a viable accumulation structure. In the name of modernisation, post-war strategies have already weakened the local communities, which were the best guarantee of 'rootedness', of the indigenous appropriation of the value generated by labour. This attack on local communities was carried out in the name of a larger, more ambitious development project at the level of a unified national economy. It was a project that suddenly, at a moment of crisis, evaporated.

## Limitations of the Free Market as a Tool of Control

Even if the North, through SAPs, finds it easy to prevent national development in the South, it still faces a real problem. Ideally, the system would not have to be policed on a permanent basis, but just during the transitional phase of structural adjustment. Once this transition was successfully completed, it would leave behind a self-maintaining system. The function which has hitherto been performed by the state – of enslaving working people – would be performed by the so-called market – in reality, the division of labour orchestrated by the new management systems – in which people would willingly seek their niches. But some kind of incentive would be needed, in the form of some possibility of accumulating value locally (not at a state level, but at a firm or household level). Once again, however, central capitalism would want to keep to the bare minimum the portion of value it abstains from grabbing. Ideally, therefore, the system which offers the incentive should simultaneously function as a means of exploitation.

One system that achieved this was centred on the exchange rate. The policy of auctioning foreign currency – on the grounds that it was a scarce resource in the domestic market – was enforced in parts of Africa in the 1980s.[16] In practice it was really the local currency that was being held up for auction, and the structural factors in the world economy ensured that it found a new level ultimately determined by the lower value of labour (in fact, also the lower value of human life) in the South. By making imports more expensive, this scheme – which amounted to a devaluation of the local currency – undermined ISI-style industrialisation, which is based on the import of intermediate goods.[17] But theoretically, this scheme could also act as a stimulus to export, for it was only by exporting that it was supposedly possible for the South to gain some benefit from its cheap human life, as a counterweight to all the disadvantages. In this sense, devaluation could be seen as an incentive, in that it offered some crumbs of local accumulation as a basis for establishing a form of dominance secured by market forces rather than by direct administration. At the same time, there was little risk of this promoting effective development at a national level: for example, when exporting was successful in Brazil in the mid-1980s, the IMF ordered an immediate increase of imports in order to sponge off 'excess' foreign currency.[18] And, more importantly, there is a fail-safe mechanism that ensures that the added value will eventually find its way to the North, because through the devaluation, the value represented by the 'debt' in hard currencies increases. The undermining of local currency also means that foreign capital can step in to take over any industries it wants, even perhaps using the advantage of being based in a country with a cheap currency, to export back to the industrial world.

Nevertheless, segments of the local ruling class could enrich themselves in these processes. As, effectively, it is those with access to international currency who have status within their own societies, this could benefit the system of domination. I have already discussed the importance of social mobility in consolidating any system. The old model saw international society as a society of states, and in this case social mobility took the form of latecomers joining the leading group as states. In the contemporary form, it is possible that social mobility may start operating at the level of élites. They could be given fairly powerful roles within the new structures, for example as World Bank functionaries, provided that they fully accept the norms of the accumulation system – which, in fact, they would have every interest in doing, since it gives them their status. Though this would give the system a 'united colours' appearance, it would actually reinforce the North–South divide by weakening the possibility of a national consensus in a Southern nation so that it could mount an effective challenge to the colour line. The privatisation of state companies, even when it occurred in the interest of local capitalists, would also weaken the national economy because individual entrepreneurs would be unlikely to stand up to the global system without state support.

A North–South consensus among élites in support of atructural adjust-ment would thus replace the nationalistic consensus of the old development projects. If this happened, it would be a big bonus for international capitalism, because at the moment there is a serious gap: in the days of the old development models, there was no need for a thought police to enforce the schemes, because they were relatively convincing, but structural adjustment, on the contrary, has been largely enforced by external agencies, and this is undoubtedly a weakness.

But it is likely, all the same, that this system will have only very limited effectiveness. The new vision may appear plausible to élites, since it presents the North and South as united within a single free-market economic model (in contrast to the division between Keynesianism for the North and develop-ment economics for the South, which was characteristic of the post-war regime). But in reality the free market is an expression of profoundly unequal power relations, and the practical consequences of this are all too obvious to the masses: to give only one example, it leads to a virtual monopoly by the North of mass consumption.

The new system has thus created a fundamental problem for the North. The 'national economy' is one of capitalism's best inventions because it provides a good basis for social control. It was very effective in the industrial-ised world in promoting consensus, and post-war developmentalism discovered a good way of spreading the benefits of this social control to the South as well. Now this has all been lost. Neo-colonialism in the form it took during the post-war long cycle, involving apparent respect for the national economy, has been under attack from structural adjustment, and if, as seems possible, change occurs through the negation of the negation, neo-colonialism could be abolished and we could end up with a disguised form of colonialism again!

The new form of direct rule which I am calling 'post-neo-colonial' would be very risky. In the past, IMF representatives have often been observed as the power behind governments,[19] and their role in imposing incomes policies[20] can be considered quasi-governmental. But this was power without responsibility. Actually to run a country would involve a qualitative change and it would expose the void at the heart of the New World Order. At the simplest level, direct rule is much more costly than indirect, and it is not at all clear where the money would come from. But even if this could be resolved, there is the problem of the conceptual void. Where could global capitalism find a new basis of social control? Contemporary development theory has invented a name for the new philosophy of social order, calling it 'governance', which in essence means keeping poor people under control without a strong state. But inventing a new term does not solve the problem. After the Bretton Woods institutions' pyrrhic victory over the South in the battle against the NIEO, they have been obsessed with 'governance', which shows that, although they are intoxicated with their own power, they are also frightened because they do not have a vision to guide them in their use of this power.

In this context, the inner weakness of SAPs is exposed. Their role is in a way far more commandist than the old statism ever was. 'Second-best' economic theory is interesting here. It argues that an economic order learns to live with its distortions, so any form of interventionism designed to secure a theoretically better system is not only futile but counterproductive. It is for this reason that liberalism attacks any state intervention in the economy (whether motivated by Keynesian or development economics). However the same argument can just as easily be turned against SAPs, in the sense that they aim to restore conditions of a free market which does not exist.[21] Their role is thus theoretically inconsistent, as long as one accepts the premises of free-market economics. It is scarcely surprising, therefore, that in practice the World Bank falls back on the old argument to justify the paradox of free-market interventionism, namely modernisation. World Bank theorists of the 1980s and their NGO mentors were based on a sort of political extension of neo-liberal theories of economic choice, so logically the transformation of society that they defended meant doing away with those aspects of tradition which contradicted this vision, such as traditional concepts of obligation.[22]

The more radical scenario would be to ditch free market economics altogether, but for the moment this is impossible, and the full social-engineering implications of SAPs cannot be followed to their logical conclusion. Instead, in what is almost like an economic equivalent of the end of the Vietnam War, the World Bank and IMF want to 'get out', but before they can do this they must construct a viable system to leave in their place. In effect, SAPs have become a piecemeal attempt to resolve this problem. But some sort of conceptual framework is necessary before this can be done. This is why in recent years the World Bank has formed such close contacts with NGOs, often appointing to its staff leading critics from development agencies. At first sight it simply seems that the Bank has found that it can silence its opponents by offering them good salaries, and there is certainly an element of this. But at a deeper level, the Bank desperately needs their ideas, in its futile quest for an idealised vision of what a particular society 'ought to' be like in a world free of distortions.

The task for SAPs is to establish the economic conditions in which such a society can become self-functioning. There must be just enough local accumulation to permit the South to maintain some non-statist institutions or social forces which can enable it to manage its own poverty. Today, it might be possible to address the problem of 'governance' by recognising and 'validating' the coping strategies which people have developed to resist social degradation, and then by calling the organisations behind these strategies 'NGOs' and constituents of 'civil society', and using them to run society in a low-cost way without the risks of post-neo-colonial direct rule. The old accumulation system, which operated through marketing boards and other similar bodies, oppressed the rural producer in such a way that it gave rise to socio-economic structures (the state, the urban economy) which acted as intermediaries to exploitation under conditions of the old long cycle, but have now become barriers to the direct incorporation of producers within the globalised economy. What is needed now is a new form of social engineering which encourages the emergence of a small-producer economy. But in practical terms, SAPs run up against unresolvable contradictions in trying to bring about this kind of change; for example, it is difficult to abolish food subsidies for the urban population, which must happen if state spending is to be slashed, just at the time when food prices are being allowed to rise in order to stimulate the producers. Many anti-SAP riots have resulted from this botched strategy.

The present system of 'governance' does not have the appearance of a stable system. It looks as though it ought to be a transition to something, but to what? Ideally, the fusion with NGOs should make it easier for the World Bank to carry out its great mission, which is to secure the long-term basis for future capital accumulation so that societies can carry on laying golden eggs for international capitalism for many years to come. Objectively, NGOs are trying to push SAPs into allowing economies to become more 'sustainable', and, when NGOs fail to target specifically the mechanisms by which capital is extracted from the South, this can all too easily become the sustainability of creating the reproduction necessary for capital accumulation at the centre to proceed into the future. I will examine the long-term implications of this issue in the final chapter. For the moment, however, few NGOs have developed an adequate theoretical framework for their actions, and the reality of what is happening with SAPs is much more prosaic.

It is true that, since the system badly needs success stories, élites have some bargaining power.[23] In Ghana, the leadership was able to get away with policies which contravene SAP dogma, on the understanding that the World Bank could claim that its 'successes' confirmed the effectiveness of Structural Adjustment.[24] However, the autonomy of élites is, in practical terms, limited by another aspect of the *de facto* role of SAPs, which is in effect to promote a kind of limited democratisation so that the different elements of Southern societies compete between themselves – and are unable to unite behind a single political programme directed against the dominance of the North. Such democratisation is safe because, although political parties can differ on many issues, they all have to articulate exactly the same policy in the areas defined by the SAPs. In practice, there is no interesting political debate because the only thing the parties cannot do is the only thing that would be worth doing: calling into question the whole neo-liberal edifice.

It might appear that this is a new form of the classic 'balance of power' policy, in which dualism is used in a new way, not to back modernisation against tradition but – by slightly increasing the power of the grassroots/traditional sector – to allow them into the picture, thus keeping both elements weak. However, if capitalism is really to aspire to be a self-reproducing regime of accumulation, the different economic sectors should have some viable relationship to one another, which this set-up does not provide. If SAPs merely lead to an extension of the classic divide-and-rule policy, they hardly have any credentials as a real system of economic management.

## Notes

1. Cf. Broad and Cavanagh 1988; the countries were: Argentina, Chile, Colombia, Costa Rica, Cyprus, Dominican Republic, Ecuador, Egypt, Guatemala, Honduras, Indonesia, Ivory Coast, Jordan, Kenya, Malaysia, Morocco, Pakistan, Paraguay, Peru, Philippines, Rwanda, Senegal, Sri Lanka, Syria, Thailand, Tunisia, Uruguay, Venezuela, Zambia.

2. Quoted in Bennholdt-Thomsen 1988, p. 55.

3. Bauer 1971, pp. 100–101.

4. Ibid., p. 133.

5. Lal 1983.

6. South Africa also received a huge infusion of IMF money in the 1980s without any significant 'structural' terms; cf. Cheru 1989, p. 81.

7. World Bank policies were employed in the 1960s to claw back concessions made earlier to Filipino élites at the time of serious guerrilla struggles. Marcos initially came to power in 1965 on an anti-World Bank platform; cf. Lichauco 1983.

8. Merlin M. Magallona, 'The Economic Content of Neo-colonialism', in Jose 1983.

9. International Bank for Reconstruction and Development 1981, p. 21.

10. Amin 1978b; originally published as *La loi de la valeur et le Matérialisme historique*, Paris, Minuit, 1977, p. 35.

11. Lipietz 1987, p. 36.

12. Campbell 1989, p. 18.

13. For an example, see Folson 1991, p. 105. In 1988, 75% of Ghana's export earnings went on 'debt' servicing.

14. Miller 1989, p. 44.

15. Killick 1987, p. 27.

16. In the Zambian case, the value of the kwacha fell from K2.20 to K15.29 to the dollar between 1985 and 1986; cf. Okogu 1989, p. 37.

17. Cf. Ohiorhenuan 1987; Kwanashie 1987.

18. Schatan 1987, p. 37.

19. Lamb 1981.

20. See, for example, Ncube *et al.* 1987.

21. In the early 1950s, J. Viner argued, in an analysis which is considered a precursor of second-best theory, that in an international context where there is protectionism the reduction of trade barriers or formation of customs unions by some actors – which in isolation would constitute fulfilment of Paretian conditions – would not necessarily increase efficiency in world production.

22. Cf. Williams and Young 1994.

23. I am grateful to Wambui Mwangi for raising this point in the context of a discussion on an earlier draft.

24. O'Malley 1994.

# 12

# Political Implications of a New Economic Order

## A New Vocabulary of Northern Dominance

When the socio-economic world system undergoes a structural change, it is plausible to expect a reciprocal change in the military–political system. It is clear that events in the 1960s and 1970s sparked off a drawn-out crisis which was as evident in the military–political sphere as in the economic and social. Efforts at restructuring Northern dominance were initially a reaction to this crisis, only later turning into a more proactive attempt to design something new.

The Vietnam War, which precipitated the decline of the old system, was connected with the apparently more 'economic' aspects of the crisis, such as the collapse of the Bretton Woods economic system. Both sides were affected: Kolko has shown that Vietnamese military strategies were dictated by economic considerations; they launched the Tet Offensive in 1968 because a dollar crisis at the beginning of that year suggested that the USA was vulnerable to domestic instability.[1]

While the Vietnam War was still going on, the Americans were unable to take the initiative in designing something new. Ultimately, a new world order would have to be post-hegemony (or rather a transition from individual US hegemony to a joint one by the industrial world as a whole). Although this was in no way predetermined, it turned out in practice that the new order was also post-Cold War. A long and complex journey was required before the new world order emerged. As many new contradictions were created as old ones resolved. I will try to trace the route that was taken.

In 1973–74, in the aftermath of the October War in the Middle East, capitalism had two priorities: to outflank the third world movement and the organisation of primary producers; and to prepare the way for a new form of interventionism which would not lead to a Vietnam-style commitment of ground forces.

To achieve these goals, it was necessary to create the economic conditions for post-hegemony. It was clearly important to confront the South with a more unified and organised Northern persona; and interdependence was managed with this in view. An élite common to the North as a whole began to emerge. To a certain extent, it occurred naturally, with groups with similar perspectives coming together, but there was an element of deliberate orchestration: for example, in the formation of the Trilateral Commission (a pressure group of influential politicians and academics) which, during 1973–74, drew up the blueprint for a summit meeting of the leading powers; this led to the first annual meeting of the Group of Seven (G7) in 1975. When Carter became president in 1976, this process took a decisive step forward, with Trilateral sympathisers, headed by Carter himself and National Security Adviser Brzezinski, holding key positions in the new administration. The objective was clearly to unify the North.

At this stage, however, the responses of Northern powers to the crisis contained a great deal of ambiguity. They adopted nationalistic policies, but it was not clear whether these represented a resurrection of the sort of nationalism which could lead to renewed competition, or were, on the contrary, precursors of a new kind of joint Northern nationalism which could place their dominance over the South on a firmer footing. In the first instance, it looked as if particular Northern powers were looking after their own interests in a post-hegemonic world. The US passed a Trade Act in 1975, punishing developing countries that were members of primary-producer organisations. New and decisive political leadership emerged in Europe, and organised in the same year an annual summit of heads of state, known as the European Council, which proved a key step towards eventual integration. At a military level, the US prepared for a new interventionism. Contingency plans for a military intervention in recalcitrant Arab states began in 1973. Remarks by Defence Secretary Schlesinger in 1974 made it seem that invasion could be imminent. Military manoeuvres began, pitting US forces against troops dressed in Iraqi and Libyan uniforms.[2] In 1975, the US House of Representatives prepared *Oil Fields as Military Objectives: A Feasibility Study*.[3] Carter developed the Rapid Deployment Joint Task Force.[4]

Though these actions appeared to be responding to individual nationalist interest, I believe that in a deeper sense they were collective. This could be seen in the new role of international regimes. After the NIEO movement had been destroyed, the IMF and World Bank emerged as the new collective organs and came up with Structural Adjustment around 1980. This was reinforced by 'debt'-related measures, such as the strengthening of the Paris and London Clubs (dealing respectively with public and commercial loans), and the adoption of a set of measures in the aftermath of the Mexican debt crisis to ensure that Southern countries could not use their collective debtor-power to threaten the banking system. And, at a military level, the whole industrial world began to adopt the new interventionist doctrine. During the Falklands War in 1982, for instance, the USA strongly backed Britain, sending out a clear signal, in what was essentially only a dress rehearsal, that it was a new era, very different from, for example, the Suez war, when the USA had been unwilling to jeopardise its credentials with the nationalist movement by backing unequivocally the old colonial powers.

## How the Change of Long Cycle Relates to the End of the Cold War

'Security' and 'stability' are key terms in theories about international relations, but ultimately they mean security and stability for capital accumulation. Since accumulation is premised on cheap and unorganised labour, this definition of security is bound to mean insecurity at a grassroots level in the South, with precarious conditions for farm labourers or factory workers and the creation of death-squads if they attempt to organise.

Patterns of order acquire stability over a certain period: the actors who count learn informal rules for such things as how to interpret each other's behaviour. Security systems are distinct in a sense from economic systems, in that they guarantee external conditions under which the latter can flourish. But the two are also directly related, with the arms economy and arms trade being an obvious example, and, more fundamentally, since the security system serves capital accumulation, and capital accumulation is organised in structures which prevail over a certain period, one can expect some correspondence between the periodisation of economic systems and politico-military ones.

However, in the case under consideration, this correspondence is not immediately obvious. The Cold War, in its time, was a security system appropriate to a particular stage in the international political economy. As I have already shown, the latter underwent a major system-change around the end of the 1970s, so one might expect the security system to have changed at the same time. But the Cold War still appeared to determine international politics for another decade. This needs to be explained.

I believe the solution to this problem is as follows: the key issue was not the Cold War but bipolarity. In substance, bipolarity ended before the end of the Cold War. It had served its purpose as the guarantor of an international 'stability' which enabled accumulation to proceed during a definite period. But by the end of the 1970s, it was no longer carrying out this function adequately, and the agenda had moved on to looking for what would succeed neo-colonialism. In a deep sense, it was already by then that a 'new world order' implied smashing the Soviet bloc. It simply took a number of years for this to happen. By the late 1970s, the world was very clearly in a transitional phase.

At the simplest level, it might seem that the stabilising role of the USSR had been functional specifically for the transition from formal colonialism to neo-colonialism, and, once this was complete, there had been no point in continuing with it. But this statement covers two distinct sets of causes: firstly, there were the negative reasons why bipolarity itself might be becoming inconvenient and needed to be got rid of; and secondly, there was the positive stimulus arising from the fact that a new long cycle in the international economy might demand a different system of international relations that did not include bipolarity. I will expand on these points.

WHY BIPOLARITY ITSELF WAS BECOMING INCONVENIENT On the one hand, the Soviet Union was performing a stabilising function by making sure local conflicts did not spill over into direct superpower confrontation. But this created the possibility that, in exchange for the stabilising services which it rendered, it could seek 'rents' or entitlements – in the form of enlarging its recognised sphere of control. On the other hand, bipolarity was not necessarily successful in controlling all the popular radical forces anyway.

What the West liked to do was to conflate these two distinct processes, making them appear part of the same phenomenon of supposed Soviet expansionism. It would present a picture with the following elements: the expansion of Soviet influence in areas such as the Red Sea – particularly Ethiopia and South Yemen; in southern Africa with its links with the radical regimes in Angola and Mozambique; in the hegemony asserted by its ally, Vietnam, over Kampuchea and Laos; in the role of Cuba as proxy in many of these conflicts; in the Soviet-backed state of emergency in India; in the expansion of the Council for Mutual Economic Assistance (CMEA) – an institution of political economy hitherto 'contained' within Europe – to parts of the third world; and finally in the invasion of Afghanistan. These developments had all occurred by the mid–late 1970s.

This picture, which was to become an important argument for the rejection of bipolarity and subsequently for the adoption of rollback, contains two key elements of distortion.

First, it mixes up popular forces with Soviet expansionism. The situations in, for example, Angola and Ethiopia were qualitatively different, in that in the former case popular forces were seeking to counter the Western agenda of replacing Portuguese colonialism by CIA-manipulated liberation movements, and they saw (wisely or not) rapprochement with the Soviet Union as a logical response; and in the latter case, the Ethiopian junta (Dergue) was merely a repressive military regime, baptised as radical by the Soviets, which was fighting *against* the popular movements.

Second, as serious Western studies of Soviet policy have shown, the Soviet Union was not impetuously challenging the superpower status quo. From the Soviet angle, the global power-struggle was conceived as a very ponderous process. The domino or 'Munich' image of a small concession leading to an immediate bandwagon effect, while having some credence in Washington, was probably not espoused from the Soviet side.[5] Soviet relations with, for example, Vietnam, were quite complex, for Vietnam was independent enough to be resentful of entanglement within CMEA.[6] The Soviet invasion of Afghanistan was probably a sign of weakness, in that it could not find any other way of controlling the situation.

However, the West could kill two birds with one stone by presenting the radical popular forces as though they were equivalent to Soviet expansionism, for it meant that it could get rid of both at the same time.

THE DEMANDS OF A NEW LONG CYCLE   The specific form of North–South relations which bipolarity helped to create was not of eternal validity for global capitalism. It fitted in with a particular level of the international-isation of capital, characterised for example by pseudo-nationalistic import substitution strategies. The new economic structure might demand a different set of world politics. In effect, the rejection of bipolarity by international capitalism, expressed most obviously in Reagan's and Thatcher's rollback policies, took place in the late 1970s and early 1980s, which was exactly the time when the new economic structure was coming in. In the remainder of this chapter, I will investigate this transition period in more detail.

In the following discussion, there are two crucial underlying contradictions which initially appeared to ease the transition, but which ultimately have proved very intractable.

First, there is no system of international relations which is appropriate to the new economic system. Establishment international relations theory has perceived the mixture of statist and post-statist elements in the contemporary system, but without being able to provide an adequate explanation for it. I believe that the explanation is simply that the current economic demands of capital accumulation require a system which is not really international at all, because it would effectively undermine the boundaries upon which inter-state relations have always been based. It is clear that neo-colonialism has always meant that, as far as the South is concerned, its participation in IR has been illusory, but – and this is what is important here – the old system of capital accumulation accommodated itself very well to the apparent autonomy of the state. Since the beginning of the transition, this has now no longer been the case. This becomes evident when we start looking for the equivalent of the military-repressive system appropriate to a post-statist economic order. There is no evidence that it exists, or can exist.

Second, the neo-colonial system of the 1960s and 1970s was abandoned, not only because it was no longer appropriate to the new long cycle, but also because its own development was exposing its flaws. The local state which had acted quite efficiently in repressing labour found its economic basis eroded by the crisis. But this takes us back to the same problem of finding a replacement system of repression.

## New Trends in Élite Southern Nationalism – Compensating for Economic Weakness by Military Troublemaking

The international deployment of capital requires not only cheap labour but also an appropriate system of class relations.[7] Part of this equation is a suitably controlled working class. All exploitative systems need to be able to keep the masses in order. Physical repression is an important aspect of this, but it always has to be supplemented by 'social control', which is the mechanism by which people police themselves because they have internalised society's norms. The colonial system was no exception – people like Frantz Fanon and Steve Biko were important in the liberation movement because they combated the ideological dimension of social control. However, it has been argued convincingly that colonialism was inefficient because it involved the colonial power in a lot of direct activity, not only in repression, but also in maintaining social control, which meant that it ran the risk of becoming the target of a *national* movement. Neo-colonialism was a big step forward from this angle, because the ultimate beneficiaries of exploitation (the Northern capitalist interests) no longer needed to get their hands dirty, as the domestic system, rather than the international one, could deal with the mass movement.

It looked like a better deal for the North, because the exploited people, using their own state, had to fund their own repression. It was not, however, as straightforward as it seemed. If the local state is to function sufficiently to maintain social order, the centre must be prepared to abstain from appropriating a certain amount of value, sufficient to fund this operation. It can, however, be taken as axiomatic that the central capitalists will extract every penny of profit they can. The problem was made particularly severe by the fact that Northern capitalism does not operate as a single enlightened operation, but rather as a number of competing interests each seeking to maximise short-term profit. Nevertheless, in principle (if we leave aside the problems of implementation) this investment would be worthwhile. However, we should now consider the problem this creates in the South. There is an economic angle that I addressed in Chapter 10, in that some bastions of anti-communism tried to exploit their usefulness to the West by pushing authoritarian development models. What concerns us here, however, is the military angle. Élites which had grown strong through repression tried to carve themselves out a local power role, or, by threatening to make trouble, to win concessions. India, which served both the USA and the Soviet Union in different ways in suppressing the grassroots, Maoist-led radical movement, is an example.

This created management problems for the North. One way in which the dangers of troublesome élite nationalisms could be contained was by manipulating the local balance of power. But this was not without some dangers of its own, since divide-and-rule policies at times gave rise to local arms races, which were profitable at one level but were destabilising at another. In some areas, such as Latin America, this was undoubtedly manageable: Brazil served as a sort of sub-imperialist power for a while.[8] Although it developed its own nationalist foreign policy in the 1970s, it scarcely represented a fundamental threat to the interests of its mentor, the USA. But, as we shall see later, South Asia was an entirely different problem.

The problem of élites also has to be seen as part of the local class relations which central capital needs for its reproduction. From this angle, it is not simply that the North must abstain from grabbing enough value to fund local repressive activities, but that it must also permit local accumulation on a sufficient scale to allow the establishment of a class system which can solve the problems of repression and social control in an ongoing, self-reproducing way. This is highly problematic.

These contradictions in North–South class relations are endemic, but there are particular problems when there is a crisis. At such moments, the local ruling élite needs to maintain its own hegemony by acting in the name of a more general interest, which involves the legitimacy of the state itself. As Sidgi Kaballo has pointed out, the failure of élites can lead to crises of hegemony and legitimacy.[9] But I would also add an international dimension: crises of legitimacy are bound up with the cyclical development of the international political economy, within which local systems are embedded.

There are two aspects to the fundamental change that was occurring to Southern states in the late 1970s and early 1980s. First, the crisis of the accumulation system had as one of its aspects the crisis of the Southern development projects, including the states which embodied them. Since the state embodied the project, the two are not really separable. Abdoun correctly made this point with respect to Algeria, before things had degenerated to the point reached today.[10] The local state helps to make a profit for the North by buying equipment, maintaining labour in order, and so on. But if it degenerates beyond a certain point, the state can even become a cost, if the North has to intervene directly to keep things in order. Second, the demands of the incipient new accumulation structure included a greatly expanded role for direct economic penetration of Southern societies; this made it difficult for the local élites to build a new statist structure to replace the one in crisis.

This process of change also had repercussions at an international level. Some Southern élites strove for regional hegemony as a way of getting legitimacy that was lacking at a societal level, or to obtain supplementary resources for papering over the cracks in development models; others tried to get concessions from the North, either by acting in its favour, as a local proxy, or by threatening to stir up trouble in the hope of being bought off. At times, the state, already armed for the purposes of internal repression, sought to convert this into a sort of economic entitlement at the level of the international system.

## The Contradictory Transition to a Post-bipolar World Order

To give concrete examples of what was going on, I will briefly take as a case study the Iran–Iraq conflict, and then look at the processes leading up to the Gulf War. Through these events, we can gain important insights into the way the North was searching for an international relations system appropriate to the current phase of international economics, and more particularly into the unresolvable contradictions carried forward from the post-bipolar restructuring of the international system, which can be expected to haunt international capitalism in the structural crises that, at the time of writing, appear imminent.

The Iran–Iraq war shows that the superpower system was simply not up to managing a conflict of this kind. The actual fighting in this conflict lasted from 1980 to 1988 and peace was formalised in 1990 only in direct response to Iraqi plans to invade Kuwait. Basically, the conflict covered the whole period of transition to the post-Cold War era.

The conflict was an international projection of the way third-world élites had responded to the problem of restructuring their own societies. In an earlier phase of the crisis, élites had typically sought to salvage the old economic models by attempting to gain an increased share of raw material rents. This endeavour collapsed in the face of central capitalism's attack on the NIEO project. But a new type of movement then emerged which based its legitimacy, not on attempting to salvage modernisation, but on the forces generated by its collapse. Modernisation had attacked the spirituality of mass cultures, considering it as part of the traditional constraints on development which needed to be uprooted in the cause of progress. Pre-revolutionary Iran was typical of this sort of modernising model, with its aura of progressive cultural nationalism, which was quite phoney and hollow. The Iranian revolution brought to power a new sort of élite which specialised in channelling – or perhaps manipulating – the popular sentiments repressed by the earlier model. Such élites aim to exploit the mass movement partly for their own benefit and partly to demonstrate to central capital that only *they* can contain these movements and hence must be paid a stipend for doing so.

In international politics terms, pre-revolutionary Iran had been a sort of regional sub-imperialist power, which professed to pursue its own national interests, but was permitted to make these claims only because, in the last analysis, it was subordinate to America. But at this time Iraq, too, was well regarded by the capitalist powers. As a modernising state, it consumed equipment and arms and, more specifically, Saddam was killing communists and fighting Islam at the same time, an ideal combination from the North's point of view. In the mid-1970s, French Prime Minister Jacques Chirac saw Iraq as a symbol of everything that should be encouraged, of the 'good' forces of rationality and industrialisation. Then came the Iranian revolution, which suddenly seemed to release the primitive, elemental forces of mass spirituality in the country. Iraq was indirectly encouraged to attack Iran, perhaps even explicitly encouraged by hints from Carter's National Security Adviser, Brzezinski.

But Iraq was never adopted wholesale as a sub-imperialist power to replace Iran. In fact, the West tried to play off the different sides while keeping them all weak. The Kurds were encouraged to keep up their struggle for independence, so that they would 'maintain a level of hostilities high enough to sap the resources of the neighbouring state [Iraq]'.[11] And at the same time Iran itself was being secretly armed, through the diversion of part of the funds supposed to be used to fund terrorism in Nicaragua. The Iran–Iraq war served in a sense to play off the different facets of élite nationalism one against the other, so as to prevent either from gaining a position where it could become effectively autonomous (either economically or militarily) *vis-à-vis* the North. But at the same time, this strategy was dangerous, for the conflict was so intense that it became destabilising, with neither superpower effectively able to control it. It was clear that bipolarity had become redundant, and a new sort of military–political world order was needed to take over from it.

This led eventually to the Gulf War, but first there was a transitional period, which can only be understood against the background of changes in the international political economy (IPE).

The portion of raw material rents which Southern states were allowed to appropriate was not necessarily lost value from the North's point of view. It can plausibly be argued[12] that, far from bringing any real social benefit to the nation, petroleum rents serve, through patronage, to maintain the power of local rulers. Objectively, they could therefore be seen as a stipend funding the regimes' repressive function. It is clear that they could also use the money to buy equipment from the North and, in the case of petrodollars, there were special channels – the Gulf regimes – for getting the money invested in the North. Petrodollars from Kuwait came to play a major role in financing the great TNCs (examples include BP, Midland Bank, Hoechst, Daimler Benz, Volkswagen, Kodak, IBM, General Electric), and clearly the local rulers, whose profits are drawn from Northern economies, have no interest in damaging the latter by their pricing policies. At the same time, it was not altogether in the interests of the industrial countries to keep petroleum prices low: high prices would favour oil companies' profit, as well as making it economically viable to exploit the oil reserves in some industrial countries, including America. For these reasons, there seemed to be plenty of scope for allowing prices to settle at a level which allowed local élites enough to fund the trappings of nationalism, while leaving a healthy profit for the North.

This balance could, however, be disrupted in certain circumstances. Reaganomics placed a great priority on curtailing inflation, and this meant forcing petroleum prices down. This also led to greater reliance by the USA on imported energy: the proportion of domestically consumed petroleum imported from abroad increased from 27 per cent in 1985 to 44 per cent by 1989.[13] At the same time, America needed more foreign investment to fund the budget deficits, and it was not clear where this money would come from. In the late 1980s, Japan was increasingly moving its capital out of the US economy, where it had played such an important role earlier in the decade.

Japan's share in funding the US deficit thus fell from a high point of 40 per cent in the 1970s to only 20 per cent in 1990. Germany, in its turn, was tied up with reunification. The solution was to get more investment from the right-wing Arab states. Indeed, it has been argued that political manoeuvrings at the time of the Gulf War resulted in a large amount of Saudi funds being diverted into US government bonds.[14] All this led to a pincer movement on oil rents going to the Arab states: simultaneously, the absolute value of oil income fell, and the *proportion* redirected to the North increased. The result was two-fold: on the one hand, the balance with the 'nationalist' élites was disturbed, as the stipend they received to fund their repressive states diminished; and on the other, popular resentment at international exploitation increased. The Gulf regimes became a symbol of this exploitation, of the feeling that people in the South were being cheated. It is not surprising that the Iraqi leadership hit on the idea of channelling this resentment and threatening military trouble to improve their bargaining position *vis-à-vis* the North.

It is clear that the very logic of this process created a strong possibility that the USA would be drawn into direct intervention in the Gulf. The discovery of detailed plans for invasion led a far-sighted observer, Ayoob, to note that the Soviet presence in the region provided only a temporary restraining factor.[15] There is a strong case for arguing that the Kuwait issue was set up as a deliberate trap for Iraq. There were certainly signals from the USA that could be interpreted as giving Iraq the green light to invade.[16]

If the intervention was indeed deliberately engineered, it seems that the USA drew up a proactive strategy for imposing a new international order. Why? A new economic system of Northern dominance had been established at the beginning of the 1980s, but the international political system had lagged behind. A change was therefore overdue. In practice, a change would occur not simply because logical elegance required it, but in response to a concrete threat which the existing order could not handle. In this instance, the danger was as follows: the end of bipolarity had left a vacuum which regional powers had attempted to fill, using the argument that they were creating regional subsystems to offset the threat of a unipolar order controlled by the USA. This is, in effect, how we can interpret Saddam's statement that 'Arabs possess an extraordinary ability to accelerate the creation of an international balance'.[17] In this way, would-be dominant powers could claim that their policies were not just defending mere national interest, but were pursuing 'milieu goals' that aimed to influence the development of the system itself.

There has long been a suspicion, particularly among many people in the developing world, that the end of the Cold War would signal a reversion to the old geopolitics, with the ideological façade slipping away and warfare being waged openly over control of resources and trade routes. As the end of bipolarity approached, American planners began using the concept of 'keeping the violent peace' to signify an essentially naval strategy of protecting sea lines of communications and access to resources and markets. This is a classically imperialist concept, which implies less of a global and more of a local emphasis in intervention, with each situation being examined for the specific threats it poses to US interests, rather than in terms of bipolarity. Once the Cold War had ended, the logical conclusions could be drawn, and a Navy/Marine Corps document of 1992 asserted that the global threat had receded in favour of a threat to 'regions critical to our national interest', and that the armed forces should prepare to 'preserve the strategic position we won at the end of the Cold War'.[18]

## The New Imperialism and Its Instability

In these circumstances, the USA urgently needed to create the impression that it was itself pursuing some wider systemic interest, and not a narrow national interest. The 'new world order' concept was created to fill this gap. According to this vision, the USA is benevolently protecting the world against the instability threatened by post-bipolar regional strongmen. The Gulf War was a demonstration of its determination to do so. Hence the slaughter, militarily unnecessary, of an estimated 125,000–150,000 Iraqi personnel. The Chairman of the House of Representatives Armed Services Committee openly said that the Gulf War experience should be 'transported around the globe'.[19] If this was done, local élites – deprived of the option of using their military muscle to make trouble – would have to accept whatever level of rents the North deigned to concede.

But there are two important reasons why this approach will not work in practice. First, the military aspect of the world order problem cannot possibly be resolved by replicating Gulf War-style intervention against other countries. Second, the military dimension is in an important sense only a symptom of a wider social problem in the world order, to which there is no obvious interventionist answer. It is important to develop more fully these two issues.

THE PROBLEM OF MILITARISM IS EMBEDDED IN THE WHOLE FABRIC OF NEO-COLONIALISM  Iraq under Saddam was exceptionally well qualified for the role of the scapegoat that needed to be 'taught a lesson', and it continued to fulfil this function until the end of the 1990s. Most of the other governments which could have been cast as 'culprits' of local power politics were allies of America and could not be attacked in this way, for the economic causes of their actions were linked to the contradictions in the IPE itself. Asia provides an example. 'Growth' in a conventional sense has always been intensive in terms of energy and raw materials. It is a hidden implication of 'NIC' development (and one which development theory itself keeps quiet about) that competition to control these resources could have a military dimension. I should emphasise that such conflict is not absolutely inevitable – popular protest movements, women's and indigenous movements would be sure to respond to such a threat by promoting an alternative vision of development, and one of the strongest arguments for sustainability is that it is far less conflictual (on an international, as well as on a domestic level) than a system premised on the depletion of scarce resources. However, in the immediate term, such conflict is very likely, particularly in areas where several would-be industrialisers co-exist. During the Cold War, the old issues of imperialist geopolitics were replaced by the peculiar geopolitics of containment, but a more straightforward interest-based geopolitics can re-emerge. And in the post-Cold War environment, it is not only the Americans who can play at keeping a 'violent peace', but local strongmen as well. In the East Asian context, this concept includes the defence of sea-lines of communications (SLOCs). And in South and East Asia, the defence establishment seems likely to push India as a counterweight to growing Chinese power, and to build privileged relations with the Association of South-East Asian Nations (ASEAN) and Japan on this basis.[20] These conflictual relations can build up their own prisoners' dilemma dynamic (see p. 286, n. 14), and it is futile to think something like the 'lesson' to Iraq could prevent this.

THE PROBLEM OF DISLOCATION WITHIN DEVELOPING COUNTRIES IS ESSENTIALLY SOCIAL RATHER THAN MILITARY When modernisation falls apart, it does not always give rise, as in Iran, to an élite specialised in manipulating the victims of modernisation; it can also create social chaos. Although most societies 'cope' quite well, this chaos could have a military expression in some places, if interest groups attempt by violent means to monopolise what is left. This could lead to a decline in the state's monopoly of violence, with social groups acquiring arms in order to enforce their entitlement to various economic goods.

If the problem of social dislocation takes a military expression, it may give the impression that it would be solved by military intervention, but practice has shown that this is not the case. In Somalia, where the former dictator had developed a false national unity by manipulating clan divisions, the situation became very serious when the alliance fell apart.[21] The United States launched its military intervention without any clear idea of whether it was stamping on a troublesome local ruler, undertaking a wider social engineering task, or doing something quite different. Not surprisingly, its intervention did nothing to resolve the crisis.[22]

Increasing social disorder in the South is inevitable. This will be produced by a mixture of factors including weakness of the economic role of the state, the continued role of the state in committing human rights abuses and other forms of repression, the effects of structural adjustment, the sudden collapse of ambitious NIC models, ecological degradation and so on. The disorder will clearly spill over into the international system. As I have already argued, such concepts as 'order' and 'security' (whether applied to domestic or international systems) essentially serve the propertied interests, and in the long term, their collapse will simply hasten the day when the masses take over responsibility for the social order themselves. Since this can only happen under the banner of radical politics, the North is sure to revert to anti-Communism as the guiding principle of its international relations at some time in the future. For the moment, however, the worst effects of the collapse of domestic and international order are being offloaded on to the masses, and the suffering this causes is in far greater evidence than the social creativity which will eventually be spawned. One of the most noticeable symptoms of these problems is people being forced – whether for political or economic reasons does not really matter – to migrate.

It is evident that the current system cannot accept the free movement of people as such movement would tend to equalise the rewards of labour and threaten the division which forms the very basis of the North–South dynamic. This gives rise to two trends in the North which at a certain level are contradictory. One is towards isolationism and fencing oneself in, and the other is towards intervention, in a proactive way preferably, so as to impose a certain stabilising order.

As far as possible, the industrial world would like to combine elements of both. The 'fortress' idea is certainly strong. The new Berlin Wall takes the form of barriers, literal and administrative, placed in the way of migrants. During the brief period 1993–96, 1,185 people are estimated to have died attempting to cross the US–Mexican border[23] – which is more than were killed during the whole history of the Berlin Wall; according to the highest figure cited by the pressure group of victims' families, the Wall accounted for the deaths of about 900 people.[24]

Ideally, the exclusionist solution should be combined with intervention to deal with the causes of the migration. After all, the American tradition of wanting to create world order is historically ingrained.[25] But here an important contradiction surfaces. If liberalism is the supposed banner of such world orders, one might expect economic liberalism to be accompanied by political liberalism, which would mean stopping the human rights abuses and therefore removing one reason for people wanting to leave. Indeed, one version of the new world order criticises the neo-realist nostalgia for the Cold War and boldly asserts the credentials of liberalism as a principle for restructuring the world system.[26] But this is obviously unlikely to work in practice. The reason is simply that the North–South divide ensures that the political benefits of liberalism, such as pluralism and the rule of law, are as unevenly divided as the economic ones. In the South, economic liberalism often requires the support of political dictatorship.

If abstract liberalism is not likely to provide the unifying principle, there is an intriguing possibility that the new management systems could provide some useful tools for the management of international relations. They might help to defuse the 'us-and-them' culture in general, as well as providing specific problem-solving techniques.

Considerable effort has been put into promoting conflict resolution as an idea. The point of departure for these endeavours is certainly correct: instead of seeing security as a zero-sum problem which brands 'someone else' as the enemy, it perceives that this 'someone else' has a similar (therefore, common) need for security, so, instead of being a factor of division, security becomes a factor of unity. In a post-Cold War world there could, for example, be a new definition of collective security where organisations are not built around the idea of defending themselves against somebody else, but simply seek to maintain the security of all their members.[27] One branch of development theory even heroically attempts to use export promotion itself as a basis for removing the economic basis of conflict. It argues that traditional, statist models of development tended to lead to trade wars, along the lines of the prisoners' dilemma, even though this was not in the 'higher' interest.[28] But now it believes that the world has moved on to a situation where a more optimistic *laissez-faire* theory is valid: the 'prisoners' delight' situation, where countries have an interest in liberalising regardless of the behaviour of other actors. According to this theory, if the international environment were sufficiently strong, loyalty to openness would yield substantial payoffs, and those countries adopting protectionist strategies would lose out. These approaches look towards a new non-conflictual global politics to replace statism and the balance of power.

There is a lot which is of interest in these ideas, and certainly grassroots movements could take up the new approaches to conflict resolution. The problem of the official discourse on conflict resolution is that it is deeply imbued with the idea of seeking the benefits of exploitation while minimising the costs. It is telling that contemporary strategies originated in the anti-Taylorist management literature of the 1960s. One proponent of the theory, J.W. Burton, mentions this connection, without apparently seeing anything worrying about it.[29]

It is easy to see the attraction of conflict resolution as a way of getting rid, at one and the same time, of class struggle and troublesome third-world nationalism, but it is less easy to see it working in practice. War and conflict, whether at an international level between rival states or at a domestic level between warlord factions, are an unmitigated evil for ordinary people in the developing world, but they have attained such a momentum that the North, whose economic exploitation ultimately caused the problems, will never succeed in imposing a managerial solution. This is another sign that today's system has got out of control. But there is a resolution implied in this progression: these evils create their own opposite in the form of a radical grassroots agenda to attack the causes of the conflicts. The North's failure to share its 'security' (alongside its failure to share wealth) will ensure that this is the only outcome.

# Notes

1. See Kolko 1986, p. 304.

2. Cf. Ramsey Clark 1992.

3. Ayoob 1988, p. 164, note 7.

4. In 1983 this became the US Central Command (CENTCOM).

5. Cf. Hopf 1991.

6. Ross 1990.

7. Cf. Petras and Morley 1981.

8. The Rockefeller Report published in 1969 emphasised the point about military regimes; cf. Rouquié 1987, p. 401.

9. Kaballo 1994, Chapter 1.

10. Abdoun 1990.

11. Quoted in Ramsey Clark 1992.

12. Cf. Sayigh 1991.

13. Carton 1991.

14. Talha 1991, p. 143.

15. Ayoob 1988.

16. Cf. Alain Gresh and Dominique Vidal, 'Golfe – Clefs pour une Guerre annoncée', Paris, Le Monde, 1991, pp. 213ff.

17. Quoted in Dannreuther 1992, p. 14.

18. Quoted in Rogers 1994, p. 18.

19. Quoted in Ramsey Clark 1992, p. 10.

20. Cf. Mohan Malik 1995.

21. Cf. Isaa-Salwe 1994; Giannou 1993.

22. Cf. Salih and Wohlgemuth 1994.

23. The figure comes from a report from the University of Houston; Le Monde 14 August 1997.

24. Cf. Libération 26 August 1997.

25. Cf. Clough 1991.

26. For a perspective along these lines, cf. Väyrynen 1993.

27. At a European level, this can be seen in the Conference on Security and Co-operation in Europe (CSCE), and one image of the new 'world order' at the outset of the 1990s would have had this as a replacement for NATO and the Warsaw Pact.

28. This assumes that each country's decision-makers have more to lose by unilaterally cutting protectionism than they would gain by a general decline in protectionism, and expect other countries to follow the same reasoning; this makes it difficult to realise (in terms of concrete decisions) the best general result.

29. Cf. Burton 1986.

# 13

# Globalisation versus Regionalism

## Significance of the Trend to an Increasingly Open World Economy

Up to now there have been three components of the international political economy (IPE): firstly, the national markets of the dominant powers, secondly an international economic system which links those national markets, and thirdly a global accumulation system which exploits Southern countries and stops them developing their own national markets. Today there are signs that the national market is being weakened. The ground for this was prepared in the Uruguay Round of GATT (1986–93) and the formation of the World Trade Organisation (WTO). Although the WTO works very much at the level of governments, there is a sense in which it is preparing for a stage of economic development which would eventually undermine national economies.

The main establishment argument for this type of liberalisation claims that significant savings would be made that would bring about an improvement in the welfare of the general population. Much was made of figures produced in an IBRD report, *Trade Liberalisation – The Global Economic Implications*, and separate OECD and GATT surveys all published in 1993, to the effect that, with the successful conclusion of the Uruguay Round, global economic welfare would increase by between US$200 and US$275 billion through more efficient resource allocation.

If we accept, for the sake of argument, that the savings issue is central to the discussion, two criticisms can still be made.

First, we can dispute the claim that savings will indeed be made. After all, the Ricardian model is highly unrealistic in that it neglects to cost retraining, transport and so on. This means that there is scope for developing a model within mainstream economics that is geared to the development of the local economy.[1]

Second, we can accept that savings can be made, but ask who will benefit. In the Ricardian model itself, the goods which are exchanged between the newly specialised economies are the product of unequal quantities of labour, as he recognises,

Such an exchange could not take place between individuals of the same country. The labour of 100 Englishmen cannot be given for that of 80 Englishmen, but the produce of the labour of 100 Englishmen may be given for the produce of the labour of 80 Portuguese, 60 Russians, or 120 East Indians.[2]

Given the structural nature of the world economy, trade liberalisation could become a mechanism for ensuring an unequal distribution of the savings resulting from specialisation. In fact, this possibility is actually confirmed by those nations which one might most expect to be coy on the subject. During the Uruguay Round negotiations, published calculations showed that the main beneficiaries would be the EU, Japan and the USA.[3] The reason why the establishment has been so open on this is that, while opinion in the South can be largely ignored, powerful interests in the North need to be convinced not only that the open economy will benefit them, but also that its benefits will be evenly distributed between the different industrial powers.

Although these two levels of critique appear mutually exclusive, this is not altogether the case if we drop the assumption that the fundamental issue is indeed savings. If we look at the question more closely, it is clear that what is really at stake is accumulation, that is, the self-expansion of capital through exploitation. Specialisation occurs not because it is more efficient in the abstract, but because it helps expand capital. It does this precisely because there is an exchange of unequal values. From the standpoint of human development in general, we can argue that increased specialisation is not the way forward, while at the same time (dealing with the situation here and now) we can recognise that the division of labour has generated a certain value, and that there is scope for campaigns to redress the inequality with which this value is distributed.

The assumption that an accentuated division of labour provides the impetus for *future* development implies that everything has already been turned into commodities and it would simply be a matter of arranging the same set of resources in more efficient ways. But experience suggests that accumulation needs to turn into commodities new areas of life, and this is the process which is really happening behind the facade of increasing efficiency through increasing trade. What is occurring is almost like a continuing form of 'primitive accumulation'. Since capital cannot break up the same areas twice – for example it cannot enclose the commons twice – it has to move on to new areas. In this context, the term 'area' has two meanings:

IN A GEOGRAPHICAL SENSE International capital can start doing in the South things which it previously did in the North, such as spreading the monetary sector at the expense of the traditional sector. But if it did this, it would face the problem that Rosa Luxemburg highlighted, and which was taken up by dependency theory, namely that tradition or pseudo-tradition needs to be reproduced in the periphery if accumulation is to continue.

IN A QUALITATIVE SENSE  New areas of life can be turned into commodities. This is a very promising area of development for capitalism. Although it is true, as I have argued in previous chapters, that new technology enabled investment to take place in the real economy (e.g. manufacturing) in the North in the 1980s and 1990s, it is also evident that there was at the same time a frantic quest for profit in all sorts of other areas, some of which are included in the term 'services': speculation, insurance, selling ideas, tourism, global communications, the entertainment and sports industries, and the spread of brand identities.

However, this area also has its problems. In particular, it can increase alienation in the South if it becomes clear to the masses there that they cannot enjoy any of the things on offer. Just tourism alone draws attention to the colour line which only people from the North can cross. Even so, capitalism probably had little option but to press ahead with this kind of development. The Uruguay Round opened up many of these issues, without resolving them. It became clear that an institutional framework would have to be set up to sort out these problems without waiting for the conclusion of a new 'round' which could take several years. It was for this reason that the WTO was established, so that it could police the dismantling of barriers to the penetration of these new aspects of capital accumulation.

Development has become post-statist, not because the state as an economic unit was inherently inefficient, but simply because the ongoing process of capital accumulation in the 1980s required, like grist to its mill, to consume large parts of the state, both in the centre and the periphery. What has been left of the state is seriously weakened, at least as an agent of economic organisation.

The liberal discourse pretends that national economic boundaries are simply a historical relic that makes no sense today. But this is not entirely true. The national economy used to be, however imperfectly, a repository of some surviving real-economy elements (in the sense that List equated 'national' and 'natural'). By destroying these, a new area has been opened up for 'commodification' or turning into commodities. This was particularly evident in the agricultural agenda of the Uruguay Round, which attacked the support previously given by Northern economies to small farmers. But the process of 'commodification' has come at an immense potential social cost, because of the damage it causes to national identities. The fundamental weakness of Ricardian theory is that it offers no guarantee that specialisation will be socially possible.

Within this context, what happened to protectionism becomes a key issue. Its real significance can only be understood if we see it, not as something purely negative (a tool for excluding a hostile external environment), but as having a positive, managerial role in capitalist development. The Northern economies needed to maintain their individual completeness and coherence while they were becoming more interdependent with one another. Trade between them developed, but the countries were not really specialising in the Ricardian sense; they were but exchanging goods from the same branch of production but with different brand identities. Even at this level, there was an implicit North–South agenda, in the sense that, since the divide was conditional on the existence of 'complete' economies in the individual Northern countries, actions to maintain these economies were collective actions in support of Northern dominance, even when expressed superficially in the form of rivalry.

## The Historical Role of the Uruguay Round of GATT

In the sphere of North–South relations, the industrial countries were using a semblance of the same sort of protectionism which they had previously used to build their own national economies, but the content was different; protectionism against fellow industrial countries was an arrangement among colleagues, which gave rise to some acrimony but whose rules were fundamentally accepted because it balanced industrial development between them. Directed against the South, protectionism does not balance industrial development, but prevents it. From this perspective, protectionism retained the same form, but changed in substance. Eventually there was also a change in form. Historically, tariffs have been a major protectionist weapon, but after the Second World War, GATT began removing them. This was necessary to push integration within the North. So to deal with the South different measures were also brought into play, in particular, quotas.

Since the end of the 1970s the situation has changed again. This is because the new management systems demand a market composed of free-floating economic actors. At the same time, these systems are supposed to be strong enough to control such a market, so, in theory at least, the latter can be safely introduced without risk of the South getting too much benefit from it. In these circumstances it has become possible to dismantle further tools of economic nationalism. The Uruguay Round was therefore much more ambitious than earlier tariff-cutting rounds of GATT in creating a 'free' market. It is clear that this market is not really free, because it actually serves to unleash the powerful economic interests which can now operate in an environment where national economic boundaries no longer present a barrier. But there were risks in this radical change: firstly that the South might be able in some way to take advantage of this new environment, and secondly that the national economy in the North, although it remains significantly stronger than in the South, might have been undermined to some degree.

These risks created the need for a different form of safeguard, which I will call the 'new protectionism'. In a sense, this protectionism operated higher up the chain: that is, at the level of ideas, software, patents and brand identities – all the things which the new management system uses to control and manipulate the 'free' market.

In some areas, such as textiles, protectionism appears not to have changed a great deal. Textiles were regulated by the Long Term Arrangement (LTA) of 1962, which originally applied to cotton yarns and garments. This was a derogation from GATT whereby signatories gave up rights under GATT in exchange for increased quotas. It was replaced in 1974 by the Multifibre Agreement (MFA). It is interesting to note that, although the mid-1970s was apparently the high point of the NIEO movement, the North managed to make the new agreement more restrictive than the old one, in that synthetic fibres were included as well. Under the Uruguay Round agreement of December 1993, the MFA was extended for another year, and then phased out over a period of a further ten years. This, remarkably, adds up to a total of 43 years during which a special textiles regime will have prevailed. The inequality of the system is starkly exposed here, in the contrast between GATT's failure to provide developing countries with effective protection for 'infant industries', and its readiness to help the North revamp its decrepit textile sector.

Other commodities were not dealt with in this way, which raises the question of why textiles were special. Conventionally, the explanation has been that it was precisely the relatively open character of the market in textiles, in comparison to other sectors which were more heavily monopolised, that made it necessary to have a more intense form of protectionism (in our definition, the 'old' protectionism).[4] Elsewhere, it is true, monopoly was more marked. The NIEO movement aimed, in effect, to institute at an international level the kind of checks and balances which limited monopoly within developed capitalist countries. As Raghavan points out, the Uruguay Round of GATT amounted to a rejection of this idea.[5] According to this analysis, the new stage of development will accentuate the power of monopoly. An indication that this may indeed be the case have been the calls for the abolition of UNCTAD – which used to monitor the activities of TNCs and propose measures to limit their abuse of power – on the grounds that the WTO's existence makes it redundant.

But this analysis is not entirely adequate. Although monopoly remains important, the new management systems have significantly altered its parameters. As I argued in Chapter 10, this makes it possible to some extent to relax direct control. As we have seen, the 'new protectionism' does not aim to hold on to the old industries lock stock and barrel, but rather to safeguard control over the core technology, which facilitates the 'putting-out' of processes into the South. This applies to all sectors of industry, including the 'old' ones like textiles which, according to product-cycle theory, should have shifted to the developing world.

A true picture of the Uruguay Round is probably that it was genuinely radical in changing some of the old forms of restriction, but it offset this by introducing new ones. The trick was that, in this latter task, it appeared to be doing the opposite, so that the new protectionism was introduced under the cloak of liberalism. The argument went like this: trade needed to encompass ideas as well as commodities, but before these could freely be traded, patent laws had to be internationalised. In practice this protected the monopoly of knowledge of the powerful interests in the North, and dealt a powerful blow to latecomers, who in the past had always had the advantage of being able to copy technology. The fact that the Uruguay Round copied American endeavours to exclude imported goods – the US trade act, the so-called Super 301 and Special 301 (1988) which extended the regime to services and intellectual property – clearly demonstrates this fact. In one sense, it is true that ideas are becoming increasingly commoditised – the 'privatisation of the intellectual commons' in Vandana Shiva's memorable phrase.[6] Those who control ideas can therefore extract monopoly rents. But perhaps even more important than the monetary value is the fact that software, patents, and so on control the overall productive economy, which means that the old forms of protectionism can be relaxed while ensuring that the South remains subservient.

Having said all this, the new system is so new that it would be premature to regard it as watertight. It is not impossible that the South could take advantage somewhere along the line. Could increased interdependence generate a certain 'spreading' of development?

In the argument about 'spreading', it is essential to clarify whether one is speaking of levelling or social mobility, because the two are diametrically opposite. Levelling would imply a homogenisation: abundant capital would flow in pursuit of abundant (therefore cheap) labour until an evening-out occurred. There is absolutely no evidence that this is objectively possible or subjectively encouraged under the current regime.

Social mobility is an entirely different matter, because it is an individual actor who moves up the system; and in this way mobility strengthens divisive systems, rather than weakening them, as levelling would. Extending this to an international level, Alfred Sauvy's analogy with the 'Third Estate' in pre-Revolutionary France shows the risks inherent in a situation in which there is no hope of improvement within the system, so the system itself becomes the target of struggle. To prevent this happening, it would therefore be highly beneficial to the centre–periphery divide to create some room for movement between the categories in the system. It is possible that, as a result of the relaxation of the old trade restrictions, there is now an opportunity for doing this.

But the analogy between domestic and international forms of social mobility is suspect, just because the centre–periphery division is closer to a racial divide than to a class one. Certainly, individuals from the Southern élites can move more freely within the international power structure, perhaps even prosper as part of (rather than simply intermediaries in) global accumulation. Whether an entire country could move up is, however, far more questionable. It is also doubtful whether a country in the North would be allowed to move down: in the last analysis, the North would probably club together to stop this happening. Both these factors make it clear that the North will not tolerate too many honorary Aryans at a country level. It is certainly true that a certain third-worldisation of particular sectors within the North already exists, and constitutes a very important feature of the present system; but against the background of all the other relevant factors, we are surely justified in seeing it more as a mechanism for stopping the South obtaining a monopoly on cheap labour than as a real loosening of the North–South divide.

This impression is reinforced if we examine another aspect of the recent development of GATT, which I shall refer to as a second form of 'new protectionism': one directed specifically against the advantage of cheap labour. It is reflected in the debate over 'social dumping'. Some Northern interests have called for trade restrictions if countries in the South use low wages or low 'social cost' to gain a competitive advantage. Other groups in the North favour indirect means, with the EU arguing for including provisions about workers' rights in trade agreements, and the USA speaking of human and social rights.[7] The purpose behind all this is to strike the right balance, so that the North can continue to exploit cheap peripheral labour, while making sure that the South does not draw structural benefits from the situation.

It is true that the GATT/WTO in some way polices this new fabric of the IPE, but what is much more important is that these organisations have been setting up a regime in which the new relationships should become self-maintaining in a systemic sense and not require too much policing. One way in which this regime operates can be seen in what has been dubbed the 'poverty trap'; if, by taking advantage of the comparative advantage of its cheap labour, a country in the South seems to be moving too fast up the system, its further progress is halted by automatic mechanisms, triggered by thresholds.

This scheme involves the institutionalisation of categories which were formerly just part of development theory. A crucial role is played by placing the South into categories: less-developed, developing and newly-industrialising countries. These categories have an established ideological role, propagating a comforting, conveyor-belt image (in its way every bit as developmentalist as supposedly discredited Rostowism), while also serving to undermine third-worldist solidarity. But today, they also have a concrete and practical function as well. Developing countries need GATT to give access to Northern markets, but the GATT package carries with it a corresponding limitation which can annul the benefits so obtained through this access: as soon as a country is promoted from 'less-developed' to 'developing', it loses the right to impose minimum local content requirements in its exported products. Malaysia is an interesting example. Its automobile industry aimed for a 60 per cent local input in order to make sure that domestic business benefited, and was not merely assembling 'kits', as has often been the case with ISI automobile projects of the past. But trade-related investment measures (TRIMs) now require developing countries to phase out both local content requirements within five years and also subsidies to industry conditional upon the use of domestic as against imported inputs.[8] As a result, the multiplier effect of the Malaysian car industry in the rest of the economy has been severely curtailed. In this sense, the system has developed a fail-safe mechanism to inhibit effective spreading.

But the rejection of social mobility – on what are, in the last analysis, racial grounds – has a cost. Regimes are supposed to create order in the international system (without the need for a supranational sovereign) because they acquire the loyalty of the participants. But GATT has a major weakness in this respect: within the South, only the élites are loyal to it, because they have achieved a sort of social mobility which is denied to the masses. Export promotion further undermines the link between what is produced and consumed, further increasing alienation. As a result, ordinary people do not identify with decisions taken at regime level. This feeling of exclusion can give birth to an opposition movement, such as the Indian peasant movement, explicitly directed against GATT, or the Mexican movement, directed immediately against NAFTA, but which also tapped into the same resentments.

At the same time, there are opportunities within the trading system for élites to threaten trouble, in pursuit of a bigger share of value. At first sight, this is not evident. The Uruguay Round was conducted like the Versailles Treaty at the end of the First World War, with all the decisions taken by the powerful few and simply registered by everyone else. The consensus voting system (different from the weighted system in the World Bank and the IMF) even makes it difficult to register a negative vote. Pro-GATT establishment writers warn, without too much circumspection, that turning up for GATT meetings 'can easily be an inefficient use of the time of many Ministers from smaller trading nations', because the deals are done between the powerful nations.[9]

Even so, there are probably openings for the South within the WTO, if the more powerful Southern actors were to threaten to create enough trouble to damage the system. The North's fear of admitting China is a graphic recognition of this danger: it has every interest in 'binding' China into the system as the best way of influencing it internally, but year after year the North hesitated about admitting it into GATT.

In fact, if the global dimension were the only dimension which existed above the national level, capitalism could probably not control things effectively enough. This is probably the reason for the existence of another level which has become increasingly important and complex in the recent period – regionalism.

## The Necessity and Dangers of a Regionally Organised Capitalism: Does It Undermine Globalism?

A key issue within the capitalist international political economy is something often referred to as the 'new regionalism'. Conventionally, this can be taken to describe not only the proliferation of regional organisations over the past decade, but also an assumption that the international system could fragment into regions, perhaps dominated by individual powers or blocs. In this sense, regionalisation could be a step backward for the IPE, away from universalism and multilateralism. What reality does this reflect? The question requires an understanding of regionalism's significance within capitalist development as a whole.

Capitalism develops in general by breaking up local self-referential systems, such as local communal systems of production and exchange. However, the pre-capitalist political economy was also characterised by long-range trading systems, which included an element of 'natural' regionalism, and these were destroyed too.

In its place, accumulation creates a new spatial organisation. This exists at two levels: firstly, the 'national' economy at the centre, and secondly, colonialism as a vertical apparatus for siphoning to the centre resources (raw materials, human labour) which are not fully remunerated. This leaves no space for a South–South dimension. The two levels are interdependent, since colonial accumulation reinforces the national economies (and bourgeois class power) in the North.

But at a particular point, both these sets of boundaries become, in their existing form, restrictions on further capitalist development, for the following reasons. In relation to the first of these dimensions, the national one, the 'complete' economies in the North, which used to provide a context for the growth of capitalist relations, begin at a particular point to become an obstacle. As we have seen, this happens because several countries are all doing the same thing, which creates overlapping capacity. The most obvious and conventional way of describing this problem is to say that it creates 'inefficiency', but I believe there may be a longer-term issue. At some point capital accumulation has to develop by consuming the state-protected element, like some insect eating the chrysalis which once shielded it, which leaves the problem of where capitalism goes once this source has been exhausted. And there is another, equally important issue: the political dimension. The nations start to compete, not only because the world is not big enough for several powers following this road, but because, as Sen points out, the existence of 'surplus capacity in substantial areas of manufacturing' reinforces a dangerous military–competitive dynamic.[10] These factors provide a powerful argument for integration between industrialised economies.

In relation to the second dimension: the colonial system, as a primarily extractive system with impenetrable vertical boundaries, also starts to restrict capitalist development, once industry and finance capital demand to move more freely in search of cheap local labour. Some new spatial organisation is clearly needed (although it is not immediately clear what form it will take).

Here, another contradiction emerges. Capitalist development on the one hand renders these changes necessary, but on the other creates a structure in which it becomes apparently impossible for them to happen: imperialism, under whose auspices the two, implicitly outdated, levels of organisation – economic nationalism at the centre, and the value pulled up through the vertical conveyor-belt from the colonies – reinforce one another.

At the same time, as left-wing theories of the 1900s perceived, imperialism paved the way for possible solutions. As was inevitable, industry began to spread to the South, creating the risk that it would spin out of control, but the very perception by the North of the danger provided the stimulus for it to resolve its differences, either through integration within the 'old world' – Europe – or, more broadly, in the creation of a 'federation of the Western States'.[11] So it became able to manage the process of shifting some industrial production to the South, while making sure that the relationship remained essentially exploitative. Eventually, Europe was revitalised both by eliminating the productive capacity previously protected by the state and by consuming the state itself. Ultimately, what emerged was the challenge to create a new systemic milieu in which the new organising power of industry and finance capital could take over the functions which the national economy and vertical integration were no longer able to fulfil.

Initially, the new organising forces were used to fuel an even more intense rivalry between nations. Germany and Japan, as revisionist powers, were able to be the most innovatory. The German *Mitteleuropa* ideas of the First World War period, and the Japanese 'flying geese' model indicate some awareness that colonialism and nationalism of the old kind were being superseded by the advent of imperialism itself. At one level this is an extension of the Listian argument – if pure globalism inhibits the development of capitalism beyond the nation, then regionalism might be necessary in order to provide some protection for the next phase. One Japanese article from 1942 remarks that 'The white world is likely to have a common prosperity sphere in Europe and another in the Western Hemisphere ... And the combination of these different Co-Prosperity Spheres will lead to the emergence of a new international order'.[12] This would transcend both the conventional national economy and conventional colonialism by establishing contiguous industrial spaces. This process, however, would occur in response to rival *regional* projects.

United States leaders felt the need to stop nationalism taking control of this process, and did so by using the threat of the Cold War. It was this that made it possible to press for the integration of the old world and to push for the dismantling of colonial exclusivity far enough to enable industry and capital to ease themselves into a new organising role. Because of the Cold War, there was no longer any real risk of nationalism taking command of the shake-up of the old system and, for this reason, there was no need to be creative in the field of any new postcolonial forms for the organisation of Northern exploitation. Instead, it was sufficient to reshape the old ones. The USA continued to rule Latin America through the Monroe Doctrine. Military treaty organisations took charge of the repressive aspect of regionalism. Above all, former colonial powers were permitted to carry forward their previous relationships with subject territories as a reward for agreeing to a division of labour in which they would suppress radical forces in their areas of influence, on the condition that these economic nexuses did not inhibit the global accumulation process (and that US investments were not barred from any of the areas).

This conservatism was only possible because pro-independence forces in the South did not take advantage of the weakening of the old structures to defend a new regional agenda. This does not mean that the third world was a passive spectator. Élites in the South correctly perceived that the Cold War was being used as an excuse to perpetuate spheres of influence in a new form, and the Bandung Conference and Organisation of African Unity (OAU) attempted to counter this danger. However, their efforts were hampered by their mindset: they still saw themselves as latecomers, who were building the national economy and would then 'join' the international one. If they had only perceived the extent to which economic development at the international level undermined their national projects, they might have perceived that, for them, development was possible only through South–South integration at a regional level. In the absence of such an understanding, America could safely defend its own version of the regional agenda during the 1960s: projects such as the Latin American Free Trade Area (LAFTA) or (in its original incarnation) ASEAN employed a spurious, Europe-derived concept of modernity that effectively isolated radicals by surrounding them with a mass of moderates. At the same time, Southern nationalism, while not focused enough to offer effective resistance to this agenda, was sufficiently entrenched to prevent the take-off of an autonomous regional economy.

Although it appeared neat in the way it operated, Northern control suffered weaknesses because of its lack of real content. It would have been dangerous to build new regional economies before the establishment of the international one because in these circumstances these would just have been a reworking of the old spheres of influence. For this reason it became necessary to establish the global economy immediately, but since this was so new it was effectively maintained by US hegemony rather than by its own systemic momentum. The regional economic systems became a kind of subset of a world economy which itself lacked real content or systemic momentum, and as such had no real identity. As the Free World (the so-called universal market) had no positive identity, it could define itself only negatively with respect to its 'other', the Eastern bloc. To a large extent, this also happened at the levels of the regions, which were in practice largely dominated by 'containment'. The problem for the future was that, when the IPE eventually had to give itself a richer content at different levels including the regional one, this process could appear regressive. Although objectively the new regional economy would be giving concrete form to the capitalist world economy, it might appear, on the contrary, that it was undermining it, and this could be confusing ideologically. It was also possible that this weakness might actually be exploited in the future by competitive nationalist tendencies in the North, so in the end the regression might even be real.

## The Disorientation of the 1970s and the Apparent Fragmentation of Global Capitalism

Regional integration always seems to be reaching out towards some restoration of the 'natural' economy, balancing trade with important elements of self-sufficiency and local particularism. But under capitalism, this never quite happens. The 1970s were a strange period because a number of the underlying problems of the real economy came to the surface in the dying phase of the postwar long cycle. The old structures were no longer valid, but the new ones which seemed to be emerging were in fact stamped with the character of a historical period soon to be swept away. During this period, there was much more apparent autonomy in the South, reflected in an upsurge of regional experiments. The following were the most interesting.

REGIONAL FORM OF THE NEW INTERNATIONAL ECONOMIC ORDER 'Collective self-reliance' and 'economic co-operation among developing countries' (ECDC) took on a regional dimension, for example in Latin America. As a result, an attempt was made to challenge the anachronistic Monroe Doctrine, not just by abolishing it, but by replacing it with new institutions, such as the Latin America Economic System (SELA), which gave expression to Latin American nationalism. Once the long cycle shifted, much of this withered.

NORTHERN RESTRUCTURING CAUSED A RE-ALIGNMENT IN THE SOUTH In the mid-1970s, there were immense structural changes. These led eventually to the creation of the EU, but in the short term they weakened the old vertical power relations, providing favourable conditions for the creation of the Economic Community of West African States (ECOWAS), the first regional organisation in Africa which grouped countries from different former empires. On the other hand, the Lomé Convention (1975) may have been one of the earliest expressions of an attempt by Europe to move towards collective hegemony.

EFFECTS OF THE SLUMP IN THE NORTH The industrial world went through a phase of stagnation before regaining its dynamism again and dictating a new agenda for reorganising capital accumulation on a global scale. During the transition, international economic activity weakened in some areas, making developing countries believe that they could reduce their vulnerability by trading with each other.

POST-VIETNAM ADJUSTMENTS IN ASIA America, through the Nixon doctrine, suddenly reduced American protection, while at the same time promising to permit capitalist development. This, together with the Japanese 'flying geese' strategy, gave fresh impetus to Asia. More specifically, the Association of South-East Asian Nations (ASEAN), founded in the 1960s but moribund, acquired a new lease of life.

ENLARGEMENT OF THE SOVIET SPHERE It appeared, in defiance of globalism, that a new form of verticality might arise, with the extension of CMEA into the South and the creation of a web of pro-Soviet governments under the auspices of the theory of the 'non-capitalist road' to development. This again reflected the temporary loss of initiative of the capitalist IPE.

STRONG SOUTHERN STATES ATTEMPT TO CATALYSE REGIONALISM Regional powers in the South were able to seek forms of integration which strengthened their own local hegemony. As the Indian ruling élite discovered,[13] the slogans of South–South co-operation promoted by the third world movement could provide an effective smokescreen for this purpose.

Many of these developments were responses to temporary opportunities. This is not to diminish the importance of such responses; on the contrary, the ability to take advantage of temporarily favourable circumstances is one of the most important skills to be used in an attempt to assert autonomy for the South. The problem was that Southern élites did not understand the broader picture of how the capitalist IPE develops through large-scale qualitative shifts, preceded by structural crises, and wrongly believed that the temporary circumstances indicated a decisive shift in the South's favour.

## The New Long Cycle and the Issue of Post-Hegemony

By the beginning of the 1980s, central capitalism was in a position to start crushing the South's attempts at autonomy, but by then a new element was beginning to create confusion in relations with the regions. For capitalism was now experimenting with a new form of regionalism which favoured central accumulation rather than restricting it. Superficially, this new form appeared regressive, in relation to the universal capitalist world market proclaimed in 1945. There were two reasons for this: first, the universal market that it promoted was a somewhat abstract declaration of intent which lacked a real content, and second, it depended on US hegemony. From the end of the 1970s the international system had been adjusting to collective hegemony instead of individual hegemony, while at the same time, once the transition to neo-colonialism had been realised and the NIEO movement defeated, experimenting with new forms of spatial organisation that reflected the new exploitative possibilities of a rapidly evolving accumulation system.

US hegemony had played a transitional role in moving the international system away from the prisoners' dilemma situation,[14] where mutual suspicion prevented the big capitalist powers from moderating their rivalry. The risk was that once the hegemony had been removed, the old rivalry would be reasserted. But this was not necessarily so, because the hegemony could be used to establish regimes – using the term in the special sense of structures, that may arise informally – which enable actors to co-operate because they gradually perceive co-operation to be advantageous.[15]

Now, the period around 1980 witnessed a form of regionalism which at first sight looked like the refutation of the old universalist order. The increasing European unity and the Pacific Economic Co-operation Conference (PECC, widely interpreted as a Japanese tool for controlling Asia), are symptoms. From a radical perspective, Marcussen and Torp's excellent study in the early 1980s proposes a model of 'a vertical division of labour consisting of the axes USA–Latin America, Japan–South-East Asia, Western Europe–Africa'.[16] From the establishment side, there is a current of liberal apologists for the period of American hegemony who regard the new regionalism as the end of a golden age. Robert Gilpin warned in the mid-1980s that the system would fragment, not because the USA had been dethroned by other capitalist powers, but because it had abandoned a commitment to multilateralism. He puts forward a curious vision of a benevolent hegemony being replaced by predatory regimes, which he attacks by an argument borrowed from imperialism theory, saying in effect that the regimes are trying to be ultra-imperialist.[17]

I would argue, though, that neither the left-wing nor pro-establishment versions of fragmentation adequately describes what was happening in the 1980s. The new situation of regimes – a relationship of roughly equal capitalist powers maintained through OECD, the G7, etc. – reflected the fact that there was by then widespread recognition that an open world market would benefit exploitation. It was a tribute to the solidity of these regimes that it became possible to experiment with regionalism without tearing the system apart. New regional structures of capital accumulation could be tried out, while the regimes themselves – in particular the Bretton Woods institutions and GATT–WTO – provided a counterweight, if there was a real risk of fragmentation.

## Towards a New Spatial Organisation of Capital – the Search for Local Peripheries

What forms could this experimentation take? Capital organises itself spatially in pursuit of cheap labour, and one new form of capital accumulation could be created around 'local peripheries', that is, South–style economies located closer to the centre, in which the industrial powers were partly competing and partly exploring collective hegemony. This new form reflects the fact that on the one hand it is not ideal to import labour directly into Northern economies (because it is hard to avoid meeting its reproductions costs); but, on the other hand, there are risks in having the work done in remote countries, because it might be difficult to keep the situation under control. Local peripheries are a compromise solution, where it is possible to avoid meeting the reproduction costs and at the same time to control the situation closely enough to prevent autonomous take-off. This could be a solution to the classic problem of imperialism, that is, to manage Asia by an indirect route, through setting up foci of semi-development elsewhere.

From the European angle, one way of preventing too much investment going to Asia would be the notion that 'Development would be kept in the family' – an idea that Gorbachev sought to exploit with his notion of Europe as a 'common home'. Around the time of the end of the Cold War, some sectors of capital welcomed this approach; for example, when the Fiat motor corporation concluded a deal in 1989 to set up a large subsidiary in the then Soviet Union, one of its executives remarked that 'Eastern Europe will become the new Korea of the motor industry, except this time cheap production will be available on our doorstep.'[18] There is clearly a racial subtext in this statement.

Since then, the appeal of this option has obviously waned, but there are other possibilities for semi-peripheries. Given the viciousness of the North–South divide, some states might prefer semi-periphery status to being in the outer limbo. In the EU context, this could include building on EU 'associate' states in the Mediterranean. French 'overseas departments' could be another example, and the Caribbean has been an area where local states have for some time cultivated this status. Trinidad sought to win concessions by serving as a bridgehead for TNC penetration of the whole region.[19] This led to Reagan's Caribbean Basin Initiative, launched in 1983. The political background behind all this was the invasion of Grenada and the perennial strategy to isolate Cuba. Within a semi-periphery, subordinate actors may spontaneously find the best way of entering exploitative relationships, and of creating 'niches' within the grand scheme of capital accumulation. One example is the promotion of 'non-traditional' exports which diversify without fundamentally altering dependency relationships.[20] Such hybrid situations do not mean that North–South polarisation does not exist; on the contrary, they confirm it, since it is precisely because of such polarisation that the privileged status of a local periphery may appear attractive to élites seeking to obtain a share of the crumbs. In a sense, the hierarchy of levels or grades of semi-peripheries can be seen as part of the new management systems, which seek to reward and integrate by promoting 'overseers'. Within this context, it is possible that the organising power of industry, specifically the new management structures, will take over the management of the international system in a post-statist sense.

The most remarkable case is NAFTA, a regional grouping established in 1992, whereby Mexico linked itself to the USA and Canada. All the concessions were made by Mexico: the initial terms included an undertaking by Mexico to relinquish taxes on automobiles and spare parts, open up its telecommunications market by 1995, immediately abandon import licenses on agricultural products, abandon the clause stipulating that US enterprises investing in Mexico have to export, immediately permit US and Canadian banks to take over Mexican banks up to a limit of 8 per cent in the sector, abandon all restrictions on the takeover of Mexican banks by the year 2000, and open up the transport market in two stages in 1995 and 1999.[21] It adds up to colonialism, without the inconvenience of the USA having to wage a new Spanish-American war to seize the territory, and, more important, without the costs of direct colonial administration.

But this example also illustrates the limitations and contradictions of the 'local periphery' scenario. Ideally, a one-off act of political interventionism would establish conditions under which economic actors would spontaneously 'self-exploit' themselves. But the reality may be very different. It is far from clear that this new setup has a coherent socio-political basis. NAFTA does not offer anything to the masses – certainly not any freedom of movement for people that is in any way equivalent to the freedom of movement of capital. As a result, humiliation is always evident, the narrowing of differentials illusory. Élites might welcome the opportunities, and in fact once they lost confidence in the old nationalist models which had previously guaranteed their status, they rushed headlong to protect their status within new ones, but ordinary people realise that there is nothing in it for them. Ultimately, this could make the USA responsible for policing the social crisis in Mexico, which means that there is no consensus among US capitalists that NAFTA is a good thing.

## Can Southern Élites Generate an Autonomous 'New Regionalism'?

Although there are risks when the central powers are too heavily involved in the issue of Southern regionalism, there are also risks when they are not involved enough. There are two key factors.

SOME INCREASE IN SOUTH–SOUTH TRADE MAY BE INEVITABLE  Production in the South is expanding not just because the South supplies the North with a useful supply of cheap manufactured goods, but also because the North can increase the value of capital by exporting it to the South. Obviously there is a certain reciprocity in these two processes, but there is no reason why the volume of production (dictated solely by the needs of capital accumulation) should exactly balance the Northern market's ability to consume them. It is quite possible that overproduction on an international scale can result. This can create the rationale for increasing South–South trade and/or economic co-operation, but this is possible only if the second factor is in place.

THE UNDERMINING OF NATIONALISM MIGHT PROMOTE SOUTH–SOUTH LINKS  The breakup of the state in the South can have a paradoxical effect. In the old long cycle, the statist focus of latecomer strategies at the individual-country level effectively undermined regional strategies. But statism has now itself been undermined by neo-liberalism. Might this remove the blockage which used to prevent South–South regional integration?

In these circumstances, it is certainly possible that the South could become more self-reliant, and the North has to make sure this does not happen. This is the main reason that it cannot afford to wash its hands of South–South developments. There is a sense in which the old 1960s regionalism was 'safe' because it fell within the parameters of the Cold War, and statist development policies effectively prevented integration between the Southern nations.

The new regionalism is much more complex. There is something in the new élite movement towards integration that the dominant powers do not like. It gives the impression that there are two conflicting agendas in the world capitalist system. The growth of the regional organisation Mercosur in South America shows how the weakening of old national economic boundaries can pave the way for a new form of integration through collaboration in infrastructure and technology. Protocols of the original Argentina–Brazil agreement of 1987 planned for co-operation in hydroelectric power schemes as well as in some key modern sectors such as biotechnology, and for the integration of transport and telecommunication systems, with the formation of joint enterprises. Trade between the four countries in the organisation – Brazil, Argentina, Uruguay and Paraguay – grew strongly in the 1980s. In the case of Brazil, intra-regional trade rose by more than half, while imports from the rest of the world actually declined.[22] As a result, the decision was taken in 1991 to set up a formal body, Mercosur, and the organisation became operational in January 1995.[23] Relations between member states are continuing to grow stronger: trade with one another as a percentage of total trade increased from 9 per cent in 1990 to 20 per cent in 1996.[24] Potentially, Mercosur could act as a catalyst for wider Latin American unity, something which is already beginning with the formation of a new organisation, the Latin American Integration Association (ALADI) to replace earlier failed attempts such as LAFTA and SELA. This type of integration reflects the desire of local entrepreneurs to explore a new and wider economic space, but it also requires a political decision to explore a new definition of community. This is not the definition of community that the grassroots would give, but grassroots movements are not hostile to Mercosur-type integration to the same extent as they are to NAFTA. There is a sense of a new period in politics, different from the authoritarianism of the past. The new set-up is democratic in the sense of greater pluralism, and a desire not to return to the military dictatorships of the past, but not in a meaningful economic sense. The new regimes are also prepared to help each other at moments of crisis.[25] This means that the USA sees it as a challenge to its own authority and has given no encouragement whatever to this form of regionalism.[26] It puts forward its own counter-schemes – in particular, a plan for the enlargement of NAFTA – as a spoiling operation to undermine the chances of deeper regional integration.

However, this convergence of regional interests is premised on systems which also marginalise large sections of the population and do nothing to reduce polarisation. In an economic sense, this mutual reinforcement of the new élite structures seeks to explore a developmental potential within a framework which is highly resistant to mass demands. Even if development occurs, it is unlikely to deliver anything to the grassroots, simply because, if the marginalised were to become consumers, this would challenge existing class power. More than anything else, the growing interdependence of élites expressed in the new regionalism is a way of consolidating their power. The new regionalism comes about precisely because the restriction of the domestic market under conditions of existing class relations means that the élites cannot achieve a greater degree of self-reliance within a single national economy.

To some extent, this form of regionalism may be compared with the successful phase of NIC models, in that, in just the same way, frenetic growth may have generated extra productive capacity that cannot be satisfied by demand within export markets. There is no sign that this is leading to the emergence of an economic form of democracy, that it is lessening polarisation in order to create a mass market. This necessarily restricts the possibility of self-related growth at a national level, but it might be possible to remove this barrier for a time, at a level of the regional élite market. By weakening the old barrier to integration, which was the discrete national economy, globalisation has created the conditions for regionalism, but the effects of this will be circumscribed unless there is a change of distribution within the societies. For the moment, regionalism acts as a way of sidestepping this demand by temporarily prolonging growth without redistribution, but at a particular point the further development of regionalism will itself become an argument for redistribution.

What is not yet clear is the extent to which the crisis of the late 1990s will reverse the recent move towards regionalism, but there may well be additional forces for regionalism which counteract whatever negative pressures arise. To give an example: the declining value of currencies which occurred in the Southern economies affected by the crisis of the late 1990s makes it very difficult to fix any of the benefits of global trade within the local economies. Devaluation is supposed to make it 'easier' to get into foreign markets, but a moment's reflection shows that this argument is spurious, and that a devalued currency merely heightens the exchange of unequal values. This poses the obvious question: what is the point of exporting? Increased regional integration would be a logical response.

## Asia and the Confrontation of Different Regional Agendas

The issues that we have looked at in Latin America can be examined in the Asian context. NIC development has gone furthest there, and at the same time, external agendas have also been more forcefully imposed. Simply because of its 'success', a major effort is required to contain Asian NIC development.

There are aspects of the NIC phenomenon which seem to push in the direction of regional collaboration. This is partly political. If we look back to the post-Cold War, pre-crisis period, it can be seen that the economic motive for co-operation was reinforced by a political dimension. ASEAN élites, who were primarily anti-communists who had done well out of the Cold War but were threatened by the re-articulation of US goals along lines of economic national interest, were seeking a strategy for reinforcing the local economy and thus giving themselves bargaining power. Part of the response was the pursuit of 'milieu goals', in other words foreign policy aiming to influence the functioning of the system itself, rather than simply maximise interests within it. Self-reliance in this sense did not mean withdrawing from the system but influencing the distribution of power within it.[27] It meant promoting a more diffuse power environment, which would necessarily favour smaller actors.

But there was also a different range of factors, affecting also the larger states. When élites aspire to nationalist development strategies, the limitations of doing this individually may become apparent. Technology is crucial for development: individual countries can get dislocated bits of technologies, but it is only through co-operation that something like a coherent technology can come about. The logic of this is so strong that it would be surprising if it did not find some practical expression. India–China relations are an example: despite acute hostility, there is a logic pushing towards co-operation. Indeed, China has always avoided being drawn into irrevocably hostile relations with India.[28] Since the improvement of relations in the 1980s, trade has not increased dramatically, but there have been complementarities of a different kind in the field of technology. Co-operation agreements were signed dealing with agricultural technique, petroleum technology, biogas, small power plants, irrigation, communications, health and population control, drug research, biotechnology, software, plasma physics and laser technology.[29] This list includes both 'appropriate' technology (indigenous, small-scale processes) and state-of-the-art technology, which the North is trying to monopolise (pharma-ceuticals, communications).

Logically, the effects of the crisis should only make such collaboration more attractive, since the costs of imported technology will effectively increase. If the South could 'delink' their own creativity, as well as their resources (genetic, raw material, and so on), this might give them a favourable position in the world balance of forces for the first time in the modern period. Such a strategy is not feasible if it is to be executed by élites alone, but a common front with grassroots forces may be possible, a point I will address in the final chapter. Present regional strategies have been worked out exclusively by the élites, but they have certain aspects which, even in the pre-crisis period, have tended towards a degree of self-reliance. It has been argued for some time, most clearly by Malaysia, that the days of pure export-led growth (in the sense of South–North exports) are numbered and that Southern interdependence is needed to counteract the threat of dependence inherent in the North–South trade still necessary to obtain technology.[30] The emphasis in the technology debate has also switched from the economistic problem of buying it to the issue of absorbing it, which implies investment in education. Hypothetically, one might move away from a pure export orientation (as would be the case if the only issue was importing the techno-logy) to seek a new equilibrium in the direction of regional integration together with a further development of the domestic Asian market.[31]

There is a supplementary argument, which is probably not consciously articulated by Southern élites, but is nevertheless pressing in the same direction. The crisis that is beginning to affect the Asian NICs is itself only a symptom of something wider, which is that the present long cycle is at a pivotal point at the time of writing and is certain to enter a declining phase. This must lead to severe structural problems in the North, which may be reflected in a decline of consumption, independently of the political will of the Northern bourgeoisie. For this reason as well, South–South co-operation is a sound strategy.

The phenomenon of a clash between conflicting agendas, which was already noted in the NAFTA–Mercosur issue in Latin America, is also visible in Asia. In a way, it is much more acute here because of the politico-military dimension. Clear battle-lines have already been drawn. For example, China's 1992 decision to extend the opening-out process to India and Central Asia is part of a strategy for reconstituting the 'natural regionalism' of pre-colonial times – the ancient Silk Road which linked China, India and the Middle East – and carries with it the clear objective of countering an external agenda for Central Asia, of which Turkey is seen as the vehicle.[32] The economic stakes in Asia are very high: intra-regional trade in East Asia increased from 30 per cent to 40 per cent of the region's total trade in the period 1970–90, and was predicted to have risen to account for a third of total world trade by the year 2000.[33] Such statistics obviously cover conflicting trends, and some of the activity they describe is probably a disguised form of external exploitation. But there is at least a risk of some of this value slipping out of control. The North needs to make sure, first, that it benefits from this trade and, second, that it stops any tendency towards the growth of self-related trade patterns which might exclude it.

However, the situation in Asia is even more complex that this. Asia's weight in the world economy means that different overlapping interests explore different dimensions of regionalism and seek to turn them to their benefit, while élites also occupy an ambiguous status. Moreover, the situation is evolving through time. For example, the agenda for controlling Asian regionalism in the 1980s and the first half of the 1990s was probably premised on an assumption of successful Asian development, whereas in the coming period interventionism will almost certainly attempt to counter the risks of a shift to regional self-reliance under conditions of decline.

The development of regional organisations illustrates some of this complexity. Although a founder member of PECC,[34] the USA was not interested in developing it during much of the Reagan period.[35] It appeared to be politics that changed the situation: around 1986, before his conversion to pan-Europeanism, Gorbachev set off alarm bells by focusing on Asia and an *entente* with China.[36] But perhaps there was also a deeper cause in that huge amounts of investment, particularly Japanese, were flowing into Asia in the second half of the 1980s, reflecting the partial failure of intra-Northern relations to contain Asian development. Action was urgently needed on the spot, hands on. The Asia–Pacific Economic Co-operation Council (APEC) was therefore founded in 1989, at the initiative of the industrial powers within the region, with a clear 'local–periphery' perspective. The US had to force Australia and Japan to let it join APEC, which was expanded to include Pacific Rim countries, defined in such a way as to take in the Western Americas.[37] After a fairly cautious start, America increased its role in decision-making, the institution being pushed strongly in Clinton's 'New Pacific Community' idea (1993).[38]

The *raison d'être* for APEC is still the search for an answer to Hobson's problem, which was that the industrial world needed to find a way of 'managing' Asian development, as it evidently could not halt it. This is reinterpreted, inadequately, in the United States context, as the industrial world having a responsibility to give 'leadership,'[39] which implies that otherwise the region would succumb to the forces of chaos.

But the question is, leadership in pursuit of what? An obvious answer has been to push an extreme free trade agenda, which would lessen the chances of a local accumulation node forming in Asia while leaving the USA with its own semi-periphery in the Americas. An 'Action Agenda' worked out by business interests even leapt ahead of its original timetable (the year 2000) for the 'liberalisation' of regional trade.

Smaller actors are left to maneouvre as best they can within these parameters. Within ASEAN there was considerable fear of being swamped by an agenda fundamentally determined by the North, and divisions arose over whether this was an inevitable change which ASEAN had to adapt to, or something which should be resisted. Malaysia, in particular, took the latter stance, consistently attempting to promote an Asian identity, in the shape of an East Asian Economic Caucus (EAEC). And, predictably, the USA has sought to undermine this. But the subtlety of the Malaysian position is to push Japan to play a leading role, with the incentive of serving as an Asian 'voice' within G7, the aim being to strengthen Asian identity in the region, and also, to some extent, to subject Japanese power to a collective vision of policy. With the aim of outflanking Japan, US policy has become more favourable to the EAEC idea. Its purpose is to 'contain' Japan locally, while using APEC's strong free-trade agenda to undermine the possibility of a regional development which could marginalise America. Japan, for its part, rejects the poisoned chalice of an enhanced Asian role because, as Noritsugu Tamaki has observed, it enjoys effective informal power in Asia through the hierarchical relationships developed by its companies. The formal recognition of its status in EAEC would add nothing, and would provide an excuse for cutting it out of markets in the Americas.[40]

The crucial point here is that, underlying all this political manoeuvring, there are objective developments within the IPE. It is clear that the new management systems are already generating control systems with features not seen in earlier stages of imperialism. The global accumulation system itself creates certain local nodes which require local integrated production systems. This economic-management imperative may push in a different direction to the agendas espoused by Northern states for politico-military reasons. For example, part of the spoiling operation for preventing autonomy in the South involves promoting a 'strong' free trade agenda; but, as I shall explain, this does not coincide exactly with the regional demands made on the new management systems by the South's élites. We should first understand the historical background. The South-centred view of regionalism has long argued for the key importance of complementarities – that is, the *managed* division of labour by which an industry is 'given' to a particular country, which is then permitted to supply products from this industry to the whole regional market.[41] ASEAN attempted this in the 1970s in the context of stagnation in the North and the Nixon doctrine. In this sense, it can be viewed as a kind of internationalised import substitution, and was not particularly successful.[42] But the new phase in capitalist organisation has probably changed all this. The current form may be a new, extended form of complementarities. ASEAN as an institution has signed a deal with the big Japanese motor corporations, whereby Toyota and Mitsubishi allow an affiliate producing a particular component to supply the whole regional market in products which ASEAN agrees to consider of local origin: diesel engines in Thailand, petrol engines in Indonesia, steering gears in Malaysia, transmissions in the Philippines.[43]

However, even if consumption becomes proportionally more geared to local élites than to export to the North, this does not necessarily mean effective autonomy.

But the new IPE is certainly not uniformly manipulable in this way, nor is the Pacific 'rim' idea merely a tool of the US for defusing local accumulation dynamics or Japanese power. The old regionalism has given way, at a 'micro' level, to the emergence of both large and small 'natural economic territories'.[44] And even the larger-scale Asia–Pacific dimension itself is not only a tool of US policy, it has a certain objective basis. East Asian entrepreneurs have been setting up turn-of-the-century-type sweatshops in the USA itself, using labour from Mexico, Central America, the Caribbean and Asia, while there is also significant East Asian investment in the Caribbean basin area (which super-ficially seems a US local periphery), for example in electronic assembly. In describing this, Gereffi correctly says that a 1990s development theory 'will have to be flexible enough to incorporate increased specialisation at the product and geographical levels, along with new forms of integration that link the core, semi-peripheral, and peripheral nations of the Pacific Rim in novel ways'.[45]

The management of all this is a very difficult challenge for the North. Industry and finance capital have developed important new organising cap-acities, but the goalposts are always moving: the more these capacities advance, the more they weaken capitalism's most effective organ of economic organ-isation and repression, the state, which, in turn, means that the management tasks become more difficult! This is true for the new regionalism at every level: its development has been so startling precisely because the new current of economic interdependence and anti-statism has weakened the old national economies and therefore suddenly removed the old resistance to regionalism. But the national economies are still necessary to fund the state which maintains social order. Perhaps repression might become less necessary if regionalism were somehow to diffuse benefits more widely. Theoretically this could happen, if regionalism were to provide the basis for a 'post-export promotion' model of development based on enlarged local consumption. It could even happen that those promoting a wider regionalism and local communities become allies in promoting development at the expense of the state, now in terminal decline as a focus for identities.

At the moment, however, the new third-world regionalism is very much an élite agenda. To a large extent, these economies have emerged in the aftermath of the NIC euphoria and the Nixon Doctrine with powerful pockets of development, grafted on top of highly distorted economies, often including archaic landholding systems. In these circumstances, regionalism appears as an alternative path to growth, at least in generating a wider *élite* market. But in the absence of wider distribution, there are obvious limits to how far this can go. If anything, the new regionalism is even more remote than the old nationalism. Mexico shows this in extreme form, and in many cases grassroots forces think in terms of a dialectic, not between the national economy and economic globalisation, but between the local community and a different vision of the global, one focused on the ecosystem and networking between grassroots groups. From this angle, the 'national' may re-emerge as the logical linking unit, but not in the conventional, homogenising definition of nation.

At the élite level, the new regionalism to some extent pushes in the direction of at least a limited creation of the missing South–South dimension in the IPE, which could be sufficient to block the central accumulation process and thereby provide a new context for grassroots struggles to develop. In the longer term, given the contradictions within the new regionalism, this could create a basis on which popular forces could build in pushing for a new autonomous economic focus. Theoretically, the shift to a South–South agenda, away from Northern markets, could be accompanied by a demand for consumption to be broadened, since poverty would once again become a constraint on growth. Whatever the future holds, these issues are of serious concern to popular movements; if Southern élite attempts to hurt central capital are successful, popular movements will be able to take advantage of the weak points in the accumulation of central capital, or, if the élites fail, they can put forward democratic demands for an alternative.

## Notes

1. An example of such an attempt would be Douthwaite 1996.

2. Ricardo 1951, p. 135.

3. See Cable 1994; a lot of this benefit would reflect the supposed advantages of cheaper agricultural goods.

4. Tussie 1987, p. 101.

5. Raghavan 1990, p. 87.

6. Shiva 1993.

7. See *Financial Times*, 24 March 1994, for a description of these debates.

8. See *Third World Resurgence*, No. 41.

9. Hoekman and Kostecki 1995, p. 37.

10. Sen 1984, p. 158.

11. Cf. Hobson 1938.

12. Article by Takahashi Kamekichi (November 1942), in Lebra 1975, p. 49.

13. Dutt 1984.

14. This model draws attention to the fact that a favourable outcome may be missed by the parties: each would tend to opt for a choice which guards against the least favourable choice of the other, and, guessing that the other will follow the same logic, can predict that the choice will indeed be this one. If one party drops its defences, either in trade or military conflicts, the result could be disastrous if the other party were to adopt nationalistic or militaristic behaviour. Hence it is the best option to do this oneself, and then a balance will be preserved, but at a cost of missing the more favourable, collaborative scenario.

15. Cf. Rittberger 1993.

16. Marcussen and Torp 1982, p. 52.

17. Gilpin 1987, p. 384.

18. *Guardian*, 11 November 1989.

19. Cf. Lamb 1981.

20. Cf. Paus 1988.

21. *Le Monde*, 14 August 1992.

22. Dávila-Villers 1992.

23. Full members are the four countries mentioned; Bolivia and Chile are associate members.

24. *Financial Times*, 4 February 1997.

25. Intra-Mercosur integration was credited not only economically, with helping Argentina out of an economic crisis, but also politically, with blocking a military solution in Paraguay.

26. It is interesting that when a series of meetings was set up in 1989 to try and reactivate the Andean Pact, the US countered with President Bush's 'Enterprise America' plan in June 1990. The US was also the only country in the world to vote against Brazil's motion establishing a South Atlantic Zone of Peace and Co-operation in the UN General Assembly in 1986.

27. Cf. Choy 1981.

28. Cf. Vertzberger 1985, p. 70.

29. Chaturvedi 1991, Chapter 8.

30. Cf. Foot 1994.

31. Cf. Park Se-hark 1993.

32. Walsh 1993.

33. Drysdale and Garnaut 1993. These authors are representative of this line of argumentation.

34. PECC has since expanded to include not only the United States, Canada, the ASEAN countries, Australasia, etc., but also Russia, China and the Latin American countries that border the Pacific.

35. Crone 1993.

36. Nguyen 1993.

37. The American members are the USA, Canada, Mexico and Chile.

38. Cf. Peng Dajin 1995.

39. Cf., for example, Hellmann 1996.

40. Tamaki n.d.

41. For a theoretical demonstration of this, see Amin 1988, pp. 315ff.

42. Cf. Ariff 1977.

43. Hill and Lee Yong Joo 1994.

44. This term often refers to the 'growth triangle', including Singapore and parts of Indonesia and Malaysia, and grouping Guangdon and Fujian provinces in China together with Hong Kong and Taiwan.

45. Gereffi 1993, pp. 65, 66.

# 14

# Future Challenge: Grassroots Movements and the Prospects for a New Social Order

## Dimensions of Change in the Period Now Beginning

Having considered the processes of change which have produced the contemporary system, I will conclude this study by considering the forces for change in the future.

I will be looking at two different kinds of change: the change between one period of capitalist development (long cycles) to another, and hypothetical change beyond capitalism into a different social system. What is needed is a framework for analysing the transforming power of human initiative within the possibilities created by capitalist development.

It is evident that at the moment two very different processes of change are occurring on a world scale. First, this particular phase in capitalist development is entering a structural crisis. This could in principle be resolved by a major systemic shake-up, involving (for example) new economic doctrines and new forms of international relations. Second, the world is also fast approaching a crisis which will not be resolved by such restructuring: non-renewable natural and human resources are being exhausted and no form of capitalism can change this. These two kinds of change are often intermingled. Let us take the Asian crisis: on the one hand, the current accumulation system – the NIC models, the reproduction of parasitic finance capital, and so on – is in disarray, to which a solution might be found (even though it is not immediately obvious how) by a different accumulation regime; and, on the other hand, profound problems of ecological devastation and human resource depletion are emerging in the midst of this crisis, and from this angle we are witnessing a failure of capitalism as a whole, not just of one of its phases.

In principle we can say that there are two ways in which renewal could occur. One, which comes out of capitalism itself, is the system's own capacity for adaptation. This route would lead to a renewal of the basis for exploitation, but would not address the fundamental issues of renewing human and natural resources. The other way forward would be towards a totally different course of development. We need to understand what form this could take, and where it could emerge from.

I believe that recent capitalist development has brought to the fore a range of grassroots forces: the so-called 'new social movements', different forms of organised activity in the parallel economy, women's movements, co-operatives, a new trade-unionism of homeworkers and others, campaigns over ecological issues, movements by indigenous peoples. In the search for exploitative renewal, capitalism must adjust to these forces and find some way of co-opting them. But by the very process of resisting such co-option, these forces are beginning to forge an alternative. First, we have to consider capitalism's agendas of co-option, because the struggle against these will be one of the most important areas of activity of the new movements in the coming period.

## Capitalism's Changed Attitude to the Unofficial Economy – from Denial to Exploitation

The rise to prominence of the informal economy and new social movements is a product of two factors: firstly, objective forces of capitalist development (independent of any attempt to encompass these within the subjective strategies of the various agencies of capitalism such as TNCs or the World Bank); and secondly the attack on the organised political left. The weakening of the organised left has caused working people's struggles (which cannot simply disappear) to appear in a different form.

I will first establish a historical framework. To recapitulate the earlier argument: ever since stratified societies came into being, there has always been some 'unofficial' grassroots sphere. From today's standpoint (although the distinction would not have been meaningful then) we could say that the grassroots fulfilled two functions, one economic and the other political. Economically, the grassroots took charge of reproducing its own labour, managed important areas of the economy and conducted the knowledge-gathering and experimentation necessary for production. The political aspect was a tendency towards rebelliousness, which was not welcomed by rulers but which was nevertheless tolerated because it was functional in purging the ruling strata of parasitic and degenerate members and therefore of helping society to continue flourishing.

Capitalism has abolished the balance between official society and the grassroots, but without altogether removing this dualism. One way in which this dualism has survived is through tradition. Dependency theory noticed that capitalism needed to maintain and reproduce the exploitative, élite parts of tradition, but there were many grassroots elements which also survived: the household, rural socio-economic structures, social support mechanisms and so on. These vestiges of tradition are strongest in the South because there capitalism has tended to be incomplete, whereas in the centre thoroughgoing capitalist markets have destroyed most of what came before. These relics can be useful to capitalism because they can provide an additional concealed support for the monetary economy which the latter neither recognises nor rewards. But these vestiges can also take a form which is not welcomed by capitalism: namely co-operatives, local economies and grassroots innovation. In an ideal capitalist world, only the aspects conducive to exploitation would be preserved, but in real terms the two are so closely intertwined that it is impossible to dissociate them. So the process of exploitative dualism has always contained the seeds of an anti-exploitative struggle. If the conditions are right – and they may be becoming right today – these seeds could germinate.

Another way in which elements of the informal economy are sustained has nothing to do with tradition. It consists of the range of coping mechanisms, devised by the workers in this sector, to circumvent the norms and legality of official society. This is useful for capital accumulation because labour conditions in this sector are so precarious that workers are responsible for most of their own production costs, and in general their activity in the informal sector provides under-remunerated inputs into the waged economy. But once more, there is a facet to this process which could be dangerous for capitalism, for it often means that workers control their own productive activity in a co-operative way, and create local, self-sufficient economic systems. They gain experience which would be highly valuable in the construction of an alternative social system.

What is important in this surviving dualism is that it shows how capitalist society carries its opposite within itself, as humans take action to provide for the developmental needs that capitalism fails to address. It is capitalism's negation of the natural human forms of social organisation that leads to the sublation (preservation in the act of destruction) of these tendencies. In this sense, there is a kind of 'natural communism' in society, which is simply the ability of working people to run things collectively and to rebel. Communism could potentially be a summation of all this, if it could promote everything which is potentially anti-capitalist within the mixed-up reality which is the informal economy. It has not often realised this potential in practice, Soviet-style communism being, for historical reasons, strongly linked with top-downism and central planning. But it remains a possibility.

In general, capitalism has coped with the parallel economy by denying its existence, and with international communism by demonising it (and refusing to admit that it came about through acts of real rebellion by the masses and through their ability to organise themselves).

This combination worked during the period of the gestation and development of imperialism. A crucial economic role was played by the state: it monopolised the official economic and social world and quietly consigned the parallel grassroots sphere to an unacknowledged limbo. The capitalist state, which was strongly normative and bureaucratic, developed new forms of social control, while international communism, in response to the threats it faced, also became very statist. It took on the view that power could only be met with power and that it had to mobilise an industrial army. This meant that it took away from the masses responsibility for development, and in practice repressed many of the innovatory and unpredictable aspects of spontaneous mass movements. Official society became very strong, which left the grassroots with little possibility of political and organisational innovation.

In the most recent period all this has changed. Capital accumulation has taken place at the expense of the state, which weakened its economic basis. Official structures have likewise been undermined in communism, so capitalism has now reversed its strategy, coping with the surviving left movement by denying its existence, and with the spontaneous grassroots movement through a kind of recognition, which aims at co-option.

At the end of the 1970s the capitalist system restructured itself in an audacious way, which in some respects was very successful. The new management systems opened up fresh opportunities for exploiting the unacknowledged, partially unremunerated parallel economy. But this change has also created dangers. If capitalism fails to mould the grassroots movements in a sense favourable to itself, it will have unleashed something which could destroy it, because their tendency towards rebellion could come to the fore. It is therefore crucial to understand the nature of the control mechanisms developed by capitalism, and the conflicts within them.

The grassroots is vulnerable to control because it lacks both a strategic leadership (communism) which could unite it around an anti-capitalist agenda, and a state which could shield it. Without these, it is apparently 'safe' to allow it to develop.

In some sense, society is left directly confronting global capitalism. The present world order is paradoxical. On the one hand it extends the global market, and turns more goods than ever before into commodities. It attacks all particularities, spreading a uniform consumer culture into new types of goods and so-called services, attacking all vestiges of self-sufficiency at a national level, promoting the homogenisation of products, eroding local characteristics, and emphasising specialisation and trade as opposed to self-sufficiency. But on the other hand there is a massive informal economy, where people resort to unofficial activities and schemes for self-sufficiency in order to make up for the inadequacies and failures of the mainstream economy. I am concentrating on economic trends since this is what the study is mainly about, but clearly the economic aspect is part of a wider trend, including all forms of empowerment: cultural groups, women's struggles against violence, and so on.

There is, however, a certain logic behind this paradox. First of all, we need to understand why the two trends have developed simultaneously. As Rosa Luxemburg explained, accumulation could not continue if monetary relations took over everything. Since monetary relations are now spreading unchecked, the simultaneous strengthening of the unofficial sphere provides a counterbalancing mechanism.

Secondly, there is a new mechanism of accumulation, namely the new management systems, which make it possible for the global economy to exploit the grassroots directly, without the intermediary of the state. Despite the apparent neatness of this solution, there are dangers. First, global society is remote, without any apparent concern for the people or any plausible vision that might lead people to believe that it might provide for them in the future. Second, it is becoming clear that the crisis which produced the new survival strategies is a crisis not of the state alone, as it first appears, but of capitalism itself.

In earlier years, it had appeared that capitalism, personified in the state, might be able to provide for the excluded. In the South this was a fiction (because the apparently national accumulation dynamic really fed the accumulation of international capital), but the myth was nevertheless important as it helped to unify society. Since the collapse of this vision, grassroots organisations have proliferated, particularly in Africa, in response to the state's 'abandonment of social welfare responsibility'.[1] Significantly, since the crisis is the revenge of the natural world as well, it was sometimes natural disasters which exposed the failings of official society. A serious earthquake in Mexico in 1985 led the way to the formation of many self-help organisations: rank and file trade unions, building co-operatives and so on.

If this process represented only the failure of the state, neo-liberalism might welcome it. But in a deeper sense, it is becoming clear that capitalism itself is being called into question, not least because there is no convincing focus for the official economy other than the national economy. Local economies are no substitute, because, to adapt Chayanov, they handle labour and resources in a fundamentally different way from capitalism.

The undermining of official economies in the South began with the crisis of the last long cycle in the 1970s and was not resolved by the subsequent restructuring; on the contrary, the restructuring created forces, notably Structural Adjustment Programmes, which undermined the state still further. The grassroots movement was therefore thrust by default into a key position. It is precisely because this development is potentially anti-capitalist that the system has to recognise it, take a stand on it, and seek to co-opt it.

The grassroots movement has developed two strategies: retreat and adaptation. Retreat can lead to further exploitation, with greater inputs of unremunerated labour, but it also demonstrates that self-sufficient economic systems are possible. Adaptation can obviously lead to further exploitation, but is also dangerous for the North in that the system has to admit for the first time that ordinary people can innovate without being told what to do.

RETREAT  As a result of the world accumulation crisis of the 1970s, cracks appeared within the textbook Southern development models, and popular strategies emerged to hold society together. Studies of Ghana in the 1970s showed that people switched from export crops to subsistence foodstuffs, that hunting was revived, that traditional craftspeople like potters, blacksmiths and tinkers re-appeared, and that people moved back to the villages.[2] To describe this, Chazan coined the interesting phrase, 'creative self-encapsulation'. Although this phenomenon was a feature of the crisis of the old long cycle, it carried on into the new one, simply because Structural Adjustment Programmes, imposed during this new phase, intensified the attack on the state; they deliberately carried on with the destructive process which had been originally caused by the objective forces of the crisis. The ability of the state to 'provide' went into reverse. Over the past decade or so, the informal sector in Africa has almost certainly become larger than the formal economy. In Uganda, for example, whereas in 1972 60 per cent of wages were enough to buy a family's food, in 1984 450 per cent would have been required.[3] In 1980s Tanzania, family wages amounted to 2,000 shillings per month, but outgoings were 5,000 shillings.[4] In both cases, the difference must have been covered by informal activities.

This situation almost certainly means that exploitation by international capitalism has increased because the hidden inputs into the reproduction of labour have grown, but there is a problem for capitalism, which is that the new set-up threatens the hierarchical structures. The parallel/unofficial economy has always been the preserve of the most marginalised, almost by definition, but this is the case only as long as the official economy is strong enough to define the rest as inferior. The change in the role of women highlights this. In an earlier period when the hierarchies were intact, it was possible to observe that 'the fact that women, supported by their men, mobilise in what is considered a natural extension of the domestic arena imposes limitations on such action'.[5] But the subordination implied in this relationship has now turned into its opposite. This is because in the past women were marginalised in relation to an official (waged, male) economy, but now this formal economy has itself become increasingly marginal. It can be hypothesised that when the marginal economy becomes the real economy, the basis of patriarchy is eroded. It is possible to study the recent rise of the informal economy in a gender-neutral way,[6] but to do so precisely misses the main point, which is the important role of women within the new social movements.[7] It is true that in the past a great deal has always happened along informal lines which has bypassed official definitions of the economy – for example, women's trading activities, which often ignore formal state boundaries – and in this sense, the 'new movements' are not really new. What has changed is that the decline of the official economy has brought about a qualitative redistribution of influence.

ADAPTATION Besides withdrawal, there is an important element of what can be called 'adaptation' in the grassroots' strategies, that is, adapting to survive within the new conditions of capitalist economy. At the most obvious level this should not only be acceptable to, but even welcomed by, the system. After a period in which they were derided in the name of modernisation, peasantry and small producers have partially come back into favour. In agriculture, there has been some recognition that development strategies based on peasant farming are potentially viable.[8] It is also being recognised that there is an important sphere in the industrial urban economy where popular small actors are at the cutting edge of new production ideas. G.S. Shieh, in a study of Taiwan, employs a useful phrase, 'grassroots R&D',[9] and the concept of 'clusters' helps to explain the innovatory skill of some small producers. It describes how, in countries like India and Brazil, small producers have come together, or 'clustered', in particular areas for the manufacture of particular products. The producers interact through mutual trust, which enables risks to be spread, and endogenous technical innovation is encouraged. The term 'collective efficiency' has been used to describe this phenomenon.[10] In India, a small city in the Punjab has emerged since the 1970s as the main supplier of knitwear and textile machinery for the whole country, while in Brazil two regions have successfully specialised in footwear. Studies of woodworkers in East Africa show that they deliberately keep the scale of production small, not because of the 'primitive' or elementary level of the organisation of their production, but because this is a rational response to an international context where external demand is so unpredictable that it is a great advantage to remain flexible.[11] This is an interesting example of successful adaptation to the cyclical facet of capitalist development.

Clearly capitalism can co-opt these initiatives within the scheme of the new management systems which have themselves been shaped by adaptation strategies adopted both by workers and by those seeking to appropriate the fruits of their labour. It is interesting to note that in both Brazil's Sinos Valley and in Agra, India, there has been a degree of accommodation with capitalist interests: the more skilled tasks were given to specialised firms, whereas 'usually the most labour intensive functions were carried out by home-based women and child workers in both clusters'.[12]

None the less, it is important to realise that, although these initiatives can be used by the dominant order, they also show that the grassroots possess an innovatory skill which in different circumstances could provide resources for another kind of development. People are simply giving vent to a long-stifled ability to organise themselves, and returning to an old historical tradition of 'collective efficiency' and 'grassroots R&D'. Under a different set of conditions, this creativity – which is at present expressed in the art of survival under capitalism – might be channelled into the task of building an alternative. These are the kind of issues which the political left has always discussed in the past, and will continue to discuss in the future.

All this makes it clear that international capital does not have the luxury of deciding whether or not it wants to co-opt these trends into its own agendas; it has to do so, or run the risk of having them used against it. It will not be enough to exploit grassroots initiatives in a piecemeal way, for what is clearly required is a strategic, conceptual framework which locates the exploitation within a coherent system. Establishment agendas must take account of the realities of popular empowerment, and seek to channel this into acceptable forms. Actually, capitalism is feeling its way towards a political economy which is partly a response to the current crisis and partly an answer to the exploitative problems of the twenty-first century. Radical forces within the grassroots movements will develop their strength, not only in protecting people's livelihoods, but in combating this agenda. Before we consider the positive content of a non-exploitative political economy of renewal, we must consider the agendas which it will define itself against.

## The Role of Empowerment in the New Capitalist Political Economy

Capitalism cannot be fully successful unless it can build the grassroots into a systemic, self-reproducing system of capital accumulation, within which actors will spontaneously find their own niches.

An important element of a new political economy of such a kind would be some acceptable definition of empowerment. The idea of empowerment was the result of an evolution in development thinking: in the early post-war period, growth and GNP were all that mattered; then came a second stage where development was assessed in terms of its impact on people, but they were still seen as passive receivers of services; and finally there was a third phase where developing the creative potential of mankind – not just in-oculating it and running literacy programmes for it – was seen, not just as a right in itself, but also as a means for realising other development goals. The key concept in this third phase is empowerment. The long-term implications of this shift would be a new form of economics which would at last abandon the *laissez-faire* ideas characteristic of the 1980s long cycle. The award of the 1998 Nobel Prize to Amartya Sen suggests that the capitalist establishment might eventually develop in this direction. As Sen says, to focus on 'capability' suggests the possibility of fulfilling potential, which in turn leads to the possibility of people choosing between different possible futures.[13] This is twenty-first century economics. Much of the intention behind it is progressive, but what is important here is to see what use the system is going to make of it.

To offer people a range of choices beyond consumerism appears to be humanising economics, but we have to ask what this represents in concrete terms. The way the establishment responds to empowerment reflects two concerns: one is to see that people have enough so that their ability to supply labour is not constrained by poverty; and the other is to ensure that their income does not rise above this level.

Exploitation simply means making people live at a subsistence level, while seeing that they produce a surplus of value over and above this subsistence, which can be taken over by somebody else. In order for people to carry on generating this surplus (which is necessary if accumulation is to become a self-reinforcing process of capital-expansion), the subsistence income they are given needs to be enough for them to have a home life, bring up children, and so on. If this is not guaranteed, accumulation will suffer.

In nineteenth-century England, there was considerable interest in defining this minimum, and eventually the concept of absolute poverty as something that should not be permitted was created. In effect, the same has now happened at an international level, particularly since the end of the 1980s, when the issue of poverty was taken up in a big way by the World Bank. In this context, empowerment seems to be a step forward, because it is not simply giving people the tools with which to combat their absolute poverty, but also helping them to liberate their human capability. But there is a hidden agenda in that the idea of absolute poverty blocks the development of an alternative, and far more radical concept, namely the idea of relative poverty. This concept would be dynamite at a global level, because it would challenge the difference in living standards between the North and the South. In a certain way, the old economics typified by Rostow was actually more progressive than the new one, because it put forward the goal – however wrong its strategy for reaching this goal – of industrialising the South in a full sense, and thereby removing the North–South divide.

For this reason, the past decade's discourse on poverty has to a large extent been conservative in that it has turned the clock back to the Victorian conception of absolute poverty, but there is one way in which the discussion has moved on: it is no longer a question of being too poor to be exploited, but of being too poor for self-exploitation. Reflecting this calculation, the UN Development Programme employs the telling term, 'Capability Poverty Measure',[14] which measures the extent to which poverty has eroded a person's capacity to lead a proper life. The new twenty-first century economics may be different from the current one in abandoning *laissez-faire*, but it will probably remain a supply-side economics in the sense that it will not envisage any shift to rising demand in the South. In these circumstances, empowerment will be an excuse for reconciling people to their loss of consumption. The insistence that poverty is a bad thing seems a welcome departure from the Eurocentrism of Rostow-style blueprints, but the hidden agenda is to use empowerment as a smokescreen for abandoning the notion of some nationally focused accumulation which would eventually lead to mass consumption. It is true that the vision of Southern national-capitalist development was largely phoney, but the question is whether, in withdrawing the Rostowite promise, any convincing alternative path is proposed. People should at least have a free choice whether to be commodity fetishists or not, and, unless the North curtails its own consumption it will sound hollow for it to tell the South that the spiritual satisfaction of fulfilling one's human potential is far greater than the pleasure of indulging one's consumer urges.

While discouraging consumption in the South, the new economics will expect the region to play a key role in the supply side by providing firstly export commodities and secondly labour.

Keeping income to the 'capability poverty' level will, in effect, mean that exports to the North are subsidised, which will bring down the cost of subsistence in the North as well. It will also supply cheap labour to the new management systems. The new economics will be post-Cold War in the sense that it is only now there is no longer a vision of an alternative social system in which capitalists are unnecessary that it is safe to lift the veil on popular creativity. It will leave people servicing what appears to be a market but is in reality an accumulation system. The people are empowered with new choices, but in reality these are limited to seeking niches within the global accumulation system which will not only absorb the surplus value they generate but has also saved itself the organisational effort of finding niches for them. In fact, when empowerment calls for people to improve their understanding of social and economic processes, and their competence to analyse problems, to exercise control over their lives and to interact in a social context on a basis of dignity and respect,[15] it sounds exactly like the jargon of the new management systems.

But management also has to face problems at a social level. One of these is to take on the tasks of organising society which the state can no longer carry out. Global society cannot do this directly but it can give a helping hand.

This is where the idea of 'non-governmental organisations' (NGO) comes in. Here again, this began as a solution to the crisis of the 1970s, but in a deeper sense it is now moving into a whole new area which it began to explore only in the 1980s long cycle. While not challenging neo-liberalism head-on, the new, NGO-based development strategies reflect some retreat from the dogmas of the pure *laissez-faire* world of isolated individual economic actors. NGOs work within the concept of 'regimes', which recognises an element of social reality which capitalism had been unwilling to recognise before, namely that in the real world people and groups organise without being told what to do: the term 'commons regimes' is sometimes used to describe the fact that in traditional society people always held some property in common, and spontaneously regulated this. It is a rebuttal of the Hobbesian notion that everything would fall apart in the absence of a sovereign which could force people to observe social order.

Up to now, these possibilities have been limited by the constraints of the 1980s long cycle, which have made it impossible to destroy the myth of the free market. Neo-liberalism is a very deficient philosophy for running society; it seems to create identities through consumerism and openings for entrepreneurship, but if these collapse (because people cannot afford the goods, or go bankrupt when they set up businesses) there is not much left. A new, acceptable definition of community might work far more effectively as a kind of social cement. At the moment, we are witnessing experiments in this direction, for example the ideology of New Labour in Britain. These experiments are certainly a response to the cracks appearing in the current long cycle as it begins to enter into its declining phase, but they might also be exploring the vocabulary of a social philosophy appropriate to an eventual new long cycle. These developments suggest that ultimately the solution for the next long cycle will be to overthrow *laissez-faire* altogether.

But, for the moment, the new agendas have to operate within the constraints of *laissez-faire*, which can be done only through difficult ideological contortions. Right-wing libertarianism provides one answer: Friedrich von Hayek spoke of 'spontaneous order', and attempts have been made to use this concept within the contemporary discourse on regimes, fusing it with elements of anarchism into a general theory of how society organises itself in the absence of authority.[16] But libertarianism is always a dangerous concept to play with. For this reason, a better solution might instead be some form of post-modernism, which, utilising the fragmenting aspect of local organisation, rejects the unifying discourse of structuralism in favour of pluralism, diversity and appropriateness to local conditions. Solidarity would be allowed to operate within, but not between, individual movements. The pluralism of civil society, with its different interest groups, would promote a fragmentation of society and inhibit the gathering-together of the forces of the poor, which in the past has been expressed in the solidarity mechanisms of the traditional left, while at the same time retaining the repressive aspects of truncated local cultures (in the name of pluralism or non-Eurocentrism) as a bulwark against the dangerous aspects of libertarianism. It would promote a vision of popular participation, freed from statist interference, which would be welcomed by part of the NGO 'community', more precisely, the Northern aid agencies, who seek a way of humanising the existing system without fundamentally challenging its premises. In such a universe, there would be regimes serving the dominant interests and others serving the poor. The term 'NGOs' is a confusing one because it brings together the organisations which facilitate exploitation and those formed by people who suffer from it. This confusion is precisely why it is useful to the system.

In its ideal form, the new political economy would therefore operate by constructing the right sort of labour, people would be directed into their appropriate niches by the operation of the system itself, and there would be no need for special politico-military bodies to order them around. The social cement would be provided by regimes (NGOs) which would ensure that basic needs were satisfied and would allow people to develop their 'capability'. This ideal model has a certain elegance, particularly in rationalising the close links between the World Bank and NGOs, with the free movement of staff between one and the other. The organisation created by the grassroots movements could constitute civil society, maintain some degree of social order and provide informal safety-nets. In this way, it would be possible to prevent social disintegration, civil wars, migration of refugees and other problems which might call for costly intervention by the North. It would certainly be a creative development in self-exploitation, if the oppressed themselves were to meet not only the economic costs of their own repro-duction (as in earlier systems), but the political costs of maintaining the system as well.

## Why the New Political Economy of Co-opted Empowerment Will Fail

Although this scenario seems neat, I believe it is almost certain to fail, because international capital is unlikely to be willing to sacrifice immediate profitability in order to fund it. There are two routes the funding could take, the direct and the indirect.

DIRECT   If NGOs were to be funded through a direct transfer of resources by the North, this would make them conform to the agenda set by the donors and might constitute a modern equivalent of the way in which the 'labour aristocracy' was channelled into acceptable directions by the bribe of better wages.

INDIRECT   The second route would be to find some way of persuading central capital to give up a portion of the value which would normally be siphoned out through the mechanisms of centre–periphery exploitation, so that local accumulation, on a strictly limited basis, could be permitted. The incorporation of ideas like 'micro-credit' into the World Bank's vocabulary shows how it is looking for 'safe' forms of limited accumulation which do not run the risk of developing into major projects at a societal level.

In practice, these solutions would almost certainly in the medium term cost the North nothing because the profits that would be generated by destroying the state would outweigh the initial outlay. Indeed, the new economics may very well lead to calls for increasing aid (in contrast to the period of hegemony of Reaganomics, which was fundamentally hostile to aid) or for writing off 'debt', even a tax on speculative capital (something which has been suggested).

But the fundamental question is this: is capitalism capable of implementing a strategic solution if, during the process of arriving at such a solution, it has to sacrifice immediate profits? The evidence so far suggests that the answer is no. And the structural crisis now beginning, which will in principle make such a solution more necessary, will also probably make it more difficult to implement such a solution, simply because profits will be harder to come by, which will increase pressure to maximise sources of exploitation that yield an immediate profit. While capitalism in some sense 'needs' an ultra-imperialist solution orchestrated not by companies but by international regimes like the World Bank, it is very unlikely to get this in practice.

But as well as this, there is also a deeper problem. Grassroots organisations have an inherent rebellious streak, which means that it is difficult to keep them within the narrow parameters of what central capital regards as safe. It is difficult to keep the identity of interest groups so separate that they do not express solidarity for each other. It is not easy to prevent micro-credit from strengthening local economies, which could eventually threaten the international division of labour. And so on.

All this suggests that the grand scenario of a regime-populated post-statist universe will come to nothing.

## The Alternative to Empowerment – a New Repressive Pact with the State

If it is true that the attempt to co-opt grassroots initiatives in a systemic sense is going to fail, there must be an alternative. It can only be repression, but this too must have a basis.

Time and again, when, in order to defuse protest, international capitalism has raised the issue of alleviating poverty at a mass level, the practical outcome has been repression. When local accumulation has been permitted (Kennedy's Alliance for Progress would be one example), it has been in the hands of the élites who have conducted the repression. By far the most plausible scenario is that it will follow the same path this time. It has the advantage of familiarity.

Repression can only be conducted either by the centre or by local élites. The first option is unacceptable as a general response (although the USA will obviously carry on invading countries where other solutions fail). So it seems that there is only one solution: the local state must be restored.

I believe this is likely to be an important feature of the coming period, as capitalism grapples with the falling-apart of the current long cycle. Statism would be far more comprehensible to capitalist decision-makers than the NGO–civil society scenario, because it offers the kind of advantage everyone can understand: keeping labour in order. The state in this new period would have two functions: to provide education, and the rest of the infrastructure necessary for effective self-exploitation, and to suppress potential rebellion within the grassroots organisation. It is not easy to supply what is required, because the economic basis of the state has been eroded. So we are looking towards a new form of statism.

Along with empowerment, there have already been signs, within the 1980s long cycle, of a new statism, and this is likely to form the basis of the new political economy.

In the most recent period, the World Bank has changed its discourse to admit the validity of some element of state intervention, but this does not mean that the argument has come full circle, with a return to earlier forms of statism. Rather it seems to me that it is an advance towards a new strategy for providing a local structure to facilitate global accumulation. The state is becoming a structure that is opposed to any meaningful definition of the interest of the nation, that represses resistance to the global economy; it can become interventionist again, but only on behalf of that economy. The critique of Ricardian economics made from the point of view of the real economy correctly criticised its unrealistic assumption that, as specialisation occurs, there is no cost in terms of conversion, for example retraining labour. Moreover, even if the domestic free market operated efficiently in permitting resources to find their way into the sectors demanded by the international market, this would not guarantee the supply side of labour. It is precisely on this basis that, for the World Bank, market integration requires 'strong policy action at the domestic level',[17] including investment in people. In effect, inconsistent plagiarism of aspects of Listianism is used to create a monstrous paradox, a form of Listianism that is opposed to the nation! While the old economics spoke of labour, the modern one speaks of 'human resources'. From capital's point of view, this is an improvement on earlier versions of capitalist macro-economics in that it points towards a more all-round exploitation of the human potential. 'Empowerment', it is now clear, has been doctored to leave an exploitative rump.

Chile is interesting as an example because it indicates the direction the new statism might take; empowerment has lost any humanistic content it originally had, leaving a framework for self-exploitation, where industries spontaneously seek their niches in the system of global capital accumulation and individual workers spontaneously seek employment within these industries. The main objective of the current phase of capitalism is to make the system self-managing, but there has to be a transitional period of brutal repression, euphemistically known as 'adjustment' during which the old form of labour organisation is smashed. However, what is interesting about the new theory is that the state does not lose its role in the more tranquil post-'adjustment' phase. Instead, it continues in a new form, so as to provide the necessary conditions for ensuring that labour of the right kind remains available. According to apologists of these models, the labour market then begins to follow the business (macroeconomic) cycle. Whereas during 'adjustment' it was skilled male workers who lost their jobs, in the more recent phase it has been the more marginal, flexible workforce of young people and women, which is just as one would expect during the down phase in a business cycle. But this, it seems, is not the full story. Using an index of 1980 = 100, wages in Chile fell from 112.4 in 1970 to 76.0 in 1990, but since then they have apparently stabilised at this low level, irrespective of the phase in the business cycle.[18] What this signifies in practice is that, with the state acting to provide a framework guaranteeing the provision of flexible, low-cost labour, the latter's price is not affected by the fluctuation of demand associated with the business cycle.

This paradoxical situation was already beginning to emerge during the Reagan–Thatcher years, when theorists began 'to argue simultaneously for a radical *laissez-faire* experiment and for greater intervention'.[19] In practice, this meant using a strong degree of statism to force resources, including human ones, into the mould required by capital accumulation. The difference is that once this is transferred to an international scene and imposed on the South, the accumulation which this statism serves, and the business cycle to which it provides a plentiful supply of labour at static cost, in the last analysis serve the needs of an external capitalism.

The role of the state has always been to protect property rights, which form the basis of the system by which those who control the wealth appropriate value. This is deceptively presented as a way of rewarding initiative. Fashionable economic theories emphasise the legal-institutional aspect of the state's role (in order to downplay the managerial role, which is more dangerous to discuss). Douglass North, who has been influential in World Bank thinking, proposed a model, premised upon neo-classical free-market economics, but where the state necessarily has a role in protecting rights. Development will not occur without 'individual capturability of the benefits to society from additions to the stocks of knowledge and technology', intellectual property rights being the main mechanism by which 'individuals' are rewarded for the 'benefits' they have brought to society.[20]

Here again the language of autonomous development is being manipulated in a deceptive way to justify a form of accumulation which is in substance international. The new statism protects not just – or perhaps not mainly – domestic rights, but international ones. While the North presents a closed-economy model, the World Bank has internationalised it in such a way that the cost–benefit analysis of the role of the state is conducted from the centre's point of view: under the euphemism of transaction costs, the Bank decides whether the benefits of having a local body to exercise social control and dragoon labour make up for the value foregone by central capital. The main aspect of the 'capturability' of intellectual property rights accrues not to local innovators but to the centre. It is perfectly clear – from a combination of US trade reprisals and the 'TRIPS' agenda of the Uruguay Round of GATT – that Southern states are forced to change their domestic legislation precisely in order to enforce this 'capturability' in the interest not of local but of global capital accumulation.

It is clear from the above analysis that capitalism, in its search for a system of social control, will be unable to place its main emphasis on the radical innovations in social engineering carried out by NGOs, but will have to opt instead for a solution which in practice leaves the grassroots confronting (rather than being absorbed by) the official society (both international and local) which protects global accumulation.

## The Probable Failure of the New Statism, and the Openings for a Mass-based Project

The need to resort to a redefinition of statism in order to maintain social control, is in itself a desperate rearguard measure, and, in the face of the mounting crisis in the NICs, it will probably fail. What the strategy lacks is the integrative power of the old nationalist strategies, with their plausible (if fallacious) argument that today's poverty was a by-product of the pattern of accumulation which would produce tomorrow's riches.

It is possible that the grassroots could put forward their own project to fill the void left by the demise of the old nationalism. At the time of writing, the prospects are good, since the current long cycle, although in a declining phase, still has a few years to run during which mainstream economics will have to continue to defend an increasingly threadbare neo-liberalism that is scarcely credible even to capitalism itself. During the structural crisis of the last long cycle, the old third-worldism had been able to take advantage of the disarray of global capitalism to occupy the high ground, but theirs was an élite agenda which was easily undermined. It could be different today.

An important element in favour of a grassroots-based alternative is that the two challenges highlighted at the beginning of this chapter – the need to respond both to the crisis of a particular phase of capitalism and to the limitations of capitalism in general – could be answered by the same set of principles. This has not been the case before. The left used to believe that the political and economic responses to the immediate stage should be fundamentally different from the policies needed in the longer term. The former would be characterised by violence and power, and by statism and centralisation, and it was only when this stage was over that society could be ruled by communal and local structures. This may have made sense in the 1930s and during the Cold War, but circumstances today are not quite the same. Now, the same key principles of sustainability and self-sufficiency may be effective in realising the twin objectives of immediate survival and long-term system-change.

Even so, there will be different stages in the process. During an intermediate period, the grassroots may still have to preserve the state as an inadequate but necessary shield behind which, to use List's phrase, a natural system of political economy can emerge. But there will be a crucial difference in that the old concept of centralism as a homogenising force will definitely end. Self-sufficient local economies driven by highly concrete and specific knowledge systems will be seen – and defended as – a rational component in human development. They have been criticised as insular, but this is not true – they can carry out cultural and economic interchange over vast distances, as traditional societies have always proved. Capitalism abolished these societies in the interests of a large, homogeneous economic space within which capital accumulation could unfold and, in doing so, destroyed an important tool of human development, namely a wide variety of socio-economic raw material upon which development strategies can draw. If true development is to be restarted, the richness of local economies must be restored.

In the rest of this chapter I will examine what is needed to regain a positive agenda for change. The main elements are: first, the forward-looking potential of tradition; second, the fusion between tradition and modernity; third, the possibility of new, co-operative institutional structures; fourth, the new definition of 'mixed' economy; and, fifth, the ability of the grassroots to influence global systemic developments. The way I have arranged these topics also reflects a progression from objective forces to conscious, campaigning agendas.

## The Contribution of Tradition to a New Definition of the National Project

Any more rational human society that is developed in the future will inevitably regain some characteristics which look 'like' pre-capitalist traditional society. Even where capitalism has been perfectly successful in abolishing all direct links with tradition, this will occur, through the negation of the negation. But this is not the only way in which it will happen. Since capitalism is not a pure system, it still coexists with parts of tradition. Some of these, such as the gender division, are harmful and limit human development at an individual level, but there are also creative elements, which are found above all in rural society in the South. Knowledge systems are an example. This suggests that it may be possible to use human resources quite differently from the exploitative way they are used in the new management systems. People are inventive. In contrast to conventional economics – which assumes that the 'problem' to be 'solved' is the allocation of a finite set of resources in the optimum way – it may be possible for society to use its human resources in such a way that they suddenly demonstrate such a wealth of creativity that the stock of resources turns out to be far greater than was assumed.

Because of its social destructiveness, capitalist development often reduced the resource base upon which future development could take place. Capitalism at all levels sought to control the people by undermining the autonomy of their knowledge systems.[21] In the periphery it often went even further, seeking to rid itself of the embarrassment of any kind of social system whatsoever, so that the land, raw materials and labour power could be 'shaken free' from the social systems which originally controlled them.[22] Later, in the post-colonial era, attempts were made to invent new rural economies, but they were not socially viable. The Green Revolution carried on the socially destructive process: in the name of modernisation, and with the argument that the rise in agricultural productivity meant that fewer people were needed in the countryside,[23] peasant farming systems were further weakened.

It has long been evident that land reform is crucial. But today it is possible to put forward an even stronger set of arguments in its favour. In the past, land reform used to be seen in terms of ownership, and the economic rationale for carrying it out used to be expressed somewhat negatively: land reform, it was said, would remove the obstacles to modernisation by abolishing the power of the conservative social strata that were opposed to it.[24] But this perspective fails to distinguish between those aspects of tradition which inhibit development and those which promote it. If we look at it from this point of view, land reform can be seen as something positive, which unleashes the human ingenuity enshrined in grassroots knowledge systems.

The case for sustainable agriculture is being made in all parts of the world today, which shows that the seeming increase in productivity arising from the mainstream 'scientific' agricultural system is not sustainable. In the South there is an added argument for not being dependent on official agricultural technology because it is a channel through which outsiders gain control, and siphon resources out of the country, to the disadvantage of poor farmers. In this way, the 'entitlements' of ordinary people, which could be used as an incentive to local food production by expanding demand, are undermined.

It is being recognised more and more by the public that ordinary people can possess scientific knowledge of enormous importance. Besides reflecting genuine admiration for grassroots initiatives, this shows that many specialists believe that mainstream agricultural development will come to a dead end if it does not take on board some of this traditional knowledge. Part of what is needed, people say, is a reassessment of ancient practices, for example the use of ridging systems in agriculture. In pre-colonial America these enabled marginal land to be cultivated very effectively,[25] while in Africa the area of contemporary Tanzania – conventionally considered to have been barren and stagnant prior to colonialism – possessed, in fact, a thriving system that, using a mixture of contour-following ridges laced with diagonal up-and-down ridges, permitted land on steep hills to be farmed.[26] But even more important than historical re-assessment is to look carefully at contemporary practices. All traditional systems have elements of sustainable agriculture that can be seen in the balance between livestock and the cultivation of crops that return nutrients to the soil, the use of mixed cropping instead of monoculture, and so on. One widespread practice is intercropping, where different crops do not follow each other sequentially, but are cultivated together, with different rooting systems reaching to different levels in the soil. This brings many advantages: one kind of plant can provide a micro-climate for another; pests are discouraged by the intermingling of different plants; the need for weeding is reduced by the use of quick-spreading crops like beans; insects which hunt pests are attracted by the cultivation of plants that they feed off, and so on.[27] As a result, intercropping systems are not vulnerable to large-scale devastation by pests or diseases, and the occurrence of these infestations at low endemic levels may in itself stimulate immune reactions. What is also important in these traditional intercropping systems is that they can be varied in response to microvariations in soil conditions. One researcher found 147 distinct intercropping patterns in three villages in Northern Nigeria.[28] It seems that, in a way, the traditional intercropping systems reproduce the conditions of the natural forest.[29] Even shifting cultivation, which modernisation presents as the epitome of primitiveness, is today increasingly seen as a flexible set of practices responding to the crucial problem of managing marginal lands, with the farmers sensitive to the minute differences between different types of soil.[30] Another crucially important issue is the management of time, which in this context means the natural cycle of time. This is particularly evident in the farming of semi-arid lands. The tree, *Acacia Senegal*, whose root systems penetrate to great depths in a symbiotic relationship with a bacteria which fixes nitrogen in the soil, is highly beneficial to marginal lands.[31] It also lies at the heart of an agro-sylvo-pastoral system in Sudan which involves a cycle of 20–30 years, with the cultivation of millet and sorghum followed by a fallow period, and then colonisation by *A. Senegal*, and finally gum arabic production.[32] 'Cyclical' here means something quite different from its meaning under capitalism where it reflects the realisation of accumulation.

The principles embodied in these traditional practices certainly answer a contemporary need. In this context, sustainability is far from being a middle-class luxury. Rather, it is a survival mechanism for the poorest people. New techniques are being constantly invented as part of the day-to-day struggle to exist in conditions of super-exploitation. A fishermen's co-operative society near Calcutta, India, which started in the 1930s, has developed recycling to such an extent that today it is fully sustainable with the production of everything it needs to feed fish and to fertilise the paddy.[33] It shows that people will recycle things when they need to do so to survive.

But, in the formulation of a grassroots blueprint for development, more is needed: we must understand how the traditional element can relate to the technology sanctioned by the official world, which clearly must be involved in the strategy. As we shall see, the interaction between the two worlds could be restructured in a way that would bring more benefits to the grassroots.

## The Prospects for an Independent Technology

What is required, it seems, is some kind of 'intermediate' solution, in which the traditional and 'modern' elements are integrated. Let us look at how this could operate in practice.

Although intermediate technology is an interesting idea, there are hidden dangers in the way it is conventionally presented. It was created largely because the official world, which wanted to control the traditional sector more effectively, had found that it could not promote modernisation without a common language in which to talk to those still immersed in tradition. For example, peasants were rejecting 'extension' contacts, which had been designed to educate them about modern agricultural practices, because the practices they were recommending lay completely outside their everyday experience.[34] Intermediate technology was initially designed to fill this gap, but it later acquired a more positive content in its own right: it became a solution for increasing employment, reducing alienation and humanising work processes.[35] But this carried with it a new danger: it was tacitly assumed that the South's technical development must always be held down to a level where it could be easily managed by the North. In this respect, the problem is similar to the one encountered with 'basic needs': Rostow had (falsely) promised developing countries that they would attain exactly the same levels as the industrial world, but then this promise was withdrawn as it became clear that, with their role in the accumulation process, they could never catch up. 'Appropriate' always implies second-rate.[36]

In response to these difficulties, some modernisers reject any definition of technology other than that officially described as advanced. From this premise, the deductions can either be pessimistic, namely that development is phoney because the South will never gain real autonomous control over this technology;[37] or on the contrary, naïvely optimistic: Arghiri Emmanuel, once a perceptive critic of the international economy, lost his credibility when he began to believe, without any real basis in fact, that the South would be able to acquire through the world market the advanced technology it needed.[38]

What is wrong in this sterile debate is the premise. It is perfectly true that the North will do everything to hang on to its technology monopoly, or the 'capturability' of its intellectual property rights, and for this reason the South cannot hope to acquire advanced technology in a complete form. But a different scenario is possible, where intermediate technology, instead of serving as an intermediary in subjugating the grassroots to the official world, does the very opposite. Although official science is geared to enriching the dominant interests, some technological information can evade Northern capital's control mechanisms; what the South needs is some kind of autonomous framework into which it can be integrated. Popular knowledge systems could provide this. In this set-up, 'intermediate' would no longer be a token of limitation but a stepping stone to independence. Indeed, it can be argued that grassroots strategies are far more effective in this way than those adopted by the NICs, simply because they are pragmatic, taking from western technology what they need.

In fact, some fusion between the NICs and popular culture is likely to happen anyway, either under the auspices of transnational capital (which may, for example, be able to appropriate the genetic resources painstakingly nurtured by popular knowledge systems) or in a way which is more advantageous to popular systems.

If the people decide to offer the fruits of their 'grassroots R&D', 'creative self-encapsulation' and 'collective efficiency' as a contribution to national liberation, they should negotiate their own terms for doing so. But before collaboration of this kind can work, it is necessary to have an alternative, progressive definition of 'mixed' technology. The term 'technology-blending' has entered into development literature;[39] it is a useful concept, but it needs to be properly defined. Such a definition should include the following elements:

TECHNOLOGY-BLENDING AS IT IS PRACTISED TODAY  Many of the crops used in contemporary inter-cropping systems are not traditional ones, but the result of some kind of 'technology-blending'. For instance, soya beans were originally introduced into Nigeria as an export cash-crop, but were converted into a consumption item for the domestic diet by women, who were carrying out pioneering work in mutual aid and the sharing of seed and technical know-how.[40] At the élite level as well, significant efforts are being made to integrate different areas of science and technique, Western or indigenous, to serve development aims. All these efforts should be supported[41]. They could lead to a redefinition of the national project, with different social strata agreeing on common goals.

A NON-EXPLOITATIVE VERSION OF THE NEW MANAGEMENT SYSTEMS  It may well make sense for a particular economy to have a mixture of labour-saving and labour-intensive technologies, so long as the former are not exploiting the latter. At the moment the value generated by grassroots R&D can easily be stolen by the global economy, but it might be possible to design an alternative economic model where this did not happen. As long as the value generated feeds into local communities, it can be perfectly acceptable to maintain labour-intensive production in some economic areas.

A CAPACITY TO OPEN UP NEW AVENUES OF LONG-TERM DEVELOP-MENT  It might be possible eventually to put an end to the separation between science and production. As today indigenous technology is regarded more favourably than in the past, the old assumption that it is inferior to mainstream science because, being practical, it is less conducive to generalisations, has been challenged. Instead, writers emphasise the ability of indigenous technology to take into account micro-variations, and its adaptability, as it is continuously tested and altered by ordinary people.[42] But this reappraisal is not enough by itself, because the problem is not only the hierarchy between the two, but the fact that they are separated. It can be argued that it is imperative to start changing this now, precisely because without this change the South's national cause cannot advance. Such a strategy would begin to put scientific development as a whole on a new footing.

An integrated project, which would be 'intermediate' in the sense of combining 'high' and 'low' elements, is therefore technically viable and desirable. But this does not mean that in practice it will be implemented, because this depends on the social balance of forces.

## The Social Basis for New Alliances

Traditional technical systems were inseparable from the reproduction of social relations. Children, for example, were socialised by being taken on long walks so that they could get to know the plants in the area and the use that was made of them; and this effected a 'transformation of space into a socially appropriated territory'.[43] The reproduction of social relations and the conservation of the land were in this sense inseparable, and the co-operative aspect of social relations was itself embedded in a certain vision of nature.[44] This implied that society held a different concept of education, one in which culture and technology were no longer separate.

It might be possible to return to a vision of this kind in the future, but at present, social relations in this pure form have been widely disrupted. This creates a problem, because it is impossible to isolate the grassroots technology, however progressive, from its social milieu. If the grassroots cannot generate the contemporary social forms for reconciling culture and technology, it is not much help that the mixed-technology model may, theoretically, work at a technical level. This means that, in one way or another, the 'social' element in grassroots structures has not only to contribute to a long-term solution but also create the means for getting there.

In a fundamental sense, the conditions of traditional society cannot be reproduced. The co-operative/local element in the new social movements fulfils a different role to the one it had in traditional society. As Appadurai says, in traditional society the reproduction of co-operative social relations was an end in itself, which was just as important as the material reproduction of the group through growing food, and so on, whereas today's co-operative relations are no longer seen as valuable in themselves, but merely as part of a strategy for survival.[45] But the implied value judgement – that the old forms were more authentic and thus superior – is questionable. In fact, traditions restricted the development of an important part of human potential, and this prevented the realisation of important human resources, for example through the way they determined women's identities in a manner external to them.[46] What is needed today is for relationships to be reinvented, not traditional ones restored. In this sense, the weakening of societal pressures is positive.

This is true, even when we are considering what may be thought of as the 'good' aspects of tradition. In the old social system, co-operative grassroots structures were strongly integrated into a system dominated by the élite. Both sides accepted their obligations to the other and the system functioned with serenity and self-confidence. But – and this was the bad side for the grassroots – they were integrated from a position of inferiority. Today the system has been destroyed, and the masses are condemned to surviving within a world that is basically hostile and alienating. There is an advantage, however, which is that there is nothing in the system today which can absorb them systemically. They have to seek a new relationship with official society, which for the first time could be one where they are no longer subordinate. Capitalism has never had a real balance between official and grassroots spheres. It has maintained the duality, but in an exploitative and unstable form, and there is little evidence that its attempt today to re-invent the relationship will work. This means that the grassroots may be able to have a far greater role, creating a new relationship which for the first time is favourable to them.

In the longer term, the grassroots may be able to remake society entirely, but first there must be some kind of transition. It seems probable that the grassroots will move gradually to impose themselves more and more during this transition.

There have been historical examples of relationships between a radically oriented official society and a mass movement, which have had acceptable results for both sides.[47] For example, nationalist governments have sought to introduce agricultural co-operatives, and peasants have taken a pragmatic attitude to these: 'If they experience them as exploitative or adversely affecting their private interests, they will reject them or act to undermine their operation', but in the contrary case they will support and participate.[48] There have obviously been significant negative aspects, with top-down models often inhibiting effective mass creativity at the grassroots level. In Ghana under Nkrumah, co-operativisation projects were very bureaucratic and failed to stimulate real agricultural development.[49] Even in a more unconventional model like Tanzania, what was supposed to be a rural class struggle was orchestrated in a top-down way.[50] In Algeria, the 'Agrarian Revolution' launched in 1971 took advantage of what were supposed to be co-operative structures to exercise control over the producers.[51] Indeed, there are many examples in the past of the state using the language of popular struggle to repress popular movements.[52] But there are also positive experiences. There are concrete cases where a would-be revolutionary state has acted as a facilitator for grassroots initiatives. A few environmental examples can illustrate this. In Burkina Faso, the radicalisation of state power, for all its imperfections, transformed a small country previously perceived as totally insignificant into an experience which excited worldwide attention; experiments with sustainable agriculture are only one example of what was achieved.[53] In Mozambique the government experimented in the countryside with multipurpose village forest zones, which combined agriculture, orchards, fuel wood and small animals,[54] while in the towns it supported a green belt which was the fruit of popular initiative, essentially undertaken by women's co-operatives.[55] In Zimbabwe, the Organisation of Rural Associations for Progress (ORAP), founded in 1981 and originally based on women's clubs, grew into a major co-operative movement,[56] propagating the use of traditional seeds and fertilisers and encouraging families to broaden their sources of food. If these mixed experiences were carefully assessed, it could open up the debate, freeing it of externally imposed definitions or false dichotomies about what constitutes revolution or radical social change.[57]

This shows that there have been positive experiences in which state power has been influenced from below so that it has adopted policies useful to the masses. It can also be helpful to look critically at the negative aspects.

## Grassroots Campaigns and the Notion of a New 'Mixed' Economics

Today, conditions may be improving for popular movements to push their agendas. Official society is certainly weaker morally than ever before. Élites have probably always enriched themselves from their role as intermediaries in exploitative systems, but in the past they could at least plausibly claim that they were being rewarded for their work in promoting the national interest. Today, this justification is wearing thin.

Recent developments have been calling into question not just the élites' justification for enriching themselves, but also the nature of the national project that has underpinned this justification. Fundamentally, as we have seen, the project was based on the homogenising nationalism characteristic of European latecomer experiences and was inherently centralist. In strongly authoritarian fashion, the latecomer models assumed that the enlightened modernising leadership knew what was best, and certainly knew better than local movements, which were steeped in tradition and could not see the complete picture. This meant that any resistance to grandiose flagship projects was by definition caused by ignorance.

These assumptions are being questioned today. The recent mobilisation, on a global scale, against hydroelectric dams is an example. Grassroots have historically held their own valid views about water conservancy,[58] and for this reason they have been less willing to accept centralised policy on dams. By extension, they have begun to challenge the centre's definition of the national interest as a whole.[59]

What needs to happen is some 'meeting of minds' where the grassroots and official society come together and gradually develop a more general social project. This project would need to contain the following elements:

VALIDATING THE GRASSROOTS ECONOMY One of the main weaknesses of modernisation was that it rejected any notion of a creative dualism between the official and informal economic spheres. In India, the Self-Employed Women's Association (SEWA) argued for the concept of the national economy to be changed, so that it would recognise and protect the informal sector. They managed to get the state to conduct a survey of the informal economy, headed by a SEWA leader, which raised some issues long neglected in mainstream economics: for example, it showed that modernisation had wrongly attacked both traditional non-monetary rights (such as usufruct), and small craft industry.[60] Implicitly, the reassertion of these would actually strengthen the nation, giving it a rootedness to counter the pull of the global economy. Gandhi had already proposed an economics where the traditional sector would have its own status, and had been ready to use women's labour as a mainstay of the anti-colonial movement for economic self-reliance. However, he became highly mistrustful when women began taking initiatives.[61] Today, real progress is being made because the issue is being raised by women's actual struggles. It is in this way that the relationship between the official and informal economic spheres will be genuinely redefined, for it is clear that change will occur only through practice, not through the formulation of new theoretical models.

LOCAL TRADING SYSTEMS   Modernisation claimed to be forward-looking in breaking the restrictions imposed by tradition and establishing a unified market within the national economy, but, in practice, the object of the market in capitalist development is to promote accumulation rather than efficiency *per se*. The problem in the South is that this accumulation is ruled by international agendas, so the market simply facilitates the siphoning of value out of the economy. So in fact, it is the defence of traditional practices which, from the point of view of the South, is forward-looking. African women's movements to defend traditional rights to trade are, in this context, progressive: in 1985, a 'women's war' in Nigeria, launched in response to state tax on market sales, culminated in demonstrations by tens of thousands of women which highlighted issues affecting the poor, including austerity, health and education.[62]

AN ECONOMICS BASED ON DEMAND   The new grassroots economics, which aims to fix value in the local community, needs to be more demand-based. The World Bank supports micro-credit initiatives from a supply-side perspective, because they 'empower' people to make their human resources available to the global economy. In contrast, the counter-agenda of the grassroots must be demand-oriented, seeing credit as a way of promoting local consumption which until now has been suppressed by exorbitant interest rates. A case study in Pakistan showed that women workers in the informal sector not only valued the greater autonomy and decision-making power they gained within the household by earning money, but acquired this new autonomy through consumption,[63] by taking decisions on how to spend the money. This is not a neo-classical definition of choice between different commodities, but rather a redistribution of power within the household, a change of social relations. Unlike in the new establishment economics where capability functions as a substitute for consumption, here the two are on the same side of the equation. It should be noted that this is not a reversion to a Keynesian perspective on demand, where everything is aggregated at a national, macro level, a level at which, in the South's case, demand cannot be protected, at least in conventional terms, against central accumulation.

RESOLVING CONFLICTS CAUSED BY HOMOGENISING NATIONALISM
At a political and cultural level, the state fails as an arbiter of conflicting interests because it suppresses plurality in the name of an abstract national interest – which is in practice the sectional interest of dominant groups. Grassroots groups can approach the situation from a completely different perspective, and fulfill urgently needed tasks of conflict resolution. SEWA's work shows that this is possible: at a time of riots in Ahmadebad,[64] it promoted dialogue between different groups,[65] carrying out a role which the state had been powerless to fulfil. Its ability to do this was clearly related to the different way it worked, as a women's organisation. Today conflict resolution is fashionable, from the point of view of donor-funding, because in a low-cost way, NGOs could render unnecessary invasions by troops from the North. But this also means that grassroots movements could take advantage of these circumstances to further their own agendas.

These examples show that there is a basis in practice for a new economics. It is possible to build a national liberation project based on grassroots economic strategies. The Palestinian movement is an example: according to Adel Samara, the development strategy for its grassroots movement, the Intifada, is 'generated' from below,[66] with its principles of 'popular protection of the economy' and 'inward withdrawal' being very much a strategic and conscious application of the 'creative self-encapsulation' to which I referred earlier. It is important to understand that its definition of withdrawal goes far beyond simply dropping out, in that it promotes the formulation of a positive new strategy of economic organisation.

## A Popular Agenda for the Global System

Although at one level the new grassroots economics develops through a dialogue between the local and the national, it also operates at quite another level, by immediately targeting the issue of the international systems. It takes up the question where the old NIEO left off, regenerating it from the grassroots in a radically new form. There are two important aspects:

RESTORING SOLIDARITY World capitalism in the 1980s had attempted to bury any sense of a common cause beneath the social Darwinism of NIC-style development, viewed as a zero-sum competition for scarce foreign investment. Today, local movements are beginning to recreate solidarity from the ashes of the old third-worldism. They learn from one another, and successes in one area are positively related to successes in another. This is in no way in contradiction with the struggle to influence national agendas.

Although plurality and local relevance lie at the heart of the new movements, the ease with which they communicate with each other means that in some loose sense they share a common agenda.

The Indian anti-GATT movement, with its re-application of the old anti-colonial slogans such as *swaraj* and 'quit India', also seeks to collaborate with movements for sustainable agriculture in different parts of the world, on the basis of a common interest in resisting the monopolistic appropriation of knowledge by transnational capital.[67] It shows perhaps that it is possible to take advantage of the positive aspects of globalism, particularly the way it has destroyed some of the narrowness of the old definitions of nationalism, in order to combat its obviously negative aspects. It is clear that the establishment definition of globalism is specious because its real purpose is solely to facilitate the predatory pursuit of accumulation by transnational industrial and speculative interests, which is the main obstacle standing in the way of a true globalism based on resource management. So today's local movements are the real inheritors of globalisation.

INFLUENCING OFFICIAL SOCIETY AT AN INTERNATIONAL LEVEL
Conventionally, international agendas are by definition formulated through negotiations between governmental élites. But in practice, particularly since the Earth Summit of 1992, UN conferences have accepted a significant input from grassroots movements. They have networked to produce a common agenda, with the internet providing the technical framework for this; but what accounts for their success is not their technical skill in creating these links, but the reality of what is being linked – the work the movements are performing on the ground. What is emerging is a new definition of democracy. The NIEO movement of the past had campaigned to democratise an international society composed of state actors, whereas the effective actors in the new setup are co-operative groupings of ordinary people.

A further qualitative shift occurred in 1998, with the undermining of the Multilateral Agreement on Investment (MAI). The MAI was a system of rules worked out between the industrial countries using their own grouping, the OECD. The rules were far-reaching: they would allow investing companies to sue the host government if they were 'discriminated' against; they would outlaw requirements that companies use local suppliers, take on local partners, or hire a minimum number of local employees; and they would combat any local rules restricting foreign ownership of media or utility companies and restrictions on investors' ability to move money across borders. In contrast with the Uruguay Round of GATT, which had been accompanied by tremendous publicity and the charade that it was serving a universal interest, MAI was worked out in an undercover way by the industrial countries alone (although it was confidently predicted that other countries would be forced to conform once it was in place). But in April 1998, the OECD was forced to postpone the negotiations, perhaps to abandon them altogether. What was responsible for this remarkable climb-down was a campaign based on networking between many groups hostile to the dominant economic agendas. Small amounts of information obtained in one part of the world were instantly published and made available to all the other campaigning groups,[68] which meant that the economic establishment's attempt at secrecy was completely undermined.[69]

It should be noted that the Asian crisis helped to undermine confidence in capital flows, and in this sense a widespread lack of conviction among investors may have contributed to the defeat of the MAI, as much as popular campaigning. But this only confirms the fact that there are many opportunities for the grassroots: the centre does not know which direction to take, so there is a chance for popular forces to articulate a positive agenda to fill this void. It is important that this is done at an international as well as a national level.

Campaigns such as the one against the MAI may seem to be merely oppositional, but there is a positive element within this negativity: the campaigning movements are in effect calling for globalism to be defined as something different from the globalism of speculative capital. Besides rebuilding the NIEO, the campaigning movements are constructing the missing South–South dimension at the level of knowledge and culture. The grassroots movements are communicating with each other and learning from each other; the slogan 'act locally, think globally' expresses the link between the two apparently opposite forces: what is required is local concreteness/pluralism combined with global consciousness.

## Why the Political Left is Still Relevant

The above examples can provide the basis of a viable and theoretically consistent strategy, which makes the popular movements aware that they are struggling for something worthwhile and workable. Such movements can win specific concessions, but the really important question is how to make the transition to the completely different, more rational social system which these movements undoubtedly imply.

Both local and international systems are controlled by those with power and wealth, and these groups will never step down simply because an alternative project can be shown to be viable.

One of the strengths of the political left is that it has always been acutely aware that vested interests have to be defeated, for they will never be convinced. This means guiding the mass movement through the necessary stages, each of which will involve accumulating strength from the struggle for reforms, without losing the perspective of eventually seizing power.

The issues around which the left can be mobilised are still there. Indeed, it is the establishment itself which indirectly provides convincing evidence that this is the case. As I argued earlier, the present order copes with the left through denial, but this denial is itself testimony to the left's continued relevance. For instance, the establishment has pronounced, with suspicious haste, that the left's approach to popular participation is outmoded.[70] The ruling orders are also keen to dub the new movements as 'sectoral' and 'post-modern', delightedly applauding 'the emergence of a plurality of social actors – indigenous people, women, ecologists and so on whose demands for recognition and social identity *are not necessarily geared towards a change in the power structure*' [my italics].[71] In such statements, the establishment unwittingly reveals the persistent fear which underlies its denial of the political left.

Today's apparently altruistic notions of popular participation are in reality seeking to do what the establishment has always done, to combat political mass movements.

Established interests have always supported small producers as a way of undercutting organised labour; in the plantation sector in Senegal, agribusiness chose to work through households, rather than organised labour, in the hope of avoiding 'Cesar Chavez'[72] and all those problems'.[73] More recently, the strategy has been updated to encompass small entrepreneurs within the new parallel economy. A school of writers studying Peru hailed the parallel economy as the 'other path', which would become a bastion against the organising power of the Maoist guerrillas known as Sendero Luminoso – (Radiant Path).[74] All this is indicative of an enduring fear on the part of the élites.

What is clear is that 'development' has not reduced the structural inequalities of power and wealth which create class divisions.

Even when the taking of power is not openly attempted, the class struggle is still there, but in a different, endemic form. It is the kind of struggle which explores the relationships of class, taking the form of a 'constant process of testing and renegotiation of production relations between classes'. In many cases, the struggle is carried out in a prudent and secretive form which, in Scott's words, 'preserves, for the most part, the on-stage theatre of power which dominates public life'.[75]

When capitalism is in a well-consolidated phase, and official society ('the on-stage theatre of power') cannot be challenged openly, this spontaneous process often becomes the main form of struggle. It provides the refuge into which the left can retreat when open organisation is difficult, and provides the base from which a resurgence can be launched when conditions are right.

Although the new social movements fall into this category of 'everyday resistance', they also take the struggle a step further, bringing an element of organisation to the process of testing the oppressive structures.

In fact, this organisational ability is not as new as it seems to the establishment, which has only recently discovered the new movements. Everyday resistance has always given rise to organisational forms. For example, one of the most established forms of struggle – trade unionism – has long been organised and has continued developing, in some respects making qualitative progress over recent years. For rapid economic change has brought with it the exploration of new forms of solidarity among working people, which highlight not only new issues, but also (and perhaps this is more important) old issues which were previously neglected. The old labour movement was narrow in some respects, for it mirrored the official world's definitions, giving priority to industrial and waged workers, as opposed to the excluded and marginalised. The left believed that large-scale factory work was the highest arena of struggle because it was most specific to advanced capitalism, and created large, disciplined industrial armies which could become armies of the class war. The assumption was that it required centralism and militarism on the left to combat the centralism and militarism of capitalist society. Taking this reasoning a step further, it was thought that the most industrialised countries would take the lead in the class struggle, so the Eurocentrism which existed within an oppressive world order was reproduced in the struggle against that system.

Today, a new unionism is arising which addresses a wider social agenda. One example is the Nineteenth of September Garment Workers' Union in Mexico, which was formed after the collapse of the official economy following the earthquake of 1985.[76] One important aspect of this new trade unionism is that it is propelled by previously marginalised groups of workers, in which women play a crucial role.

The objective processes of class-formation which underlie this new unionism are also continuing. Electronics companies in Asia seek to exhaust the labour of young women quite rapidly, but in practice many of the women have held on and resisted dismissal. In this process, continuity and a strong collective spirit have developed. Vivian Lin's study showed that, although money was the initial motive behind the women's decision to seek waged employment, companionship was viewed as a major positive factor, with some women refusing promotion out of solidarity with fellow-workers.[77] (Promotion is an important anti-solidarity tactic of the new management systems.) In this way, working people are making sense of an epoch of rapid social change, appropriating the experience conceptually at a collective level. This change is another demonstration of the 'complementary opposite' which capitalism always carries within it.

The labour movement in the past had some justification for focusing on building industrial armies in the core workplace: capitalism has implicitly confirmed that this was a weak point, because otherwise there would have been no reason for inventing the new management doctrines. But by marginalising black and women workers, the labour movement laid itself open to being outmanoeuvred by capitalism through these new strategies. Anyway, it must be recognised that a new reality is in place today, where capitalism's hold over the core workplaces is fairly consolidated; treating these as the main focus of labour organisation is no longer an option. In the future, labour struggles will have to adapt to this, because it is the marginal areas of the world economy, on which capital accumulation more and more depends, that will increasingly become the point of weakness for capitalism. Although it is very complex, this change will eventually strengthen the left movement, because it will not be as easy for the dominant system to co-opt working people in the marginal sectors as it was for them to buy over the relatively privileged labour within the core economic sectors.

It might appear today that the organised left has abandoned the scene and that, in its absence, the forces of social development are pushing ahead, continually testing the limits of the relational phenomenon that is class. Although there is an element of truth in this image, it is far from the whole story. To a certain extent, left-wingers have deliberately shifted to a new strategy of working within new social movements, and this is reflected in the way in which these movements have developed. The leftists who work within them include people who wanted to carry on doing political work after their organisations were smashed by the repressive state, people disillusioned by the top-downism of existing organisations, and, importantly, people who are still members of leftist organisations which have decided to reduce their public profile for a while and work at the grassroots.

This approach is a logical response to a situation of repression. It occurred in some countries some time ago, before becoming in the early 1980s a generalised defensive phase for the left. It was a tactical retreat into a scattered form of activity, but because it led the left to work among the most marginalised, it was also, in fact, a step forward. As a response to the right-wing dictatorship that took power in 1964, radicals in Brazil undertook the 'work of the ants': popular education centres, advice and support centres, projects based on communities, self-help and education.[78] Although repression seemed to reflect the strength of the dominant order, in reality it exposed new areas of the system's weakness: the remoteness and hostility of state power weakened the official system because it left unanswered so many social needs. Radicals identified these areas and naturally began to work in them.

Building radical forces within the unofficial economy and grassroots social structures is a viable alternative to a strategy centred in industrial armies. It will need a change of outlook, but it may have strengths which the earlier strategies did not have. Notably, it raises long-term qualitative issues – sustainability, women's rights, and so on – as part of the immediate struggle in a way which earlier strategies did not.

It undoubtedly implies very different methods of working. Although the concept of a relationship between vanguard and masses still exists, it is today being framed in a new way. A different technique of mobilisation needs to be learned. An important element in it is the method associated with Paulo Freire, which has exercised a considerable influence on radical work within the new movements, and has led to a new role for intellectuals working within them. The researchers who have brought the new social movements to world attention have participated themselves in the movements, not just studied them. This points towards a radical interpretation of empowerment. The outside facilitator sets in motion a process leading to the generation of new ideas from within the mass movement. Key techniques could include the role of history/local studies, and the relationship between immediate and strategic interests. For example, in a case study of Participatory Action Research in a native American village in Mexico, researchers initially helped local people to produce a manual in their own language so that they could run a co-op to market tomatoes (a cash crop). After a while, however, a local leader began a movement to stop growing the cash crop and switch instead to cultivation of maize, a subsistence crop.[79] Other approaches to integrating research with social change have also been developed. Research carried out by the Society for the Promotion of Area Resource Centres (SPARC), founded in 1984, was the catalyst that got women pavement-dwellers in Bombay, India, to organise themselves.[80] Constantly harassed by threats of demolition from a government that was doing nothing to remove the problem,[81] pavement-dwellers responded with a community survival system based on mutual support. The wider lesson learnt from the experience was that practical needs provide a focus for struggles which can then move on to formulating 'strategic interests', with a structural dimension.

The fact that many of the new social movements are the result of conscious political work does not mean that they are phoney or manipulated. They develop their own momentum, and it is precisely this unpredictability which gives them their strength. In northern Mexico, Maoists from the 1968 student movement began political work organising squatters.[82] This produced a range of new forms of democratic political and social organisation, and despite state repression and the killing of a number of leaders, the movement acquired its own momentum and proved unstoppable. The federal government was eventually forced, in 1989, to yield to a number of concrete demands to improve the living environment, education, and so on, of the squatters. It is interesting to note that the movement, under its own momentum, became concerned about ecological issues, winning backing from the local state leadership for popular teams to scout for sources of pure water so that they could plant fruit trees and irrigate vegetable gardens.

What is good about empowerment is that it emphasises the positive in human creativity. Anisur Rahman, for example, argues, in a study of the emergence of building co-operatives in Mexico in the mid-1980s, that orthodox definitions of poverty, which stigmatise people as victims, inhibit the development of the elements that could serve to change this state of affairs.[83] In its doctored version of empowerment, the establishment has seized on this emphasis on the positive in order to distract attention away from the negative forces (exploitation) which prevent people from realising their potential. The establishment is seeking to bolster its own definition of empowerment, using external funding to win the new social movements over to acceptable identities or perhaps to win over to its side an élite within them, the modern equivalent of the worker aristocracy. The situation is complicated by the fact that many grassroots groups are probably repeating, parrot-fashion, the language of governance and post-modernism in order to get the funds offered by Northern donors, without necessarily believing a word of it.

But ultimately, this attempt at co-option will fail because it fails to make sense of people's reality. The left's strength has always been its vision of giving downtrodden working people the confidence to stand up to the oppressor, and to fight back by any means necessary, and the Freirean method simply takes this one step further by addressing the internalised expressions of this oppression. It is likely that the NGOs will increasingly face fierce internal debates over the direction they should take. All this will be a new arena for left politics to develop.

## The Organised Left and the Revolutionary Potential of the Immediate Future

The left still exists in a conventionally organised form, in the shape of large political parties, perhaps more than is often realised. The US élite wanted us to believe that the left was dead – the journal *Problems of Communism* closed down immediately after the fall of the Berlin Wall – and it may suit both sides to maintain this fiction for a while. There have been some extremely strange developments in the last few years, with political forces from a Marxist–Leninist background seizing power in countries like Ethiopia, Eritrea and Congo (Kinshasa) with the connivance of the US administration. This is a kind of international version of 'preserving the on-stage theatre of power'. Any political force which is good at organising society has been supported for performing a useful service in preventing social collapse, floods of refugees and calls for an unpredictable, Somali-style US military intervention leading to GIs returning in coffins. At least in some areas, the official attitude has been that as long as Marxist–Leninists do not proclaim their beliefs from the housetops, they can go on practising their activities. It is hoped that they will be corrupted by power, by post-modernism or by World Bank and NGO involvement, and this may, indeed, happen to some of them. At the same time, this is clearly a situation which can be exploited tactically.

Indeed, the left has been learning new ways of working. One of the most important changes has not been the collapse of the organised left *per se*, but the collapse of the idea that it could set up a distinct international system of political economy largely fenced off from capitalism, and eventually defeat it through competition. It is probable that this was never feasible, even in the past. For example, even strongly pro-Soviet states in Africa remained, in common with other types of African regime, 'thoroughly integrated into the international capitalist order'.[84] If the left has stopped deceiving itself and is finding new ways of operating within capitalism, this is a healthy step, bringing radicals closer to the grassroots movements which are expanding by finding a way of surviving at a day-to-day level within capitalism. The old vision of separation should be replaced by a different sort of 'parallel universe', that is, the grassroots movements, local economies, and so on, which exist within the system and get stronger by combating it.

The left at a state level is being forced to adapt to these circumstances. China was always sceptical of the possibility of building a self-contained political economy cut off from world capitalism.[85] Since the anti-Communist rollback of the 1980s, it has not only avoided direct challenges to capitalism, but even perhaps has developed what could be seen as a strategy of luring the enemy in deep, or waging a guerrilla war behind the enemy's lines. Deng Xiaoping's aphorism, 'Observe developments soberly, maintain our position, meet challenges calmly, hide our capacities, bide our time, remain free of ambitions, never claim leadership',[86] could be interpreted to mean this.

The important question, however, is whether this option of working within the system will make organised socialism more responsive to demands from the grassroots movements. At present, the Chinese system seems hostile to independent movements within the country, and if this is the case it is more likely to influence the new social movements as an external factor – perhaps by weakening capitalism at an international-systems level – rather than playing a central role in their development. It is possible, however, to envisage some new fusion of statism and grassroots initiative. Cuba used to have a monocrop agriculture based on state farms, but in the 1980s it grew dissatisfied both with its subordinate place in the international division of labour and with its dependence on imported inputs, which became increasingly unsustainable. Its response was to invest heavily in technology, in a form which stimulated sustainable grassroots development. Biofertilisers and natural predators on pests are now being manufactured in decentralised, local centres, with the use of this 'high' technology being blended with traditional farming practices, which some farmers still remember using before the introduction of 'modern' methods. It is necessary to have small production units because the application of biological methods implies a close knowledge of precise local conditions. For this reason, state farms have been leased in parcels to collectives, but according to a sustainable management logic, not one of privatisation for its own sake.[87] Statism has provided positive support here, which shows that its role, however transitory in a long-term developmental sense, can at times be crucial.

It is possible to make a fairly confident prediction that there will be an upsurge of radical struggle in some areas in the coming period. Since international capitalism develops unevenly, the struggle will be concentrated in certain places, but for a number of reasons, it is not possible to identify where exactly this will happen.

Historical experience of revolutionary situations suggests that they mature very rapidly, which is why they are often very exciting. This is partly because qualitative change occurs through a transformation of opposites: oppression, which causes people to withdraw from politics into day-to-day survival, can suddenly spark off radical challenges to the system itself, with even revolutionaries taken by surprise by the rapidity of this transformation. There is a certain kind of organised resistance, found in the grassroots movements, which involves a new way of organising society as a whole; at present it is only latent, but it could form a realistic basis for taking over control of important areas of social life. The organised left has itself opted for a mode of action which downplays (without completely abandoning) the idea of directly challenging the system. Far from boasting, as it did in the past, it keeps a low profile, which makes it difficult for anyone not directly involved with the grassroots in a particular place to assess the real degree of political organisation. Finally, crises which may precipitate rapid social change are increasingly linked to shifts in the international economy; we can gain some knowledge of how these complex factors operate – which has been the purpose of the present study – but cannot be sure where and when they will converge geographically.

There were major weaknesses in understanding the reality of peripheral capitalism in the past, and left movements sometimes paid a heavy price.[88] But it is not just a question of absorbing some static 'idea', because the reality which needs to be understood is above all dynamic. Social classes themselves do not merely 'exist', but assert themselves in actual practice, particularly in the dynamic context of conflict;[89] and this is precisely the kind of situation that will arise in the coming period.

As an example, India is extremely rich in both grassroots movements and organised radicals – it could therefore function as a kind of laboratory of social development. Left groups such as the various sections of the Communist Party of India (Marxist-Leninist) are learning to operate within a social reality where there is, for instance, some coming together of anti-GATT peasant movements with other popular movements, such as those organised by dalits and other out- or lower castes.[90] Women's informal-sector struggles, movements in defence of tribal lands or anti-dam protests will add to this complexity.

These are broadly all movements of working people. Each has its own particular interests and logic, but they can converge around some common goals – a new, plural societal project serving working people's interests. Its political economy would have many new features: local economies, popular knowledge systems and all the other elements which we have discussed so far, or which are yet to emerge. At the moment, the left is experimenting how to strike a difficult balance: it must resist the tendency to write off its traditional values, while at the same time being open enough to absorb fundamentally new inputs from the grassroots movements. In India, there are so many different left groups partly because they are answering these problems in different ways.[91] There will be many controversial and difficult questions, which are already dividing opinion:[92] for example, should the left demand that India use the possibilities opened up by the Uruguay round of GATT to launch a South-centred assault on the world trading system, or, on the contrary, link up with the grassroots protests which reject GATT in its entirety?[93] New and complex issues like this will recur all the time. This is all part of social development.

The left has had to retreat for a time from organising an alternative political economy, and is working instead on the terrain of capitalism. But even though this terrain has been defined on capitalism's terms, the things which seem to make the system strong can change quite suddenly into its weak points. What is a nightmare for the system is when the organised left acts as catalyst for social movements. The best example is Mexico, where the Zapatistas have done this, not only at a national level but to some extent internationally too. The same objective conditions are found elsewhere: Indian radicals have made explicit parallels with Mexico. In both cases, oppressive social structures, by marginalising the masses, make the reliance on export markets self-reinforcing.[94] Ultimately, the globalised consumer culture which seeks to make people loyal to capitalism is quite hollow. In a sense, the spread of interdependence has only served to increase the tangibility of the North–South divide, and the globalisation of culture works only to a point 'beyond which popular rejection sets in. The false premises of cultural imperialism become objects of bitter jokes in the reality of abject poverty, hunger and perpetual denial of minimum livelihood to millions of people.'[95]

The period of retreat can undoubtedly be the basis of moving forward. What is at stake is to understand the possible operation of an alternative social system, which effectively integrates the grassroots in a way capitalism can never do. This will never be easy. But objectively, the process is already beginning.

One of the big lessons of the twentieth century is that the radicals cannot just address the problems created by some mythical pure, economistic capitalism. They must deal with a really existing capitalism which exploits different groups of people in different ways and constantly suffers its ecological limitations. But this realisation takes us only part of the way. The impurity, the complexity which make up the reality of *contemporary* capitalism, reflect the fact that oppressive structures stored up from much earlier in the history of social development, and which capitalism took over, have been dumped in the lap of the present generation. These have to be unpicked: the limitations on personal development inherent in forcing people into subordinate roles according to their ascribed characteristics: 'racial', gender or whatever. This means not only re-creating (through the negation of the negation) the functioning balances of traditional grassroots structures, but in some ways doing things better than they did. There is no doubt that the social movements of the past two decades have posed some of the necessary questions for making this advance, for example on the gender issue.

The left has become plural and diffuse: this is true both within individual countries, where there are often several tendencies; and also internationally, where there is no clear ideological centre. This diffuseness can be seen as something positive: as a survival method in response to repression and a way of accumulating the variety of responses that produce the raw material of future development.

But this should not be taken as an excuse for abandoning the search for 'big' unifying ideas about the nature and tendencies of the system, or for convincing alternative social projects. To work towards these is in fact an urgent necessity. This can be done through a process of networking and discussing the ideas which have emerged out of the practice in different areas. This book is conceived as a contribution in one small area, namely the understanding of international systems, and hopefully it will be discussed and pulled to pieces and integrated with other contributions.

The history of the socialist movement does have the positive things which make it still relevant to serve as the core of a more generalised process of renewal. There has always been an orientation to uphold the rights of the poorest and most oppressed sectors, including their right to fight back, an orientation to criticise and refute all attempts to justify oppression and exploitation. We can emphasise two positive issues in Marxism's attitude to mass movements. First, Marx himself always criticised the fashion for 'enlightened' individuals to dream up ideal future societies, and his book *The Civil War in France* shows clearly how he regarded the organisational forms of mass initiatives as the basis for appreciating the direction of social change. If we were to rewrite this book for the contemporary situation, it would necessarily be international in scope, and would probably take the form of a survey of the new social movements, which would provide much richer material for such an analysis than anything available in Marx's time. Second, when considering the kind of social organisation that will be capable of effecting the transition to post-capitalism, the crucial problem is to provide some counterbalance to the abuses which may arise in a state machine which is still condemned to exist during a transitional period: authoritarianism or bureaucracy. Here again, there is an approach within the Marxist tradition that can be adapted to take account of the new reality. Lenin, in his last years, argued strongly for independent organisations of workers *within* the socialist state. This has interesting implications for the grassroots movements. While any movement to establish an alternative power will necessarily draw its strength from the new grassroots struggles, it is also clear that the social movements will have to maintain a distinct identity. What is needed is some new relationship between official and non-official society on a different basis. In the longer term, the relationship of pre-eminence would be reversed, with the non-official world dominant, but in the immediate term the relationship would keep the state machine in check. In general, the point is for the raw material of future socio-economic development to continue to emerge from the base. The source of new ideas and new practices must be mass initiatives, the real social movement. And this must continue under a new social order.

## Notes

1. Wangoola n.d., p. 29.
2. Chazan 1982.
3. Mamdani 1991.
4. Maliyamkono and Bagachwa 1990, p. 61.
5. Moser 1987, p. 319.
6. Maliyamkono and Bagachwa's (1990) study (see note 4) effectively does this, and would seem to underestimate the level of the informal economy by failing to link it with the wider household issue.
7. See, for example, Agarwal 1990, p. 115.
8. Jonsson 1991.
9. Shieh 1992, p. 214.
10. Nadvi and Schmitz 1994.
11. See Sverrisson 1993.
12. Nadvi and Schmitz 1994, p. 16.
13. Amartya Sen, 'Development as Capability Expansion', in Griffin and Knight 1990.
14. It is based on three criteria: the proportion of children under 5 who are underweight, the proportion of births unattended by trained personnel, and female illiteracy. United Nations Development Programme 1996.
15. For a survey of these changes, see Ghai 1990.
16. Cf. the argument of Oran Young, in Krasner 1983, p. 98.
17. World Bank 1995, p. 118.
18. Paredes and Riveres 1994, p. 71; the authors are typical apologists of the Chilean model.
19. Hall 1983, p. 8.
20. North 1981, pp. 6, 16.
21. Cf., for example, Zelem 1991.
22. Blakie 1985, pp. 119, 53, 57.
23. Cf. Delpeuch 1985.
24. Baran 1973.
25. Pierce 1991.
26. Koponen 1991.
27. Belshaw 1980, p. 197.
28. Richards 1985, p. 64.
29. Glaeser and Phillips-Howard 1987.
30. In some cases manure and green manure are burned, which has the effect of releasing phosphorus, while in others manure is dug in to conserve nitrates, a final cash-crop of pigeon peas serving to fix nitrogen before soil returns to bush; Richards 1985.
31. See Grainger 1989, p. 67.
32. Le Houérou 1989, p. 146.
33. Feyerabend 1994.

34. See, for example, Buntzel 1980.

35. Cf. Dobrska 1981 for a positive statement of this orientation.

36. As, for example, when British political élites refer to the need to shift unemployed people into appropriate housing.

37. Cf. Kunio 1988.

38. Emmanuel 1981.

39. See, for example, Bhalla and James 1988.

40. Cf. Rau 1991.

41. See, for example, the symposium published in Ewusi n.d.

42. Cf. Fre 1990.

43. Bergeret and Ribot 1990, p. 66.

44. The baobab tree, the most nutritious, is a treasure tree, the gateway to an invisible world, 'more than a tree, a member of the village community'; the ficus is a social tree, under which meetings are held, and it can't be private property; the proprietor of a tamarind tree can't monopolise its fruits, they must be shared.

45. Appadurai 1990.

46. Cockburn 1986.

47. See, for example, Petras and Gunle 1987.

48. James and Havens 1981, p. 223.

49. Beckman 1981.

50. Siddiqui 1990.

51. Abdoun 1990.

52. See, for example, Guisse n.d., p. 95.

53. L'Évènement, Paris, No. 401, July 1992.

54. Wisner 1984.

55. Rau 1991.

56. See details in Rau 1991, p. 174; Ghai 1990.

57. See, for example, Introduction to Mandaza 1986.

58. See Irayagolle 1978.

59. Cf. Gadgil and Guha 1994, p. 110.

60. Shramshakti 1988.

61. Cf. Sharma 1981, pp. 65–6.

62. Rau 1991, p. 155.

63. Ayub 1994.

64. The riots began on a caste/class issue, but had been sidetracked into a Hindu–Muslim confrontation.

65. Cf. Rose 1992.

66. Samara 1992, pp. 342–5.

67. See, for example, Third World Resurgence, 1993, p. 39.

68. Drohan 1998.

69. Financial Times, 30 April 1998.

70. As an example of this discourse, cf. Stieffel and Wolfe 1994, pp. 181ff.

71. Schejtman 1997, p. 49.

72. César Chavez: an organiser of heavily exploited, mainly Hispanic, agricultural workers in the south-west USA, who led several legendary campaigns, particularly in the 1960s and 1970s.

73. Mackintosh 1989, p. xv.

74. For a critique of this literature, see Mitter 1989.

75. Scott 1986, pp. 18, 21.

76. Benaria 1989, p. 256.

77. Cf. Lin 1987.

78. Cf. Landim 1993.

79. Fals-Borda 1993.

80. Bapat and Patel 1993, p. 41.

81. 27,000 pavement dwellers were found by SPARC to be living in just one area of Bombay; ibid., p. 193.

82. Moguel and Velasquez 1992, for the following details.

83. Rahman 1991.

84. Ottaway and Ottaway 1986, p. 166.

85. Cf. Friedman 1979.

86. Quoted in Garver 1993, p. 5.

87. Cf. Rosset 1996; this article is the source for the details in the following paragraph.

88. Cf., for example, Tornquist 1984, p. 239.

89. See Pearce 1979.

90. Cf. Le Monde, 14–15 August 1994.

91. See Gupta 1993.

92. Elements of this struggle can be seen, for example, in India, with the campaigns of different Communist Party of India (Marxist–Leninist) groups against Communist Party of India (Marxist) administrations, or conflicts within the Communist Party of the Philippines over attempts to incorporate a mixed-economy model within its broad front organisation, the National Democratic Front.

93. Omvedt 1993; Panda 1993.

94. 'Mexican Pointers for India', 1995.

95. CPI(ML)–Janashakti 1994.

# Bibliography

Abdel-Fadil, Mahmoud (1975) *Development, Income Distribution and Social Change in Rural Egypt 1952–70*, Cambridge, Cambridge University Press.

Abdel-Malek, Anouar (1972) *La Dialectique sociale*, Paris, Seuil.

— (1983) *Contemporary Arab Political Thought*, London, Zed Books.

Abdoun, Rabah (1990) 'Algeria: The Problem of Nation Building', in Azzam Mahjoub (ed.), *Adjustment or Delinking – The African Experience*, Tokyo and London, UNU Press/Zed Books.

Addo, Herb *et al.* (1985) *Development as Social Transformation*, London, Hodder & Stoughton/UNU.

Adedeji, Adebayo (1984) 'The Economic Evolution of Developing Africa', in M. Crowder (ed.), *The Cambridge History of Africa*, Vol. 8, Cambridge, Cambridge University Press.

Aganbegyan, A. (1988) *The Economic Challenge of Perestroika*, Bloomington, Indiana University Press.

Agarwal, Bina (1988a) 'Neither Sustenance nor Sustainability', in Bina Agarwal (ed.), *Structures of Patriarchy – The State, the Community and the Household in Modernising Asia*, London, Zed Books.

— (ed.) (1988b) *Structures of Patriarchy – The State, the Community and the Household in Modernising Asia*, London, Zed Books.

Agarwala, A.N. and S.P. Singh (eds) (1958) *The Economics of Underdevelopment*, Delhi, Oxford University Press.

Ahooja-Patel, K. *et al.* (eds) (1986) *World Economy in Transition*, Oxford, Pergamon Press.

Alaux, J-P. and P. Norel (eds) (1985) *Faim au Sud, Crise au Nord*, Paris, L'Harmattan.

Alavi, H. and T. Shanin (eds) (1982) *Introduction to the Sociology of 'Developing Societies'*, Basingstoke, Macmillan.

Alschuler, L.R. (1988) *Multinationals and Maldevelopment*, Basingstoke, Macmillan.

Altvater, E. (1992) 'Fordist and Post-Fordist International Division of Labour and Monetary Regimes', in M. Storper and H. Scott (eds), *Pathways to Industrialisation and Regional Development*, London, Routledge.

Amadiume, Ifi (1987) *Afrikan Matriarchal Formations*, London, Karnak.

Amin, Samir (1973) *Neo-Colonialism in West Africa*, New York, Monthly Review Press.

— (1978a) *The Arab Nation*, London, Zed Books.

— (1978b) *The Law of Value and Historical Materialism*, New York, Monthly Review Press.

— (1980) *Class and Nation – Historically and in the Current Crisis*, London, Heinemann.

— (1981) *L'Avenir du Maoisme*, Paris, Editions de Minuit.

— (1983) 'L'Art – Intégration ou Révolte', in *Waraango*, Senegal.

— (1988) 'Le Commerce interafricain', reprinted in Samir Amin, *Impérialisme et Sous-développement en Afrique*, Paris, Anthropos.

Amsden, Alice (ed.) (1980) *The Economics of Women and Work*, Harmondsworth, Penguin.

Anon. (1992) 'The Current Crisis, a Crisis for Over-Production of Capital', in *Social Relations*, Milan, March.

Anyang' Nyong'o, P. (ed.) (1987) *Popular Struggles for Democracy in Africa*, London and Tokyo, Zed Books and United Nations University Press.

Apffel Marglin, F. and A. Marglin (eds) (1990) *Dominating Knowledge – Development, Culture and Resistance*, Oxford, Clarendon Press.

Appadurai, Arjun (1990) 'Technology and the Reproduction of Values in Rural Western India', in Apffel Marglin and Marglin (1990).

APSP (1982) *Black People and the US Economy – Our Case for Reparations*, Oakland, Calif., Burning Spear.

Archetti, P. *et al.* (eds) (1987) *Sociology of 'Developing Societies' – Latin America*, London, Macmillan.

Ariff, Mohammed *et al.* (eds) (1977) *ASEAN Co-operation in Industrial Projects*, Kuala Lumpur, Malaysian Economic Association.

Asad, T. and R. Owen (eds) (1983) *Sociology of 'Developing Societies' – The Middle East*, London, Macmillan.

Aseniero, George (1985) 'A Reflection on Developmentalism', in Addo 1985.

Ayo, E.J. (1988) *Development Planning in Nigeria*, Ibadan, University Press.

Ayoob, Mohamed (1988) 'The Iran–Iraq War and Regional Security in the Gulf', in Yoshikazu Sakamoto (ed.) *Asia – Militarisation and Regional Conflict*, Tokyo and London, United Nations University Press and Zed Books.

Ayub, Nasreen (1994) *The Self-Employed Women in Pakistan – A Case Study of the Self-Employed Women of the Urban Informal Sector in Karachi*, Karachi, Pakistan Association of Women's Studies.

Azar, E.E. and J.W. Burton (1986) *International Conflict Resolution – Theory and Practice*, Brighton, Wheatsheaf.

Baduel, P.R. (ed.) (1991) *Crise du Golfe – La Logique des Chercheurs* [Revue du Monde musulman et de la Méditerranée, hors série].

Bahr, Hans-Dieter (1980) 'The Class Structure of Machinery: Notes on the Value Form', in P. Slater (ed.) *Outlines of a Critique of Technology*, London, Ink Links.

Baily, M.N. and A.K. Chakrabarti (1988) *Innovation and the Productivity Crisis*, Washington, DC, Brookings Institution.

Ball, M. (1969) *The OAS in Transition*, Durham, NC, Duke University Press.

Bandyophadyaya, J. (1982) *North Over South*, Brighton, Harvester.

Banque Mondiale (1990) *Rapport sur le développement dans le monde*.

Bapat, Meera and Sheela Patel (1993) 'Beating a Path: Towards Defining Women's Participation', in *Adult Education and Development*, Bonn.

Baran, P.A. (1958) 'On the Political Economy of Backwardness', in A.N. Agarwala and S.P. Singh (eds), *The Economics of Underdevelopment*, Delhi, Oxford University Press.

— (1973) *The Political Economy of Growth*, London, Penguin [first published 1957].

Bauer, P.T. (1971) *Dissent on Development – Studies and Debates in Development Economics*, London, Weidenfeld and Nicolson.

Beckman, Björn (1981) 'Ghana 1951–78 – The Agrarian Basis of the Post-Colonial State', in Judith Heyer *et al.* (eds) *Rural Development in Tropical Africa*, London, Macmillan.

Bell, Daniel (1965) *The End of Ideology – On the Exhaustion of Political Ideas in the 1950s*, New York, The Free Press [first published 1961].

Bell, David A. (1984) *Employment in the Age of Drastic Change*, Tunbridge Wells, Abacus.

Bello, W. and S. Rosenfeld (1990) *Dragons in Distress – Asia's Miracle Economies in Crisis*, London, Penguin.

Belshaw D. (1980) 'Taking Indigenous Technology Seriously, the Case of Inter-Cropping Techniques in East Africa', in D. Brokensha *et al.* (eds) *Indigenous Knowledge Systems and Development*, Lanham, Md., University Press of America.

Benaria, L. (1989) 'Gender and the Global Economy', in A. MacEwan and W.K. Tabb (eds), *Instability and Change in the World Economy*, New York, Monthly Review Press.

Bennholdt-Thomsen, Veronika (1988) '"Investment in the Poor": an Analysis of World Bank Policy', in Maria Mies *et al.*, *Women: The Last Colony*, London, Zed Books.

Bennis, P. and M. Moushabeck (eds) (1993) *Altered States*, New York, Olive Branch.

Benson, I. and J. Lloyd (1983) *New Technology and Industrial Change*, London, Kogan Page.

Bergeret, Anne and J.C. Ribot (1990) *L'Arbre nourricier en Pays sahélien*, Paris, Editions de la Maison des Sciences de l'Homme.

Bergsten, C.F. and M. Noland (eds) (1993) *Pacific Dynamism in the International Economic System*, Washington, DC, Institute for International Economics.

Berri, D. and J. Ozawa (1997) 'Pax americana and Asian Exports: revealed trends of Comparative Advantage Recycling', in *International Trade Journal*, Spring.

Bettelheim, Charles (1965) 'Les Cadres généraux de la Planification chinoise', in C. Bettelheim *et al.*, *La Construction du Socialisme en Chine*, Paris, Maspéro.

Bhalla, A.S. and D. James (eds) (1988) *New Technologies and Development*, Boulder, Colo., Lynne Rienner for the ILO.

Bin Yu (1993) 'Sino-Russian Military Relations', in *Asian Survey*, March.

Blakie, Piers (1985) *The Political Economy of Soil Erosion in Developing Countries*, London, Longmans.

— and H. Brookfield (1987) 'The Farmer, the State and the Land in Developed Market Economies', in P. Blakie *et al.*, *Land Degradation and Society*, London, Methuen.

Blakie, P. *et al.*, (1987) *Land Degradation and Society*, London, Methuen.

Bleier, Ruth (1984) *Science and Gender: A Critique of Biology and its Theories on Women*, Oxford, Pergamon Press.

Blum, William (1986) *The CIA: A Forgotten History*, London, Zed Books.

Borrus M. *et al.* (1988) 'Creating Advantage: How Government Policies Shape International Trade in the Semiconductor Industry', in P.R. Krugman (ed.) *Strategic Trade Policy and the New International Economics*, Cambridge, Mass., Massachusetts Institute of Technology Press.

Boyer, R. and D. Drache (eds) (1996) *States Against Markets – the Limits of Globalisation*, London, Routledge.

Brac de la Perière, Robert-Ali (1990) 'La Révolution des Semences pourrait améliorer toute l'Alimentation humaine', in *Le Monde diplomatique*, May.

Brandt Commission (1980) *North–South*, London, Pan.

Braverman, H. (1974) *Labour and Monopoly Capital*, New York, Monthly Review Press.

Brewer, A. (1980) *Marxist Theories of Imperialism – A Critical Survey*, London, Routledge and Kegan Paul.

Broad, R. and J. Cavanagh (1988) 'No more NICs', in *Foreign Policy*, Fall.

Brokensha, D. *et al.* (eds) (1980) *Indigenous Knowledge Systems and Development*, Lanham, Md., University Press of America.

Brookings Institution (1949) International Studies Group, *Major Problems of US Foreign Policy 1949–50*, Washington, DC, Brookings Institution.

Brugger, Bill and D. Kelly (1990) *Chinese Marxism in the Post-Mao Era*, Stanford, Calif., Stanford University Press.

Bruhat, Jean (1976) *Histoire d'Indonésie*, Paris, Presses universitaires de France, third edition.

Bruntland, G.H. (1987) *Our Common Future*, Oxford, Oxford University Press for World Commission on Environment and Development.

Buchholz, Jurgen (1984) 'Grune Revolution oder okologischer Landbau – Beobachtungen in Bangladesh und Rwanda', in K. Fiege and L. Ramalho (eds), *Landwirtschaft = Hungerwirtschaft? – Umbruche und Krisen in der Agrarsystem der dritten Welt*, Saarbrucken, Breitenbach Verlag.

Buntzel, Rudolf (1980) 'Outline for a Rural Development Strategy for Africa with Special Reference to Tanzania', in Johan Galtung *et al.* (eds), *Self Reliance – A Strategy for Development*, London, Bogle.

Burton, J.W. (1986) 'The History of International Conflict Resolution', in E.E. Azar and J.W. Burton, *International Conflict Resolution – Theory and Practice*, Brighton, Wheatsheaf.

Cable, V. (1994) 'GATT and After', in *The World Today*, February.

Caldwell, M. (1977) *The Wealth of Some Nations*, London, Zed Books.

— and E. Utrecht (1979) *Indonesia – An Alternative History*, Sidney, Alternative Publishing Co-op.

Campbell, B. (1989) 'Indebtedness in Africa – Consequence, Cause or Symptom of the Crisis', in Bade Onimode (ed.) *The IMF, the World Bank and the African Debt – The Social and Political Impact*, London, Institute For African Alternatives.

Carton, B. (1991) 'Guerre pour le Pétrole', in G. Selys and B. van Doninck (eds), *La Guerre du Pétrole*, Brussels, EPO.

Casson, M. *et al.* (eds) (1986) *Multinationals and World Trade*, London, Allen and Unwin.

Castel, Odile (1988) 'Les Firmes multinationales et la stratégie d'industrialisation engagée au sein du système socio-économique mexicain', in *Revue Tiers-monde*, January–March.

Castro, Fidel (1983) *The World Economic and Social Crisis*, Report to the Seventh Summit Conference of Non-aligned Countries, Havana, Council of State.

Césaire, Aimé (1972) *Discourse on Colonialism*, New York, Monthly Review Press.

Chacel, J. *et al.* (eds) (1988) *Brazil's Economic and Political Future*, Boulder, Colo., Westview Press.

Chandra, Bipan (1979) *Nationalism and Colonialism in Modern India*, Delhi, Orient Longman.

Chang, Gordon H. (1990) *Friends and Enemies: The US, China and the Soviet Union 1948–72*, Stanford, Calif., Stanford University Press.

Chaturvedi, G. (1991) *India–China Relations*, Agra, M.G. Publishers.

Chayanov, A.V. (1966) *On the Theory of Peasant Economy*, Manchester, Manchester University Press.

Chazan, Naomi H. (1982) *Development, Underdevelopment and the State in Ghana*, Boston, Mass., Boston University African Studies Centre, Working Papers (New Series) No. 58.

Cheru, Fantu (1989) 'The Role of the IMF and World Bank in the Agrarian Crisis of Sudan and Tanzania – Sovereignty vs. Control', in Bade Onimode (ed.), *The IMF, the World Bank and the African Debt – The Social and Political Impact*, London, Institute For African Alternatives.

Choudhury, G.W. (1975) *India, Pakistan, Bangladesh and the Major Powers*, New York, Free Press.

Chowdhury, A. and I. Islam (1993) *The Newly Industrialising Economies of East Asia*, London, Routledge.

Choy, Chong Li (1981) *Open Self-Reliant Regionalism – Power for ASEAN Development*, Singapore, Institute of South-East Asian Studies.

Clairmonte, F. and J. Cavanagh (1981) *The World in Their Web – Dynamics of the Textile Multinationals*, London, Zed Books.

Clairmonte, F.F. (1986) 'Transnational Conglomerates', in K. Ahooja-Patel *et al.* (eds), *World Economy in Transition*, Oxford, Pergamon Press.

Clark, C. and S. Chan (1992) *The Evolving Pacific Basin in the Global Political Economy*, Boulder, Colo., Lynne Rienner.

Clark, Ramsey (1992) *The Fire This Time*, New York, Thunder's Mouth.

Clarke, I.M. (1986) 'Labour Dynamics and Plant Centrality in Multinational Corporations', in M. Taylor and N. Thrift (eds), *Multinationals and the Restructuring of the World Economy*, London, Croom Helm.

Cleary, Thomas (1988) Preface to Sun Tzu [Sun Zi], *The Art of War*, Boston, Mass., Shambala.

Clough, M. (1991) 'US Policy Toward the Third World in the 21st Century', in T.G. Weiss and M.A. Kessler (eds), *Third World Security in the Post Cold War Era*, Boulder, Colo., Lynne Rienner.

Clutterbuck, R. (1984) *Conflict and Violence in Singapore and Malaysia*, Singapore, Graham Brash.

Cockburn, C. (1986) 'The Relations of Technology', in R. Crompton and M. Mann (eds), *Gender and Stratification*, Cambridge, Polity Press.

Cohen, D. and J. Daniel (eds) (1981) *Political Economy of Africa*, Harlow, Longmans.

Cohen, R. (1987) *The New Helots*, Aldershot, Avebury.

— (1991) *Contested Domains – Debates in International Labour Studies*, London, Zed Books.

— *et al.* (eds) (1979) *Peasants and Proletarians*, London, Hutchinson.

Cole, Sam and Ian Miles (1984) *Worlds Apart – Technology and North-South Relations in the Global Economy*, Brighton, Wheatsheaf for UNITAR.

Cole, H.S.D. *et al.* (1973) *Thinking About the Future – A Critique of the Limits to Growth*, University of Sussex, Science Policy Research Unit.

Cook, Ian G. *et al.* (eds) (1996) *Fragmented Asia – Regional Integration and National Disintegration in Pacific Asia*, Aldershot, Avebury.

Cook, P. and C. Kirkpatrick (1995) *Globalisation, Regionalism and Third World Development*, Manchester, Institute for Development Policy and Management, Discussion Paper No. 42.

Cornevin, M. (1980) *Histoire de l'Afrique contemporaine*, Paris, Payot.

Coward, Rosalind (1983) *Patriarchal Precedents – Sexuality and Social Relations*, London, Routledge and Kegan Paul.

Cowling, K. and R. Sugden (1987) *Transnational Monopoly Capital*, Brighton, Wheatsheaf.

CPI(ML)–Janashakti (1994) *Statement of Preparatory Committee for All-India Convention*, Hyderabad, January (duplicated).

Crabb, Cecil (1965) *The Elephants and the Grass – A Study of Nonalignment*, New York, Praeger.

Crane, George T. (1990) *The Political Economy of China's Special Economic Zones*, Armonk, M.E. Sharpe.

Crockatt, R. (1993) 'Theories of Stability and the End of the Cold War', in M. Bowker and R. Brown (eds), *From Cold War to Collapse*, Cambridge, Cambridge University Press.

Crone, Donald (1993) 'The Reorganisation of the Pacific Political Economy', in *World Politics* 45, July.

Cumings, Bruce (1984) 'The Political Economy of China's Turn Outward', in S.S. Kim (ed.), *China and the World*, Boulder, Colo., Westview Press, third edition.

Cutrufelli, Maria Rosa (1983) *Women of Africa*, London, Zed Books.

D'Onofrio-Flores, P.M. and S.M. Pfafflin (1982) *Scientific–Technological Change and the Role of Women in Development*, Boulder, Colo., Westview Press for UNITAR.

Dannreuther, R. (1992) *The Gulf Conflict – A Political and Strategic Analysis*, London, Brassey's for IISS.

Dávila-Villers, D.R. (1992) 'Competition and Co-operation in the River Plate: the Democratic Transition and Mercosur', in *Bulletin of Latin American Research*, Vol. 11, No. 3.

Day, R.B. (1981) *The Crisis and the Crash*, London, New Left Books.

De Janvry, Alain (1981) *The Agrarian Question and Reformism in Latin America*, Baltimore, Johns Hopkins University Press.

Deere, C.D. (1979) 'Rural Women's Subsistence Production in the Capitalist Periphery', [1976] in Robin Cohen *et al.* (eds), *Peasants and Proletarians*, London, Hutchinson.

Delpeuch, Bertrand (1985) 'L'Espoir déçu de la Révolution verte', in J-P. Alaux and P. Norel (eds), *Faim au Sud, Crise au Nord*, Paris, L'Harmattan.

Dennis, Caroline (1987) 'Women and the State in Nigeria – the Case of the Federal Military Government 1984–85', in Haleh Afshar (ed.), *Women, State and Ideology*, Albany, NY, State University of New York Press.

Dickens, P. (1988) *One Nation? Social Change and the Politics of Locality*, London, Pluto Press.

Dickens, Peter (1991) 'The Changing Geography of Japanese foreign direct investment in Manufacturing Industry', in Jonathon Morris (ed.), *Japan and the Global Economy*, London, Routledge.

Dikötter, F. (1992) *The Discourse of Race in Modern China*, London, Hurst & Co.

Dinham, B. and C. Hines (1983) *Agribusiness in Africa*, London, Earth Resources Research.

Diop, Abdoulaye-Bara (1981) *La Société wolof – Tradition et Changement. Les Systèmes d'Inégalité et de Domination*, Paris, Karthala.

Diop, Cheikh Anta (1989) *The Cultural Unity of Black Africa – The Domains of Matriarchy and Patriarchy in Classical Antiquity*, London, Karnak House.

Dirlik, Arif (ed.) (1993) *What is in a Rim? – Critical Perspectives on the Pacific Rim Idea*, Boulder, Colo., Westview Press.

Dobrska, Z. (1981) 'The Problem of Technological Choice', in D. Seers (ed.), *Dependency Theory – A Critical Reassessment*, London, Pinter.

Dos Santos, T. (1970) 'The Structure of Dependency', in *American Economic Review*, Vol. LX, No. 2, May.

Douthwaite, R. (1996) *Short Circuit – Strengthening Local Economies for Security in an Unstable World*, Totnes, Green Books.

Doz, Y. (1987) 'International Industries: Fragmentation versus Globalisation', in B.R. Guile and H. Brooks (eds), *Technology and Global Industry*, Washington, DC, National Academy Press.

Drohan, M. (1998) 'How the Net killed the MAI', 29 April, labornews@labornet.org

Drysdale, P. and R. Garnaut (1993) 'The Pacific: An Application of a General Theory of Economic Integration', in C.F. Bergsten and M. Noland (eds), *Pacific Dynamism in the International Economic System*, Washington, DC, Institute for International Economics.

Du Bois, W.E.B. (1970) 'Address to the Nations of the World' [1900], in *W.E.B. Du Bois Speaks*, New York, Pathfinder.

Dumont, René, and Nicholas Cohen (1980) *The Growth of Hunger*, London, Marion Boyers.

Dupré, G. (ed.) (1991) *Savoirs paysans et Développement*, Paris, Karthala/Orstom.

Dutt, Srikant (1984) *India and the Third World – Altruism or Hegemony*, London, Zed.

Dutt, R.P. (1936) *World Politics 1918–1936*, London, Gollancz.

Eatwell, J. *et al.* (1987) *The New Palgrave Encyclopaedia of Economics*, Vol. I, London, Macmillan.

Edwards, V. and T. Sienkewicz (1990) *Oral Cultures Past and Present*, Oxford, Blackwell.

El Ayouti, Yassir (1971) *The United Nations and Decolonisation – the Role of Afro-Asia*, The Hague, Martinus Nijhoff.

Emmanuel, A. (1981) *Technologie appropriée ou Technologie sous-développée?*, Paris, PUF.

Environmental Information Center, Tokyo (1994) *Energy Demand Forecast and Environmental Impact in China*, Tokyo.

Epstein, G. (1996) 'International Capital Mobility and the Scope for National Economic Management', in R. Boyer and D. Drache (eds), *States Against Markets – the Limits of Globalisation*, London, Routledge.

Epstein, Leon D. (1964) *British Politics in the Suez Crisis*, London, Pall Mall Press.

Eteng, Inyang (1981) 'Indigenization for Lumpen-Bourgeois Development in Nigeria', in O. Nnoli (ed.), *Path to Nigerian Development*, Dakar, Codesria.

Ewusi, Kodwo (ed.) (n.d.) *Towards Food Self-Sufficiency in West Africa*, Tema, Ghana.

Fals-Borda, Orlando (1993) 'Building Countervailing Power in Nicaragua, Mexico and Colombia', in P. Wignaraja (ed.), *New Social Movements in the South*, London, Zed.

Feldman, R. (1975) 'Differentiation and Political Goals in Tanzania', in I. Oxaal et al. (eds), *Beyond the Sociology of Development*, London, Routledge and Kegan Paul.

Fevre, Ralph (1985) 'Racism and Cheap Labour in UK Wool Textiles', in H. Newby et al. (eds), *Restructuring Capital – Recession and Reorganisation in Industrial Society*, Basingstoke, Macmillan.

Feyerabend, G. (1994) 'People's Empowerment – a Condition for a Sustainable, Equitable and Liveable World', in Philip B. Smith *et al.* (eds), *The World at the Crossroads*, London, Earthscan.

Fiege, K. and L. Ramalho (eds) (1984) *Landwirtschaft = Hungerwirtschaft? – Umbruche und Krisen in der Agrarsystem der dritten Welt*, Saarbrucken, Breitenbach Verlag.

Folson, Kweku G. (1991) 'Structural Adjustment in Ghana', in B. Turok (ed.) *Alternative Strategies for Africa*, Volume 3, London, Institute For African Alternatives.

Folta, Paul H. (1992) *From Swords to Plowshares – Defense Industry Reform in the PRC*, Boulder, Colo., Westview Press.

Foot, R. (1994) 'Thinking Globally from a Regional Perspective: China, Indonesia and Malaysia in the Post Cold War Era', SOAS, October (duplicated).

Forbes, Jack D. (1988) *Black Africans and Native Americans – Color, Race and Caste in the Evolution of Red-Black Peoples*, Oxford, Blackwell.

Foreman-Peck, James (1986) 'The Motor Industry', in M. Casson *et al.* (eds), *Multinationals and World Trade*, London, Allen and Unwin.

Forrester, T. (ed.) (1985) *The Information Technology Revolution*, Oxford, Blackwell.

Franck, T. and E. Weisband (1971) *Word Politics – Verbal Strategy Among the Superpowers*, New York, Oxford University Press.

Frank A.G. (1972) *Lumpenbourgeoisie–Lumpendevelopment– Dependence, Class and Politics in Latin America*, New York, Monthly Review Press.

— (1978) *World Accumulation 1492–1789*, New York, Monthly Review Press.

— (1981) *Crisis in the Third World*, London, Heinemann.

Fre, Zeremariam (1990) 'Pastoral Development in Eritrea and Eastern Sudan – Implications for Livestock Extension Programmes', Reading University, Ph.D thesis.

Freeman, C. (1989) 'New Technology and Catching Up', in R. Kaplinsky and C. Cooper (eds), *Technology and Development in the Third Industrial Revolution*, London, Frank Cass.

— *et al.* (1982) *Unemployment and Technical Innovation – A study of Long Waves and Economic Development*, Westport, Conn., Greenwood.

Freire, P. (1972) *Pedagogy of the Oppressed*, Harmondsworth, Penguin.

Friedman, E. (1979) 'On Maoist Conceptualisations of the Capitalist World System', in *China Quarterly*.

Fröbel, F., J. Heinrichs and O. Kreye (1980) *The New International Division of Labour – Structural Unemployment in Industrial Countries and Industrialisation in Developing Countries*, Cambridge, Cambridge University Press.

Furtado, Celso (1976) *Economic Development of Latin America*, Cambridge, Cambridge University Press, 2nd edition.

Gadgil, Madhav and Ramachandra Guha (1994) 'Ecological Conflicts and the Environmental Movement in India', in D. Ghai (ed.), *Development and Environment*, Oxford, Blackwell/ UNRISD.

Gaignard, R. (1968) 'Sous-développement et Déséquilibres régionaux au Paraguay', in *Revista Geográfica*, No. 69, Rio de Janeiro, December.

Galtung, Johan *et al.* (eds) (1980) *Self Reliance – A Strategy for Development*, London, Bogle.

Ganguli, B.N. (1977) *Indian Economic Thought*, New Delhi, Tata/McGraw Hill.

Garver, J.W. (1993) 'The Chinese Communist Party after the Collapse of Soviet Communism', in *China Quarterly*, March.

Gbagbo, Laurent (1978) *Réflexions sur la Conférence de Brazzaville*, Yaoundé.

George, Susan (1988) *A Fate Worse than Debt – A Radical New Analysis of the Third World Debt Crisis*, Harmondsworth, Pelican.

Gereffi, Gary (1993) 'Global Sourcing and Regional Divisions of Labor in the Pacific Rim', in Arif Dirlik (ed.), *What is in a Rim? – Critical Perspectives on the Pacific Rim Idea*, Boulder, Colo., Westview Press.

Ghai, Dharam (1990) 'Participatory Development – Some Perspectives from Grass-Roots Experiences', in K. Griffin and J. Knight (eds), *Human Development and the International Development Strategy for the 1990s*, Basingstoke, Macmillan for the United Nations.

— and C. Hewitt de Alcantara (1991) 'The Crisis of the 1980s in Africa, Latin America and the Caribbean', in D. Ghai (ed.) *The IMF and the South*, London, Zed Books.

Ghai, Dharam (ed.) (1991) *The IMF and the South*, London, Zed Books.

— (ed.) (1994) *Development and Environment*, Oxford, Blackwell/UNRISD.

— and J.M. Vivian (eds) (1992) *Grassroots Environmental Action – People's Participation in Sustainable Development*, London, Routledge.

Ghose, A.K. (1984) 'The development strategy and rural reforms in post-Mao China', in K. Griffin (ed.), *Institutional Reform and Economic Development in the Chinese Countryside*, London, Macmillan.

Giannou, C. (1993) 'Reaping the Whirlwind – Somalia After the Cold War', in P. Bennis and M. Moushabeck (eds), *Altered States*, New York, Olive Branch.

Gifford, P. and W.R. Louis (eds) (1982) *The Transfer of Power in Africa – Decolonisation 1940–60*, New Haven, Yale University Press.

Gilpin, Robert (1987) *The Political Economy of International Relations*, Princeton, Princeton University Press.

Ginzberg, E. et al. (1986) *Technology and Employment*, Boulder, Colo., Westview Press.

Gittings, J. (ed.) (1991) *Beyond the Cold War*, London, Catholic Institute for International Relations.

Glaeser, B. and K. Phillips-Howard (1987) 'Low-energy Farming Systems in Nigeria', in B. Glaeser (ed.), *The Green Revolution Revisited – Critique and Alternatives*, London, Allen and Unwin.

Glaeser B. (ed.) (1984) *Ecodevelopment – Concepts, Projects, Strategies*, Oxford, Pergamon Press.

— (ed.) (1987) *The Green Revolution Revisited – Critique and Alternatives*, London, Allen and Unwin.

Golub, P. (1998) 'Quand l'Asie orientale vacille', in *Le Monde diplomatique*, July.

Goonatilake, Susantha (1982) *Crippled Minds – An Exploration into Colonial Culture*, New Delhi, Vikas.

— (1984) *Aborted Discovery: Science and Creativity in the Third World*, London, Zed Books.

Graham, Ronald (1982) *The Aluminium Industry and the Third World – Multinational Corporations and Underdevelopment*, London, Zed Books.

Grainger, Alan (1989) *The Threatening Desert*, London, Earthscan–UNEP.

Gran, Peter (1979) *Islamic Roots of Capitalism – Egypt 1760–1840*, Austin, University of Texas Press.

Greenberg, Stanley B. (1980) *Race and State in Capitalist Development – Comparative Perspectives*, Yale, Yale University Press.

Greene, Felix (1970) *The Enemy – Notes on Imperialism*, London, Cape.

Grevemeyer, J.H. (ed.) (1981) *Traditionale Gesellschafter und europäischer Kolonialismus*, Frankfurt-am-Main, Syndikat.

Griffin, Keith (1978) *International Inequality and National Poverty*, London, Macmillan.

— (ed.) (1984) *Institutional Reform and Economic Development in the Chinese Countryside*, London, Macmillan.

— and J. Knight (eds) (1990) *Human Development and the International Development Strategy for the 1990s*, Basingstoke, Macmillan for the United Nations.

Gromyko, A. (1964) Speech to the Supreme Soviet of the USSR, 13 December 1962, in *The National Liberation Movement Today*, London.

Grunwald, J. and K. Flamm (1985) *The Global Factory – Foreign Assembly in International Trade*, Washington, DC, Brookings Institution.

Guha, R. (1983) *Elementary Aspects of Peasant Insurgency in Colonial India*, Delhi, Oxford University Press.

Guile, B.R. and H. Brooks (1987) *Technology and Global Industry*, Washington, DC, National Academy Press.

Guisse, Youssouph Mbargane (n.d.) *Philosophie, Culture et Devenir social en Afrique noire*, Dakar, Nouvelles éditions africaines.

Gupta, Tilak D. (1993) 'Recent Developments in the Naxalite Movement', in *Monthly Review* 45, September.

Hall, Peter (1983) *Enterprise Zones Revisited*, University College London, Development Planning Unit, Occasional Paper No. 3.

Hansen, Bent and Girgis Marzouk (1965) *Development and Economic Policy in the UAR (Egypt)*, Amsterdam, North Holland Publishing Co.

Harding, Sandra (1986) *The Science Question in Feminism*, Ithaca, NY, Cornell University Press.

Harris, Nigel (1987) *The End of the Third World*, Harmondsworth, Penguin.

Harris, S. and G. Klintworth (eds) (1995) *China as a Great Power*, Melbourne, Longmans.

Hart, J.A. (1990) 'Interdependence and Increased Competition among the Industrialised Countries – Implications for the Developing World', in D.C. Pirages and C. Sylvester (eds), *Transformations in the Global Political Economy*, Basingstoke, Macmillan.

Hartland-Thunberg, P. (1990) *China, Hong Kong, Taiwan and the World Trading System*, New York, St. Martin's Press.

Hartsock, Nancy (1983) *Money, Sex and Power – Toward a Feminist Historical Materialism*, New York, Longman.

Harvey, Patricia (1954) 'The Planning of the New Order in 1940', in A. Toynbee and V.N. Toynbee (eds), *Survey of International Affairs – Hitler's Europe*, London, Oxford University Press.

Haupt, G. and M. Reberioux (eds) (1967) *La deuxième Internationale et l'Orient*, Paris, Editions Cujas.

Havnevik, K.J. (ed.) (1987) *The IMF and the World Bank in Africa*, Uppsala, Scandinavian Institute of African Studies.

Hayek, F. von (1939) 'The "Paradox" of Savings', in F. von Hayek, *Profits, Interest and Investment*, London, Routledge.

— (1973) *Law, Legislation and Liberty*, Vol. 1, London, Routledge.

Hayes, P.M. (1973) *Fascism*, London, G. Allen and Unwin.

Heiduk, Gunter and Yamamura Kozo (eds) (1990) *Technological Competition and Interdependence*, Seattle, University of Washington Press.

Hellmann, D.C. (1996) 'America, APEC and the Road Not Taken: International Leadership in the Post-Cold War Interregnum in the Asia Pacific', in I. Yamazawa and A. Hirata (eds), *APEC – Co-operation from Diversity*, Tokyo, Institute of Developing Economies.

Henderson, J. and M. Castells M. (eds) (1987) *Global Restructuring and Territorial Development*, London, Sage.

Hettiarachchy, T. (1992) *Working in the Zone*, Asian Human Rights Commission.

Heyer, Judith *et al.* (eds) (1981) *Rural Development in Tropical Africa*, London, Macmillan.

Hill, R.C. and Lee Young Joo (1994) 'Japanese Multinationals and East Asian Development – the Case of the Automobile Industry', in L. Sklair (ed.), *Capitalism and Development*, London, Routledge.

Hindess, B. and P.Q. Hirst (1977) *Mode of Production and Social Formation*, London, Macmillan.

Hobson, J.A. (1938) *Imperialism – A Study*, London, G. Allen and Unwin, 3rd edition.

Hoekman, B. and M. Kostecki (1995) *The Political Economy of the World Trading System*, Oxford, Oxford University Press.

Hogan, Lloyd (1984) *Principles of Black Political Economy*, London, Routledge and Kegan Paul.

Hopf, T. (1991) 'Soviet inferences from their victories in the periphery: visions of resistance or cumulating gains', in R. Jervis R. and J. Snyder (eds), *Dominoes and Bandwaggons*, New York, Oxford University Press.

Hopkins, T. and I. Wallerstein (eds) (1996) *The Age of Transition*, London, Zed Books.

Hu Jichuang (1981) *A Concise History of Chinese Economic Thought*, Beijing, Foreign Languages Press.

Hua Wu Yin (1983) *Class and Communalism in Malaysia*, London, Zed Books.

Hunt, E. and H.J. Sherman (1986) *Economics*, New York, Harper and Row, fifth edition.

Hussein, Mahmoud (1971) *La Lutte de Classes en Egypte*, Paris, Maspéro, second edition.

Hymer, S.H. (1990) 'The Large Multinational "Corporation": an Analysis of Some Motives for the International Integration of Business', in M. Casson (ed.), *Multinational Corporations*, Aldershot, Edward Elgar.

Ikeda, S. (1996) 'World Production', in T.K. Hopkins and I. Wallerstein *et al.* (eds), *The Age of Transition*, London, Zed Books.

Ilyenkov, E.V. (1982) *The Dialectics of the Abstract and the Concrete in Marx's Capital*, Moscow, Progress.

International Bank for Reconstruction and Development (1981) *Accelerate Development in Sub-Saharan Africa – An Agenda for Action*, Washington, IBRD.

Irayagolle, Gamini (1978) *The Truth about the Mahaweli*, no place of publication.

Isaa-Salwe, Abdisalam (1994) *The Collapse of the Somali State*, London, HAAN.

Itoh, Motoshige (1990) 'The Impact of Industrial Structure and Industrial Policy on International Trade', in Gunter Heiduk and Yamamura Kozo (eds), *Technological Competition and Interdependence*, Seattle, University of Washington Press.

Itoh, Makoto (1990) *The World Economic Crisis and Japanese Capitalism*, Basingstoke, Macmillan.

Izzeddin, N.M. (1975) *Nasser*, London, Third World Centre for Research.

Jaffe, H. (1985) *A History of Africa*, London, Zed Books.

Jalée, Pierre (1969) The Third World in World Economy, New York, Monthly Review Press.

James, C.L.R. (1982) *Nkrumah and the Ghana Revolution*, London, Allison and Busby.

James, F. and A.E. Havens (1981) 'Peasant Movements and Social Change – Co-operatives in Peru', in J. Petras et al., *Class, State and Power in the Third World*, Montclair, Allanheld, Osman.

Jervis, R. and J. Snyder (eds) (1991) *Dominoes and Bandwaggons – Strategic Beliefs and Great-Power Competition in the Eurasian Rimland*, New York, Oxford University Press.

Jones, Charles A. (1983) *The North–South Dialogue*, London, Pinter.

Jonsson, U. *et al.* (1991) 'What is Wrong with a Peasant-Based Development Strategy', in M. Morner and T. Svensson (eds), *The Transformation of Rural Society in the Third World*, London, Routledge.

Jose, Vivencio R. (ed.) (1983) *Mortgaging the Future – The World Bank and IMF in the Philippines*, Quezon, Foundation for Nationalist Studies.

Joseph, W.A. *et al.* (eds) (1991) *New Perspectives on the Cultural Revolution*, Cambridge, Mass., Harvard University Press.

Julien, Claude (1972) *L'Empire américain*, Paris, Grasset, second edition.

Kaballo, Sidgi (1994) 'The Political Economy of Crisis in Sudan 1973–85', Leeds University, Ph.D thesis.

Kakabadse, Mario A. (1987) *International Trade in Services – Prospects for Liberalisation in the 1990s*, London, Croom Helm, for Atlantic Institute for International Affairs.

Kapchenko, N. (1975) 'Socialist foreign policy and the restructuring of international relations', in *International Affairs*, Moscow.

Kautilya (attrib.) (1962) 'Arthasastra', in T.N. Ramswamy, *Essentials of Indian Statecraft*, London, Asia.

Kazziha, Walid (1979) *Palestine in the Arab Dilemma*, London, Croom Helm.

Keal, P. (1983) *Unspoken Rules and Superpower Dominance*, London, Macmillan.

Kegley, C.W. and E.R. Wittkopf (1979) *American Foreign Policy, Patterns and Process*, New York, St Martin's Press.

Keynes, J.M. (1919) *The Economic Consequences of the Peace*, London, Macmillan.

Khanna, Ashok (1996) 'Equity Investment Prospects in Emerging Markets in Colombia', in *Journal of World Business*, Summer.

Killick, Tony (1987) 'Reflections on the IMF/World Bank Relationship', in K.J. Havnevik (ed.), *The IMF and the World Bank in Africa*, Uppsala, Scandinavian Institute of African Studies.

Kim, S.S. (ed.) (1984) *China and the World*, Boulder, Colo., Westview Press.

Kim Young-Ho (1987) 'Towards an Articulation of Dependency and Development Paradigms: Development of Semi-Development in the Korean Economy', in Kim Kyong-Dong (ed.), *Dependency Issues in Korean Development*, Seoul, Seoul National University Press.

Kim Kyong-Dong (ed.) (1987) *Dependency Issues in Korean Development*, Seoul, Seoul National University Press.

Knox R. (1862) *The Races of Man*, London, Henry Renshaw, 2nd edition.

Kobayashi, H. (1996) 'The Postwar Economic Legacy of Japan's Wartime Empire', in P. Duus *et al.* (eds), *The Japanese Wartime Empire 1931–45*, Princeton, Princeton University Press.

Kojima, K. (1977) *Japan and a New World Economic Order*, Boulder, Colo., Westview Press.

Kolko, G. (1969a) *The Politics of War – Allied Diplomacy and the World Crisis 1943–45*, London, Routledge.

— (1969b) *The Roots of American Foreign Policy*, Boston, Beacon Press.

— (1986) *Vietnam – Anatomy of a War 1940–75*, London, Allen & Unwin.

Kolko, Joyce (1988) *Restructuring the World Economy*, New York, Pantheon.

Kolkovitz, R. (1967) *The Soviet Military and the Communist Party*, Princeton, Princeton University Press for RAND Corporation.

Koponen, Juhani (1991) 'Agricultural Systems in late Pre-Colonial Tanzania', in M. Morner and T. Svensson (eds), *The Transformation of Rural Society in the Third World*, London, Routledge.

Krasner, S.D. (ed.) (1983) *International Regimes*, Ithaca, Cornell University Press, p. 98.

Krugman, Paul (1994) 'The Myth of Asia's Miracle', in *Foreign Affairs*, November–December.

Kumar, Shive (1979–80) *Peasantry and the Indian National Movement 1919–33*, Meerut, Anu Prakashan.

Kunio, Yoshihara (1988) *The Rise of Ersatz Capitalism in South-East Asia*, Singapore, Oxford University Press.

Kwanashie, Mike (1987) 'Structural Adjustment – Capital Accumulation and Employment', in Phillips and Ndekwu (eds), *Structural Adjustment Programmes in a Developing Country – The Case of Nigeria*, Ibadan, Nigerian Institute of Social and Economic Research.

Lal, D. (1983) *The Poverty of 'Development Economics'*, London, Institute of Economic Affairs.

Lam, D.K-K. and I. Lee (1992) 'Guerrilla Capitalism and the Limits of Statist Theory', in C. Clark and S. Chan, *The Evolving Pacific Basin in the Global Political Economy*, Boulder, Colo., Lynne Rienner.

Lamb, Geoff (1981) 'Rapid Capitalist Development Models – a New Politics of Dependence?', in D. Seers (ed.), *Dependency Theory – A Critical Reassessment*, London, Pinter.

Landim, Leilah (1993) 'Brazilian Crossroads', in P. Wignaraja (ed.), *New Social Movements in the South – Empowering the People*, London, Zed Books.

Latané, J.H. and D.W. Wainhouse (1941) *A History of American Foreign Policy*, New York, Doubleday, Doran.

Latin American and Caribbean Women's Collective (1980) *Slaves of Slaves*, London, Zed Books.

Lauren, Paul G. (1988) *Power and Prejudice – The Politics and Diplomacy of Racial Discrimination*, Boulder, Colo., Westview Press.

Le Houérou, Henry (1989) *The Grazing Land Ecosystems of the African Sahel*, Berlin, Springer-Verlag.

*Le Monde diplomatique* (n.d.) 'Le Libéralisme contre les Libertés', Paris, Le Monde.

Lebra, J.C. (ed.) (1975) *Japan's Greater East Asia Co-Prosperity Sphere – Selected Readings and Documents*, Kuala Lumpur, Oxford University Press.

Leffler, M.P. (1994) 'National Security and United States Foreign Policy', in M.P. Leffler and D. Painter (eds), *Origins of the Cold War*, London, Routledge.

— and D. Painter (eds) (1994) *Origins of the Cold War*, London, Routledge.

Lehnerd, A.P. (1987) 'Revitalising the Manufacture and Design of Mature Global Products', in B.R. Guile and H. Brooks (eds), *Technology of Global Industry*, Washington D.C., National Academy Press.

Lenin, V.I. (1965) 'The Second Congress of the Communist International', in V.I. Lenin, *Collected Works*, Vol. 31, Moscow, Progress.

— (1970) *Imperialism, the Highest Stage of Capitalism*, Beijing, Foreign Languages Press.

Lerner, Gerda (1987) *The Creation of Patriarchy*, Oxford, Oxford University Press.

Lewis, W.A. (1955) *The Theory of Economic Growth*, London, George Allen and Unwin.

— (1958) 'Economic Development with Unlimited Supplies of Labour', in A.N. Agarwala and S.P. Singh (eds), *The Economics of Underdevelopment*, Delhi, Oxford University Press.

Liao Kuang-sheng (1984) *Antiforeignism and Modernisation in China 1860–1980*, Hong Kong, Chinese University Press.

Lichauco, Alexandro A. (1983) 'The International Economic Order and the Philippines Experience', in Vivencio R. Jose (ed.), *Mortgaging the Future – The World Bank and IMF in the Philippines*, Quezon, Foundation for Nationalist Studies.

Lietaer, B. (1997) 'Global Currency Speculation and its Implications', in *Third World Resurgence*, No. 87/88.

Light, M. (1988) *The Soviet Theory of International Relations*, Brighton, Harvester.

Lin, V. (1987) 'Women Electronics Workers in Southeast Asia – The Emergence of the Working Class', in J. Henderson and M. Castells (eds), *Global Restructuring and Territorial Development*, London, Sage.

Lindberg, S. and A. Sverrison (eds) (1997) *Social Movements and Development – The Challenge of Globalisation and Democratisation*, Basingstoke, Macmillan.

Linear, M. (1985) *Zapping the Third World – The Disaster of Development Aid*, London, Pluto.

Lipietz, A. (1987) *Miracles and Mirages – The Crisis of Global Fordism*, London, Verso.

List, Friedrich (1983) *The Natural System of Political Economy*, London, Frank Cass [first published 1837].

Liu Fu-Kuo (1996) 'Industrial Development and the Impetus to Regional Economic Integration in Pacific Area', in Ian G. Cook et al. (eds), *Fragmented Asia – Regional Integration and National Disintegration in Pacific Asia*, Aldershot, Avebury.

Lockwood, W.W. (1954) *The Economic Development of Japan, Growth and Structural Change 1868–1938*, Princeton, Princeton University Press.

Louis, W.R. and R. Robinson (1982) 'The US and the liquidation of the British Empire in tropical Africa 1941–51', in P. Gifford and W.R. Louis (eds), *The Transfer of Power in Africa – Decolonisation 1940–60*, New Haven, Yale University Press.

Lundestad, G. and O.A. Westad (1993) *Beyond the Cold War*, Oslo, Scandinavian University Press.

Luxemburg, R. (1972) *The Accumulation of Capital – An Anti-Critique*, New York, Monthly Review Press.

MacDonald, Douglas J. (1991) 'The Truman Administration and Global Responsibilities', in R. Jervis and J. Snyder (eds), *Dominoes and Bandwaggons – Strategic Beliefs and Great-Power Competition in the Eurasian Rimland*, New York, Oxford University Press.

MacEwan, A. and W.K. Tabb (eds) (1989) *Instability and Change in the World Economy*, New York, Monthly Review.

Mackintosh, Maureen (1989) *Gender, Class and Rural Transition – Agribusiness and the Food Crisis in Senegal*, London, Zed Books.

Madan, G.R. (1966) *Economic Thinking in India*, Delhi, S. Chand and Co.

Mahjoub, Azzam (ed.) (1990) *Adjustment or Delinking – The African Experience*, London and Tokyo, Zed Books/United Nations University Press.

Maliyamkono, T.L. and M.S.D. Bagachwa (1990) *The Second Economy of Tanzania*, London, James Currey.

Mamdani, Mahmood (1991) 'Uganda: Contradictions in the IMF Programme and Perspective', in D. Ghai (ed.), *The IMF and the South*, London, Zed Books.

Mandaza, Ibbo (ed.) (1986) *Zimbabwe – The Political Economy of Transition*, Dakar, Codesria.

Mao Zedong (1977) 'On the Ten Major Relationships' (April 1956), in *Selected Works of Mao Tsetung*, Beijing, Foreign Languages Press.

Marcussen, H.S. and J.E. Torp (1982) *The Internationalisation of Capital*, London, Zed Books.

Mariátegui, José Carlos (1971) *Seven Interpretive Essays on Peruvian Reality*, Austin, University of Texas Press [first published 1928].

Marx, K. (1965) *Oeuvres, Economie Tome I*, Paris, Gallimard.

— and F. Engels (1969) *Selected Works*, Volume I, Moscow, Progress.

Massarat, Mohsen (1980) 'The Energy Crisis', in P. Nore and T. Turner (eds), *Oil and the Class Struggle*, London, Zed Books.

Meadows, D.L. *et al.* (1972) *The Limits to Growth*, London, Earth Island.

Medvedev, J.A. (1992) 'Improvisation et Echec des Réformes agraires', in *Le Monde diplomatique*, June.

Meillassoux, Claude (1986) *Anthropologie de l'Esclavage*, Paris, Presses universitaires de France.

Meister R. (1994) 'Beyond Satisfaction: Desire, Consumption and the Future of Socialism', SOAS, September (duplicated).

Merchant, Carolyn (1990) *The Death of Nature*, New York, Harper.

Meyns P. (n.d.) *Nationale Unabhangigkeit und landliche Entwicklung in der 3. Welt – Das Beispiel Tanzania*, Berlin, Oberbaumverlag.

'Mexican Pointers for India – "Welcome to the Nightmare"' (1995) in *Towards New Democracy* (CPI-ML), Vol. 9, No. 1–3, January–March.

Mies, Maria (1986) *Patriarchy and Accumulation on a World Scale*, London, Zed Books.

— *et al.* (1988) *Women: The Last Colony*, London, Zed Books.

Miller, Morris (1989) *Resolving the Global Debt Crisis*, New York, UNDP.

Mitra, Subrata and Claudia Werde-Bruniger (1984) 'Towards a new international economic order', in N. Schofield (ed.), *Crisis in Economic Relations between North and South*, Aldershot, Gower.

Mitter, Swasti (1986) *Common Fate, Common Bond – Women in the Global Economy*, London, Pluto.

— (1989) 'On Organising Workers in the Informal Sector', Brussels, ICFTU (duplicated).

Moguel, Julio and Enrique Velasquez (1992) 'Urban Social Organisation and Ecological Struggle in Durango, Mexico', in D. Ghai and J.M. Vivian (eds), *Grassroots Environmental Action – People's Participation in Sustainable Development*, London, Routledge.

Mohan Malik, J. (1995) 'India's Relations with China Post-Soviet Union', in S. Harris and G. Klintworth (eds), *China as a Great Power*, Melbourne, Longmans.

Molineu, Harold M. (1986) *United States Policy Toward Latin America – From Regionalism to Globalism*, Boulder, Colo., Westview Press.

Morgan G. (1985) 'From West to East and Back Again: Capitalist Expansion and Class Formation in the Nineteenth Century', in H. Newby (ed.), *Restructuring Capital*, Basingstoke, Macmillan.

Morgan, W.B. (1978) *Agriculture in the Third World – A spatial analysis*, London, Bell and Hyman.

Morner M. and T. Svensson (eds) (1991) *The Transformation of Rural Society in the Third World*, London, Routledge.

Morris, R.B. (ed.) (1982) *Encyclopedia of American History*, New York, Harper and Row, 6th edition.

Morris-Suzuki, T. and T. Seiyama (1989) *Japanese Capitalism Since 1945*, Armonk, NY, M.E. Sharpe.

Moser, C. (1987) 'The Experience of Poor Women in Guayaquil', in E.P. Archetti *et al.* (eds), *Sociology of 'Developing Societies', Latin America*, London, Macmillan.

Mukherjee, Ramakrishna (1974) *The Rise and Fall of the East India Company*, New York, Monthly Review Press.

Mureau, A-M. (1989) 'La Construction navale, Moteur de l'Industrialisation', in J-L. Maurer and P. Regnier (eds), *La Nouvelle Asie industrielle*, Paris, Presses universitaires de France.

Murray, P. and J. Wickham (1985) 'Women Workers and Bureaucratic Control in Irish Electronics Factories', in H. Newby *et al.* (eds), *Restructuring Capital*, Basingstoke, Macmillan.

Myers, R.H. (1996) 'Creating a Modern Enclave Economy', in P. Duus *et al.* (eds) *The Japanese Wartime Empire 1931–45*, Princeton, Princeton University Press.

Nabudere D.W. (1979) 'Generalised Schemes of Preferences in World Trade', in D.W. Nabudere, *Essays on the Theory and Practice of Imperialism*, London, Onyx Press.

— (1990) *The Rise and Fall of Money Capital*, London, Africa in Transition.

Nadvi, Khalid and Hubert Schmitz (1994) 'Industrial Clusters in Less Developed Countries – Review of Experiences and Research Agenda', Institute of Development Studies, Sussex, Discussion Paper No. 339.

Nag, Kalidas (1923) *Les Théories diplomatiques de l'Inde ancienne et l'Arthacastra*, Paris, Librairie orientale et américaine.

Naoroji, Dadabhai (1962) *Poverty and Un-British Rule in India*, Delhi, Government of India (first published 1901).

Naughton, B. (1991) 'Industrial Policy During the Cultural Revolution', in W.A. Joseph *et al.* (eds), *New Perspectives on the Cultural Revolution*, Cambridge, Mass., Harvard University Press.

— (1994) 'The Foreign Policy Implications of China's Economic Development Strategy', in T.W. Robinson and D. Shambaugh (eds), *Chinese Foreign Policy – Theory and Practice*, Oxford, Clarendon Press.

Ncube, P.D. *et al.* (1987) 'The IMF and the Zambian Economy – A Case', in K. Havnevik (ed.), *The IMF and the World Bank in Africa*, Uppsala, Scandinavian Institute of African Studies.

Nester, W.R. (1992) *Japan and the Third World*, Basingstoke, Macmillan.

Newby, H. *et al.* (eds) (1985) *Restructuring Capital – Recession and Reorganisation in Industrial Society*, Basingstoke, Macmillan.

Ng, Cecilia and Maznah Mohamed (1988) 'Primary but Subordinated – Changing Class and Gender Relations in Rural Malaysia', in Bina Agarwal (ed.), *Structures of Patriarchy*, London, Zed Books.

Nguyen, Hung P. (1993) 'Russia and China – The Genesis of an Eastern Rapallo', in *Asian Survey*, March.

Niem, Beth (1980) 'The Female-Male Differential in Unemployment Rates' [1975], in Alice Amsden (ed.), *The Economics of Women and Work*, Harmondsworth, Penguin.

Nikitin, P.I. (1983) *The Fundamentals of Political Economy*, Moscow, Progress.

Nnoli, Okwudiba (1981) 'A Short History of Nigerian Underdevelopment', in O. Nnoli (ed.), *Path to Nigerian Development*, Dakar, Codesria.

— (ed.) (1981) *Path to Nigerian Development*, Dakar, Codesria.

Nore, P. and T. Turner (eds) (1980) *Oil and the Class Struggle*, London, Zed Books.

North, Douglas C. (1981) *Structure and Change in Economic History*, New York, W.W. Norton.

Nouvel Ordre international et Non-alignement – Recueil de Documents (1982) Paris, Editions du Monde arabe.

Nwoke, Chibuzo (1987) *Raw Materials and Global Pricing*, London, Zed Books.

O'Malley, K. (1994) 'A Critical Assessment of the Impact of Ghana's Economic Recovery Programme', Birkbeck College, London, research paper, April.

O'Neill, H. (1980) 'The Need for Economic Co-operation among Developing Countries', *Institute of Development Studies Bulletin*, Sussex, January.

— and K. Mustafa (eds) (1990) *Capitalism, Socialism and the Development Crisis in Tanzania*, Aldershot, Avebury.

Odle, Maurice (1981) *Multinational Banks and Underdevelopment*, New York, Pergamon.

Ohiorhenuan, John (1987) 'Re-colonising Nigerian industry: the First Year of the Structural Adjustment Programme', in Adedotun Phillips and E.C. Ndekwu (eds), *Structural Adjustment Programmes in a Developing Country – The Case of Nigeria*, Ibadan, Nigerian Institute of Social and Economic Research.

Okogu, B. (1989) 'Structural Adjustment Policies in African Countries: A Theoretical Assessment', in B. Onimode (ed.), *The IMF, the World Bank and the African Debt*, Volume 1, London, Zed Books.

Oliver, N. and B. Wilkinson (1988) *The Japanization of British Industry*, Oxford, Blackwell.

Omvedt, G. (1993) 'The Dunkel Draft and American Imperialism', in *Frontier*, 15 and 22 May; D. Panda, 'Confronting the Dunkel Draft', in *Frontier*, 31 July and 7 August; S.C., 'MNCs on the Side of the Dalits?', in *Frontier*, 21 August.

Onimode B. (ed.) (1989) *The IMF, the World Bank and the African Debt – Volume 1: The Social and Political Impact*, London, Institute for African Alternatives/Zed Books.

Organisation of American States (1978) General Assembly, 8th Session, *Proceedings*, Vol. I, Washington DC, OEA/Ser.P/VIII-0.2.

Ottaway, M. and D. Ottaway (1986) *Afro-Communism*, New York, Africana, 2nd edition.

Oxaal, I. *et al.* (eds) (1975) *Beyond the Sociology of Development*, London, Routledge and Kegan Paul.

Palloix, Christian (1975) *L'Internationalisation du Capital*, Paris, Maspéro.

Paredes, Ricardo and Luis Riveres (1994) 'Chile', in Ricardo Paredes and Luis Riveres (eds), *Human Resources and the Adjustment Process*, Washington DC, Inter-American Development Bank.

Pareti, M. et al. (1965) *History of Mankind*, Volume II, London, Unwin Bros for UNESCO.

Park Se-hark (1993) 'Trade, Inter-Industry Linkages and Structural Change in Selected Asian-Pacific Economies', in Takao Sano and Chiharu Tamamura (eds), *Inter-Industry Linkages in Economic Interdependency in the Asia–Pacific Region*, Tokyo, Institute of Developing Economies.

Patrick, H. (1976) *Japanese Industrialisation and its Social Consequences*, Berkeley, University of California Press.

Paus, Eva (ed.) (1988) *Struggle Against Dependence – Non-traditional Export Growth in Central America and the Caribbean*, Boulder, Colo., Westview Press.

Pearce, A (1979) 'Industrial Protest in Nigeria', in R. Cohen *et al.* (eds), *Peasants and Proletarians*, London, Hutchinson.

Peng, Dajin (1995) 'The Rise of a Pacific Community? Evolution and Trends of Asia-Pacific Economic Co-operation', Princeton University, thesis.

Perlman, Michael (1987) *Marx's Crisis Theory*, New York, Praeger.

Petras, James F. *et al.* (1981) *Class, State and Power in the Third World*, Montclair, Allanheld, Osmun.

— (1987) *Capitalist and Socialist Crises in the Late Twentieth Century*, Totowa, NJ, Rowman and Allanheld.

Petras, James F. and M. Morley (1981) 'The US Imperial State', in James F. Petras *et al.*, *Class, State and Power in the Third World*, Montclair, Allanheld, Osmun.

Petras, James F. and S. Gunle (1987) 'A Critique of Structuralist State Theorising', in James F. Petras *et al.*, *Capitalist and Socialist Crises in the Late Twentieth Century*, Totowa, NJ, Rowman and Allanheld.

Petrella, R. (1996) 'Globalisation and Internationalisation – The Dynamics of the Emerging World Order', in R. Boyer and D. Drache (eds), *States Against Markets – the Limits of Globalisation*, London, Routledge.

Phillips, Adedotun, and E.C. Ndekwu (eds) (1987) *Structural Adjustment Programmes in a Developing Country – The Case of Nigeria*, Ibadan, Nigerian Institute of Social and Economic Research.

Pierce, F. (1991) 'Ancient Lessons from Arid Lands', in *New Scientist*, 7 December.

Pinchbeck, Ivy (1981) *Women Workers and the Industrial Revolution*, London, Virago [first published 1930].

Pine, F. (1982) 'Family structure and the division of labour: female roles in urban Ghana', in H. Alavi and T. Shanin (eds), *Introduction to the Sociology of 'Developing Societies'*, Basingstoke, Macmillan.

Pirages, D.C. and C. Sylvester (1990) *Transformations in the Global Political Economy*, Basingstoke, Macmillan.

Portes, Alejandro and J. Walton (1981) *Labor, Class and the International System*, New York, Academic Press.

Post, K.W.J. (1979) 'The Alliance of Peasants and Workers', in R. Cohen *et al.* (eds), *Peasants and Proletarians*, London, Hutchinson.

Potts, L. (1990) *The World Labour Market – A History of Migration*, London, Zed Books.

Preston, D. (ed.) (1987) *Latin American Development*, Harlow, Longman.

Qi Luo and C. Howe (1993) 'Direct Investment and Economic Integration in the Asia Pacific', in *China Quarterly*, December.

Queuille, P. (1969) *L'Amérique latine – la Doctrine Monroe et le Panaméricanisme*, Paris, Payot.

Rada, Juan (1985) 'Information Technology and the Third World', in T. Forrester (ed.), *The Information Technology Revolution*, Oxford, Blackwell.

Raghavan, C. (1990) *Recolonisation – L'avenir du Tiers-monde et Négotiations commerciales du GATT*, Brussels, ARTEL.

Rahman, Mohamed Anisur (1991) *Towards an Alternative Development Paradigm*, Institute for Development Alternatives, Dossier No. 81.

Rau, Bill (1991) *From Feast to Famine – Official Cures and Grassroots Remedies to Africa's Food Crisis*, London, Zed Books.

Remington, R.A. (1971) *The Warsaw Pact – Case Studies in Communist Conflict Resolution*, Cambridge, Mass., MIT Press.

Ricardo, David (1951) *On the Principles of Political Economy and Taxation – The Works and Correspondence of David Ricardo, ed. Sraffa*, Vol. 1, Cambridge, Cambridge University Press.

Richards, Paul (1985) *Indigenous Agricultural Revolution – Ecology and Food Production in West Africa*, London, Hutchinson.

Rigby, P. (1985) *Persistent Pastoralists*, London, Zed Books.

Rittberger, Volker (ed.) (1993) *Regime Theory and International Relations*, Oxford, Clarendon Press.

Roberts H. (1983) 'The Algerian Bureaucracy', in T. Asad and R. Owen (eds), *Sociology of 'Developing Societies' – The Middle East*, London, Macmillan.

Robinson, T.W. and D. Shambaugh (eds) (1994) *Chinese Foreign Policy – Theory and Practice*, Oxford, Clarendon Press.

Roddick, J. *et al.* (1988) *The Dance of the Millions – Latin America and the Debt Crisis*, London, Latin America Bureau.

Rodinson, M. (1972) *Marxisme et monde musulman*, Paris, Seuil.

Rodney, W. (1972) *How Europe Underdeveloped Africa*, London and Dar-es-Salaam, Bogle l'Ouverture and TPH.

Rogers, Paul (1994) 'Power, Poverty and International Security', in G. Tansey (ed.), *A World Divided – Militarism and Development After the Cold War*, London, Earthscan.

Roland, G. (1989) *Économie politique du Système soviétique*, Paris, l'Harmattan.

Rose, Kalima (1992) *Where Women Are Leaders – The SEWA Movement in India*, London, Zed Books.

Ross, R. (1990) 'China and Vietnam – from Co-operation to Conflict', in H. Harding (ed.), 'China's Co-operative Relationships', no place of issue (duplicated), Vol. 2.

Rosset, Peter M. (1996) *Cuba: Alternative Agriculture During Crisis*, Washington D.C., World Resource Institute, September.

Rostow, W.W. (1960) *The Process of Economic Growth*, 2nd edition, Oxford, Clarendon Press.

— (1984) *The Barbaric Counter-Revolution*, London, Macmillan.

Rouquié, A. (1982) *L'État militaire en Amérique latine*, Paris, Seuil.

— (1987) *Amérique latine*, Paris, Seuil.

Roxborough, I. (1987) 'Populism and Class Conflict', in P. Archetti *et al.* (eds), *Sociology of 'Developing Societies' – Latin America*, Basingstoke, Macmillan.

Rozman, G. (1987) *The Chinese Debate on Soviet Socialism, 1978–85*, Princeton, Princeton University Press.

Rubinstein, W.D. (1986) *Wealth and Inequality in Britain*, London, Faber and Faber.

Saffioti, H. (1978) *Women and Class Society*, New York, Monthly Review Press.

Sakamoto, Y. (ed.) (1988) *Asia – Militarisation and Regional Conflict*, London and Tokyo, Zed Books and United Nations University Press.

Salih, M.A. and L. Wohlgemuth (eds) (1994) *Crisis Management and the Politics of Reconciliation in Somalia*, Uppsala, Nordiska Afrikainstitut.

Samara, A. (1992) *Industrialisation in the West Bank*, Jerusalem, Al-Mashriq Publications).

Sampson, A. (1981) *The Money Lenders*, Sevenoaks, Hodder and Stoughton.

Sano, Takao and Chiharu Tamamura (eds) (1993) *Inter-Industry Linkages in Economic Interdependency in Asia–Pacific Region*, Tokyo, Institute of Developing Economies.

Sapir, J. (1980) *Pays de l'Est vers la Crise généralisée*, Lyon, Federop.

Sayigh, Yezid (1991) 'The Arab Regional System and the Gulf Crisis', in J. Gittings (ed.), *Beyond the Cold War*, London, Catholic Institute for International Relations.

Schaller, Michael (1979) *The US Crusade in China 1938–45*, New York, Columbia University Press.

Schatan, J. (1987) *World Debt – Who is to Pay?*, London, Zed Books.

Schejtman, A. (1997) 'Peasants and Structural Adjustment in Latin America', in S. Lindberg and A. Sverrison (eds), *Social Movements and Development – The Challenge of Globalisation and Democratisation*, Basingstoke, Macmillan.

Schmitter, P.C. (1990) 'Sectors in Modern Capitalism – Modes of Governance', in R. Brunetta and C. Dell'aringa (eds), *Labour Relations and Economic Performance*, Basingstoke, Macmillan.

Schofield, N. (ed.) (1984) *Crisis in Economic Relations between North and South*, Aldershot, Gower.

Schwartzman, S. (1988) 'High Technology versus Self Reliance', in J. Chacel *et al.*, (eds) *Brazil's Economic and Political Future*, Boulder, Colo., Westview.

Scott, Joan W. and Louise A. Tilly, (1980) 'Women's Work and the Family in Nineteenth Century Europe', in Alice Amsden (ed.), *The Economics of Women and Work*, Harmondsworth, Penguin.

Scott, James C. (1986) 'Everyday Forms of Peasant Resistance', in James C. Scott and B.J. Tria Kerkvliet (eds), *Everyday Forms of Peasant Resistance in South-East Asia*, London, Frank Cass.

— and B.J. Tria Kerkvliet (eds) (1986) *Everyday Forms of Peasant Resistance in South-East Asia*, London, Frank Cass.

Seers, D. (ed.) (1981) *Dependency Theory – A Critical Reassessment*, London, Pinter.

Seidman, A. (1979) 'The Distorted Growth of Import Substitution: The Zambian Case', in B. Turok (ed.), *Development in Zambia*, London, Zed Books for University of Zambia.

Sekgoma, G.A. (1982) 'Decolonisation: towards a global perspective 1940–78', in T.S. Shaw and 'Sola Ojo, *Africa in the International Political System*, Washington D.C., University Press of America for Department of International Relations, University of Ife, Nigeria.

Selys, G. and B. van Doninck (eds) (1991) *La Guerre du Pétrole*, Brussels, EPO.

Sen, G. (1984) *The Military Origins of Industrialisation and International Trade Rivalry*, London, Pinter.

Sen, Gita, and Caren Grown (1987) *Development, Crises and Alternative Visions*, London, Earthscan.

Shambaugh, D. (1991) *Beautiful Imperialist – China Perceives America 1972–90*, Princeton, Princeton University Press.

Shanin, T. (ed.) (1971) *Peasants and Peasant Societies*, Harmondsworth, Penguin.

Sharma, Radha Krishna (1981) *Nationalism, Social Reform and Indian Women, 1921–37*, Patna, Janaki Rakashan.

Shaw, T.S. and 'Sola Ojo (1982) *Africa in the International Political System*, Washington, D.C., University Press of America for Department of International Relations, University of Ife, Nigeria.

Sheahan, J.B. (1986) *Alternative International Economic Strategies and their Relevance for China – World Bank Staff Working Paper 759*, Washington, World Bank.

Sheehan, N. (ed.) (1971) *The Pentagon Papers as Published by the* New York Times, New York.

Shieh, G.S. (1992) *'Boss' Island – The Subcontracting Network and Micro-Entrepreneurship in Taiwan's Development*, New York, Peter Lang.

Shishido, T. and R. Sato (eds) (1985) *Economic Policy and Development: New Perspectives*, Dover, Mass., Auburn House.

Shiva, Vandana (1993) 'Why We Should Say "No" to GATT–TRIPs', in *Third World Resurgence*, No. 39.

— (1988) *Staying Alive – Women, Ecology and Development*, London, Zed Books.

Shivji, Issa G. (1976) *Class Struggles in Tanzania*, London, Heinemann.

Shoukri, Ghali (1981) *Egypt: Portrait of a President*, London, Zed Books.

*Shramshakti – Report of the National Commission on Self-Employed Women and Women in the Informal Sector* (1988) New Delhi.

Siddiqui, Rukhsana A. (1990) 'Socialism and the Ujamaa Ideology', in N. O'Neill and K. Mustafa (eds), *Capitalism, Socialism and the Development Crisis in Tanzania*, Aldershot, Avebury.

Sigrist, C. (1981) 'Akephale politische Systeme und nationale Befreiung', in J.H. Grevemeyer (ed.), *Traditionale Gesellschafter und europaischer Kolonialismus*, Frankfurt am Main, Syndikat.

Simai, Mihaly (1990) *Global Power Structure, Technology and World Economy in the late Twentieth Century*, London, Pinter.

Simon, D.F. (1984) 'The Role of Science and Technology in China's Foreign Relations', in S.S. Kim (ed.), *China and the World*, Boulder, Colo., Westview.

Simons, G. (1987) *Eco-Computer – The Impact of Global Intelligence*, Chichester, John Wiley.

Singham, A.W. and S. Hune (1986) *Non-Alignment in an Age of Alignments*, Westport, Conn., Lawrence Hill.

Sklair, L. (ed.) (1994) *Capitalism and Development*, London, Routledge.

Slater, P. (ed.) (1980) *Outlines of a Critique of Technology*, London, Ink Links.

Smirnov, A.D. *et al.* (eds) (1981) *The Teaching of Political Economy – A Critique of Non-Marxian Theories*, Moscow, Progress.

Smith, Philip B. *et al.* (eds) (1994) *The World at the Crossroads*, London, Earthscan.

Snowden, Frank Jr. (1991) *Before Color Prejudice – The Ancient View of Blacks*, Cambridge, Mass., Harvard University Press.

Solodovnikov, V. and V. Bogoslovsky (1975) *Non-Capitalist Development – An historical outline*, Moscow, Progress.

Srinivas, S. (1998) *The Information Technology (IT) Industry in Bangalore: A Case of Urban Competitiveness in India?* London, University College London Development Planning Unit, Working Paper no. 89.

Stewart, Michael (1986) *Keynes and After*, Harmondsworth, Pelican.

Stieffel, M. and M. Wolfe (1994) *A Voice for the Excluded – Popular Participation in Development, Utopia or Necessity*, London and Geneva, Zed Books and UNRISD.

Storper, M. and H. Scott (eds) (1992) *Pathways to Industrialisation and Regional Development*, London, Routledge.

Su Shaozhi *et al.* (1983) *Marxism in China*, London, Spokesman.

Sumiya, Toshio (1989) 'The Structure and Operation of Monopoly Capitalism in Japan', in T. Morris-Suzuki and T. Seiyama, *Japanese Capitalism Since 1945*, Armonk, N.Y., M.E. Sharpe.

Sutela, P. (1991) *Economic Thought and Economic Reform in the Soviet Union*, Cambridge, Cambridge University Press.

Sverrisson, A. (1993) 'Intermediate Production Enterprises – A Challenge to Policy Makers', in M. von Troil (ed.), *Changing Paradigms in Development – South, East and West*, Uppsala, Nordiska Afrikainstitut.

Sweezy, Paul M. (1968) *The Theory of Capitalist Development*, New York, Monthly Review Press.

Szentes, Tamas (1988) *The Transformation of the World Economy*, London and Tokyo, Zed Books and United Nations University Press.

Tadesse, Zenebeworke (1982) 'Women and Technology in Peripheral Countries', in P.M. D'Onofrio-Flores and S.M. Pfafflin, *Scientific-Technological Change and the Role of Women in Development*, Boulder, Colo., Westview Press for UNITAR.

Takashi, F. (1993) 'Inventing, Forgetting, Remembering – Toward a Historical Ethnography of the Nation State', in H. Befu (ed.), *Cultural Nationalism in East Asia*, Berkeley, University of California Press.

Talha, L. (1991) 'Pour quelques pétrodollars de surplus', in P.R. Baduel (ed.), *Crise du Golfe – La Logique des Chercheurs, [Revue du Monde musulman et de la Méditerranée, hors série]*.

Tamaki, Noritsugu (n.d.) 'Japan's Strategy in the Asia Pacific Region', Chuo University, duplicated.

Tansey, G. (ed.) (1994) *A World Divided – Militarism and Development After the Cold War*, London, Earthscan.

Taussig, M.T. (1980) *The Devil and Commodity Fetishism in South America*, Chapel Hill, University of North Carolina Press.

Taylor, A.R. (1982) *The Arab Balance of Power*, Syracuse, N.Y., Syracuse University Press.

Taylor, M. and N. Thrift (eds) (1982) *The Geography of Multinationals*, London, Croom Helm.

*The Taiping Revolution* (1976) Beijing, Foreign Languages Press.

*The Middle East and United States Foreign Policy* (1957) Washington, D.C.

Thorner, D. (1971) 'Peasant Economy as a Category in Economic History', in T. Shanin (ed.), *Peasants and Peasant Societies*, Harmondsworth, Penguin.

Thornton, A.P. (1959) *The Imperial Idea and Its Enemies,* London, Macmillan.

Thurlow, L.R. (1985) 'The Case for Industrial Policies in America', in T. Shishido and R. Sato (eds), *Economic Policy and Development: New Perspectives*, Dover, Mass., Auburn House.

Tissier, Patrick (1976) *La Chine – Transformations rurales et Développement socialiste*, Paris, Maspéro.

Toffler, A. (1980) *The Third Wave*, London, Collins.

Tornquist, O. (1984) *Dilemmas of Third-World Communism*, London, Zed Books.

Townsend, Peter (1979) *Poverty in the United Kingdom – A Survey of Household Resources and Standards of Living*, Harmondsworth, Penguin.

Turok, B. (ed.) (1991) *Alternative Strategies for Africa*, Volume 3, London, IFAA.

Tussie, D. (1987) *The Less Developed Countries and the World Trading System*, London, Pinter.

USSR Institute of Economics (1957) *Political Economy*, London, Lawrence and Wishart.

UNCTAD (1979) *Economic Co-operation among Developing Countries: Priority Areas for Action*, Manila, TD/244.

United Nations (1991) *The World's Women 1970-90*, New York, UN ST/ESA/STAT/SERK/8.

United Nations Development Programme (1996) *Human Development Report 1996*, New York, Oxford University Press.

United Nations Economic Commission for Africa (1979) *Annual Report*, E/CN.14/725.

United States Government (1957) *The Middle East and US Foreign Policy*, Washington, D.C.

Uno, Kozo (1977) *Principles of Political Economy – Theory of a Purely Capitalist Society*, Brighton, Harvester.

Väyrynen, R. (1993) 'The Nature of Conflict in the Future of International Relations', in G. Lundestad and O.A. Westad (eds), *Beyond the Cold War*, Oslo, Scandinavian University Press.

Vernon, Raymond (1989) *Technological Development – The Historical Experience*, Washington, D.C., World Bank.

Vertzberger, Y. (1985) *China's Southwestern Strategy*, New York, Praeger.

Villaschi, A. (1994) *The Newly Industrialised Countries and the Information Technology Revolution*, Aldershot, Avebury.

von Troil, M. (ed.) (1993) *Changing Paradigms in Development – South, East and West*, Uppsala, Nordiska Afrikainstitut.

Walsh, J.R. (1993) 'China and the New Geopolitics of Central Asia', in *Asian Survey*, March.

Waltz, Kenneth (1979) *Theory of International Politics*, Reading, Mass., Addison Wesley.

Wamba-dia-Wamba, E. (1987) 'The Experience of Struggle in the People's Republic of Congo', in P. Anyang' Nyong'o (ed.), *Popular Struggles for Democracy in Africa*, London and Tokyo, Zed Books and United Nations University Press.

Wangoola, Paul (n.d.) *On the African Crisis, Popular Participation and the Indigenous NGOs in Africa's 'Recovery' and Development*, no place of issue, African Association for Literacy and Adult Education.

Ward, Kathryn B. (1984) *Women in the World-System – Its Impact on Status and Fertility*, New York, Praeger.

Waring, M. (1989) *If Women Counted – A New Feminist Economics*, San Francisco, Harper and Row.

Warnock, P. (1987) *The Politics of Hunger: The Global Food System*, London, Methuen.

Weeks, J. (1975) 'Imbalance between the centre and periphery and the "employment crisis" in Kenya', in I. Oxaal et al. (eds), *Beyond the Sociology of Development*, London, Routledge and Kegan Paul.

Weigel, A. (1989) *Unified Theory of Global Development*, New York, Praeger.

Weiss, T.G. and M.A. Kessler (1991) *Third World Security in the Post Cold War Era*, Boulder, Colo., Lynne Rienner.

Westad, O.A. (1993) *Cold War and Revolution – Soviet–American Rivalry and the Origins of the Chinese Civil War*, New York, Columbia University Press.

Weston, R.S. (1972) *Racism in US Imperialism – The Influence of Racial Assumptions on American Foreign Policy 1893–1946*, Columbia, University of South Carolina Press.

White, John (1974) *The Politics of Foreign Aid*, London, Bodley Head.

Whiting, A.S. (1989) *China Eyes Japan*, Berkeley, University of California Press.

Whyte, M.K. (1978) *The Status of Women in Preindustrial Societies*, Princeton, Princeton University Press.

Wignaraja, P. (ed.) (1993) *New Social Movements in the South – Empowering the People*, London, Zed Books.

Williams, D. and T. Young (1994) 'Governance, the World Bank and Liberal Theory', in *Political Studies*, Vol. 42, No. 1, March.

Williams, Eric (1994) *Capitalism and Slavery*, Chapel Hill, University of North Carolina Press.

Williams, G. (1981) 'Nigeria: the neo-colonial political economy', in D. Cohen and J. Daniel (eds), *Political Economy of Africa*, Harlow, Longmans.

Winch, Peter (1970) 'Understanding a Primitive Society', in B.R. Wilson (ed.), *Rationality*, Oxford, Blackwell.

Wisner, B. (1984) 'Ecodevelopment and Ecofarming in Mozambique – Some Personal Observations', in B. Glaeser (ed), *Ecodevelopment – Concepts, Projects, Strategies*, Oxford, Pergamon Press.

World Bank (1995) *World Development Report 1995 – Workers in an Integrating World*, Oxford, Oxford University Press.

Wu Dakun (1983) 'The Asiatic Mode of Production in History as Viewed by Political Economy in its Broad Sense' in Su Shaozhi *et al.*, *Marxism in China*, London, Spokesman.

Yachir, F. (1988) *The World Steel Industry Today*, London, Zed Books.

Yahuda, M. (1993) 'The Foreign Relations of Greater China', in *China Quarterly*, December.

Yamazawa, I. and A. Hirata (eds) (1996) *APEC – Co-operation from Diversity*, Tokyo, Institute of Developing Economies.

Yeats, Alexander J. (1991) *China's Foreign Trade and Comparative Advantage – World Bank Discussion Paper 141*, Washington, D.C., World Bank.

Zaalouk, M. (1989) *Power, Class and Foreign Capital in Egypt*, London, Zed Books.

Zelem, Marie Christine (1991) 'L'Évolution des Techniques fromagères dans le Cantal, France du XVIII au XIX Siècle', in G. Dupré (ed.), *Savoirs paysans et Développement*, Paris, Karthala/Orstom.

Zietz, J. and A. Valdes (1988) *Agriculture in the GATT: An Analysis of Alternative Approaches to Reform*, Washington, D.C., International Food Policy Research Institute, Research Report No. 70.

# Index